W. H. SMITH

STUDIES IN POLITICAL HISTORY

Editor: Michael Hurst

Fellow of St John's College, Oxford

1. W. H. SMITH

from the painting by George Richmond.

W. H. SMITH

by

VISCOUNT CHILSTON

LONDON: Routledge & Kegan Paul
TORONTO: University of Toronto Press
1965

First published 1965
in Great Britain by
Routledge & Kegan Paul Ltd
and in Canada by
University of Toronto Press

Printed in Great Britain by
John Wright & Sons Ltd
Bristol and London

CONTENTS

CONTENTS

PLATES

CARICATURES BY HARRY FURNISS

PREFACE

T HE contemplation of a career crowned by such material success and irradiated by such domestic happiness—whilst lacking none of the drama and struggle and sorrow of all human existence; the daily company of a personality so resolute, upright and courageous, yet so disarmingly modest, humane and even humble, has made the writing of the life of W. H. Smith a singularly moving and memorable experience. The fact that his letters and speeches so frequently convey, in a totally frank and unaffected manner, his own sense of wonder and humility at the mystery of life and of the Providence which had raised him from a comparatively modest background to great wealth and eminence in the commercial sphere as well as to some of the highest positions in the State, far from reducing his stature in our eyes, increases it and singles him out—whatever his shortcomings in imaginativeness and *esprit*—as one of the very few men of his own or any other time who can truly be called good as well as great.

Some present-day readers may indeed find the frequent religious invocations and the open sifting of his conscience distasteful or embarrassing; but these must make allowance for what was pretty common practice in his day among all sorts and conditions of people, but more especially among the Nonconformist circles in which he was reared. Moreover he was an intensely religious man by nature and his early struggles of conscience between wanting to become an Anglican clergyman and not displeasing or disobeying a much loved father, who disapproved, were a really agonizing experience which filled his whole horizon during his formative years.

These things apart, his letters are so eloquent, so spontaneous and so highly individual that to read them seems to bring him back to life more than any description can do. This is my excuse for quoting so freely from them and thus, whenever possible, allowing the man himself to give his own account of the events in which he was involved.

The only other biography of W. H. Smith has, until now, been that published by Sir Herbert Maxwell in 1893—barely two years after his subject's death. The value of that book, consequently, was consider-

ix

ably impaired not only by lack of perspective, but by the impossibility of alluding to certain events owing to so many of the protagonists being still alive at the time. An important case in point is that of Lord Randolph Churchill's resignation—a subject of perennial fascination. Equally and for the same reason Maxwell was unable to give any idea of Smith's relations with such great contemporaries as Salisbury, Balfour, Chamberlain and Goschen.

Maxwell appears to have been given access by Smith's widow, Lady Hambleden, to a great many of the letters to which I, through the kindness of their grandson, have also been given access. But there are a great many more letters which Maxwell either did not see or did not like to use—for the reasons already given—and which I have both seen and used. Again, there appear also to have been a fair number of letters which Maxwell saw and quoted, but which now seem to be missing from the Hambleden Papers. Some of these I have taken from his pages 'on trust'; for it must be said that there are letters 'quoted' by him which do not exactly correspond with those that I have seen—or which he has telescoped one with another. I have not thought it necessary, however, to draw attention to these various discrepancies between his quotations and the originals, nor to those undated letters which Maxwell has in my opinion wrongly placed.

My foremost thanks are due to the Honourable David Smith, C.B.E., the present chairman of W. H. Smith & Son, for making this book possible by allowing me the unfettered use of his grandfather's papers—even to taking them to my home to work on—and for many other personal kindnesses. I also want to thank Mr. F. Seymour Smith, who has charge of the archives at Strand House, for his great help and kindness; Mr. Robert Blake; Mr. Michael Hurst, Fellow of St. John's College, Oxford, for reading and advising on the drafts; Miss W. D. Coates, Registrar of the National Register of Archives, where the Hambleden Papers were deposited, and her assistant Mrs. Lamb, who had the task of sorting and arranging the Papers, both of whom rendered me enormous assistance and showed me great kindness at all times; and Mrs. D. M. Teer who has patiently and efficiently typed all my drafts and the final manuscript.

Grateful acknowledgments are due to Her Majesty the Queen for gracious permission to quote from the Royal Archives and also to Mr. Mackworth Young, Librarian at Windsor Castle. Lord Salisbury has, for the second time in a few years, accorded me the privilege of seeing the relevant correspondence among his grandfather's correspondence and I am again very grateful to Dr. J. F. A. Mason, Librarian of Christ Church, Oxford, who has charge of them, for his help and kindness. Lord Harrowby—also a grandson of W. H. Smith—has, in conjunction with his co-trustees of the Harrowby MSS Trust, been particularly kind and helpful in granting me special facilities for seeing Smith's correspondence with the third Earl, for copying family photographs and in giving me personal information. Finally my thanks are due to the Trustees of the British Museum for access to the Balfour Papers and to Birmingham University for access to the Chamberlain Papers.

CHILSTON

Chilston Park
near Maidstone
Kent

I

IN THE SHADOW OF FATHER

━━━━◆❖◆━━━━

W H. SMITH always showed great interest in and curiosity
about the origins of his family; but not for the sort of
reasons which might have been supposed in the case of a man who
rose from a very modest social position to great wealth and high
office in the State. He was not a snob; but he knew that there was a
mystery somewhere in his immediate ancestry and this intrigued him.

The mystery centred round his grandfather, Henry Walton Smith,
who was said to have come from an old, propertied family from
Devon or Somerset, to have been educated at Harrow and to have
served in the Navy; but later to have been disinherited for marrying
beneath him. Indeed, W. H. Smith's father left a memorandum saying
that his father had been 'an officer in the Navy' and in applying for a
grant of arms in 1842 described himself as 'Youngest son of Henry
Walton Smith, late of Hinton St. George, in the County of Somerset,
Gentleman deceased'.

For many years the family legend ran to the effect that Henry
Walton had been penalized by his family for a *mésalliance*; that his
wife, *née* Anna Easthaugh, had proved her illiteracy and low origin
by signing the marriage register only with a cross; that the couple
were thereafter so destitute as to have to 'go into service' separately
and that after Henry Walton's death his widow appeared never to
have received any help or notice from his family.

That was about as much as was known until W. H. Smith's grandson, the 3rd Viscount Hambleden, instituted researches into the
beginnings of the firm and into the identity of his great-great grandfather, which were carried out shortly before the outbreak of the
Second World War and were brought to a close partly by that event
and partly by reason of their appearing to have reached the limit of
their usefulness. The results were, indeed, far from conclusive, but
they did produce certain interesting new facts. For they established
the date of Henry Walton Smith's birth as 1738—which made him

54 years old when he died in 1792 (not 35 as hitherto thought)—and they established the date and place of his marriage as October 27th, 1784, at Christ Church, Spitalfields—and that his wife had in fact signed with a cross. No evidence was found either of his having been educated at Harrow or of his having served in the Navy; but definite evidence was found of his having spent at least sixteen years of his life as secretary or assistant to Charles Rogers, the art collector and connoisseur (whose collection of pictures and manuscripts, bequeathed to William Cotton, ultimately became known as the Cottonian Library at Plymouth), which certainly suggests a man of culture and education.

Whether there is any particular significance in the fact of Rogers' death having taken place in the same year as that in which Henry Walton got married it is hard to say. Sir Herbert Maxwell quotes[1] a very worried—and, incidentally, very well expressed—letter from Henry Walton to Anna from which, though there is no date, it seems clear that Rogers is dying and that the couple are not yet married. But this letter seems now to have disappeared. At any rate, with Rogers gone and possibly having bequeathed his secretary a little money, it was evidently possible for the couple to marry and to set up in business together.

Whether Henry Walton's and Anna's first choice of a business venture was that of a news agency is not known, for the first definite proof of the existence of such a business in their name is found in the year 1792 when they are so described in a London Directory and their address given as 4 Little Grosvenor Street (now Broadbent Street). Then, all in this same year, occurred first the birth of their second son and third child, William Henry, who was later to lay the foundations of the firm's greatness, and very shortly after that the death of Henry Walton Smith himself. As William Henry later wrote to his own son: 'The trade has been wonderfully preserved in the family for three generations. . . . By one awful affliction it was nearly destroyed by the sudden death of my father in 1792, when I was only 39 days old.'

The widow Anna Smith must have been a woman of considerable character, for she thereupon gallantly—and evidently very success-fully—carried on the business by herself; for she is found in a London Directory of 1805 described as a 'newsvendor, of 4, Little Grosvenor Street, Grosvenor Square'. Indeed, she successfully carried it on for twenty years before increasing years and increasing business obliged her, in 1812, to call in her younger son William Henry, who had already set up as a goldsmith, to help her. Four years later, in 1816,

---

[1] Sir Herbert Maxwell, Bart. *Life & Times of the Rt. Hon. W. H. Smith, M.P.* (William Blackwood & Sons, 1893).

she died, leaving in her will to her two sons 'the Goodwill of and in my News-Walk or Business of a Vendor of Newspapers by me . . . for many years carried on in Little Grosvenor Street' and enjoined them to carry it on as 'Co-Partners'. This will, made in the year of her death, she managed to sign with quite a clear, well-formed hand.

The two brothers, Henry Edward and William Henry, duly obeyed this injunction, describing themselves as 'Newspaper Agents, Book-sellers and Binders'. But William Henry quickly asserted himself as the moving spirit and chief controller of the business, working early and late with almost frenetic energy at the parcelling and addressing of newspapers to be sent off by the mail-coaches to their various destinations in the country. In 1817 he took a wife in the person of Mary Anne Cooper—marrying her at St. George's, Hanover Square, despite the fact that she came of a strict Wesleyan family—and in the following year, 1818, he acquired number 42 Duke Street, Grosvenor Square, as a combined family house and shop, though the old house at Little Grosvenor Street was kept on for a further two years—possibly to accommodate his brother. Here his two elder children were born—Mary Anne[1] and Caroline.[2]

Then in 1821 the brothers opened a 'reading-room' at 192 Strand, where—all types of journal still being expensive—for one and a half guineas annually no less than 150 newspapers, reviews and magazines could be browsed over by the subscribers. These premises gradually became the chief centre of the business owing to the convenience of being near to the offices of the principal newspapers and, though Henry Edward appears to have stayed on at Duke Street, William Henry soon moved to the Strand with his family to 'live over the shop'. Here on June 24th, 1825, was born his first and only son, William Henry II, the subject of this book—and later four more daughters.[3]

Newspapers in those days were a comparatively expensive com-modity, burdened as they were with taxes and restrictions of various kinds, and to make a good living out of the handling and distri-bution of them, as the Smiths were trying to do, required quite exceptionally hard work and perseverance coupled with a capacity for audacity and swift initiative. For there was a tax on paper, as well as a duty imposed on every copy of every newspaper, and the sheets, before going through the press, had all to be sent to Somerset House to receive the official stamp; and there was also a tax on advertisements, payable by the publisher. The newspaper tax, from

---

[1] Married the Rev. William Beal.   [2] Married R. M. Reece.

[3] In 1849 the firm moved from 192 to 136 Strand and in 1852 to No. 186, which remained the headquarters of the rapidly expanding business till the move to Strand House, Portugal Street, in 1920—where it still is.

a ½d. or 1d. in the early eighteenth century had gradually risen to 3½d. to 4d. for each copy by the time the Smiths became active in the field. It was reduced again in 1836, but it was not until 1855 that it was finally abolished altogether. Nevertheless, despite these difficulties, the business of the brothers Smith prospered—entirely owing to the extraordinary energy and resource of the younger, William Henry.

Indeed, the basis of the firm's success lay in William Henry's idea of sending newspapers destined for the country and the big provincial centres by the fast morning mail-coaches immediately after their publication, instead of letting them wait for the night mails, which made the newspapers already nearly a day old before they started out and anything up to two days old before they reached their destination. For, hitherto, country readers of the few newspapers then in existence depended upon the Post Office for their delivery and the Post Office sent out its country mails only at night. But Smith's undertook to deliver newspapers to country readers without the intervention of the Post Office at all, by organizing a service of swift-horsed carts, which collected the papers from the publishing offices and delivered them to the mail-coaches, ready wrapped and addressed.

When delay occurred at the newspaper office—as was often the case with *The Times*—and the mail-coach had already left, Smith's carts had orders to gallop after them, catch them up and hand over their parcels of newspapers *en route*. Sometimes they even went the whole way, obtaining relays of horses as they went along, and carried out the delivery entirely themselves—admittedly at great expense, but at the same time giving great satisfaction and earning great prestige and confidence in their firm with the country newsmen and their customers.

When George IV died in 1830 Smith chartered a special boat and delivered the news in Dublin a full twenty-four hours ahead even of the Royal messengers: and with the coming of the railways he not only immediately made the fullest use of their normal services, but never hesitated to order special trains to ensure swifter delivery in exceptional circumstances to big provincial centres. Thus, as early as 1828, when *The Times* was late coming off the press, we hear of his sending it to Birmingham by special express 'where it arrived in time for the inland mails, by which the subscribers . . . in Birmingham, Liverpool, Chester, Warrington, Manchester, Rochdale, Preston, Lancaster, etc., obtained their papers 14 hours before the arrival of the London mail'. Again, in 1847, he is employing nine special engines to take his newspapers to Liverpool, Manchester and Birmingham: later the same year he sends another special train to

2. William Henry Smith the Elder.

The Start

Throwing out Papers

Folding Van

Guard's Van

The Arrival — Scramble for Papers

3. Despatching newspapers to the country (from *The Graphic*, 1875).

Carlisle and the following year one to Edinburgh and Glasgow, which got the papers to those cities respectively one and a half and two hours earlier than the mails which had left London the previous evening. Meanwhile, as a partner in all this high-powered drive and bold endeavour, William Henry found his brother sadly wanting. Perfect organization and clockwork precision and punctuality were of the very essence of the business as visualized by William Henry and Henry Edward appears to have possessed neither the gift nor the inclination for the exercise of such qualities. He had remained at Duke Street where his role was to prepare the addresses for the country parcels of newspapers, then send them on to the Strand, where William Henry saw to their dispatch by the mail-coaches. But he appears to have driven his brother to distraction by not delivering on time and thereby jeopardizing the dispatch to the early mail-coaches—and thus the whole success of the enterprise. William Henry was a man of irascible temper, ambitious as well as meticulous to a fault, so that, though his brother was technically the senior partner, the situation became too much for him. Consequently, in 1828, he appears to have succeeded in persuading his brother to let him buy him out and thereafter became sole proprietor of the concern.

Under his rigid, relentless and almost ferocious rule the business now achieved such prodigious efficiency that it not only prospered greatly but rapidly began to overtake its principal rivals in the trade. For Mr. Smith worked daily at the office from cockcrow onwards, not only directing and managing on the spot, but himself joining in the manual labour of addressing, packing and dispatching alongside his humblest apprentice. He was in fact known to be the quickest packer in the establishment and there was a standing offer of an extra shilling to any employee who could beat him to it.

Setting himself such exacting standards it goes without saying that he was just as or more exacting towards his staff. Indeed, he was evidently severe and intolerant of shortcomings to a degree which was remarkable even in those days. Had he not been such a man, however, it is extremely doubtful whether he could have brought the business to that high point whence his son was able to step off and undertake those great imaginative strokes which soon afterwards made the firm world-famous. For, in those early days, when competition was keen and profits small, it required such unremitting labour and vigilance for a 'newsman' to hold his own—let alone pull ahead of his competitors.

The stern régime and prodigious activity of this fast-growing enterprise formed not only the background of the younger Smith's early life, but, from an astonishingly early age, the very scene of it—for even while still at school, as we shall see, he began to take a part in it. Meanwhile, that he was a precocious boy as well as a devoted brother is shown by the first extant letter from his hand—an excellent copper-plate hand—written to his elder sister Augusta, when he was nine years old.

My very dear Sister,

I feel great pleasure addressing you on your birthday and I wish that you may have many far happier days than this and I congratulate you on being eleven years old and I hope that you will accept this Geranium as a token of my affection and I wish that you will be joyful on this always happy day and that you might prosperously go on.

I am

Your most affectionate
brother W. H. Smith.

July 24th 1834
192, Strand.

Soon after this his father engaged a tutor for him in the person of the Reverend William Beal, of Trinity College, Cambridge; and shortly after this again the said Beal became his brother-in-law as well by marrying his eldest sister, Mary Anne. This was in 1838 and in the same year Beal was appointed by the Duke of Bedford to be headmaster of the newly revived Tavistock Grammar School. As a result young William had his first, only and brief experience of school, being sent there as a boarder early in 1839, when he was not quite fourteen years old. Before he arrived Mrs. Beal, with sisterly solici-tude, wrote him some advice to enable him to hold his own with the other boys in the matter of the curriculum. He was to work up 'composition & letter writing which I think you will find more diffi-cult than anything else . . . I would advise you to translate as much of your Delectus as you can do properly into the best English and practise writing remarks & thoughts upon these sentences. I will send you one or two as a pattern. Get up as much as you can well do of your Latin Grammar as most of the boys are before you in Latin, also get up your Euclid. . . .' However, he more than held his own, gaining a medal at the midsummer examination of that year.

Indeed, his letters from school reveal an extraordinary degree of maturity, including a lively interest in politics as well as a constant concern for the welfare of the family business, of which he obviously already had a remarkable understanding. Thus he writes to his formidable father in terms of complete assurance and equality (April 13th, 1839):

. . . I see that a very important debate comes on tonight in the Commons, and I should think one very likely to influence the fate of

6

the Ministry. . . . I should like to be with you tomorrow morning to
see what help I could render and I can assure you that often of a
morning when up at 6 o'clock learning my lessons, I have thought of
the Strand & you & could imagine how busy you were at any particular moment when I was enjoying myself. I suppose that you have
not yet had any occasion to use the Preston route, as I have not heard
anything of it. The Newspapers I can assure you are very welcome
reminding one of one's work at home. . . . Although away from
you & the business my mind frequently reverts to you, hoping that
you are well in health and especially that you do not work so much as
you did.

William evidently regarded his going to school in this far-off part
of the country as a kind of intelligence mission on behalf of the family
firm, noting with an already professional and critical eye the organization of newspaper delivery to these parts, the efforts of rival
agencies in the field and the general efficiency of public services. For
he writes scornfully in one letter to his father of the 'absurdity of
Post Office arrangements in the South West' and in another the
following extremely detailed information (April 23rd, 1839):

. . . In Bridgwater I observed a placard, announcing to the world, that
John Tiver, bookseller, received the Times daily at one (or two)
o'clock. We left Bridgwater at 2 by one of the coaches that wait the
8 o'c London train, this I found carried a parcel of about a dozen
papers from Westley's for a Mr. May of Taunton wh. had been enclosed
in Tiver's parcel, and had come down by the 8 o'c train. There are no
other papers carried to either Bridgwater, Taunton or Exeter . . . so
you see these are all the wonderful exertions of Mr. Westley wh. are
advertised in the Times; indeed it must be at a terrible expenditure of
trouble that he can arrange to send not quite a quire of papers, and all
folded too, by 8 o'c from the terminus at Paddington. If he was but to
make the least exertion he might very well get a good business in that
part of the country.

Further on in the same letter he writes: '. . . you gave me a little
account of your domestic budget and now I must open mine, to commence in a business-like way I should tell you what linen I had
procured according to orders, but that I suppose you wd. not listen
to, besides perhaps I shd. then make my financial disclosure rather
too long a one. . . .' Nevertheless, he then goes into a detailed account
of the state of his wardrobe and probable expenses in that connection.
In another, undated, letter of this year he again shows his intense
interest in the business at the Strand: '. . . I suppose you have by this
time sent out nearly all the quarterly accounts. I can assure you that
I did not forget them when the time drew nigh, for it was just as our
examination took place. . . .'

But, immediately after the midsummer examination in which he had so distinguished himself and having barely had time to settle into the school life, he was suddenly removed and once again placed under a private tutor at home—this time the Reverend Alfred Povah, of Wadham College, Oxford. The reason for this curious policy is supposed to have lain in the influence of his mother and again of her mother. Her family, the Coopers, were, as already said, Wesleyans of the early and stricter kind, and her mother, Mrs. Cooper, a widow, extremely devout, visited her a great deal and exerted a strong influence over her. Mrs. Cooper is thought to have been obsessed with the perils of public schools through the risk of bad companions and 'worldly' influences as much as through the risk of contamination by the usually prevailing Anglicanism of such places—the more so since young William already showed signs of sympathy with the Established Church.

However, the whole question of the religious affiliations of the various members of the Smith family at this time is curiously difficult to unravel. Mr. Smith senior would seem to have been baptized and reared as a member of the Church of England and we know for a fact that he was married at St. George's, Hanover Square. Moreover, according to a letter written some seventy years later by one of the daughters, Emma Sercombe, to Lady Hambleden, all the children were baptized at the same church. Yet—presumably under his wife's and mother-in-law's influence—Mr. Smith constantly attended Methodist services and subscribed liberally to the funds of the Wesleyan Society, without ever becoming a member of it. His children, too, as we shall see, seem to have been required to divide their allegiance between the two faiths and though certain of his daughters evidently shared his son's predilection for the Church of England, even that one (Mrs. Beal) who was married to an Anglican clergyman showed a quite remarkable ambivalence in her feelings in the matter.

Although young William was also complaisant enough to attend Methodist services with his parents and more nonconformist sisters, he did not share their suspicions of the Church of England. On the contrary, as he grew up, a fervent desire grew in him not only to drop Methodism and become an out-and-out member of the Church, but even to take Holy Orders in the Church. Indeed, by the time he was sixteen he had confessed this wish to his father and with it his longing to go to a university to prepare for it. But Mr. Smith would not for one moment entertain any of these proposals, partly no doubt influenced by the strong views of his wife and mother-in-law on Anglicanism and Anglican seats of learning, partly because he considered a university unsuited to his son's station in life and partly—

perhaps principally—because he had already decided on quite other plans for his son. In fact, he gave him to understand, that, if he persisted in such a course, he need not expect a shilling from his father; whereas if he came into the business, he might count on being made a partner as soon as he came of age.

After two years at home spent in the consideration and discussion of these agonizing problems—as well, presumably, as in imbibing some learning from Mr. Povah—William was allowed to return to Tavistock Grammar School, at the age of seventeen, not this time as an ordinary pupil, but as a private pupil of his brother-in-law, the headmaster. But he now began to worry about another aspect of his relationship with his father. For, he began to realize that the latter was going to ruin his health by overworking himself, which was not only distressing to him—for he was extremely devoted to his father despite their clash of wills—but also alarming, because it meant that his father would become increasingly dependent on him for help in running the business. This is apparent from a letter which he wrote to his mother shortly after returning to Tavistock School for the second time (January 22nd, 1842):

> . . . I am sorry to hear that Father feels the "push" of the Season. I had hoped that some arrangement would be effected by which the work would be rendered more easy to him, rather than otherwise. It is true that I had some misgivings when I left town, lest he should take too much upon himself; but still so many assurances were given by him to me that such would not be the case that I had almost succeeded in persuading myself that Father for the first time in his life would take a little care of himself on that score.

This situation led to further disturbance of his education in that he now felt obliged to divide his time between snatching a little tuition from Mr. Beal at Tavistock and then hurrying back at intervals to the Strand to help his father in the business. A most peculiar and unsatisfactory kind of arrangement, one would think, for everybody concerned. Through it all his sister, Mary Anne Beal, bombarded him with warnings and advice about his still unabandoned resolve to join the Established Church and take Holy Orders—a surprising attitude, as already remarked, in one who had not only been baptized into that Church but had married one of its ministers. Thus, in an undated letter of 1842, she writes:

> . . . It is a very serious matter to think of causing a division, even the least division in the family, for family love & unity are beyond price. . . . I do think it advisable that you should not be hasty to do anything that might in the smallest degree pain such inestimable parents as we have the happiness to possess. . . . I would wait and be very careful

before taking any decided step and be very sure of your motives in leaving Wesleyanism for the Church, do not deceive yourself but be thoroughly convinced that it is a matter of conscience and not resulting from pride in any form. . . .

And in another letter of about the same time, referring rather gratuitously to 'Your wayward thoughts and desires respecting the Church', she writes:

. . . be assured there is *no* state of life without its trials, and those of a Minister are sometimes both severe and perplexing. . . . I am free to confess that I think the life of a good country clergyman as a very happy one, perhaps I am inclined to think it happier than any other, but as I said before it cannot be free from its trials. What I would have you do is attend cheerfully to business and during the leisure allowed you keep up what you know and increase your store of good & judicious reading . . . at any rate till you are 21 or 22 . . . and if Providence has called you there will be some opening made in some way or another if the Ministry is the field in which you are destined to be useful and happy. . . .

Indeed, he received more sympathy and understanding in this tremendous and agonizing problem—for such it was for a youth who loved his father as much as his own soul's ambition—from his sisters Emma and Augusta. It must have been an enormous boon to him to be able to open his heart to them without reserve. In fact it bound him to Augusta, who never married, in a very special relationship which was to last till her death forty years later. William Beal, too, made up for his wife's nagging and lengthy exhortations by being sympathetic and helpful—though it could be argued that as a clergyman of the Church of England it was practically his duty to be so. At any rate, he wrote to William at about this time.

Would you like me to name to your Father the subject of *your*, & Augusta's and Emma's, going to Church every Sacrament Sunday? I feel very confident indeed that both with your Father and Mamma I could gain it for you all. With this stipulation, however, that so long as you are under age, this shall be the *last* concession made to you in these matters—viz. that one Sunday in a month, and *that* the Sacrament Sunday, shall be at your own disposal, but that the other three, you all consent willingly and regularly to go wherever your Father thinks you get the most wholesome spiritual food.

For a man of Mr. Beal's particular cloth this may not seem to be a particularly valiant piece of championship either for poor William or the Church. But it has to be realized that in those days the notion of filial piety and obedience tended to be exalted above almost every other consideration. Even the exemplary William could not forbear from a rather sardonic vein when writing a joint letter to his sisters Emma and Augusta (September 9th, 1842):

> . . . Have you heard from Mr. Beal on a particular subject? Did you expect anything of the kind? I was quite surprised when I heard from him about it and Father's approbation too . . . Father says that there is a slight difference between the young Gen'tn [generation] but you must wait till Sunday, when, if you'll go to Church in the morning, you shall hear it all in the afternoon and then by attending Methody or other Chapel in the Evening you will cover your double sin, and go to bed a Xtian. . . .

At the same time the pursuit of his heart's desire made him very wary, for he wrote to his 'dearest Gussie' (Augusta) in an undated letter of this time: '. . . of course you only let him [their father] know as much as you *discreetly* can of the contents of our notes. . . . I have a note this afternoon from Mr. Beal dated Liskeard. He says he is better but writes I think rather wildly. He wants me to write him confidentially on my own concerns, but I do not esteem it safe to do so while he is so excitable, as he might use my letter in a way I should not like. . . .'

Nevertheless, it has to be admitted that Beal's intercession had won a small, but by no means insignificant, concession from their father for William and his sisters. Mr. Smith was not after all himself a *bona fide* Wesleyan and it would not be unreasonable to expect that, when he was not actually under heavy pressure from his wife and mother-in-law, he would be inclined to be tolerant and even perhaps rather sympathetic to his children's aspirations. But he remained inflexible in his resistance to William's desire to take Holy Orders. This, however, was not so much inspired by sectarian prejudice as by his pride in and ambition for the business, which, by his own extreme diligence and active foresight, he had raised from a very modest scale to one of considerable importance and value.

One outward sign of Mr. Smith's comparative affluence was that at about this time he gave up living with his family over his Strand office and bought a quite grand suburban villa with large private grounds at Kilburn—known as Kilburn House. Yet in so doing he made his already arduous life even more arduous by the daily travelling to and fro from his comparatively distant home. In fact he began to realize what William had already realized, that he was ruining his health and that he would soon be compelled to hand over the reins—and he would want his son to be the one to take them.

The whole family was worried to death about Mr. Smith's health, his excitability and his fanatical application to his business, so William, being a dutiful and devoted son, as well as showing himself

11

to be scarcely less capable and mature a manager than his father, found himself willy-nilly already accepting and fulfilling the role for which the latter had cast him. It meant, of course, the final abandonment of any attempt at a regular schooling for him, for it was becoming farcical for him to continue racing backwards and forwards over the two hundred odd miles between London and Tavistock at intervals of only a few days. Certainly his mother and sisters looked to him to jump into the breach—at any rate until Father could be persuaded to employ a paid, professional manager.

'. . . I am sorry dear Father is so extremely diligent in business', wrote Emma to William, 'but the time *will come* when in some way our God will answer our earnest and united prayers.' And again: '. . . Gussie and I really think that if you feel your health perfectly equal to this second voyage it would be better *not* to leave Father for more than four or five days. We fear after all this excitement must tell upon his health.'

William did find this routine a strain on his constitution—which was never really very robust; nevertheless he was exhilarated by the amount of responsibility which now devolved upon his young shoulders, as may be seen from the following undated letter from the Strand to his sister Mary Anne Beal:

> . . . I never remember such a period of excessive excitement and hard work. I have been *in* town, with Father, once at 3 o'clock in the morning and every other day since the beginning of the season before 5 . . . and we have had 9 Special Express Engines to Liverpool, Manchester & Birmingham and they will run every day this week.— All this I have mainly to arrange and I can assure you it has worn me not a little. Constant excitement and anxiety during the days and short disturbed nights & the consequences are gradually making me feel as low and nervous as I was a few months back, but I hope it will be quieter again shortly.
>
> I have had an interview with the great George Hudson,[1] the Railway King. The Times wrote for a man to come up to town on my representation who knew something of the railways down in the North and we went together to see this great man and to remonstrate with him concerning some errors in the arrangement of the trains. We . . . had a good opportunity of seeing his character of which I have not formed a very favourable opinion . . . at first he was disposed to treat

[1] Born 1820, the son of a Yorkshire farmer; inherited a large fortune and through his friendship with George Stephenson decided to promote the still embryonic rail connections between the industrial North and Midlands. Opened his first railway in 1839—the York and North Midland—and in 1843 amalgamated three lesser lines into the Great Midland Railway. M.P. for Sunderland and three times Mayor of York, he was finally discredited and ruined; but not before he had made himself a millionaire and controlled a quarter of the railway line mileage in Britain. Died 1871.

me slightingly and I felt rather angry and in the course of conversation brought in the names of the conductors of the Times & Chronicle which had such a magical effect upon the honourable gentleman that both my companion and myself could hardly refrain from laughing in his face. . . .

Meanwhile Mary Anne continued to bombard her brother with homilies and warnings about his and his sisters' religious veerings: '. . . I am rather grieved to hear you say that you are all getting higher & higher in Church views. I had hoped the late doings at Oxford[1] would have tended to moderate your views and to shew you the danger of extremes. Do not, pray do not suffer yourselves to be beguiled into a semi-popish spirit. . . . If there are those who are bigoted Wesleyans you I fear are in much danger of becoming bigoted Church people, but my dear brother & sisters too remember that after all it is religion of the heart that is all important. . . .' Or again (April 1st, 1844): '. . . You are getting by half too high Church for us . . . pray do not hold any extreme views or make of too great importance those parts of religion wh. were meant to be secondary. . . .'

However, there now unexpectedly appeared to be a very good chance of William being able to fulfil his unrelinquished ambition of becoming a clergyman—without defying his father. For Mr. Smith suddenly seems to have reached such a pitch of fatigue and despondency as actually to have contemplated selling the business. Mary Anne wrote:

> I am most sincerely delighted at the encouraging prospect of affairs. You have now certainly a far greater likelihood of reaching your long cherished hopes and wishes—all I can say is May it please God to grant your desire and that you may live to be the useful minister of a nice little parish of your own.
>
> I am very, very thankful dear Father has determined to relieve himself but I shall not be fully able to believe he will sell the business he has so long cherished until I hear of some very decided move in that direction & I shall be most thankful to hear of it.

Mary Anne's caution was fully justified, for Mr. Smith as suddenly threw off this defeatist mood as he had succumbed to it and returned to his labours with redoubled fury, more than ever resolved to make his son an active partner in the concern. With this reversal of mood the former alarm among his family and friends revived. Besides, Mrs. Smith's health and spirits were being affected by worry about

---

[1] The 'Oxford Movement' initiated by 'Tracts for the Times', between 1833 and 1841 and written by Newman, Pusey, Keble and Williams. The last and most celebrated was Newman's 'Tract 90' on the Thirty-Nine Articles, published in 1841.

her husband, who now became lame. '. . . Does Father think of taking her away anywhere and himself going with her, for the sake of his poor leg?' asked Mary Anne of William.

At this point—early in 1845—Mr. Smith's friend and trustee Mr. Sercombe (whose son Rupert afterwards married his daughter Louisa) wrote to him urging him to rest and 'by advertisement or otherwise get a respectable business man, who understands your kind of business and who would take your morning work . . . this would save your health and in all human probability prolong your valuable life'. He also tactfully suggested that pushing William's nose too hard against the grindstone might easily induce in him a disgust for business as well as injure *his* health. To everyone's surprise Mr. Smith seemed impressed by this advice and, though he did not hire a manager, he agreed to take steps to render his own and his son's lives somewhat less gruelling. This development is described by William in a letter to Mary Anne (April 22nd, 1845):

> . . . We have at last made an alteration—a decided and I hope an effectual one.
>
> Father has long felt that his late attack of lameness resulted from over-work, and therefore has so far overcome his natural predilections as to determine on doing less—on giving up packing up altogether—on playing the Gentleman Tradesman. In order to carry out this idea he has resolved to dine *here* [at Kilburn] regularly at 4 o'clock, excepting on Saturdays—and he has purchased me a Horse,—a very beautiful one indeed—on which I am to ride backwards and for-wards—if necessary, to stay for a short time after he has left, if not to leave with him or when I choose.
>
> I hope to have some little time to myself—some little time to see my friends. . . .

Nevertheless, the new scheme of things did not live up to its promise. Mr. Smith could not reduce his tempo and inevitably bent the neck of his long-suffering son to the same yoke as he had imposed upon himself—until the boy's health broke down. Doctors ordered William to rest 'if he did not want to ruin his health for life' and packed him off to Ramsgate to recuperate. In every way things now began—in this autumn of 1845—to move towards a crisis. Mr. Smith was penitent at first and again thought of selling the business and William again thought his chance had come to become an Anglican priest. But this time it did not appear that Mr. Smith's giving up the business was synonymous with William's getting his freedom. William described the current phase in this letter to Mary Anne (October 28th, 1845):

> He [Father] had felt the pressure of the business—had been worried by it and had suffered in his nerves to some extent during my absence

from town . . . and the prospect of the future being so doubtful, he
began to think that there was no absolute necessity for him to labour
on, and after turning the matter over in his mind a great deal, and
very frequently representing to me what an enormous fortune I should
have in a few years, if I could continue the business, he at last made
up his mind to retire as soon as he could possibly get things in
order. . . .

The next question is what am I to do? I think without any cant,
that these circumstances have occurred most providentially and that
an opening now presents itself sufficiently distinctly to authorize me
without presumption to express my wish to enter the Church and if
possible to follow it up.

Father has still a great wish that I should go on with the business
but seems aware of my desire to do something else and is afraid to
press the subject lest the result might realise the Doctor's prediction
. . . I have not yet told him what I wish to do but he knows. Mamma
has been trying to get my views and intentions out of Sisters, but they
are quite dumb always avoiding a reply to my question . . . if I was
to say anything prematurely she would tell her Wesleyan acquaintances and having her prejudices worked upon would excite Father
dreadfully before he wd give me an opportunity of telling him all I
wish. . . .

During the last year or so both Father's and Mamma's prejudices
have increased to a most distressing extent. They are now dreadfully
bigoted. . . . Altogether the spirit of Wesleyanism has changed very
much for the worse during the last two or three years. They have been
preaching most violently against the Church.

I do not think that Father can absolutely refuse to accede to my
wishes. . . .

He wrote again shortly afterwards (November 6th):

. . . Don't be afraid that I am becoming a Puseyite, a Newmanite, or
Roman Catholic . . . I am only confirmed in my dislike for Wesleyanism as now carried out by preachers and people and in my decided
preference for the Church. . . .

Father does not say much of selling now . . . I don't think . . . that
even if I go out of it he will really sell the business—he may perhaps
take someone in . . . whom he could manage completely but he wd
never give up altogether the influence and income which the business
gives. . . .

Feeling that this was the best opportunity he was ever likely to
have, William now set about formulating his grand design for formal
submission to his father—and of this there remains among his papers
an undated pencil draft: '1st. It has been my wish for many years to
enter the Ministry from I trust a sincere desire to do good. 2) But
hitherto I have perceived no providential opening and therefore have
been silent. 3) Now, however, providence has presented an oppor-

tunity for decision on these points arising from the late turn in your mind, which I had never expected. 4) I ask, therefore, will you permit me to enter the Church?...'

We do not know the manner or the terms of his father's outright rejection of this appeal. As no letter is now to be found it may have been verbal—or if in a letter William may have destroyed this out of chagrin. Certain it is, however, that it did meet with absolute rejection. There is an undated note from Mary Anne: 'Your kind letter this morning grieved me, but I cannot say the result surprised me. I deeply sympathize in your disappointment, but cheer up my dear brother, your other request will most likely meet with a favourable hearing'. This 'other request' presumably refers to his simply becoming a member of the Church without entering the priesthood. At any rate William submitted and an old family friend wrote: '... from what I know of you, had you acted contrary to your Father's wishes, *you* would not have been *happy*, therefore I cannot but think you have come to a right determination upon the matter'.

But some idea of the greatness of the sacrifice and of the self-discipline and submission which he imposed upon himself can be gained from an entry in a journal which he kept intermittently at this period. Whilst on holiday at Rydal in the Lake District in the summer of 1846, the year of his coming of age, he wrote under the date August 8th:

> The past twelvemonth has been one of great importance to me and as far as man may be permitted to judge, determining the particular course of life I shall lead, and the objects to which my best energies are to be devoted.
> The decision on these most serious matters was not, perhaps in accordance with the hopes and desires I had long cherished.
> Those who have a natural claim upon my respect and obedience so strongly opposed the schemes I entertained and in such a feeling, as to render it impossible for me to carry them into effect. ...

Describing then how many of his friends, well qualified to judge, had thought him well fitted to be a minister and how he had believed his own strong wishes to be 'an indication of the will of Providence', he continues with a controlled overtone of bitterness:

> But it is not so—at least apparently—for he whose power is absolute in the matter—under Providence itself—by the strong expression of his wishes and intentions obliged me to yield my own desires and views, and adopt his instead.
> By this I do not mean that he acted otherwise than from the kindest motives, as he no doubt considered the course of life he contemplated for me the best and the most useful and that in fact for which I am designed. ...

16

He therefore concludes that he 'may not idly regret long cherished hopes, which it may be I have not been justified in entertaining, but it is my duty to acknowledge an overruling and directing Providence in all the very minutest things, by being in whatsoever state I am, therewith content. . . .'

There is no indication in the letters or journal of there being any exact date marking an abrupt transference of William's allegiance from Methodism to the Church of England. Again, out of consideration for his parents' feelings, it appears to have been a gradual and very tactful operation. For whilst on his holiday in the Lake District he noted under the date line 'Kendal, August 2nd': 'Attended St. Thomas's Church in the morning . . . Trinity Church in the afternoon . . . and the Methodist Chapel in the evening. To perpetuate my remembrance of *this* service would be unkind.' But by January 29th, 1847, he could write to Mary Anne: 'I am going on very comfortably with Father now, seldom or never going to Chapel or asked to do so. It appears understood I may do as I like, without remark on either side.'

Meanwhile, in another entry in his journal for August 1846, he shows how quickly he mastered his disappointment and how resolutely he determined to make the best of the new turn of events:

The last few weeks have been marked with very important and serious events. First came the decision affecting my future life—of the results of which no one can form an estimate. Then my coming of age on the 24th June was a serious event, as with the liberal means afforded me by my Father and the general though tacit concession of freedom of thought and action—the undefinable difference in the manner in which I am received in Society—the acknowledgement that I am a man—all have opened up fresh responsibilities and duties—without removing any that previously existed. . . .

But a few days after . . . the partnership question was debated in the best and most liberal spirit by my Father. . . . On the 30th ulto., Mr. Ford[1] waited upon us by appointment to take our joint instructions as to the Partnership, which gives me £500 a year clear, board and lodging; a comparative interest in the capital of £2,000, for seven years, but liable to six months notice on either side.

These terms, with which was coupled an express declaration that they were only temporary—as a prelude to much greater concessions— are extremely liberal and considerate.

From this it is plain that far from harbouring any animosity against his father for frustrating his most cherished hopes, his gratitude and continuing affection were as strong and unfeigned as ever. This did not, however, prevent him from seeing his father's foibles

[1] William Ford, family lawyer and close life-long friend of W. H. Smith.

17

and occasionally laughing over them. Thus he wrote to Gussie (November 26th, 1846): '. . . Things go on pretty smoothly. Father is of course a little testy, but generally manageable. He came down on Monday for half an hour, walked into the Counting House, bowed to the people, then walked upstairs, had his leg dressed and then got into the carriage (which was waiting for him all the time) vowing "the place stunk"—"couldn't breathe", and he "would not come down again for some time", "it was wretched"—"such a noise too". So he has not been here since, and won't be, at all events till next Monday.'

Indeed, Mr. Smith senior now became increasingly eccentric, irascible and difficult. But, though it was hard going for William, he was probably not alone in feeling immensely relieved when his father allowed him, as junior partner, to take over the early work in the Strand—which in such a business was of course the main burden of the day. Mr. Smith would drive over from Kilburn later in the day and expend his habitual terrorism upon a staff already somewhat relaxed. His son's gentler though none the less firm hand also did much to offset the effect of his outbursts and to create a happier spirit in the place. William, moreover, had long been known to members of the staff, not only as a pleasant, energetic boy, working side by side with them, but also as an outstandingly capable organizer, who, as we have seen, had at 14 a complete grasp of the business and at 19 could stand up to an arrogant magnate like George Hudson, the Railway King.

Nevertheless, these first two years of his full-fledged partnership were anxious ones owing to the counterpart in England of the political upheavals on the Continent in the shape of the second flare-up of the Chartist Movement and the onset of a widespread financial and commercial depression marked by the end of the great railway speculation boom and the fall of its central figure, George Hudson. Allusions to these things are to be found in William's correspondence at the time, as when his brother-in-law Rupert Sercombe wrote (September 20th, 1847): '. . . truly matters wear a *very, very* gloomy aspect. . . . It is very deplorable to hear of the difficulties of so many old and respectable houses and I see no immediate prospect of alleviation, but fear with you that many strange events await us.' And William to Gussie several months later: 'We have been flogging along pretty miserably since—I can hardly say when. In fact there is so much to be said and done here and at Kilburn by everybody that we have no time to think about our misfortunes, or we should be able to feel them more acutely. . . .'

When the Chartists staged a huge demonstration on April 10th, 1848, and planned to march on Westminster and present a monster petition to Parliament, the Government's security measures proved too much for them, the demonstrators dispersed after a few clashes with the police and the rolls comprising the petition were sent to the House of Commons in a series of cabs. Of this Mary Anne wrote from the country to William (April 14th):

> ... I am very glad Monday passed off better than you expected and hope there will be no recurrence of such a meeting or at least that the agitators will not be able to get up a disturbance. I suppose both you and dear Father are kept pretty close prisoners. Practically we know nothing of these things here. Our quiet village is just as it was when Louis Philippe ruled France.[1] There has been no sensation created by any of the political events that have been so lately occurring—I mean among the cottage population—of course in Society it is one great theme of conversation.

Soon after these excitements there was a severe outbreak of cholera in London and Mr. Smith senior wrote to his son (August 30th, 1849): 'Keep your place at the Strand well aired & fumigated—ease our Servants as much as possible & keep them in good spirits, teach them not to alarm themselves though the pestilence is really awfully increased since we left London.'

Yet, despite the cares of business and his own rather exceptionally serious cast of mind, William had time for other no less serious but more human interests, as this letter (February 5th, 1848) to his sister Gussie shows:

> ... My numerous engagements have prevented me from seeing those angels H. A. D.—E. W. and A.H. or any others, of whom of course I ought to dream every night.
>
> Thank Lucy for her charming *little* note; if she wants to write three a day to me it could not possibly fatigue her I should think. I will write her a line with a report of the flirtation association for the promotion of sighs, groans and tears between young people of both sexes meeting tonight at Elliotts. When you can find yourself strong enough to take two minutes out of your twelve hours sleep bestow them on paper for my benefit—for I am dismal—very—sometimes—and in love.
>
> P.S. Keep that secret—that is don't tell anybody but Mamma, Lucy, Cari and Prisci.

We do not know whether the object of his love here referred to was in fact the girl who was eventually to become his wife. Possibly it was a little before the time when he could have met her. Nevertheless it is a fact that in this February of 1848 he took a step which was to have far-reaching consequences for his life in two ways. For it was at this

[1] Louis Philippe, 'King of the French' since 1830, abdicated as a result of the Revolution in Paris and fled to England on February 24th, 1848.

time that he gave thirty guineas to the funds of King's College Hospital, the managing committee of which he was to join in the following year and with which he was to be closely connected throughout the rest of his life. Moreover, this connection brought him acquaintance with one of the hospital's leading lights, Robert Cheere, who in turn introduced him to the family of Frederick Dawes Danvers, a former clerk to the council of the Duchy of Lancaster.

William quickly became on intimate terms with the Danvers family, which included several attractive daughters and with the eldest of whom, Emily, he probably fell in love at first sight. But in fact she married in 1854 an acquaintance of his who had been courting her longer—a man named Benjamin Auber Leach, who held an appointment in the old India House. As Leach died only a year after the marriage, Emily returned again to her family and soon afterwards a baby girl was born. After a decent interval William was therefore free to pay his court to her—and in due course to make her his wife. Nevertheless, before this happy outcome was reached, it is reasonably deducible from certain hints in his letters and journal that he was jealous of Auber Leach from the start and that the latter's success in winning Emily was a blow and a torture to him. The impression is cumulative—from a number of oblique allusions—and therefore it would be impracticable to try to provide the evidence here, because so much irrelevant and otherwise uninteresting material would have to be reproduced; but it is there none the less.

Meanwhile, once the political and economic malaise of the later 1840s had passed and the boom which was to last for the next twenty years had begun with the 1850s, William found distraction from his love-sickness and also abounding interest in the exhilarating tempo of the business. '. . . I don't know how it is', he wrote to Gussie (September 5th, 1851), 'but I am very jolly—quite comfortable, and people tell me I am getting fat—do you think so?' In another letter to her (September 15th) we have a glimpse of the kind of thing he was now having to do—and how he did it.

> . . . Master Willmer [firm's agent in Liverpool] being very naughty and Ford our Solicitor having gone down to Liverpool to look after him I was telegraphed for on Friday evening to go down "directly". I therefore sent a man on horseback to Kilburn for a couple of shirts—greatly to Sarah's dismay—and bowled away for the Mail Train. After having a good deal of crying—I can assure you it is no joke to see an old man cry and to feel that you have even in the proper line of Duty caused him to do so—we patched up matters once more and I returned by the Express, getting to Kilburn at 11 o'clock, having had enough travelling—some 700 miles since Thursday night at 6 o'clock.

4. Emily Smith (*née* Danvers).

5. Emily Smith, with her daughter by her first marriage, Mary Auber Leach, *circa* 1867, from the painting by Buckner.

But his main preoccupation was that of trying to keep his father away from the business, partly for his health's sake and partly because his spasmodical and rather terrifying appearances at the office must have been disturbing in every sense. Fortunately, however, Mr. Smith was beginning to be more amenable to the idea of withdrawal. The death of his wife in March 1851—though she had been even more of an invalid than himself and her passing seems to have caused but few demonstrations of grief from her family—must have lowered his health and spirits more than usual. For William wrote to Gussie (July 20th, 1852):

> ... Father is, he says, going to take a house near a Station for six weeks by way of change. This will be pleasant for me as it will be the only Country I shall get. . . . He is not to work, so Todd says, for some months to come and I incline to think he will submit.
>
> I don't wish Father to return, if it can be avoided. I am not going to oppose anything; like a well-trained child I submit to my betters, only muttering that I will have my own way when I can, but if he comes, really and truly I do not think he ought to be alone more than two or three days at the outside.

Then, early the following year, he writes again to Gussie (February 2nd, 1853): 'Father proposes to go down to Torquay; and you must keep him as long as you can. He is *much* more reasonable than he was. . . .' When, later that year, Mr. Smith suffered some kind of heart attack, fit or stroke, a family friend wrote to William (December 30th, 1853): '. . . I feel deeply for your constant anxiety relative to your excellent Father's health and I hope from my heart that you may be spared from a recurrence of that most distressing attack. . . . That long continued attention to great business has a very bad effect at last—and the only thing now is to keep him from resuming it. . . .'

How close William was to Gussie and how much relief he got from opening his heart to her is evident from the following revealing and moving letter of about this time, written to her in pencil *en route* to Dublin (March 3rd, 1853):

> My dear Gussie,
>
> I am flying along the London and North Western by Express Train somewhere near Tring at this moment and probably near Rugby before I have done. . . .
>
> I am going to Dublin as we are rather anxious about the state of accounts there. Father wishes me to stay a fortnight but I don't think I ought to be away from him more than three days at the outside, and I therefore think of leaving Dublin again on Friday, even if I have to return next week. I have not told him so, because it is best to let him think he is having his way. Although in really good health, as far as I can see, and you know I have so nervous a disposition with regard

21

to him as anyone can have, he chafes under the small annoyances of business, so as to become nervously irritated beyond anything I ever remember,—giving three people notice to leave in one day and such like things—but he is most kind and considerate to me. Still, all this occasions anxiety to one, and I am almost afraid to go away not knowing what violent changes may take place in my absence, in his desire to 'get rid' of the business.

I find too that his excitement is much greater when I am away and increases in proportion to the length of time, as everything comes before him. . . .

I sometimes feel that Father's happiness, in his later days and the comfort of the family depended upon me, and then I feel and know I am absolutely blind and can really do nothing whatever of my own judgment; but I know also that if I and we all desire absolutely and without reservation to be guided aright, that guidance will be granted to us, and we need not and ought not to fear or doubt in the darkest night of uncertainty and human difficulty. . . .

I have gone on writing this without quite intending it;—just as I would talk with you, as I could fancy I was now doing—but there is solid pleasure in the conviction that we are of one mind in these things—wherever we are we can think of each other and we can pray . . . do not think I am at all low or sad. With the exception of very transient occasions, I never felt greater reason for cheerfulness.

Another, undated, letter to Gussie during this same trip shows the strong compassion which always, throughout his life, tempered his firmness and sense of duty.

. . . really to spend nearly a week in Dublin in such weather, your occupation being the agreeable one of taking the means of subsistence in the most complete and legal manner from the head of a family— probing his necessities, his home secrets, the affairs of his connections as well as his own—and then making as a gratuity and on certain conditions an allowance per week, as to a servant . . . and the agree-able taste of giving his Brother and his Nephews to understand that I being Master in the place of Johnston, and things being as they are, they must look for another shelter and make or find a home for themselves. . . .

. . . but it is not pleasant to talk over and settle these contingencies before the face of a man like Johnston 'for our legal security', who really shows himself willing to do all he can to repair the evil he has done us. However these are things which become a matter of necessity and can no more be avoided than the necessity of submitting to medical treatment in illness can be. . . .

You need not show this to the Governor. . . .

The 'Dublin House', as it was called, was the first of the wholesale houses to be instituted to serve the needs of outlying provinces when the volume of business had begun to become too big to be handled from a single source of supply in London. Others soon followed at Birmingham, Manchester and Liverpool. For the wholesale side had been started in London quite early on in the reign of the elder W. H. Smith, when he had extended the business from supplying his own individual customers within a limited area of the metropolis to supplying country newsagents, wholesale, who in turn retailed to their local customers. The Dublin House had been an already existing business which the Smiths had bought up in the Dublin bankruptcy court in 1850 and which, as can be seen from the above references in William's letters, was at first unsatisfactorily and dishonestly run by one Johnston. After the latter's removal, William, in 1856, appointed Charles Eason, hitherto bookstall manager at Victoria Station, Manchester, who had attracted his attention by his efficiency and high moral character, to be head of the Dublin House. The choice proved to be well justified, for under Eason's careful and scrupulous management the Irish business grew rapidly and continuously during the next thirty years, until, in 1886, it was transferred—lock, stock and barrel—to him and his son, under circumstances which will later be described.

II

THE GREAT COUPS

⟶✦⟵

BEFORE beginning to relate the story of those bold strokes which, under William Henry II's inspired direction, expanded the business to undreamt-of proportions, we can get a glimpse of the working of the original and main business of newspaper distribution as it was shortly after William Henry I's retirement from a journal called *The Leisure Hour* of October 1860, entitled 'Smith's Express Newspaper Office', describing the visit of their correspondent to 186 Strand at 4.0 a.m. on a Saturday morning:

> . . . a large hall, forming all the back part of the extensive premises (behind the counting houses), and surrounded by two galleries, was occupied by above a hundred and sixty men, either at the long tables or benches which run along the floor, or darting from post to pillar. The galleries were also filled by circles of most active coadjutors, from whom every now and then small parcels or reams of wet journals were showered upon the heads of claimants or clamants below. And it was this incessant clamour for supplies from every corner, and apparently addressed to nowhere, that struck me as the most remarkable feature of the labour. To witness perfect order emerge from such a scene of apparently utter confusion was like conjuring. Suppose twenty individuals scattered about at the tables marking up packages of the newspapers, some almost too heavy to be lifted, and others perhaps consisting of not more than a quire or two; and suppose twenty voices to be uttering or bawling the words, 'a hundred Times', 'ten Fields', 'three Eras', 'twenty Telys' [Telegraphs], 'fifteen Stars', 'fifteen Standards', 'four Presses', 'three Critics', 'two Gasses', 'twenty Revs' . . . 'three Mists' [Economists], 'two Worlds', 'six Ill. News and six Ill. Times', etc.; and to such a babel what was the reply? The flying about in all directions of the supplies still wanted and their alighting upon the benches into the hands whence the vocal calls have proceeded! By them they were immediately disposed of, folded up into oblong square bundles; and when the entire order was completed according to a list before every packer, the same was by another

24

prompt assistant wrapped in strong brown paper covers, ready
addressed, then corded, and despatched to the outer door, where the
light flying carts were waiting for their several cargoes.

... I ought to have stated that every ten or fifteen minutes the
vehicles (conspicuously painted 'Express Newspaper Office', with the
proprietors' name and address), with piles of the 'Times' had been
driving rapidly up and down from Printing House Square with loads,
as fast as they could be got from the machine. . . .

Contemporaneously, trucks and porters are delivering deposits of
other journals; . . . men staggering in under heavy burdens and
others going out with packages of all sizes, look as if inextricably
complicated and yet the whole in perfect order. The outgoers find the
conveyances for the different Northern, Great Western, South
Eastern, etc., stations, waiting for their freight under the superin-
tendence of a manager, who has all their hours of starting marked,
and all the number of parcels that are to be sent to them. His charge is
a very important one, and calculated to minutes. The time necessary
for the transit from the Strand office to the rail runs nearly as close
as a horse-race. Where needed, in consequence of streets being paved,
or obstacles from buildings, or laying down gas or water pipes, or any
other interruption of the right of way, previous surveys are made,
routes changed and farther time allowed, as the case may be. Sometimes outriders are sent to clear off such hindrances as London is
exposed to from locks of market carts, wagons, cabs, and all the
interruptions of its mighty traffic; that is, as the morning advances,
for the earliest despatches up to six o'clock are little likely to fall in
with aught in the way before them. In this work sixty horses are
employed and their sleek condition does credit to their feed and
efficiency. . . .

By five o'clock the absolute whirl all about the spectator is enough
to excite that sort of giddiness which is felt in factories where a
complication of steam and endless wheels are at fight, only here it is
the human agency that is getting through the wonderful task, and
with a degree of steady speed which is difficult to reconcile with the
nature and amount of the labour. And so good-humouredly too.
Everybody looked as if almost at play—jocund, laughing at petty
contretemps and joking at awkward mishaps and their instant
remedies. It was an excellent sign of the relations between masters and
men. I should not look for a strike, hardly for a dismissal, in this
admirably conducted establishment. . . .

On this Saturday morning a hundred and twenty thousand public
journals were, between four and nine o'clock, thus transmitted to a
hundred and nine railway stations. . . .

His father's increasing absence from the Strand not only greatly
facilitated for William the actual running of the office, but also gave
him the opportunity to consider ways and means of widening the
scope of the business. Hitherto—apart from one or two temporary

excursions into the fields of stationery, bookselling and binding—it had been almost wholly confined to that of distributing newspapers; but in this trade they had considerable competitors, the largest and most powerful of whom, Clayton's, still outdistanced them. William saw that by extending his operations to another and wider field he might outflank this mighty rival.

Bookstalls—of a sort—had already become a familiar feature of the principal stations of the rapidly extending network of railways with their ever-growing number of passengers. For the most part, however, they tended to be a combination of book and newspaper stall and general refreshment booth run by local tradesmen. There were no regulations controlling these stalls, the goods which they offered for sale or the people who ran them. Consequently they were frequently run by disreputable, illiterate and untrained people and the literature which they offered tended to be cheap, trashy and often near-pornographic. There was naturally no lack of sale for this and many people patronized these stalls precisely for the reason that such material was unlikely to be obtainable from a reputable bookseller. Nevertheless, protesting letters were already appearing in the newspapers and so many complaints were being received by the railway companies from the more fastidious section of travellers as to lead them to advertise for tenders for the rent of stalls on their stations in the hopes of entrusting them, not only to more scrupulous, but to more business-like hands.

Young William had taken due note of the prevailing circumstances and within a very short time of his entry into partnership had begun to buy up some of the stalls of local men on stations and to open negotiations with the railway companies for the right to erect his own bookstalls. In the matter of the provision of better reading material he had been preceded—by a very short head—by one or two other firms. In 1847 Messrs. Simms and McIntyre had initiated a 'Parlour Library', and Messrs. Routledge a 'Railway Library', both designed to meet the requirements of railway bookstalls. The books were for the most part reprinted English works whose copyright had expired or been transferred, foreign works in translation and American works unable to claim copyright protection. Even when Smith appeared on the scene in the following year the books on his bookstalls, were, at first, principally reprints—often pirated American reprints; though this fact did not by any means necessarily reflect upon their literary quality.[1]

Indeed, all the circumstances suited Smith exactly. They gave him the opportunity he had been seeking for extending the scope of the

[1] For some of the facts in this paragraph I am indebted to James T. Barnes: *Free Trade in Books: a Study in the London Book Trade since 1800;* p. 105 seqq.

family business and at the same time offered him a most satisfying
outlet for his missionary instincts—in this case in the substitution of
good light literature for trash and pornography. Nevertheless, despite
his worthy aims, he encountered the strong opposition of his father,
who mistrusted the idea of going beyond what he regarded as the
legitimate business of the firm—the distribution of newspapers—and
who was sceptical of the profits to be derived from bookselling.

But William's determination soon prevailed. He made an offer to
the London and North Western Railway for the rent of the bookstall
at Euston Station and this being accepted he opened it, on his own
entirely new lines, on November 1st, 1848. Meanwhile he concluded
a lease with this company which gained him exclusive rights for the
sale of books and newspapers throughout their network. This coup
earned for him the sobriquet of 'the North Western Missionary'. Two
weeks later he concluded a similar contract with the Midland Railway. Barely three years later, in 1851, Smith's railway bookstalls
were such an established institution that we find the great Gladstone
himself suggesting to Murray, the publisher, that perhaps 'the
individual [Smith] who rents the whole of the North Western Railway Bookstalls . . . would be competent, without binding himself, to
given an opinion "concerning the popular demand" for Gladstone's
Letters to Lord Aberdeen'. Six months later he again asked Murray
whether Smith might not be prevailed upon to sell at a reduction
several hundred copies of a pamphlet of his (Gladstone's) whose sale
had ceased at the original price.[1]

It was not long before the contrast between the quality of the
literature and of the service offered by W. H. Smith & Son on the
London and North Western and Midland stations and the quality of
that offered by the stalls on other lines began to be publicly commented upon. *The Times* sent a correspondent to investigate conditions at all the larger railway stations and he published his findings
in a lengthy and typically ponderous report in that newspaper on
August 9th, 1851. First, he said, he visited all the termini in London
and found it 'a painful and humiliating inspection'. 'With few
exceptions, unmitigated rubbish encumbered the bookshelves of
almost every bookstall we visited. . . . The purchasers were not few
or far between, but the greater the number, the more melancholy the
scene. . . .'

But, 'as we progressed north, a wholesome change became visible
in railway bookstalls'. Finally, at Euston, 'we poked in vain for the
trash. If it had ever been there, the broom had been there before us
and swept it clear away. . . .' The correspondent admitted that: 'At
first the result was most discouraging. An evident check had been

[1] Ibid.

given to demand; but as the new proprietor was gradually able to obtain the assistance of young men who had been educated as booksellers, and as public attention was drawn to the improvement in the character of the books exposed for sale, the returns perceptibly improved and have maintained a steady progressive increase greatly in excess of the proportion to be expected from the increase of travelling up to the present time. . . .'

One after another the great railway companies now ceded to Smith's the exclusive right to erect and run bookstalls at their stations. About 1852 the whole of the London and South-Western system was acquired, the London and Brighton a few years later and the Great Western in 1862. Such sudden and tremendous expansions called for considerable capital expenditure—apart from the problem of finding suitable staff in sufficient numbers to man so many new stations and enough literature to stock them. But William, despite the unrelenting opposition of his father, quietly and confidently pursued his object—sometimes acquiring outright monopoly on a whole network or at other times merely buying out the local man on a local station when the opportunity arose.

It soon became necessary, therefore, to create a separate 'book department' in connection with the bookstalls and to appoint a special manager for this department. From the well-known house of Messrs. Ward, Lock and Co. William obtained such a man in the person of Jabez Sandifer, who, from then onwards for the next forty years, developed this side with great shrewdness and ability, becoming one of the mainstays of the firm and in due course a partner.

Despite all William's and Sandifer's good intentions and precautions regarding the quality and nature of the literature dispensed at their bookstalls it was not always possible to please everybody and indeed, both now and later, indignant letters were received from time to time complaining of particular books bought off the stalls. What was probably one of the earliest of these came from no less a person than William's rival for Emily Danvers' affections, Auber Leach, and it is possible to suppose that the latter may not have been entirely innocent of some devious motive in writing it. At any rate, William's already mixed feelings about this acquaintance cannot have been much improved by such a pompous epistle (dated October 1853):

My dear Friend,
    I was very sorry to see on one of your bookstalls at Waterloo Station three copies of Byron's 'Don Juan'. I mention it as I suppose with your press of business you cannot check all the books which pass muster for your stalls. I believe that even Byron's publisher protested against the publication & his statue was refused room at Westminster Abbey in consequence.

Much was said some few years ago about the vile character of the literature sold at the railways—but I question if anything more poisonous was admitted to any station & perhaps the danger from Don Juan is greater from the fact of Byron being its author.

You must excuse my drawing your attention to this but you may accept this either privately or publickly—privately as from a friend or publickly as from one who considers it his duty to do all the little he can to stop the stream of iniquity which seems to threaten us, in the shape of immorality flowing from the press. . . . If you accept this as the latter form I may follow it up by one on the subject of Alexr. Dumas' writings.

Believe me,
Yours very truly,
B. Auber Leach

Almost simultaneously with the great bookstall venture another field of business was entered upon at William's instigation—again in face of dogged opposition from his father. At the beginning of the railway movement advertising on railway stations had been in no less primitive and ill-regulated a state than had been the bookstalls. But the railway companies soon became as alive to the great possibilities of their huge, blank station walls as did the tradesmen and manufacturers who wished to advertise their goods. The former therefore began to advertise for tenders for the use of them from those contractors who, to save them trouble, would make their own arrangements with individual advertisers. Again, in almost every case, Smith & Son were the successful tenderers.

But again the initial outlay of capital was very heavy and for a time the returns were so invisible or insignificant that old Mr. Smith fretted and fumed at the rent paid to the railway companies and at the cost of providing frames for advertisements, of printing, agents and bill-posters. But William's serene confidence again won the day and by 1854 the balance sheet of this particular branch at last showed a slight profit—albeit it was only £130 on an expenditure of £9,800! But thereafter the business and the profit increased by leaps and bounds from year to year, so that a new department—the Railway Advertising Department—had to be created to deal with it.

Already by 1854, therefore, the business consisted of three great branches, each in process of swift and sometimes sudden expansion— the newspaper agency under the direct control of the younger Smith, the bookstall trade under Sandifer, and the railway advertising department under yet other direction. In fact William was already beginning to find the strain of such widespread responsibility too much for him. His father—though he did not formally retire till

1857—was rapidly fading from the picture and when William at about this time happened to renew acquaintance with an old Tavistock school-fellow, William Lethbridge, he persuaded the latter, who was at that time an assistant master at Rossall School, to give up schoolmastering and join the firm, which he duly did shortly afterwards. He soon became a partner, and one upon whom William—especially after he had entered politics—came to rely absolutely for the next thirty years.

With old Mr. Smith's virtual disappearance—despite spasmodical incursions into the office, which caused nothing but unhappiness and confusion in the later years—all the details of planning and organization devolved completely on his son, who thus became to all intents and purposes the managing head of the firm. However, before taking leave of 'William Henry I', a proper tribute to his great work must be paid. For his early exertions, his energy, pluck and indefatigability, his single-minded devotion to his guiding principle of 'first on the road' had secured for the firm that standing and those resources without which—as William would have been the first to admit—his son's great imaginative strokes would not have been feasible. Likewise when great opportunities arose—as they now began to do—William was able with complete confidence to take the fullest advantage of them.

For, besides the expansion of the firm in these years along the—to the elder Smith's mind highly unorthodox—lines just described, the whole of the newspaper and news-agency business in England received a sudden and extraordinary stimulus through the abolition of the newspaper stamp-duty by John Bright's Act of 1854. The immediate effect of this was a reduction in the price of newspapers and an enormous increase in the demand for them. It was then that the great standing of W. H. Smith & Son—and the confidence of others in their ability to handle the increased demand—was proved beyond question.

For, on June 21st, 1854, a remarkable circular was issued from the office of *The Times*. This intimated that the proprietors of that mighty organ had determined that for the future 'all papers required by Messrs. Smith & Son for distribution in the country shall be delivered to them by the Publishers before any other Agent is supplied. "The Country" is understood to include all railway stations, and to exclude London and the Metropolitan districts, as defined by the Post Office. Messrs. Smith & Son will distribute for the London Agents, at a fair price, the Papers required by them for the service above defined.'

The importance of this circular can scarcely be overestimated, for it virtually amounted to a charter of monopoly in agency for the foremost newspaper in the world.[1] Every wholesale agent was now obliged to come to Smith's for his supply of *The Times*. Indeed, the firm was placed practically out of reach of the competition of Clayton's or of any of those others who had once been its bugbears. But this enormous privilege carried with it certain burdens and embarrassments. Long before they had been granted the monopoly Smith's had found—and become resigned to the fact—that the handling of *The Times* involved them in certain special problems. For *The Times* was always the latest of the newspapers to go to press, because it was the only one which gave a full report of Parliamentary proceedings and when the House of Commons sat late the paper did not make its appearance till after the morning mail-trains had left. The elder Smith had long ago evolved a procedure for overcoming this challenge to his efficiency by sending to receive the paper straight from the press and employing fast carts and special express trains to get it into the country on the same day.

Nevertheless, despite what Smith & Son had been able to achieve on their own account when acting as one among many newsagents, when the whole of the distribution of *The Times* came to be channelled through them it was inevitable that the effects of that paper's late publication should be magnified and cause delay and disruption all along the line. At the same time *The Times* publishers themselves refused to make any changes in their organization or arrangements to make matters at all easier for the agents: indeed, they seemed rather to take a perverse pleasure in being a law unto themselves and making things difficult for those whose job it was to distribute their newspaper.

Matters came to a head very shortly after Smith's had been given the monopoly in agency—in fact it was because of their new status that they were appealed to by indignant wholesalers and agents to protest to *The Times*. The following letter to Smith's from a firm called 'The English & Foreign Newspaper and Advertisement Office', dated December 11th, 1854, is worth quoting as an example of the feeling engendered by the lackadaisicalness of *The Times:*

Gentlemen,
   The complaints respecting The Times are now getting so heavy and the loss both ourselves and our Agents experience daily is so great we must ask you to represent the matter to the Manager at the first interview you have.
   We should think that if properly represented—and your own Business must furnish some strong cases—the time to supply the Country should be made an hour later, giving the Country the Papers

[1] At about this time the total circulation of the six leading London daily newspapers was only about 75,000, of which *The Times* accounted for 50,000.

printed up till 8 o'clock. London People can surely wait an hour and this hour will make all the difference to the Country—in some cases saving 12 hours.

This hour would do a great deal for the Country and I am sure the other members of the Trade who do Country Business would be in favour of it. I am sure our Town Business would not suffer the least by the delay. . . .

There is another point to arrange—what is Country and what is Town? Many Papers given off for town supply are sent to Greenwich, Vauxhall and such distances by some Agents. Is this the instruction of the Times? . . .

Messrs. Smith's having duly passed this complaint to *The Times*, the latter condescended to revise their definition of 'Town delivery' to include all places within a circle of 6 miles from the General Post Office, plus a number of places beyond it. But they added stiffly that '. . . the proprietors do not deem it expedient to make any change in the system of Publication . . . and they reserve to themselves the right of revoking this present concession to the demands of the town trade', if they should find that it resulted in the environs being supplied earlier than the town itself, which result they would regard as 'injurious to the interests of the Times'.

Another firm of newsagents, invited by William Smith to say if they were satisfied with existing arrangements for the publication of *The Times* wrote (December 11th, 1854): 'We have only to express our entire satisfaction and our increased confidence in *your* arrangements. If however yr. enquiry refers to the *publication* of the paper itself I must say we have reason to regard it as very far from equitable and in many cases inflicting very gross injustice. . . .' When publication was at all later than usual, they complained, they were put at a grave disadvantage by not getting their allocation in one lot—though 'we can at most times purchase outside the office what cannot be obtained within'. To this *The Times*'s retort was that as they did not undertake to supply their paper direct to the public 'the subsequent apportionment of the numbers rests entirely with the Trade, for the exercise of whose discretion in the matter the Proprietors cannot hold themselves in any degree responsible'.

A few years later (1860) there were further tussles between *The Times* and Smith & Son over the price at which the paper was to be sold—*The Times* insisting that Smith's should pay a bulk price for it and sell it at a price (3d. a copy) which Smith complained would cause him to 'lose one clear penny on every copy'. But the manager of *The Times* replied rather sanctimoniously that this loss could 'only result from your having demanded and received from the public your customers a higher price than that marked on the paper. . . . It is true that we have acquiesced in this practice and have derived a benefit from it, tho' not to the same extent that you have. What we propose now is that we shd. both forgo this benefit. Your sacrifice may be greater but so has been your gain.' Smith submitted, but not without emphasizing 'the magnitude of our sacrifice'.

However, to offset the impression of stolid arrogance and rigidity conveyed by the above correspondence it must be said that, at about the time it began, *The Times* had immensely increased its prestige by its enterprise in sending out to the Crimea the very first and one of the greatest of war correspondents, William Howard Russell, whose daily, fearless dispatches, sent by telegraph from the theatre of war, brought the horrors of the war home to the British public in a way never before experienced. So great was the interest—and the indignation against those held responsible for the war's mismanagement—that the circulation enormously increased, thereby benefiting as well their sole country agents, W. H. Smith & Son.

Incidentally, the war in the Crimea brought about the only exception, at least hitherto, in the firm's rule against Sunday work. For, in September 1855, shortly after the Battle of the Alma, the dispatches containing the list of killed and wounded arrived late on a Saturday night, and, after consultation with his father, William called upon the staff to sacrifice their Sunday rest in order that special supplements might be distributed in London and the provinces. Indeed, in the ordinary way the firm refused to handle Sunday newspapers at all and it is said that a member of the Royal Family who asked, among other papers, to be supplied with the *Observer* met with a flat refusal—even despite threats to cancel the whole order.

In the same vein, William, as soon as he took virtual charge of the business, set about shortening the hours of work in the Strand office. Saturday half-holidays were almost unknown in the 1850s; but William was a pioneer in the establishment of what is now a universal practice. He also organized periodical excursions on the river for the whole staff in the Strand and, what was bolder, encouraged the formation of a debating society for the discussion of social questions. With himself he was harder. For the first few years of his 'reign' he continued to rise each week-day at 4.0 a.m., swallow a cup of coffee and drive to the Strand by 5.0 a.m. Like his father before him, he would then take off his coat, roll up his sleeves and take part in the sorting and packing.

All this hard work did not preclude a certain amount of social life and William's observations and judgments in this sphere, shrewd and humorous as they often were, are valuable for any attempt to draw him 'in the round'. Thus he writes to Gussie (May 14th, 1853):

... You all wanted to know about the Boltons. The two girls dined with us last night. Bolton himself was shut up in bed with a cold. They were not extravagantly dressed, both extremely sensible and nice, but there is nothing to excite one in their characters as they come out on such occasions beyond their real worthiness. There is no real interchange of sympathy and I am not surprised Miss Bolton is still only Miss Bolton.

Edgar Silver came up to dine. He is very good, forcible, warm-hearted, but looks at the table or the ground most fearfully. Not really shy, but very apparently so—quite careless I believe of the society of ladies—preferring independence of position, even if it resulted in isolation, but he is a very worthy fellow, and I think my friend. . . . The other people were Lucy,[1] Rupert,[2] Edwin,[3] and our Father,—so you can imagine the group—as Father & Rupert said very little indeed, I found it rather hard to keep things going. . . .

In the autumn of 1854 he began his lifelong habit of taking an annual continental holiday by visiting Dresden and Leipzig and in the following year by going to Paris. 'The air makes me happy and I am at liberty and at rest—wonderful sensations', he wrote to his sister. Neither the first nor the last Englishman to experience this reaction.

At this time he began again to commit his inmost thoughts, hopes and fears to his journal. Before quoting some of this material it should be repeated, by way of a background and perhaps even as a possible explanation of some of the remarks, that the girl whom he loved, Emily Danvers, married Auber Leach in July 1854 and that in January 1855, the latter died. There could, it is true, be various explanations of the 'sin' to which William is referring, but there is a strong probability that it concerned his passion for Emily, which, in view of Leach's so recent death and of Emily's carrying his child, he felt ashamed to indulge, even in thought. Nevertheless, it seems clear from some of the entries that from the moment of her becoming a widow he determined to lose no time in making her his wife and that with this in mind he decided at least on sounding her feelings about such a possibility—even before any idea of a formal engagement could decently be entertained. So to the journal:

March 17. 55
. . . I know the Sin which most easily besets me, and I have now solemnly vowed never again to give way to it, even by thought and by desire. . . . O Lord! deliver me and keep me for ever from my greatest enemy my own evil heart—& make me do all thy will.
March 18
I am thankful that this day I have been preserved from open and wilful sin, and I do trust that I may be preserved by the Holy Spirit

[1] His sister. [2] Her husband, Rupert Sercombe.
[3] Edwin Sercombe, husband of his sister Emma.

from again relapsing into the enjoyment or the indulgence of the thoughts that have haunted me. . . .

March 19

Again I have reason for great thankfulness that I have not been led into the temptation that most easily besets me;—but the world has had the dominion in its care & anxieties. I have also been depressed and not sufficiently trustful with regard to my future domestic life. It is very difficult for man to draw the line between the intelligent exercise of the personal duties and responsibilities devolving upon him—his own part in working out the designs of providence—and that anxious care which becomes sin. . . .

March 28

. . . I now contemplate a step which may affect my whole life in this world and the next. I have made it a subject of prayer that I might be guided aright whatever that guiding may result in.

March 31

. . . The events of the past 48 hours call for great thankfulness. I have entered upon the development of my hopes and fears and hitherto I have been preserved from present disappointment. May everything that is within me praise His holy name in whom I will trust for ever and ever. . . .

April 2

I have made the attempt and not been repulsed. . . . I did not doubt I should be guided aright, but I had not dared to hope that even so far I should not meet with a check. I pray earnestly that my Father and my Friend would take me and this my very earnest desire into His keeping and entirely Direct all that is to happen concerning me:— and I pray also that He will bless *her* with all spiritual blessings. . . .

April 12

I have passed through a day of much care and anxiety and occupation. It has also been marked by a step which may affect my future life. Oh that I could more entirely trust in Him who has the disposing of events. . . .

April 16

I am thankful that I have not been so desponding today as I have been in former days, but on the other hand I am aware of ideas and schemes within me which may not proceed so entirely from a desire to render Glory to my God, as they ought to do. . . .

But this crisis in his inner life did not in the least deflect him from the pursuit of his aims in business or in other fields of public activity. For in this year, 1855, he entered upon his first connection with public business by allowing himself to be elected a member of the Metropolitan Board of Works, the body set up by the Act of that year, which was a sort of forerunner of the London County Council. Also, in the following year, national politics loomed for the first time on his horizon, for he was approached by the Liberal party at Boston, Lincolnshire, to ascertain if he were willing to stand in conjunction with a Mr. Ingram, who at that time represented the borough.[1] He appears to have been ready to accept the invitation on certain conditions, which are referred to rather cryptically in a draft reply: '. . . The most important question after all is whether or no the Party is strong enough to return a Second Member on the principles on which alone I can stand, and which are politically and religiously liberal.'

His definition of Liberal principles, which follows, shows that his Liberalism was in reality of that mildest, Whiggish variety which in his own, as in so many other cases, was to become merged in the more progressive form of Conservatism. Thus, although he declared himself in favour of abolishing Church Rates, he was opposed to Disestablishment; though advocating the promotion of popular education by fresh legislation, he would not have made it compulsory; though of the opinion that naval and military expenditure should be reduced, it must not be brought below the point of complete efficiency; and he could not look with favour on the introduction of vote by ballot.

Meanwhile, he was working as hard as ever at the Strand and travelling for the firm to Dublin, Liverpool and other outposts where the firm had established footings. 'My dear Ducky,' he wrote to Gussie from Dublin, 'I just write you a line to say that I am well and very cross, for the Irish are fast exciting all the dormant decision and anger in my character. I verily believe if I stay here much longer I shall be thought a fiend at the least for I do insist upon their doing that which is right in my own eyes this instant; —and they always want to do something else tomorrow. . . .' An echo of these sentiments is found in a letter to him from his father at this time, referring to a letter from a clergyman 'asking me for another hundred pounds to help to pay off the debt on his Church—it is just 38 days since I sent him a cheque. Really this beats the Wesleyans—surely Mr. W. must be a native of Ireland, no Englishman could have such a stock of assurance—I have answered him with a refusal.' Evidently old Mr. Smith, with the death of his wife, had undergone a revulsion of feeling in his religious allegiance.

At the end of 1856 William was again ill from overwork, as appears from a letter to him from his brother-in-law, Rupert Sercombe (December 3rd, 1856): 'I have often feared you were taxing your strength too severely and that you enjoyed far too little relaxation' and begs him 'not to sacrifice your health to the demands of business, however pressing they may at first sight appear. . . .' Apart from his natural and inherited propensity towards driving himself, his longing for Emily—for whom he must, out of regard for propriety, still

[1] Until the Reform Act of 1884 Counties and the majority of Boroughs still returned two (sometimes even three) members each.

wait—must have increased the strain immeasurably. In all his letters of this year and the next there are continual references to visits to the Danvers family and to 'Mrs. Auber Leach'.

In the following spring, 1857, there was another prospect of his standing for Parliament. Rupert Sercombe wrote from Exeter, where he lived, about a plan evidently concerted between the brothers-in-law for William to stand as a Liberal for the second seat at Exeter. Rupert, as a local man, was evidently acting as intermediary with the local Liberals. 'I suppose', he wrote (March 6th, 1857), '. . . I may speak of you as in politics moderate, leaning to the Reform side of the House, in short a Russellite—in favour of national Education, gradual extension of the Franchise, vote by ballot & etc. . . .'

But the plan failed for the same reason as had the earlier attempt at Boston, for Rupert wrote only two days later (March 8th): 'With those few parties to whom I have spoken on the subject your candidature is regarded *very favourably*, but as regards numbers, parties are so nicely balanced here that it is considered the Liberal Party has no chance of carrying two members except in case of a split among the Tories. . . .' So William did not proceed further. It may be added that in this same year William helped both Rupert and his father John Sercombe over some financial difficulties and when the latter repaid him with interest added, he sent back the interest.

By this time it was quite clear that there was not only a secret agreement between William and Emily to get married as soon as they could, but that it had been communicated to her parents, who were equally enthusiastic. Thus, in an undated letter to Emily, Mrs. Danvers writes: '. . . He [William] seems very sensible & reasonable & quite enters into my wish of keeping it quiet for the present, of course it will ooze out by degrees & that will be the best way. You will of course give up black-edged paper at once. . . .' And a week or two later, the same to the same: '. . . He is getting quite brave, he kissed me yesterday before Papa & Georgina. I am glad he seems happy with us—this opening is very gratifying, especially to me who have such a horror of reserved manners. I feel sure you will have a husband anxious to show the Christian feeling, in everything he does. There is really genuine love in his heart to God & Man.'

At last, on February 25th, 1858, William formally proposed to Emily and was accepted. 'All right!', he scribbled to Gussie, 'It is done for ever. Come and help us to buy the ring.' But Emily was very shy and sensitive. 'She shrinks from going up in the carriage', William wrote again next day, 'as she does not wish the engagement known until after she has left:—and she therefore wishes to meet you at King's Cross Station. . . .' The plan seems to have been for Emily to flee from any unwelcome publicity by going to stay with relatives near Bedford, William travelling with her as far as Bedford town, where he was to stop in a hotel, and Gussie acting as chaperon for the journey. At his hotel William wrote the following letter to his fiancée and personally delivered it at the house outside the town where she was staying:

> My dearest Emily,
> I cannot write this for the first time without thanking you again for the joy you have given me,—a new life has commenced with me— there is a pleasure in existence which with all the hope I indulged I never even imagined, and to crown all there is the assurance that our love for each other is a blessing conferred directly from Him who mercifully provides for the happiness of his Children in this World as well as the next.
> I went last evening to Lancaster Place and was most kindly & warmly received by your Father . . . without giving me time to say much your Father grasped my hand and in kinder terms to myself than I can repeat, welcomed me as a member of his Family. . . .

Emily's late husband's father, William Leach, was also pleased, declaring that though her engagement 'can hardly fail to call forth mingled feelings . . . I regard the object of your choice with very sincere affection'. William refers to this agreeable circumstance in a long letter written the next day from the Swan Hotel, Bedford, to his favourite sister:

> My dearest Gussie—not less dear that I have found one whom I can love with a different and—you won't grudge her—a stronger affection: Indeed I am sensible of the fact that love begets love even for those who were much loved before. One's capacity is increased—but I must not go on or the paper will be exhausted with that which may appear foolishness to some. . . .
> I saw Mr. Leach this afternoon and at first he appeared greatly surprised—but not at all grieved—not a shadow of sorrow. He spoke most affectionately of dear Emily and said it would be a great comfort to them all to know that she had one to love and to protect her and her Child who was so warmly esteemed by Auber. He expressed an earnest hope and belief that our union would be abundantly blessed and sent a most affectionate message to Emily. Is it not a great cause for thankfulness that we have already so many assurances that the step is one to which we have been alike guided by Providence. There is no misgiving or hesitation of any kind.
> The old man seemed greatly touched when I said how thankful I should be if he allowed me to look up to him as a sort of Father-in-law and that Emily would be still more his daughter in heart than she had been. . . . We parted very happily. He promised to write to Emily

tonight. I made him do this because I knew it would be a great comfort
to her to get it before she saw me in the morning. I have written to
her tonight to tell her of this and of her Father's & Mother's kindness
to me last night that she may have the only assurance that seemed
to be wanting before she slept,—and I have just returned from taking
it out to Mr. FitzPatrick's house which is a mile out of the town. Of
course I only left the letter and did not allow myself to be known as
leaving it, as it would have been unkind to let her know even that I
was outside. Thankfulness is now the expression—and the only one
I can give of all that I feel.

Before I left town this evening, and I was very much pressed in
many ways, Sir Thomas Phillips[1] asked me to dine with him on
Monday evening, and as I value him most of all the King's College
Hospital men and I should like to retain his friendship I thought it
best to accept his invitation even although it will keep me from home
until late in the evening. Will you explain this to Father and tell him
that it is from no want of affection for him that I stay away for a third
night from the dinner table.

I think I ought to be careful now of really good friends and good
men for Emily's sake as well as my own—and Sir Thomas is thoroughly one of that sort. He has an income of about £4,000 a year—and
being unmarried three fourths of it goes in building schools and
Churches and in quiet charity in his own County.

Your ever affectionate brother
William

His family and friends seem to have been particularly pleased at
the turn events had taken. His sister Caroline Reece wrote to him
(March 1st): '. . . I have long wished you to be married because I
believe you to be peculiarly suited for domestic happiness—& you
are capable of returning with full interest the warm devotion of a
tender affectionate wife.' An old family friend, Lady Crosbie, wrote:
'We often feared that your business had driven all other thoughts out
of your head—at least thoughts of marriage.' And the Reverend
William Ince,[2] his contemporary and lifelong friend: 'You have really
had for so many years past the wear & tear of an unceasing busy life
that you have fairly earned the enjoyment of domestic bliss & quiet
by your own fireside.' As for his father, William told Emily (March
9th) of his 'wonderful preservation from attacks. . . . He has not
been so free from them for a long time as he is now and he appears

---

[1] Born 1801, died 1867. Lawyer, Mayor of Newport, large coal-owner and
landed proprietor in Wales. Knighted for his courage, when Mayor of Newport,
in repelling an attack by 7,000 Chartists under John Frost in 1839. Gave large
sums to various charities.

[2] At this time Fellow and Tutor of Exeter College, Oxford; later Canon of
Christ Church, in which Cathedral he delivered a eulogy on Smith after his
death in 1891.

to feel almost as warmly about our marriage as I do. Have we not the promise of happiness?'

But he felt it his duty to warn her of what he imagined to be the defects in his character. Thus (March 4th):

> ... I could not help thinking over the wonderful change that has taken place in my prospects during the last few days ... and then I came to think of myself and to fear that I had not been sufficiently ingenuous with you. There are some points in my character which I am not afraid to tell you of because you love me enough to try to do me good ... Very likely I do not perceive the worst in myself but I know this—I have not the strong stern determination to do always that which is right, by God's help, which I admired so much in Auber, and which I see in so many men around me. I am inclined to be easy with myself. ... In good truth, in some things I have really a *weak* character, and I want you to be the means of strengthening it. ...

Nobody else, however, least of all Emily—seemed to agree with this rather depressing estimate of his character and those who were in a better position than most to know something about him—his own employees—wrote what was obviously a testimonial from the heart.

> On an occasion like that of your Marriage when you are surrounded by the affectionate sympathy of your family and the felicitations of your numerous friends, it would be strange if we the Assistants in your Establishment, who have so many opportunities of witnessing your excellencies and so many proofs of personal kindness, could be mere silent spectators of your joy.
>
> Permit us, then, Dear Sir, to unite our congratulations with theirs, congratulations we venture to hope not less hearty that they come from men in our position, nor less sincere that they are voicelessly expressed. ...

They were married on April 13th, 1858, at St. James's, Paddington, and went, for the first part of their honeymoon, to the Isle of Wight. Here William, whose thoughts were still always largely of his father, heard from Gussie (April 14th):

> Dear Father continues very well. I am quite surprised when I look at him to see how well he is after so much excitement. We need not have been so anxious about him, he seems in so much better health than he was a little more than a twelvemonth ago. ... The Servants very much enjoyed their treat last evening. We went down into the Kitchen to see them drink to the health of Mr. and Mrs. William Smith; it was a very pleasing sight.

And William wrote back (April 15th):

I am sure you will be as glad to hear again of us as we are of you and of dear Father! . . . I am very thankful to have such good accounts of him. Indeed, everything has been most favourable and as if a direct blessing forwarded all our hopes and plans. . . . We are . . . very happy, very quiet as we are and both feel the great comfort of the rest we so much desired and which is not a bit less sweet than we pictured to ourselves it would be. . . .

Writing to his wife's sister-in-law, Charlotte Leach, from Bonchurch (April 22nd) he describes his honeymoon as 'a sort of long summer's day in one's existence to be gone back to and compared with other days when one may want to illustrate anything peculiarly happy and beautiful'. And a week later from Bath to Gussie (April 30th):

We are very happy with our little daughter [Mary Auber Leach] and she appears to be very happy with us,—but for the present I am doubtful if she does not prefer the society of some little boys whom she has found here, and who are very humble subjects—but she is very loving and told her Grandmamma in whose room she is sleeping that 'she intended to be kind today to Papa'. . . .

We intend spending some days at Clevedon if all is well and we continue to get good accounts from you of Father and from Mr. White of the Strand. He writes to me every day and at present everything appears to go exceedingly well. Do you think anything exists at present in fact or in my Father's mind which should hasten our return?

The extreme devotion to his father and solicitude for his well-being which he had always shown was not even temporarily forgotten or diminished during these honeymoon weeks. Thus in another long letter to Gussie devoted almost solely to his father's condition, doctors and treatment, he writes: 'Only remember that expense on Father's account is no consideration with me, and if he disliked spending the money, I would willingly incur *any* cost or responsibility myself that you thought would add to his comfort or safety.' Again (May 4th): 'I am very thankful to hear the continued good accounts of dear Father. It really seems as if my Marriage was the commencement of a happier season for all of us. For a very long time I have not been so free from care and anxiety and I have never had such a sense of blessing. I ought to be and I am very thankful for I have not deserved all this. . . .'

In August William had to be temporarily parted from Emily through having to go to Dublin on business and thence he wrote to her (August 17th): '. . . I strolled out on to the Pier where crowds of people were walking up and down, arm in arm, listening to the music, and I fancied I was almost the only person who was really alone. I

am not at all sorry you are becoming so necessary to me—and I am
sure you will not be. . . .' He was so full of gratitude and wonder at
his new-found happiness that he delighted to describe it either to his
wife or to his favourite sister. Thus to the latter (September 8th):

> Somehow or other occupation increases upon me, and every day
> passes into night, and night brings sleep with a consciousness that I
> had better, if I could, have done something which however has been
> left undone. Instead, however, of being exhausted with it, I do not
> think I was ever better, certainly I have never felt so well as I have
> done for a period of months together, and I have rarely indeed the
> sense of weariness which used to be so common.

This complete harmony, mutual trust and devotion and complete
dependence upon one another continued, happily to relate this year,
next year and throughout all the years to come—unabated by time,
custom or familiarity. From Lyme Regis (October 25th, 1858): 'The
place is a very pretty one . . . but somehow or other I have changed—
and I want someone to be with me to thoroughly enjoy that which, a
year or two ago, I should have been charmed with *alone*. . . .' From
Dublin (August 4th, 1859): '. . . I was almost always thinking of you
when I was neither reading nor sleeping and I could not help wishing
that I had you with me to point out the beauties of water, wind &
cloud, of bright sunshine and dark shadows, of green hillsides and
grand, gloomy-looking mountains. . . .' From London (September
2nd, 1859): 'I cannot tell you how much you are grown with and
become necessary to my very thoughts . . . the nights are so odd
without you. I am really beginning to sleep badly alone just as I
feared I should with you before I married.' Writing a birthday letter
to Gussie in the following year (July 23rd, 1860) he reverts humor-
ously to the same subject—as well as to others:

> . . . May you be happy and be sleepy, at this time, for many a long
> day to come. You will say it is all very well for me to write about
> sleep. I like it myself. I own I do. I have improved in that accomplish-
> ment since I became joined to a woman. I only wonder what I should
> arrive at if I was a Woman myself.
> I came up this morning from T. Wells with Captain Lidgett & his
> wife . . . the Captain introduced me to his wife as Mr. Smith, and she,
> gentle creature, in an undertone, before she took my hand (not
> knowing what degree of pressure to put into the squeeze) said 'Which
> Mr. Smith, my dear, what Mr. Smith, my dear'; at last the good
> creature was comforted with a description of me before my face, and
> they both said they would be glad to see me. . . .

William and Emily wrote to each other daily when separated from
one another—not only in these first years, but throughout the rest of

their married life. The sanctity of this institution may be gauged from the following extracts. Thus William writes (August 26th, 1862): 'You are a precious woman, are you not, to keep me going backwards and forwards between the Hall door & the breakfast table, looking for letters in the box which never come—fidgetting and worrying and being cross, but quite resolved that nothing had happened because *then* I should have certainly heard from somebody.—Still you are a darling to rectify the fault which I am sure was not yours—and I have been very kind and considerate to everybody since and have let two fellows stay who had notice to leave. . . .' Similarly, two years later, from Dublin (November 11th, 1864): 'This morning again I was without a letter, and I became angry and insisted with the Porter that you *had* written. At last a letter was found. . . .'

Shortly after his marriage William took a house at No. 1, Hyde Park Street, which must have been considerably more convenient for him than living out at Kilburn, with the lengthy and tiring treks between that suburb and the Strand—as well as pleasanter in every way for Emily. Here their first child, also Emily,[1] was born in 1859 and their second, Helen,[2] in 1861. Meanwhile, old Mr. Smith had gone to live with his unmarried daughter Augusta (Gussie) at Bournemouth. William and Emily paid them frequent visits there and often left their children with them for short sojourns. After one such visit Mr. Smith wrote (September 29th, 1859): 'I was very glad to hear of yours and Emily's safe arrival & that Baby is doing pretty well. . . .' Then, enclosing a cheque for £80, he asks William to cash it for four £10 notes and eight £5 notes 'which please cut in half, sending first part on Saturday & the other on Monday'. So the care and meticulousness in small things that had made the business what it was, was still much in evidence—as was also his pride in it, as appears in a letter of a few days later (October 1st, 1859), complaining that his instructions for the delivery of his own newspapers were not being obeyed and adding tartly: '. . . I really hope my old business is not generally conducted in this neglectful & blundering way.'

The young couple were apt to worry dreadfully when they left their children behind. Thus William to Gussie (March 19th, 1861):

. . . It would be some sacrifice of comfort on Emily's part and on my own to go away [to Bournemouth] from this comfortable home [Hyde Park Street] which I like more every day I live in it, and it *is* a greater comfort to be able to get to or from one's business at any time of day or night without anxiety or fatigue or loss of time—but we do not live now for ourselves alone,—and if the dear child's health

[1] Married 1887 Admiral Sir William Dyke Acland, 2nd Bart.
[2] Married 1896 Henry Sydney Seymour, a cousin of the Duke of Somerset.

requires it the sacrifice must be made, and the sooner done the less will be anxiety. . . .

In the following year, whilst his family were in the country and he was left in town, he wrote to Emily (August 23rd, 1862): 'Kiss Mary Auber and the two little darlings for me. Tell them that you and they together have quite ruined me for a Bachelor's existence. I am worse off than a Fish out of water.'

Meanwhile—especially as his father finally retired at about the time of his marriage—he had to give every bit as much time and attention to the business as before. In fact in the very month of his marriage, in April 1858, he was involved in a tough dispute with the proprietors of the *Standard* newspaper—then a Radical organ— which evidently gave rise to the idea that his firm were refusing to supply the newspaper to clients owing to political prejudice. But in a circular to clients, which shows the highly developed sense of respon- sibility which infused all that he did, he made a point of denying this imputation and explaining the real reasons.

> . . . In order to remove any conjectures or inferences which the continued non-supply of the Paper by us may create, as to the personal or political hostility on our parts to the Proprietors or the principles which the journal advocates, we feel bound to explain that we have repeatedly intimated to the Publisher of the paper our wish and desire to receive it on the same terms on which we are now supplied with all the Daily Papers. . . .

but

> . . . the Proprietors thought fit to erect a new difficulty by raising the cost of the Paper to us to a price which would prevent supplying it upon uniform terms with others of the same class and by confining the distinction to ourselves, purposely expose our customers to a disadvantage by the sale of it, as compared with those Agents who buy at the Office direct. . . .

Two years later he writes to his wife from Dublin (June 20th, 1861), giving a further instance of this conception of himself as a servant and benefactor of the public, as well as some interesting details of the overhead expenses of his firm: 'A meeting of the Managers of the Irish Railways was fixed for today . . . to consider the question of the carriage of our Newspaper parcels. We must pay nearly £10,000 a year for Carriage, and a reduction or modification of these charges may result in a saving of perhaps a fourth or a fifth of this amount, of which I should give part to the public and keep a portion myself.'

Then, in 1861, he decided to stake a part of his growing capital on one more venture—an expansion of the firm in one more new direction, though in a sense it grew logically out of the railway bookstall business and like that venture had the same missionary and semi-philanthropic appeal to him. He came to realize that there was a real demand among people living in remote country districts for a supply of books on loan and, true to his principles, felt that it was his duty to endeavour to satisfy it. However, he first approached the problem in comparatively modest and indirect fashion by entering into negotiations with the then leading firm in the circulating and lending library business, Messrs. Mudie, with the view of acting as agents for the latter in the provinces. In fact in 1859 a 'Midland Counties Branch' of Mudie's had been opened experimentally at the Birmingham branch of W. H. Smith & Son's.

But, when further negotiations on these lines came to nothing, he set about founding his own circulating library. Like the earlier ventures—the bookstalls and the railway advertising—it naturally required a considerable outlay of capital and, though it eventually proved successful, it always remained the least remunerative department. In a letter to Eason (January 1861) Smith writes that 'the great outlay of capital which the new hires and the Library require from me makes me very short of money just now. . . .'

But an even more successful and much more profitable venture was his actual entry into the publishing business on his own. Hitherto it had always been one of his cardinal rules not to have the smallest property in any publication which he handled, because he held it important to be free to deal impartially with every publishing house. But a time came when the supply of literature for his railway bookstalls ran low—or rather the public began to fret at the lack of variety and the prices of the assortment on the bookstalls, the mainstay of which had long remained the rather heavy collection of Murray's 'Traveller's Library'—and sales began to decline rather disturbingly.

Cheapness having hitherto always gone hand in hand with nastiness, the first requirement was to try to produce light, but good literature—good novels and romances—at low prices. Accordingly, in 1854, Smith acquired the copyright of the celebrated and numerous novels of Charles Lever, the Irish writer, whose works were extremely popular (as well as quite unexceptionable) from the 1840s onwards. At the same time Sandifer, the manager of the bookstall department, was charged with getting them specially printed and published in a form both attractive and cheap enough to appeal to the travelling public. But, as Smith still did not want to engage in competition with established publishing firms, but only to supply the peculiar requirements of those who patronized his railway bookstalls, he made an arrangement with Messrs. Chapman & Hall that the books should appear under their name.

45

Success was so immediate that the copyrights of other authors were acquired and the fame and popularity of Smith's 'yellow-backs', as they were called, spread throughout the land. The profits, too, were immense: the books sold off as fast as they could be printed at 2s. a-piece, and the cost of production was only 9d. But, characteristically, Smith began to feel alarmed and despondent, as he found that the venture had exceeded his expectations and even his intentions, in that his cheap novels were driving other works off the stalls. His clerks in charge of the bookstalls, since they received a commission on sales, naturally aggravated the process by pushing the popular yellow-backs, and thrusting other less attractive wares out of sight.

Smith would, on principle, never interfere with the freedom of management of his clerks at the bookstalls; but, as soon as some other firms had entered the field and appeared to be providing an adequately similar service, he himself withdrew from it. In 1883 the copyrights acquired by him were sold for around £10,000. Perhaps it was the spectacular success of this venture which caused him to write to his wife a few years after its launching (April 10th, 1866): 'All is going well at the Strand—only too prosperously.'

46

III

'ENTRY INTO PARLIAMENT'

───── ✦✦ ─────

URING these years Smith was deepening and widening his
interest in educational, ecclesiastical and philanthropic affairs.
King's College Hospital remained, as always, one of his primary
philanthropic interests and he was already making generous dona-
tions to a number of schools and churches. In 1861 he took a further
step in the same direction when he accepted an invitation to a meeting at Fulham Palace at which the so-called 'Bishop of London's Fund'
was first set on foot for the purpose of 'improving the dwellings of
the poor'—a mild phrase to describe the appalling state of affairs
then prevalent in this sector of national life.

The chief resolution at this meeting was moved by Lord Sandon, at
that time M.P. for Liverpool and later to become 3rd Earl of
Harrowby, and was seconded by Smith. Each evidently made a great
impression on the other and their lifelong friendship, founded upon
a similarity and seriousness of outlook and a general interest in
philanthropy and education, was born in that instant. Subsequently
an inner working committee of the Fund was set up, of which
Sandon became Chairman and Smith a member—alongside a number
of other distinguished men of the day.

Many years later Sandon—or rather Harrowby as he by then
was—told Sir Herbert Maxwell that Smith had impressed him as
being 'a man of very taking appearance, with very dark hair and
bright eyes, and a calm and resolute look.[1] In 1882, when he left the
Commons for the Lords, Sandon wrote to Smith that 'an intercourse
such as ours, of more than twenty years, with a constant similarity of
aim, unbroken by a single disagreement . . . has certainly been one
of the blessings of my life . . .'.

The continuity of this great friendship was naturally assured when
Smith decided once again to try his hand at the game of national
politics by agreeing in 1865 to stand as Conservative candidate for

[1] Maxwell, I, 105.

47

Westminster. In this connection Maxwell relates an amusing anecdote which was told him by Sir Edward Levy-Lawson,[1] who was a personal friend of Smith. Levy-Lawson was editor and proprietor of the *Daily Telegraph*, which was at that time a Radical-Liberal paper, and calling one day on the Liberal Prime Minister, Lord Palmerston at the House of Commons, remarked to him that there was 'a young man in the Strand who would be heard of some day, and should be seen to, as he would make an excellent candidate'. 'Ah', replied Palmerston, 'I wish you'd tell Brand[2] about him, will ye?' Lawson did so, but apparently nothing was done, for some time afterwards Smith came up to him in the street and said:

'My dear Lawson, do you know what I have gone and done, I've accepted an invitation to stand for Westminster.'
'Delighted to hear it', replied Lawson, who assumed Smith was still a Liberal; 'You're the very man of all others we should like to have. Rely upon me to do all in my power for you.'
'Oh, but I am the Conservative candidate, you know?'
'Whew! that alters matters rather. Then rely upon it, I'll do all I fairly can to keep you out!'

What had caused Smith in these few years thus to change his political allegiance? In the first place the metamorphosis was really a scarcely perceptible one, since, when earlier putting himself forward as a Liberal, it was as such a qualified one as to make him barely distinguishable from a Conservative, and now in presenting himself as a Conservative he was carefully—and foolishly—insistent that he be described as a 'Liberal-Conservative'—a label which of course irritated both parties. Moreover, Palmerston's peculiar blend of firm leadership and very un-doctrinaire Liberalism was coming to an end with his own waning life and his more moderate followers, fearing the greater scope which his disappearance would afford to the Radicals, saw themselves brought to a fresh appraisal of their true political principles.

Finally, though 'Pam' himself was a Whig aristocrat, his genial and robust personality caused his appeal to the country at large to be much more broadly based than could ever have been the case with other members of his caste. Thus, though Pam could consider without any qualms the candidature of 'a young man in the Strand', his fellow Whig patricians were outraged when that same young man's name was put up for the Reform Club—as it was in 1862,

[1] Created Baron Burnham in 1903. Transferred his paper's (*Daily Telegraph*) support from Gladstone to Beaconsfield in 1879. After 1886 definitely Unionist and Imperialist.
[2] Henry Brand, M.P. for Lewes; Liberal Chief Whip and later Speaker of the House of Commons, 1872–84; created Viscount Hampden, 1884.

when Smith was still thinking of himself as a Liberal—and they black-balled him as a presumptuous 'tradesman'. Smith has left no record of his feeling about this rebuff, but, even allowing for his exceptionally magnanimous and forgiving nature, it is not unlikely to have influenced his change of allegiance.

But at any rate for the time being he continued to flatter himself that, even if he accepted Conservative support, he could maintain an attitude of independence from any irksome or disagreeable party ties. This emerges in the letter which he wrote to his sister Gussie, announcing his decision to stand for Westminster (March 31st, 1865):

> I remember Father has very often talked of the famous election contest in Westminster when Sir Francis Burdett stood, and when the Troops were firing in St. James's Street and Father as a boy had to run into Courts and back-ways to escape being shot.[1]
>
> Would it interest him to know that that little boy's son,—myself— has been seriously invited to stand for Westminster by a body headed by the Twinings, Stilwells and Sambroke, and that the subject is being seriously considered upon this understanding that whether I decide to stand or no, on private grounds upon which I am quite uncertain, I should not think of doing so at all unless I am absolutely assured of success in a contest, if any takes place.
>
> If I go to Parliament it will be as an independent man and the printed paper I send you contains a general sketch of my opinions. None but the Committee who have asked me and two or three intimate friends know anything at all about the affair and it will remain undecided for some time. . . .
>
> I should like to know what Father thinks about it if he is well enough to be spoken to on the subject.
>
> I can afford the expense and my business will be well managed. . . .

And again he writes to her on April 4th:

> . . . I have taken no decisive step as yet, but the address slightly modi- fied is being privately circulated in order to ascertain what amount of support I am likely to get. Unless that is satisfactorily shown to be very promising indeed, I shall not go further in the matter.
>
> A contest would be expensive, but when a man once becomes a Member for Westminster he may retain his seat pretty nearly for life if his personal or moral character is good and he attends reasonably to his duties.
>
> I am anxious beyond everything to do what is really right, and if Father really disapproved of the step, which is much less mine than

---

[1] The celebrated 'Westminster Election' of 1807. Burdett was elected and remained M.P. for Westminster for the next thirty years. He was at this time a Radical Whig of advanced views and was twice imprisoned on political charges. He married Sophia Coutts, the banker's daughter, and they had a daughter who became the celebrated Baroness Burdett-Coutts.

my neighbours', I would at once give up the idea altogether, but I confess I should like to be in Parliament.

However, his father did not disapprove in the very least: on the contrary he was enthusiastic and offered to pay all expenses. It was only sad that he was destined to live just long enough to see his son defeated and not long enough to see his second and successful attempt three years later. For, unfortunately, the 1865 attempt was a forlorn hope. Indeed, there had not been for many years a single Conservative member for any of the Metropolitan constituencies. At Westminster, in this year, there were three candidates for the two seats—Captain Grosvenor, kinsman of the Marquess of Westminster, the representation of hereditary Whiggism and a moderate Liberal; John Stuart Mill, the famous philosopher, free-thinker and advanced Liberal; and Smith, professing a 'Liberal-Conservative' faith, known to the few as a practical philanthropist and steady churchman—to the many as the owner of the bookstalls.

Levy-Lawson of the *Telegraph* was as good as his word. He gave the support of his paper to Mill, discounted Grosvenor and treated Smith's candidature as a farce, writing (May 6th) that 'in the category of political nobodies we must include Mr. Smith' and later (July 6th) that '. . . Mr. Smith issues an address from Westminster, so liberal in its tone that it ought to have been dated from the Reform Club . . . yet this gentleman is accounted a champion of Conservative principles, simply because he is opposed to two candidates of advanced Liberal views.' In this address Smith had declared himself 'unconnected with either of the great political parties' and that he would desire to enter Parliament 'as an independent member at liberty to vote for measures rather than for men'. He added that he would 'not be a party to any factious attempt to drive Lord Palmerston from power, as I feel that the country owes a debt of gratitude to him for having preserved peace and for the resistance he has offered to reckless innovation in our domestic institutions'.

Smith's ambiguous attitude and unwillingness to commit himself to the party which he was ostensibly representing caused some anxiety and heartsearchings among orthodox Conservatives and the controllers of the party machine. George Cubitt,[1] who afterwards became his intimate friend and had at that time much influence in the party organization of London was dismayed at the ambivalence of Smith's address to the electors and consulted the Conservative Whip, Colonel Taylor,[2] as to the prudence of sponsoring such a

[1] M.P. West Surrey, 1860–85; for Mid Surrey 1885–92; created Baron Ashcombe 1892.

[2] Colonel T. E. Taylor, Conservative Chief Whip, 1859–68.

candidate. 'Take him,' Taylor is supposed to have said, 'I don't fancy his politics much myself, but you'll get nobody better.'

Meanwhile Smith himself had no desire to try to enjoy the best of both worlds or to appear to angle for Conservative support under false pretences, so he wrote a most commendably and utterly frank letter to Taylor:

My dear Sir,   April 26, 1865

I have been so heartily and so handsomely supported by the Conservative party that I am anxious there should be no misunderstanding as to the position I should occupy with reference to it if returned to Parliament for Westminster.

You are fully aware of the independence of party ties which I felt it necessary to stipulate for when it was proposed by the Committee that I should stand for Westminster, but I am not sure that your friends would gather as much from my address. It will be well, therefore, to repeat that I am not a member of the Conservative party as such—nor am I a member of the Liberal party, but I believe in Lord Palmerston, and look forward ultimately to a fusion of the moderate men following Lord Derby and Lord Palmerston into a strong Liberal-Conservative party, to which I should be glad to attach myself.

Such an expectation may be chimerical, but I cannot help indulging it, and I wish to stand by it.

In the meantime, I am pledged to oppose Baine's bill [for extension of the suffrage in boroughs], the Ballot, and the unconditional abolition of Church-rates and all similar radical measures.

May I ask you to make this matter clear to your friends who have so generously offered their support to me, as I would rather retire now than fairly lay myself open to the reproach of obtaining party support under false pretences. . . .

To which Colonel Taylor replied—very magnanimously in the circumstances, one may feel: 'I consider your letter an extremely fair one, and I shall advise the Westminster Conservatives to give you their unreserved support.' But, despite this, many held aloof and Smith's campaign got off to a slow and lukewarm start and there was some difficulty in getting together a good election committee until Earl Percy[1] was persuaded to become its chairman. Then the outlook brightened considerably, Smith appeared to make an excellent impression and offers of support rolled in in gratifying numbers.

But these appearances were sadly deceptive. On polling day Smith wrote to Gussie from his Committee Rooms in Cockspur Street (July 11th, 1865): 'Things are looking a little badly for us—not very much so, but enough to render it very possible that we may be

---

[1] M.P. N. Northumberland; Lord Privy Seal, 1878–80; succeeded father as 6th Duke of Northumberland, 1867.

beaten. You must prepare my Father for it.' Another note was sent to his wife on the same day: 'I think you may have a disappointment. Men have broken their promises to a considerable extent, and we are dropping behind. Don't be discontented; it is all for the best. I will let you know later.' Finally a further note to his sister from his house in Hyde Park Street where he had gone to carry the news to Emily:

The close of the Poll made:

Grosvenor	4,384
Mill	4,379
Smith	3,812

So I was 572 behind and am left out in the cold; but although disappointed, I am not at all castdown about it. I will come to you tomorrow morning. Let me know how my Father is.

Yet, one letter of sympathy, which he received on this occasion may well have influenced the whole of his future course and contributed to the final solution of the question of his political allegiance. Disraeli—though the long Liberal ascendancy and a combination of ill-luck and excessive loyalty to Lord Derby had deprived him of the enjoyment of supreme power—had led the Tory party in the Commons for the last seventeen years and, in hopes of a triumphant future, never neglected any opportunity of attaching to himself, by timely and subtle gestures, men whom he judged to be of potential value to his cause. Thus, on the very day of the declaration of the poll at Westminster, he wrote to Smith (July 12th, 1865):

Grosvenor Gate,
Dear Sir,   July 12, 1865
    Before I leave town today for my own County, I must express to you my great regret at the termination of the Westminster contest, conducted by you with so much spirit, and evidently with such a just expectation of success.
    I hope yet to see you in the House of Commons, and, in the meantime, I trust you may find some dignified consolation and some just pride in the conviction that you possess the respect and the confidence of a great party.
                            I have the honor to be, Dear Sir,
                                Your faithful servt.
                                    B. Disraeli.

Smith wrote an extremely graceful, but cleverly non-committal reply:

1, Hyde Park St.,
Dear Sir,   July 12, 1865
    I am grateful to you for the expression of your sympathy with me under my defeat. Seeing that I had not identified myself with the party, I confess I felt surprise at the warmth and earnestness with

which the Westminster Conservatives supported me, and the ready response to our united efforts caused me to be sanguine as to the result.

But I am amply repaid for my labour or vexation through which I have passed by the confidence of the friends I have made in this contest, and the expression of your own kindly feeling.

I have the honor to be, Dear Sir,

Yours very faithfully,
William H. Smith

At the same time his friend Lord Sandon was exerting his influence in the opposite direction, trying to bolster him in the independent attitude which had cost him so dear, by writing soon afterwards (August 7th, 1865): '. . . I feel sure that freedom from all unnecessary party tie is important at this juncture of public affairs.'

A couple of weeks after the close of this episode—on July 28th, 1865—old Mr. Smith died at Bournemouth at the house to which he had retired under the care of his unmarried daughter, Augusta. His son must have felt the loss particularly keenly, since, as is evident from all his diaries and letters, he was singularly devoted to the irascible yet warm-hearted old gentleman and 'Father' always remained his first care and anxiety—even after he himself had acquired a wife and children. '. . . There is great kindness and great feeling visible on every side of us', he wrote to Gussie. 'Many shops had their shutters up yesterday and old friends and customers have written most kindly. I will show you their letters . . . as to any notice in the papers of his death in the shape of a paragraph speaking of his life and work—I have not prepared or sanctioned anything of the sort—and I do not feel sure that he would have liked it. . . .'

To his wife in the country he wrote: '. . . All the Servants must have mourning given to them . . . Coachman to bring up the Carriage and Horses . . . my Father's Carriage and Horses will arrive . . . on Thursday and must be provided for . . . Black Pad Cloths, Rosettes &c have been ordered for the two pairs of Horses, and Reid must see that they are turned out properly. . . .'

Augusta inherited the house at Bournemouth and spent the rest of her life there. The pleasant old house at Kilburn with its spacious grounds had been so closely built around in recent years that it was given up when old Mr. Smith retired from business in 1858. As his son had put it at the time: 'I can't even kiss my sister without being seen from a dozen windows.' Meanwhile, he himself acquired a country residence called Cecil Lodge at Abbots Langley in Hertfordshire, which served as a healthy home for his wife and children and a retreat for him at a reasonable distance from London.

In these years Smith seems to have been obliged to be separated from his family rather frequently, partly owing to business visits to Ireland and to other branches of the firm and partly as he took trips to the Continent, probably on doctor's orders, and Emily was either too tied to her young family or herself not strong enough to travel. Nevertheless, she and his children were constantly in his thoughts and he wrote daily without fail—whether he were only 20 miles away in London or as many hundred somewhere abroad. He had an engaging style and his descriptions of people and places were often shrewd and amusing, yet full of warmth and love of life.

In the autumn following the election fiasco and his father's death, on October 1st, 1865, a son, their first, was born to them and christened Henry Walton after the mysterious grandfather. Just before this event he was travelling on the Continent and writing from Strasbourg (September 14th, 1865) he recounts how on his journey he had 'a young French officer and his wife who when we three were left alone in the Carriage, as we were from Nancy to this place, became as we often have been to each other, my darling, so that to make them still more happy I went to sleep or appeared to do so,—and read diligently and looked out of the window more earnestly. I do like to see people happy, don't you? He is going to Africa in a fortnight, which I am not—am I, my darling?' And from Munich next day, describing the company at his hotel: 'English dressed with the most perfect propriety—and so wretched looking—so much afraid of themselves;—Germans who are self-content and have no fear that anyone can doubt they are the first people in the world.'

In the midst of his own happiness and prosperity he never forgot others and there are frequent references to such benefactions as his paying for holidays abroad for his sisters and their families or his paying the rent of a house for an old uncle. However, in the early part of the following year, a shadow fell on his own happy household when little Henry Walton, who had never really thrived, died aged only four months. Smith wrote to their closest friend, Miss Emily Giberne (February 7th, 1866): 'We are in trouble. Our little boy has been taken from us—quite gently, slowly and happily painlessly—but he has gone like a breath or a shadow . . . he is taken from the sorrow to come and we have one of our own in heaven to welcome us when we are there. . . .'

The General Election of July 1865, which had temporarily dashed Smith's hopes of entering Parliament, had resulted in the return of Lord Palmerston once again at the head of the Whig-Liberal majority. But when, only three months later, Palmerston died, he was succeeded in the premiership by Earl Russell (better known as Lord

John Russell) and party politics immediately took on a very different complexion. Sir Herbert Maxwell has well expressed this new situation in writing: 'With Lord Palmerston's firm will and quaint, genial personality there was lost that sense of security which made moderate men of both parties feel safer under a strong Liberal administration than under a weak Conservative one.'[1] Among others, the appraisal pretty well covered Smith's particular case and must have been another contributory cause of his abandonment of his ultra-independent stance.

For not only had Russell always represented a more positive form of Liberalism than Palmerston ever had—he had been the mover of the First Reform Bill in 1831—but the moving spirit and leader of the House of Commons (also Chancellor of the Exchequer) was none other than Gladstone, who, by his close association with the Radical John Bright and his menacing utterances about universal franchise was already sending shudders down aristocratic and bourgeois spines alike. Now, therefore, the first gesture of the Russell Government was to announce a Bill for the extension of the franchise, which was duly introduced in the Commons by Gladstone on March 12th, 1866. It was an extremely mild measure judged by subsequent events and standards, but it was defeated owing to the revolt of a section of the Whigs (nicknamed the 'Cave of Adullam'), who combined with the Conservatives in opposing it. The Government, having staked their life on the Bill, resigned and the Conservatives, though in a minority in the House, came in under the premiership of Lord Derby, but with Disraeli as the moving spirit in the role of Leader of the House and Chancellor of the Exchequer.

The rather unexciting content of Russell's Reform Bill, which only proposed to enfranchise a small fraction of the working-class, would probably have aroused little feeling among the masses at large, had it not been for the insistence of Robert Lowe, the leader of the 'Adullamites', on basing his opposition to it on arguments tending to the exacerbation of class rivalry. Consequently, by the time the Bill was defeated, and the Liberal Government with it, the nation was in a state of fever which their Conservative successors found themselves compelled to allay by some prompt reformist remedy of their own. This remedy was supplied by Disraeli's famous Reform Bill of 1867, which, though considerably modified during its passage through the Commons, far outstripped Russell's Bill in scope and audacity by adding nearly two million voters to the register and enfranchising the artisans of the towns.

We do not know whether Smith, like so many other Liberal-Conservatives and Conservative-Liberals at this time, was shocked

[1] Maxwell, I, 129.

by these strange goings-on and the startling policy of the new Tory saviour—though he did tell his friend and solicitor Ford in a letter at about this time that he was in 'favour of the extension of the suffrage'. At any rate, it did not appear to deflect him from his resolve of identifying himself henceforth rather more positively with the Conservative party. For when in 1867 an invitation came to him to stand for Middlesex on 'unmistakable Liberal principles', he firmly declined it, declaring that if he stood at all it could only be as a Conservative. This was promptly followed by an invitation to contest the same county as a Conservative, but, having placed himself in the hands of the party managers, he was advised to decline. When yet another invitation arrived to contest Bedford in the Conservative interest, he replied that 'my Westminster friends have so strongly remonstrated against the proposal to commit myself as a candidate for another constituency at the general election . . . that out of regard to personal considerations . . . I feel bound to refrain from severing myself from them'.

Finally, in the autumn of 1867, a requisition, with 3,000 signatures, inviting him to stand again for Westminster, was presented to him on behalf of the Conservative party in the borough, by a deputation headed by the Earl of Dalkeith,[1] and this invitation he accepted. But Westminster was not the same constituency as the one he had courted in 1865, for the effect of 'household suffrage', introduced by Disraeli's Reform Bill, was almost as incalculable as it was in most other constituencies. 'I am obliged to speak doubtfully of everything now', he wrote to Gussie (January 11th, 1868), 'as it is probable I shall be involved in an Election Contest again. I hope not to begin with the meetings or anything of that sort until October, but if either Capt. Grosvenor or Mr. Mill go to work sooner, I must do so too'.

However, there were distinct signs that the sitting member, John Stuart Mill, had alienated many people by his recent unorthodox actions and attitudes and so, all through the winter of 1867–8 and the succeeding summer, Smith and his friends worked hard, holding meetings and canvassing the voters. Here he was enormously helped by the devoted and unswerving support of a remarkable character named the Honourable Robert Grimston,[2] a popular sportsman and barrister (in that order) with immense drive and panache, who was a neighbour of Smith in the country, was a co-director with him of a telegraph company and generally a close personal friend. Grimston

[1] M.P. Midlothian 1853–68 and 1874–80. He was defeated by Gladstone when the latter contested his seat in the famous 'Midlothian Campaign' of 1880. Succeeded father in 1884 as 6th Duke of Buccleuch and 9th Duke of Queensberry.

[2] Third son of 1st Earl of Verulam. (See *Life of the Hon. Robert Grimston* by Frederick Gale (Longman's Green, 1885).

had supported Smith in his earlier attempt, but had not had time sufficiently to organize the effort. This time he flung himself unreservedly—and entirely voluntarily—into the fray, becoming chairman of the key Ward of St. George's, Hanover Square, where he was of great value in bringing over the more aristocratic elements, who might otherwise have stood aloof from the 'newsagent'. On the other hand, Smith's reputation as a good, paternalistic employer probably stood him in good stead with the newly enfranchised artisans, in whose political sagacity Disraeli claimed to place so much confidence—not without justification, as events were ultimately to prove.

During this summer of 1868 Emily Smith, who was expecting another child, was up in Yorkshire, while her husband sweltered through a phenomenal heatwave in London. On July 18th he wrote to her: 'It is all right. The meeting has gone off very well indeed. Lord Dalkeith took the Chair and Grimston, Lord Sandon and several others were there and they were all very enthusiastic.' Then on July 22nd he wrote again: '. . . the worry of the coming Election is upon me as thickly as ever. People writing all sorts of letters and calling as thickly as flies. But I keep extremely well with it all.' And on July 30th: '. . . I have been driven a good deal today—heaps of people coming one after another to prevent me from working until I have felt savage—but not with you my dearest love.'

On August 12th the child was born—a boy who was to be named Frederick (Freddy) and who was to become his heir and a man of great qualities in his own right. After his sad experience with the first little boy Smith seemed apprehensive about the prospects of boys in general. '. . . Emily has got through her trouble safely somewhat earlier than we expected and . . . we have a son again', he wrote to Gussie (August 12th). 'This time the boy looks healthy and well, but I am hardly yet able to say that I am glad. I did not desire it, altho' we shall be very thankful if all goes on well with him. I have always felt there is a greater risk in every respect with boys than with girls, and we have both been very well content with our girls. . . .' The same curious theme recurs in a letter to Ford (August 14th): '. . . I was not at all expecting another boy, imagining they were all to be girls, but I trust this little fellow will live. He looks like it, which our first never did. . . .'

As the election approached, Smith's feelings went through a variety of conflicting emotions, as these excerpts from his letters to Emily reveal. November 10th: 'I don't want people . . . to suppose I sulk if I lose the battle or am too much elated if I win.' November 11th: 'I certainly hope to succeed, but the relief of rest will be so great that if I fail I shall be compensated by a return to home comforts.'

November 12th: 'If I go down home on Tuesday evening beaten I shall not feel I am disgraced, and I intend to put a good and cheerful face upon it. It will all be for the best, and I shall be quite content to spend more time with my family and with you. . . . Everything is going well with me at present, but it is quite impossible to tell what the issue may be.'

The nomination took place on November 16th—not, as had been the almost immemorial custom, in Covent Garden, but on hustings erected at the base of Nelson's Column in Trafalgar Square. On that day Smith wrote to Gussie: '. . . I have never passed through such a fortnight of hard labour as the past has been, but am very well all things considered. . . . My *promises* of support are very satisfactory, but I shall only feel assured of success when there is a majority declared in my favour.' But certain people—quite unwarrantably—assumed that he was prepared to use any means to ensure his own success. Such a one was George Smalley, the London correspondent of the *New York Tribune*, a great admirer of Mill, who described seeing the latter trying to address the electors in Trafalgar Square, where 'there was the usual howling mob'. 'It had been given out beforehand that Mr. Mill should not be heard. Mr. W. H. Smith's army of news agents were there to prevent him, nor could the best efforts of a body of resolute working men obtain silence. . . .'[1] That Smalley was not alone in entertaining this notion subsequent events were to prove.

On polling day, from the very start, Smith obtained a lead which was maintained to the end. The result was beyond the expectations of his staunchest adherents—and certainly beyond his own. The figures that look so small to modern eyes reveal how limited still was the franchise—even after Disraeli's great extension of it. They were:

Smith (Cons.) 7,698
Grosvenor (Lib.) 6,505
Mill (Lib.) 6,185

Thus Smith had a majority of 1,193 over Grosvenor and of 1,513 over Mill. This marked indeed a turning-point in London's political history, for, besides the victory in Westminster, the Tories won one of the four seats in the City of London, thus breaking the solid phalanx of metropolitan Liberalism. Mill was openly castigated by his own side for the indiscretion of his pronouncements and of his associations—especially with Charles Bradlaugh, the celebrated atheist revolutionary. The *Pall Mall Gazette* wrote that '. . . at Westminster the Conservatives, if they had only known their strength, could have put in two Conservatives instead of one; and if both

[1] George W. Smalley: *London Letters*, I, 280 (Macmillan, 1890).

Liberals had been ousted, Mr. Mill would have been mainly to blame'. Even more vindictively the *Daily News* wrote that Mill 'has neglected nothing which could prejudice against him men whom, for the sake of his party and his cause, he might at least have abstained from offending . . .'.

Most other Liberal newspapers were generous towards Smith as being the best type of man to whom to lose the seat, if lost it must be. But there were naturally exceptions to this general tendency. Thus, for instance: 'Westminster has shown herself incapable of keeping a great man when she has got one, and has raised a wealthy newsvendor to temporary prominence, and even to such kind of notoriety as attends those whose names get somehow embedded in the world-wide fame of an opponent.'

But, despite the Conservative triumph at Westminster and in the City of London, the party in general suffered such a severe defeat throughout the country (the Liberals had a majority of 115 in the new House) as to justify the derisory description of Disraeli's much-heralded household suffrage as 'a leap in the dark'. Nevertheless it was ironical that his bitter rival and successor as premier, Gladstone, was defeated in the working-class constituency of South-West Lancashire—though he had prepared for the *contretemps* by getting himself nominated for Greenwich, where he had a comfortable majority and so was able to accept the Queen's invitation to form a ministry without delay.

As already indicated, Mill's many friends and admirers were not disposed to accept the great man's ignominious defeat without a show of defiance. Accordingly a petition was filed against Smith's return, on the grounds of bribery, treating and undue influence by the candidate and by other persons on his behalf. Smith himself was not in the least alarmed, for he obviously had a completely clear conscience, writing to his wife (December 9th, 1868): 'From what I hear, I think it likely the Petition will be presented, but it is not certain yet, and I do not think they have any matter which cannot be explained honorably and to all the world. I am very much less concerned about it than I was—indeed I cannot be said to be at all so.' In fact, as Parliament assembled the following day, December 10th, Smith duly took his seat for Westminster as though nothing were amiss, for the petition was not to be heard till February. 'I went down to the House to take my seat and shall be sworn tomorrow. It was a strange and almost solemn feeling to enter those doors for the first time.'

Nevertheless, his situation was embarrassing and frustrating. 'The Petition is of course a bother,' he wrote to Gussie (January 31st, 1868). 'I am neither fish flesh nor fowl. I don't like to make arrangements as if I was an M.P. or to appear in that capacity and so for a time I am in a state of suspended animation or animation in suspense.' Moreover, however clear his own conscience might be, there were certain awkward facts in the case to be got over. There was at that time no statutory limit to election expenses and, candidates being to a much greater extent in the hands of their agents than now, the latter had to be supplied with as much money as they might ask for and which they doled out to a horde of assistants and active partisans.

Smith was known for a very rich man, so that even if there was no dishonesty of any kind, there was the natural temptation to be lavish to make doubly sure of victory—and lavishness there had undoubtedly been. While the published expenses of the Liberal candidates, Grosvenor and Mill, only amounted together to £2,296 2s. 7d., those of the Conservative, Smith, mounted up to the huge total of £8,900 17s. 7d. The dynamic and devoted Bob Grimston, moreover, had also shown the most astonishing lack of judgment and discretion in bringing in, as a sub-agent, a certain Edwards—a tenant of his brother, Lord Verulam—who had not long before undergone eighteen months' imprisonment for his part in certain malpractices at the 1862 election at St. Albans, which had resulted in the temporary disfranchisement of that borough. This is presumably the 'most energetic lieutenant' referred to by Grimston's biographer; though of Grimston himself he says that: 'He knew the boundary line between fair hard canvassing and bribery as well as he knew the popping crease at cricket and it was certain that he was wide awake to all the snares which are laid by opponents in the path of a committee man.'[1]

Nevertheless, the same authority describes a trap into which Smith—and Grimston with him—all but fell. This was in the shape of an ostensible invitation to address a Conservative Working Men's Association at a public house in the West End. On arriving there quite a different kind of place and quite a different kind of company from that expected was found, a lot of champagne was uncorked and handed round and a glass was put into Smith's hands. He was obliged to deliver some kind of address, but withdrew, greatly disgusted, as soon as he possibly could. Grimston was later approached by a dubious character who tried to inveigle him into sending ten pounds to the landlord of the pub to 'cover the expenses' which sum could of course afterwards have readily been represented as a bribe. Fortunately Grimston refused and later the landlord came before the committee of inquiry and swore that he never asked for or expected to be paid a farthing by Smith or his party.

[1] Frederick Gale: *Life of Hon. Robert Grimston*, 203.

The proceedings on the petition against Smith's return opened on February 12th, 1869, and lasted seven days, and though the charges relating to bribery and treating broke down and were abandoned by the petitioners' counsel, the suspense remained intense up to the very last. Not till the closing sentences of the judge's summing up did he give the slightest indication of the judgment he was about to deliver. He said that:

> What struck against Mr. Smith was the enormous amount of expenditure. That expenditure had been called extravagant on one side and profuse on the other, and it might be described by a stronger term. At any rate it was not creditable, and its extent was almost beyond belief . . . He had never formed any other opinion of Mr. Smith than that he intended this election should be carried on legally and that the law should not be transgressed; but intentions were nothing if bribery were done. . . . If he was convinced that any illegal act had been done by a canvasser of Mr. Smith's, the election would be declared void, whatever Mr. Smith's intentions were. But the connection of agency must be made out clearly, for it would be unjust to accept a light proof of agency when the law was so harsh as to make the act of one person to affect the seat of an honest man.

The judge then declared Smith duly elected, though he declined to make any order as to costs. Indeed, only Smith's high-standing reputation for integrity had saved him from the consequences of his agents' indiscretions and extravagances. As *The Times* remarked in a leader on the case: 'A good character has to Mr. Smith at any rate, proved better than riches. It may be a question whether the latter won the seat for him, but there can be no question that the former has saved it.'

In spite of his earlier professed equanimity about the whole affair, Smith evidently felt the strain of the rather protracted proceedings very acutely, for he was stricken with that extremely painful affliction of the nervously oppressed—erysipelas—and was unable to be in court for the summing up, news of which was promptly brought to him by his friend George Cubitt, the M.P. for West Surrey.

Smith made his maiden speech on April 1st, 1869, on the second reading of a Bill dealing with the valuation of property in the metropolis, which was moved by George Goschen,[1] then President of the Poor Law Board, with whom Smith was later to have many, but never entirely felicitous dealings as a Cabinet colleague. Smith was neither now nor later much of a speaker; but on this particular

[1] First Lord of Admiralty 1871–4; left Gladstone and joined Liberal-Unionists 1886 and became Chancellor of Exchequer, 1887–92. Again First Lord of Admiralty, 1895–1900; created Viscount Goschen, 1900.

subject he was well-informed, he had something to say and he said it. A month later he spoke again on the question of 'Pauperism and Vagrancy', his views revealing the tremendous transformation which has taken place between the thinking of those times and our own. In other words he was not afraid—any more than most of his colleagues on either side of the House would have been—to declare that the relief of the able-bodied poor should be conditional upon their working and to insist that no precedent should be set up which implied the 'have-nots' having any inherent claim upon the 'haves'.

Nevertheless, he had a lively conscience and always took the utmost pains to gain practical experience of such problems. Thus he writes to Emily (November 22nd, 1869): 'Our dinner at St. Clement's Vestry is 6.30 this evening. I wish I could be down with you instead but this and others are some of the penalties to be paid for my M.P.ship. Tomorrow morning I am going to the distribution of pauper outdoor relief at St. James's; it is weary work to go from place to place on this subject but I am right I think in doing it.'

In individual cases of distress—once convinced of their genuineness—he was charmingly warm-hearted and, what is even rarer, scrupulously considerate of people's pride and feelings. Of this the following letter from him to his solicitor Ford gives an excellent example.

Private and Confidential   9 Eastern Terrace,
                                                                            Brighton
                                                                         Nov. 21, 1869
My Dear Ford,

I want you to be a party with me to a conspiracy if you will.

I think I have mentioned to you once or twice that a young Barrister named Sladen of Stones Buildings is married to one of my wife's sisters. With a gross income of about £300 a year—and two delicate children—they have rather a hard time of it, and when work is slack they comfort each other in a sorrowful sort of way—but they are too proud and I respect them for it to accept anything from their sisters who are better off.

Just now there is sickness and therefore extra sadness: and so I want you if such a thing is possible to send in a couple of dummy sets of papers to Sladen's chambers with a 10 or 15 guinea fee on each.

He is I think an equity draughtsman—at all events he is at the Chancery Bar: and I fancy the work he has is chiefly settlements and conveyances.

I think you will understand what I want to do.

There has been a time when all of us have been very much down on our luck, and a good strong gleam of light even if it had been artificial would have done us an uncommon deal of good. Just old phrases but they mean realities we are both acquainted with.

If you can carry out the scheme no one will be injured excepting to the extent to which you have trouble in assisting at the deception— but no clients of yours will suffer from work less well done than it might be and Sladen's self respect won't be affected.

Yours sincerely,

William H. Smith

I shall be in the Strand tomorrow between 1 and 2 but I don't want to talk there about these things.

We do not know whether the charitable deception was successfully arranged, but from glimpses obtained of Ford in other contexts—as well as from Smith's slightly diffident approach—we can sense the frown of disapproval upon the brow of a typically rigid Victorian, imbued with *laissez-faire* ideas and inwardly deploring this sign of 'weakness' in his employer.

Smith's interest in the general problem of the management of the poor was so great that, at the beginning of the following year, 1870, he went so far as to go to Paris to find out for himself what they did about it there. It was not a particularly auspicious time to make inquiries into the workings of a régime which was already in a shaky state and which within a few months was to collapse altogether under the strain of war and unpopularity: nevertheless Smith prosecuted his inquiries with characteristic thoroughness and indefatigability. The account of these which he sent to his wife is humorous as well as historically interesting.

Paris 15th Jany. 1870

I wrote very hurriedly yesterday, as I had been kept out by my friends much longer than I expected. Maynard took me first of all to M. Dubard, an Officer of the Guard. From him we all went to his brother: we had a long conversation with him. He is assistant to the Procureur Imperial, who holds an analogous position to our Attorney-General, and he introduced me to the Chief of the Municipal Police of Paris—a Mons. Nuss. He was very courteous, gave me a lot of information, and knew everything himself about our system, which he thinks a bad one. But first of all I had been to the Hotel de Ville, and saw the sous-chef in the Secretariat of the Prefect of the Seine. From him I went to the Chief of the Bureau of the Assistance Publique, and he talked to me for half an hour, and gave me permission to visit everything and to ask any questions I liked. He gave me great reports to study, and I am to return with any written questions, to which he will give me written answers. Nothing could exceed his kindness and readiness to give information. From him I went to the Palais de Justice, to encounter again my friend the Procureur's adjoint, and he took me by a tortuous dirty route, by which I fancy many troubled persons have passed in troubled times to the Prefecture of Police.

I have told you of M. Nuss, whom I saw there: from him I went to the Chef of the 1st Division of Police, to get permission to visit the Dépôt de Mendicité, and it was his volubility which nearly destroyed me. He wanted to tell me everything, and for full half an hour he poured out a torrent of words, and every time I said 'Oui, vraiment', meekly, he began again, until it got dark, and I became fairly alarmed lest I should be detained until the post had gone, and you cannot imagine the strain of mind in the endeavour to mentally translate and follow the stream of what was really very useful, only it was too much. . . .

I am not surprised you tell me to keep out of harm's way. The news in the English papers looks very threatening, but since I have been here there has not been the slightest appearance of dangerous excitement. On Wednesday there was danger, and on that day and during part of Thursday the troops were consigned to their barracks and had 92 rounds of ball-cartridge served out to each man. On Monday I begin the tour of visits to the different Institutions.

Jan. 17

. . . We start directly to visit one of the district bureaux de bien-faisance, then we go to one of the large Hospitals, questioning as we go; then we go to Mr. Gardiner, an English Clergyman, who has been long here, to pump him as to the condition of the Paris poor—from him we hope to get the names of some French Protestant Clergy who can give similar and independent information. I think this will be as much as we shall do today—and tomorrow I go to the Dépôt de Mendicité at S. Denis, and I hope also to see the head of the whole administration, to ask questions arising out of the observations we may make in the meantime. So my work will go on. I hope to finish on Wednesday evening, after dining with the Guard.

Next day he visited two hospitals—'one a very large one and the newest in Paris'—which seem to have impressed him very favourably; but he remarked at the end of the letter: 'Paris is quiet, but it is very curious quiet, the more one sees of it'. The day after that he was being conducted 'to the houses of the poor . . . that we should see the application of the system from beginning to end', but he added: 'The difficulty I shall find will be in digesting and arranging all this information in my own mind.'

Finally, on January 20th, there is this rather harrowing description:

. . . I wonder what they [his own children] would have said if they had been with me yesterday at the Hospice des Enfants Assistés. It was most interesting, but in some respects a most painful sight. One room which was called the Crêche, for newly born infants—or infants at the breast—contained about 50 cots, and when we were there, there were about 25 babies in the room. There was a Sister of Charity and a clerk engaged in marking them—i.e. each child when received has a necklace and distinguishing mark, corresponding with a register, placed round its neck—and secured so that it cannot be taken off except by pincers.

There was a row of wet-nurses advancing in order with their little bundles, and the printed paper with particulars, which is affixed to the cap of the poor little baby when taken in at the door, was exchanged for this necklace. On a sort of ottoman in front of the fire lay a row of something. As I got near to it, I found it was a row of very young babies not many days old—all dressed alike as a short bundle, labelled on their caps, all turned the same way—and looking less like babies, except for their poor little mouths and faces, than anything you can conceive. There was one just dressed, which certainly had not been born many hours, which its mother will probably never see again, and which certainly had never seen its mother, for its eyes were not yet open. This side of the picture was painful, and the sense that although there was great care it was a general and not particular care that was taken of these poor things.

Today I have been again to the Bureau de Bienfaisance, and have by the kindness of the Sisters of Charity seen the whole working of the system. I am afraid it could not be carried out at all without them. I have also been since the morning to S. Denis to see the Dépôt de Mendicité of Paris, and there I saw misery enough to make one sad, especially as it was of the hopeless kind springing from past errors, infirmity or incompetence of some kind or other in most cases, and the place smelt—stank, most abominably, as you know how. I went also this morning with the Visitor to see a poor family receiving relief in one of the old houses in Paris, and you can only imagine it,—I cannot describe it.

In Parliament, during the Session of 1869, all minor issues had been overshadowed by the debates on Gladstone's Bill to disestablish and disendow the Irish Church. This was seen by all the more conservative and moderate sections of opinion as ushering in a new epoch of almost untrammelled radicalism—especially now that the genial and easy-going figure of Lord Palmerston had vanished from the scene to be replaced by the fanatical Gladstone, who had introduced into his Cabinet the leader of the extreme Radicals, John Bright. Moreover, public interest was intensified beyond this by the mere fact of the enormous wealth—some sixteen millions—of the Church which was to be the victim of the Bill. The significance of the issue, as seen by the sister Church of England and by all the Conservative elements in the country, was well summed up by the Bishop of Peterborough (Dr. Magee) in the House of Lords:

... You will always observe in history that corporate property is always the first to be attacked in all great democratic revolutions. Especially is this so in the case of ecclesiastical corporate property, because ecclesiastical corporations for the most part are very wealthy, and at the same time are very weak . . . Revolutions commence with sacrilege, and they go on to communism; or to put it in the more gentle and euphemistic language of the day, revolutions begin with the Church and go on to the land. . . .

But despite a struggle in both Houses, ending with the usual dire threats against the Lords, the Bill was passed. The Conservative opposition in the Commons had fought the Bill, but in a rather dispirited fashion. Disraeli was absent from the House owing to illness throughout the Committee stage of the Bill; Stafford North-cote,[1] who should have been his lieutenant, was never noted for dynamism and was besides much abroad on foreign missions; and Gathorne-Hardy,[2] the next in order, though genial and reasonably able, was also lacking in drive. Under such circumstances it is not uncommon for some of the younger and more dynamic members of a party to feel dissatisfied with the performance of their leaders and to form from among their own number a substitute spearhead of opposition to the Government. Exactly the same thing happened ten years later when Lord Randolph Churchill and his friends became exasperated with Northcote's leadership—or lack of it—in opposition to Gladstone's next Government. The figures who now, in 1870, took upon them this role were however very different from those who were to form the 'Fourth Party'. They were extremely earnest, extremely pious men of a highly conventional type—not well-liking, slightly cynical *farceurs* as Churchill's men inclined to be. The two senior parliamentarians in this group were Richard Assheton Cross,[3] a worthy but mediocre statesman who was to adorn every Conservative administration for the next thirty years, and Lord Sandon, who as Smith's life-long friend, has already been described—and the junior one was of course Smith himself. At any rate these three, with a few other undistinguished hangers-on, took up their position on that bench below the gangway in the House which has always implied some degree of independence from strict party discipline and, with Disraeli's full approval, constituted themselves into a ginger-group.

In startlingly swift justification of the Bishop of Peterborough's prognostication about despoliation of the Church being inevitably followed by an attack on private property in land, the first Bill to be

[1] Sir Stafford Henry Northcote, 8th Bart., M.P. North Devon; President of Board of Trade, 1866; Chancellor of Exchequer, 1874–80; Secretary of State Foreign Affairs, 1886; created Earl of Iddesleigh, 1885. Died 1887.

[2] Gathorne Gathorne-Hardy, M.P. Leominster & Oxford University; Home Secretary, 1867–8; Secretary of State for War, 1874–80; for India, 1878; created Earl of Cranbrook, 1878. Died 1906.

[3] M.P. (Cons.) Preston, 1857–62; for S.W. Div. Lancs., 1868–85; for Newton Div., 1885–6; created Viscount Cross, 1886, Home Secretary, 1874–80 and 1885–6; Secretary of State for India, 1886–92; Lord Privy Seal, 1895–1900.

laid before Parliament in the Session of 1870 was the first in the long series of Irish Land Bills. Though Smith did not speak in the Debates on this Bill it first aroused his interest in a subject which was to dominate politics for the rest of his career. But immediately after this another Bill was presented on a subject in which he was already deeply interested and upon which he was extremely well-informed.

This was the Elementary Education Bill, introduced by W. E. Forster,[1] Vice-President of the Committee of Council on Education, with whom Smith, despite their difference of party, became on terms of close friendship. Forster's origins were rather similar to those of Smith: he was brought up a Quaker and came from a family of wool merchants, had played a notable part in restraining the Chartists in Bradford and had written and lectured on philanthropic subjects before becoming M.P. for Bradford. He had married a daughter of the famous Dr. Arnold, whereupon he had left the Society of Friends and joined the Church of England. This similarity of background and interests drew the two men together. Thus Smith wrote to Emily (July 29th, 1870): '. . . I am very glad I was in the House last night as Forster with whom you know I like to work came to me and expressed a wish I & Sandon should hear his statement on Education and then I had to say a word. . . .'

The most controversial point in Forster's Bill was that dealing with the future of religious instruction in schools. Hitherto primary education had been supplied by voluntary schools, the majority conducted on Church principles, aided by a small State grant. In his Bill Forster had doubled the State grant to the existing Church schools so as to enable them to become a permanent part of the new system, while he introduced publicly controlled schools only to fill up the large gaps in the educational map of the country. The battle raged, however, over how much—if any—religious teaching was to be given in these publicly-controlled schools. Upon this the Opposition in the House of Commons was divided. The young Conservatives, among whom were Smith, Cross and Lord Sandon, were in favour of voluntary religious instruction; but Disraeli and Gathorne-Hardy stood out for the full Church of England teaching. Yet others, of course, wanted the total prohibition of all religious instruction in the publicly-controlled schools. But the Government, supported by the advanced section of the Opposition, adopted a middle course, which, while it gave school boards power to forbid religious teaching altogether, also empowered them to permit schoolmasters to read and expound Scripture without the introduction of creeds and catechisms.

But the most important alteration in the Bill which Smith and Sandon were chiefly instrumental in inducing the Government to

[1] M.P. (Lib.) Bradford, 1861–86; Chief Secretary for Ireland, 1880–2.

accept was the withdrawal of the clause constituting twenty-three school boards for the metropolis and substituting one—creating a single board for the whole of London. Their experience in the management of the Bishop of London's Fund convinced them that only the setting up of a single central board would attract the best, most responsible and disinterested types of men. They therefore urged this course upon Forster, not so much across the floor of the House, but in private interviews rendered that much more easy by their friendship with him.

The result was the establishment of the London School Board of which Smith and Sandon almost inevitably became members—together with such distinguished contemporary figures as Lord Lawrence, the recent Viceroy of India, who became chairman; Professor Thomas Huxley, the great biologist; Sir Charles Reed, noted philanthropist and antiquary; Hepworth Dixon, the historian and traveller; Samuel Morley and McCullagh Torrens, both philanthropists and politicians of note and one or two of the Nonconformist leaders. The extreme seriousness with which Smith approached this new task may be seen from the following excerpt from a letter from him to Ford, dated September 12th, 1870:

> ... I am concerning myself about the election of the School Board for London and if I hear favourable accounts from Armstrong,[1] to whom I have written, I shall stand, and Lord Sandon with me, as candidates for Westminster. It is a bold thing to do, but I have two great objects in view—to show my earnest interest in education, and to endeavour to prove that popular election may result in the creation of a Board in London as strong in position, character and fitness for its work as the House of Commons itself. Forster very strongly pressed me to engage in the work, and I like him, and like to work with him.

Meanwhile the Franco-Prussian War was running its brief but catastrophic course. France had declared war on Prussia on July 15th, 1870, and Smith wrote to Emily on July 28th: '. . . There is no news from the War today but a sense of danger—as if it was coming—and we shall hear before very long of some terrible collision between the two Armies.' On August 2nd: '. . . Men think more and more gloomily as far as the future of Europe is concerned. We are not afraid for England but we shall have to fight or to arm for fighting. . . .' And on August 8th, as the Prussians advanced relentlessly into the heart of France: '. . . from Paris I hear today people—the common people—are walking about that City in tears and a state of

---

[1] Proprietor and editor of *The Globe* and later of *The People;* created Sir George Armstrong, Bart., 1892.

great excitement. A fresh battle must be fought almost directly and the Emperor's life probably depends upon the result of that battle. At any rate we must give up all idea of going through France just now and I must look out for some other means of getting a holiday.'

The question of religious education in board schools, which aroused so much excitement in the country during the passage of Forster's Education Bill and which, it was fondly hoped, had been laid to rest by the compromise already described, was now revived in an acute form within the narrower limits of the London School Board. Here Smith, as a member of this newly-constituted body, at once came into his own as a man who could hold deep convictions of his own and yet be capable of reconciling the conflicting opinions of his colleagues. For he framed a resolution advocating the adoption of a by-law ordering that the Bible should be read, and instruction in religious subjects given therefrom, in the board schools generally, whilst those interested in particular schools might show cause for exemption from the whole or part of this by-law; and in all schools it was to be understood that the spirit of the Act was to be observed, and no proselytism allowed. This proposal, though opposed by Professor Huxley and two other ardent secularists, was seconded by Samuel Morley, and being supported by Roman Catholic, Baptist and Wesleyan members, was carried by 38 votes to 3.

Smith's perennial concern for the poor of London had convinced him that emigration offered one of the best solutions wherever the circumstances rendered it practicable and the people showed the willingness. He therefore took an active part in the affairs of the British and Colonial Emigration Society and in particular of the 'East End Emigration Club', paying the fares of a substantial portion of the emigrants out of his own pocket. Thus on June 26th, 1870, he went down to Gravesend to see off 1,197 emigrants to Canada, the expenses of about 280 of whom he had defrayed himself. Moreover, when he visited Canada two years later he made careful inquiries about the whereabouts, welfare and prospects of these people.

In the following year, May 1871, he raised in the House of Commons the question of the operation of the Poor Law within the metropolis and moved for the appointment of a Royal Commission to inquire into the policy and administration of the law. His well-known connection with practical philanthropy, combined with the alarming increase in the number of persons who were receiving relief out of the rates, enabled him to make out a formidable case for inquiry, for he was able to show that, whereas in the preceding ten years of general prosperity the population of London had increased 16 per cent, pauperism had risen in the prodigious ratio of 64 per cent. But he was unable to persuade the House to adopt his resolution, which, after a long discussion, was withdrawn.

As his involvement in public affairs increased Smith withdrew increasingly from an active share in the management of the family business. The first partnership deed between him and William Lethbridge had been signed in June 1864 for five years. But when Smith was sure that he was going to be an M.P.—that is after the petition against his return had been successfully disposed of, in February 1869—a memorandum was added divesting him of all profits and emoluments from the sale of newspapers to Government offices. From then on, as his public and political responsibilities increased, he was always particularly anxious to remove any possible grounds for the charge that he might be making his political career serve his business interests or using office under the Crown to obtain special advantages in this respect.

Notes among his personal papers suggest that in 1867 he seriously contemplated making Sandifer and White the working heads of the News Department and all the Railway Superintendents and Travellers limited partners by giving them an interest in the business. Again, in 1876 it was proposed to form the business into a limited liability company but nothing seems to have come of this. What he did do, however, was to take in a further partner in this year in order to make up for his own withdrawal from active management, in the person of a young man named Charles Awdry, who had joined the firm six years earlier on coming down from Oxford. Awdry had had a good all-round record at Oxford and had intended becoming a barrister till he was approached by Smith. He became one of the most successful and highly respected heads of the firm and was followed by his eldest son, who also became a partner until his untimely death in the First World War.

IV

"TRAVELS AND TREASURY"

SMITH was always interested in comparing the conditions, remedies and methods prevailing in his own country with those prevailing in other countries, but it was doubtless his special interest in emigration as a solution to the overcrowding and pauperism in London which decided him in 1872—before he should become shackled with the cares of office—to make a tour of Canada and the United States. His wife Emily could not well leave her young family, so it was with a heavy heart rather outweighing a natural sense of excitement and adventure that he sailed in the Royal Mail Steamer *Moravian* on August 15th. 'Brougham to the train', he noted in his journal, 'and coachman drove so slowly that anxiety lest I should lose it almost drove out of my head and heart the pain of parting.' His fellow-passengers were some acquaintances called Russell-Gurney—'and it was a comfort to find them almost as sad at leaving as I was'.

Next day he wrote from near Liverpool:

My darling wife,

I cannot tell you what a comfort it was to me to get your precious letter this morning. I never knew before the pain of parting or I would not deliberately have inflicted it upon you: but there is hope now before me and I believe it will grow and increase day by day until we are once more brought together. . . . I go into Liverpool very shortly and at 3.0 embark on board my floating hotel for the next ten days. I promise you I will try not to do too much or work too hard. Your love and my children's will hold me back if I am tempted.

Later, on board, he wrote again:

. . . It has been such a strange day and I think it will prove to be a strange night—to me. . . . I had a kind of something in my throat which you understand and which made me know what it is to be heart sick. . . .

I found my Cabin—such a little thing—and I am very glad indeed that I am alone in it for how two persons could exist together in it I cannot understand. . . .

71

Don't imagine my darling that I am miserable. I do feel the separation very much indeed now and then, but every hour brings the time nearer when by God's mercy I hope to rejoin you all again and I am rejoicing in that. I don't think we shall ever again be separated in this way.

'A dirty night for our first at sea', he records on August 17th. '. . . We are well away from land and out in the Atlantic. . . . Quiet prevails, with interjected sighs—almost groans. Food—dry toast and tea.' The menu for breakfast had included beef-steaks, mutton and pork chops. Next day: 'Very much the same. A serious tone prevails, and we speak respectfully of the Atlantic. Very few passengers visible. Food—still tea and toast. Have come to the belief that we are all in the habit of eating a great deal too much and that so many meals on board ship are quite unnecessary. Night—roll, roll. . . . Children cry, and their mothers can't attend to them, and we have a lively night. An old lady in the cabin has a silver bell, which she is constantly ringing to assure the stewardess that she hears the water bubbling about the ship, and she is sure it is sinking. We are all grave, and most of us selfish. Captain read service in cabin; could not venture down. . . .'

And so it went on, with the children crying, the emigrants sea-sick and home-sick and Smith trying to comfort them and the old lady ringing her silver bell, until they landed at Quebec on August 27th. That same evening Smith dined with the Governor-General, Lord Dufferin,[1] and made the acquaintance of the latter's private secretary, a remarkable young man named Jacob Luard Pattisson, who not many years later was to become Smith's own private secretary and general factotum—for the rest of Smith's life.

From Quebec he went on to Montreal, whence he wrote (September 1st) the following description of local ways, which obviously afforded a strong contrast to those to which he was accustomed in England.

I wanted a bath early, so I told the chamber-maid last night, and she promised to speak to the man. No women attend upon men in their bedrooms in Canada, but they look after their rooms when they are out of them. At 7 I rang: boy answered. 'I want a bath.' 'Oh, do you? Very well,' and went away: at 20 minutes past no bath. I rang again. An old man came this time. I said, 'I ordered a bath a long time ago, and it has not come yet.' 'Did you? How long?' 'More than half an hour.' 'Oh, I don't call half an hour a long time.' 'Don't you?' said I; 'then we do in our country.' 'Ah, but it is Sunday morning, you

[1] Frederick Temple, 1st Earl and later 1st Marquess of Dufferin and Ava; later Ambassador at St. Petersburg and Constantinople, H.M. Commissioner in Egypt and Viceroy of India, 1884–8.

know.' 'Well, never mind, bring the water and the towels.' 'You can't have any towels. The chambermaid keeps them, and she has gone to breakfast.'

Is not this a free country?

. . . I have spent a very quiet afternoon in my room, making use of the church service so long used by my dear love. . . .

After careful descriptions of the city and surrounding country he concludes (September 2nd): '. . . I am learning a great deal, seeing very much that is interesting and making the acquaintance of every man of note almost in Canada; but with all this qualified enjoyment and sense of acquisition, I am looking forward so gladly and so hopefully to the bright November day of my return. . . .' He went twice to look at Niagara Falls, of which he gave a lengthy but extremely good description, and then moved on to Toronto (September 7th). '. . . There I met a gentleman who reminded me he had sat next to me at Drapers Hall two years ago, and told me what I had said to him. He took me up to Professor Goldwin Smith and introduced me to him, and we had a long talk about the politics of Canada and the United States. The Professor says Canada enjoys a perfect constitution, complete liberty, and there is only the drawback of corruption, which exists more or less everywhere. . . .'

Goldwin Smith was a celebrated contemporary figure. He had been Regius Professor of Modern History at Oxford, but he was a fervent Radical and even Republican. Indeed, so strong were his feelings against monarchy, privilege and all hereditary institutions that he left England to live in the purer atmosphere of North America. He was for a time a great admirer of Gladstone, but, like some other well-known Radicals, turned violently against him when he brought in the Bill of Home Rule for Ireland and began to express open sympathy for the Queen.

Meanwhile, Smith's brother-in-law, Juland Danvers,[1] had written to him (August 26th): '. . . You will be in the "Dominion" of Canada and in the States at interesting political times, electioneering going on in both. I hope you will have an opportunity of seeing how the Ballot is worked. The first trial here, at Pontefract, was not very encouraging, except for the absence of rioting and drinking. It did not bring the Electors out.' For Gladstone's Liberal Government, in the face of grave doubts and forebodings on many sides, had just brought in and passed the Ballot Act, under which, for the first time in English history, voting was made secret.

After this (September 9th) Smith was visiting 'the great Normal Schools here, where masters and mistresses are educated and trained'

[1] Government director of Indian Railway Companies and later Secretary Public Works Department; made a K.C.S.I. in 1886.

and then on to a champagne lunch given in his honour by the Board of Trade, where 'everybody was very kind, very demonstrative, and very anxious to show that Canadians and Englishmen are one and the same people'. After that again to a dinner given in his honour by the Directors of the Grand Trunk Railway—'more champagne and more speeches—and more heat, for it is very hot and muggy here—'. As he wrote a few days later (September 12th):

> The very kindness one encounters makes one long for home more I think. Nothing is more fatiguing than to have a lot of people one after another keeping one constantly in conversation, giving one no rest from 10 in the morning until 12 at night and delighting to do one honour and kindness. I long for rest—to be with you quietly sitting by my side or lying by me. It will come soon—the time will pass swiftly.
>
> What I am seeing here, however, greatly impresses me with a sense of the great changes which are coming over society.
>
> Every man woman and child can earn here much more than is necessary for food lodging and clothing if they have fair health. The commonest labourer will get six and seven shillings a day and food is cheaper than it is in England. The country appears healthy, but in one little town I visited in the backwoods . . . there were four doctors, all of whom appeared to be living very comfortably. . . .
>
> If it were not for the different kind of houses they have, the distances between them, the very bad roads, some not paved or stoned at all, but simply the sand and earth which has existed since the flood—one would sometimes imagine oneself at home. The people are very 'English', live a family life, conduct their religious services exactly as we do, dress as we do, and with one or two additions to the course, they eat and drink as we do. I am sure you would like them.

In a later letter (September 19th) he remarks: '. . . I have been going about seeing everything I can in the shape of schools, charities, and public buildings, until my eyes ache and both my ears and tongue are tired. . . . There is much to learn, to see, to appreciate, and I may never have another chance, and so I want to absorb all I can.' Crossing the border into the United States he embarked upon a similar programme there—first in New York and then in Chicago. Writing from the latter on September 29th, he noted that it was

> . . . the place that has had the biggest fire that ever was known. It burnt an area covered with houses 5 miles long by 3 wide. . . . All wooden houses are to be moved beyond what are called the fire-limits of the city, and I saw one going down the street today on rollers to its new location. It would be quite impossible in England, and would have to be taken down to be rebuilt, but it is a business here to move houses as we move furniture. I visited the water-works which were burnt, but at work again in a week. Fancy a city with the gas and water-works all burnt in one night! More corn and pigs than in any

other place I have ever seen; but I did not see one child at play, or one face without marks of care, anxiety and excitement—the police only excepted, and they took life easily. . . .

I went to Church this morning but the services don't improve upon one. Professionals sing in the choirs and the congregations leave everything to them . . . but imagine while the offertory was being collected the piece 'Angels ever bright and fair' was sung by one of the professionals. It was too opera-like. This evening I shall try a dissenting Chapel. . . .

I went last night to the First Baptist Church as it is termed and I did not find it a great improvement over the Episcopal.

There is something about our Cousins' way of doing everything almost which grates upon one.

Leaving Chicago he now began to travel steadily through the Middle West towards California. Passing through the plains of Nebraska in his Pullman railway carriage he wrote from near Cheyenne on October 3rd:

. . . We have seen many droves of Antelopes[1] which scudded away at our approach generally as quickly as the wind—but some stopped to look at us apparently knowing man could not shoot or hunt them from the train. Every minute almost we pass the bones and horns of buffalo[2] which have been killed or have died on the plains.

At Sidney half an hour ago . . . there was a barrack post of U.S. troops quartered there to keep the Indians in check for the protection of the Railway. . . .

I have been called off to look at a village of prairie dogs.[3] They are dust color and look something between a Marmot and a dog. They live in earth mounds which they throw up and in the day time sit on the top and bark. . . .

I have seen Buffalo trails—where they follow one after the other from feeding grounds to water. . . .

On October 7th he reached San Francisco, delighted to be rid of the swaying and noise of the train and to have a bath. He presented letters of introduction to notable citizens. 'The talk was of wheat, of diamonds, and of gold. . . . Why won't you believe we are the richest people under the sun? I politely believe my friend, but he is angry because all my friends do not understand it.' Turning from these arrogant Americans he set himself to explore the Chinese quarter of the city, culminating in a visit to a 'joss-house', where with mingled fascination and disgust he watched a Chinaman 'at his devotions'.

[1] Popularly known as 'Pronghorns': soon to become almost extinct till reintroduced in recent times into Texas.

[2] The American Bison—at this time rapidly becoming extinct through indiscriminate slaughter. A few thousand are preserved today in 'parks' and 'reserves'.

[3] Marmots.

Nevertheless, he had to admit that 'My ideas about the Chinese are greatly changed. They are a remarkably quiet, steady, hard-working body of men, as exhibited in California, and people there say they would gladly give us back all the Irish who have invaded the country in numbers, and substitute Chinamen for them. No doubt a large part of the great prosperity of the State is owing to these people. . . .'

After a few such days in 'Frisco' he joined some American friends on an expedition to the famous Yosemite Valley. Of this he wrote the following lively account to Ford (October 15th):

. . . It has been unlike anything I have ever seen before. The Trees are the strongest possible proof that this is not a 'New World'. I rode into one which was lying prostrate, the heart of which had been burnt out by the Indians: and then there were 3 feet of the bark or skin under my horse's feet and nearly as much above . . . the plains are one vast wheat-field . . . the land bears the same crop every year without change or manure. Their cattle also are very fine and thrive upon the yellow burnt up grasses and shrubs which they pick among the bush.

Grapes, pears and apples are also very good and there is still Gold to be had for the washing when water is to be had, but that at this season is a scarce commodity.

There are some drawbacks—Bears are not uncommon,[1] Rattle-snakes are easily to be found . . . and then as if to keep you dirty when there is the Pacific Ocean tempting you to wash and be clean and cool, there are Sharks so plentiful in the Bay of San Francisco that not a single bathing machine is to be seen.

The town or City of S. Francisco is a marvellous one. It is little more than 20 years old and yet covers many miles, has 150,000 inhabitants and some of the largest Hotels in the States. Its streets also are wide and handsome. . . .

I get on very well with the people and don't dislike them but I am not more republican than I was and the people themselves are not generally satisfied with the general working out of their own institutions although there is no disposition to change them. There is a general belief that every public man is corrupt and a languid regret is expressed that it is so. Grant[2] will be elected President again. . . .

After this he parted from his American friends and made a detour to Salt Lake City, 'the capital of Mormondom', as he called it. Here he was at once fascinated and repelled by a Mormon religious service, which he described as follows (October 20th):

. . . I went to the Tabernacle to morning service—mid-day I should say. It is a very large, plain building, holding 6000 people, the roof

---

[1] They still are: but probably only owing to the Yosemite Valley having become a 'National Park'.

[2] General Ulysses Grant, the great commander of the Union armies in the Civil War. Elected President of U.S.A. 1868 and for a second term in 1872.

supported without a pillar or buttress, of great span, resembling an inverted dish-cover. The organ is a very fine one, built on the spot. There is a sort of low Exeter Hall Orchestra raised step by step, one level behind the other.

There were three pulpits or stands, one on each step or stage, and the preacher, Orson Pratt, took his place at the middle one. His text was from the Word of God as revealed to Joseph Smith, page so-and-so, on the 27th December 1832, and he read it. He said the Latter-day Saints believed the Bible which he had, the Revelations to Joseph Smith, and the Book of Mormon, each and all, one as much as the other, and he went on to a defence of polygamy on the grounds that under the Old Testament dispensation it was permitted, and also that as other Christians permitted widowers to marry again, and they might therefore have two or three wives in heaven, it was certainly right to have two or three on earth. Much more was said which I shall not repeat, but the congregation received it all.

While the singing and preaching proceeded, bread and water were partaken by the members as a sacrament. I never saw such women as in that place, so plain, so vacant-looking, or so superstitious. Poor creatures! The system is described by those who have courage as a hell upon earth; and although the ground bears fruit and the valley teems with produce, the human beings who have adopted the so-called religion look either half-crazed or entirely knavish.

A meeting of gentiles against Mormonism was held last Thursday in the streets. It was the first open meeting. Threats had been uttered that it would be broken up, and the chairman announced that the first person disturbing the meeting would be shot. It was known there was a body of men armed, prepared to obey his orders, and so everything passed off peacefully.

I spent the evening quietly in my room. There was not much to choose between the countenances of the gentile miners who are attracted to Salt Lake by the silver-mines and those of the Mormons. A stranger unarmed is perfectly safe. If you want to incur danger show a six-shooter revolver and instantly every man will produce and cock his weapon. By the way, highway robbers are called road-agents in these parts. Robbers is an offensive term. And so two road-agents relieved the Stage last week of the trouble of carrying some bullion from the mines near Virginia City to Reno. . . .

Leaving the Mormon capital, Smith began to work his way eastwards—and homewards—passing through the desolate plains of Colorado, where again he observed large herds of bison and prongbuck, through Kansas, Oklahoma and the eastern states, with many curious and amusing adventures too numerous to recount (including a short interview with President Grant in Washington), until at last he found himself back in New York again. From here he wrote to Emily (November 5th):

77

My very precious wife

. . . Today I write for the last time and I hardly know how to do so. I am so glad my separation from you is coming to an end. . . . The interval will be very like the time before we were married, only I know now to what love—if I can know—I am returning; then it was expectation, now it is reality. My dear love, I get impatient . . . I go in a fast vessel but it will not be fast enough for me.

Apart from the longed-for reunion with his wife and children, Smith had something else to look forward to on his return from America. For in the previous year he had bought, from Sir Dudley Marjoribanks,[1] a new and more spacious country home called 'Greenlands', near Henley-on-Thames, and during these past months an army of architects and workmen had been improving and altering it to his taste. Shortly before his return from the States Juland Danvers had reported (October 21st, 1872):

. . . I joined them today in their visit to Greenlands, 'them' meaning Emily and the three elder children. We started in gloom and wet but arrived there in sunshine. The place was looking extremely pretty, the bright tints of autumn (some of which I trust will keep themselves for you) adding brilliancy to the scene. The workmen had all but cleared out and there is every prospect of a country house, replete with comfort and elegance, being ready to receive you and an eager group with loving hearts being ready to smother you, this day month. . . .

I was sitting just now in the drawing room downstairs with Emily, after the girls had gone to bed. She was tired after her day's work and was reclining, if not napping on the sofa . . . Reinhart [?butler] came in and, as if touched by a magic wand, Emily was wide awake in an instant and in another moment on her feet with 'a letter from William' written 400 miles on your journey to 'Cisco' or 'Frisco', I forget which it is. . . .

He had also had reports on the progress of his business affairs from his partner, William Lethbridge, which were equally gratifying. The latter wrote to him in the States (August 21st):

. . . All things here have gone on quietly. The Stations [Railway Bookstalls] are doing well, money comes in very fairly. Chapman [& Hall, publisher] is of course in his chronic state of tightness. Cockett has accepted our proposition. The printers ask still for the 9 hours which I propose to give them on the terms usually adopted in the trade i.e. with its disadvantages as well as its advantages. White [head of Newspaper Dept.] goes off on his holiday . . . on Friday, but everything goes smoothly. I have had a talk with Monger [head of Packing Dept.] and he is of opinion that our hands are well satisfied as a body with their pay and position, so I have satisfied myself at present by telling him to keep his eyes & ears well open. . . .

[1] M.P. for Berwick, created Baron Tweedmouth, 1881.

Soon afterwards he reported again (September 4th):

> ... the strike of Carpenters is over, the affair being compromised, next week we shall begin the 9 hours (i.e. 54 hours per week) system in our works both Printers & Carpenters.—Things go on very quietly & comfortably. ...

Meanwhile his relationship with Forster continued to be one of the most interesting and characteristic features of this period of Smith's career. For Forster, though in most things standing much farther to the Left than many of his colleagues, had never been forgiven by the Radicals and the Non-conformists for what they considered to be the 'compromises' inherent in his Education Act of 1870. So much so that his own constituents at Bradford carried a vote of censure on him at his first meeting after the Act was passed. He also had to suffer a fearful campaign against him from the 'Birmingham League', directed by that increasingly powerful figure Joseph Chamberlain. Though Forster stood his ground he let it be known that he hoped and intended to amend his Act by the introduction of compulsion within a year or two, when increased school-accommodation might justify it.

Smith, who had so sympathized with his aspirations and had developed such a personal respect and affection for him, felt in honour bound to try to help him and to go along with him. The following excerpts from his letters to Emily give a good idea of the trend of his feelings.

Nov. 30. 71
... I found a note from Forster asking me to go and see him and I spent quite an hour with him this morning. He was very civil and very confidential and we are to meet again soon and talk over matters.
Jan. 4. 72
... I saw Forster this morning ... I am going to get up a fresh agitation if I can to help him and the Education Act, but I don't like the job.
Jan. 23. 73
... I had a long talk with Forster and a very confidential one. He is not at all happy but is quite staunch to his principles.

But by this time the strength and prestige of the Government was rapidly declining, the Conservatives were steadily winning one by-election after another and Forster never got the chance to put his plans into effect. Indeed, early in 1873, the Government were defeated on the Irish University Bill and Gladstone resigned, suggesting that Disraeli should take office with a minority administration. But Disraeli sensibly refused, thereby forcing Gladstone, who feared to risk a dissolution, to continue with a re-shuffled cabinet. This, however, could not last long and when yet another by-election went against the Government, Gladstone finally declared his intention of dissolving Parliament (January 24th, 1874). A general election almost immediately followed in which the Conservatives gained a substantial majority and Gladstone resigned.

Before passing on to recount Smith's part in the ensuing famous administration of Disraeli it is right to describe an important achievement of his in the sphere of metropolitan amenities rather than in politics. During the recent building of the Thames Embankment below Westminster Bridge a slice of land valued at £5,000 a year had been reclaimed from the river. On this land the Government proposed to erect some public offices; but Smith countered this by tabling a motion that an address be presented to Her Majesty, praying that the land, which had been reclaimed at the heavy expense of the ratepayers, should now be reserved for their advantage as a breathing place and pleasure-ground. Although the motion was violently attacked by both Gladstone and the Chancellor of the Exchequer, Lowe, on the grounds that it was 'flatly contrary to the law of the land' which required Crown property to be put to profitable use, when a division was taken the Government were defeated by 158 votes to 108. Nevertheless, the question was shelved for the time being. This was in 1870.

In the following year Smith, however, returned to the charge, giving notice of his intention to move that 'it was desirable that the ground reclaimed from the Thames between Whitehall Gardens and Whitehall Place should be devoted to the purposes of public recreation and amusement'. Apprehensive of a further defeat in the House, Gladstone decided to refer the question to a Select Committee. That body reported in favour of the disposal of the ground in the manner advocated by Smith and endorsed by the vote of the House. But no action followed as the Treasury would not budge on the question of principle relating to the disposal of Crown property.

Indeed, when a new Committee was appointed in 1872, they reversed the decision of the former Committee and recommended the appropriation of nearly all the ground in dispute for the erection of public buildings. Thereupon the Chancellor of the Exchequer prepared and brought in a Bill to give effect to this recommendation; but the only result was that the Government suffered another defeat—this time on the motion of Sir William Harcourt[1] who carried a resolution against them to the effect that it was not desirable to proceed further in the matter that year.

[1] M.P. (Lib.) Oxford; Home Secretary, 1880–5; Chancellor of Exchequer, 1886 and 1892–5.

In fact, settlement of the matter did not come till 1873. Smith continued his pressure until the Crown Commissioners finally agreed to his proposal by offering to hand over to the Metropolitan Board of Works almost the whole of the ground for a payment of £3,270—an arrangement which was confirmed by Parliament and carried out. Then, when the ground had been duly laid out as public gardens, Smith, who had by this time (May 1875) become Secretary to the Treasury, was appropriately invited to declare the gardens open—the seats for which he presented as a gift. The whole episode was typical of his tenacity as well as of that paternalistic attitude which had spread from his own employees to his fellow countrymen as a whole.

It was an undoubted tribute to his merits too when, in the autumn of 1873, his friends and colleagues on the London School Board tried to persuade him to take on the chairmanship of it. But this was something which he was quite determined to avoid at all costs, for he wrote to Emily (December 2nd, 1873): 'I think . . . I have escaped the School Board even for a few weeks. I said positively that nothing would induce me to take it [the chairmanship] permanently and my friends gave way and I think I shall escape being nominated.'

In spite of the unpopularity into which Gladstone's Government had fallen and the many and continuing Conservative gains at by-elections, nothing in particular appeared likely to bring affairs to a crisis as the new year 1874 opened and Parliament had been called for February 5th. But on January 24th Gladstone suddenly issued a manifesto announcing, with his usual flowery circumlocution, that he had decided to seek a fresh mandate from the country—'to pass from a state of things thus fitful and casual to one in which the nation will have a full opportunity of expressing will and choice as between the political parties', as he put it.

Owing to the excellent impression made by Smith since his election for Westminster in 1868 his chances of holding that seat at the coming general election were considered rather more than good. However, in the intervening time the Ballot Act had become law, and no one could be certain how the new secrecy of the vote would affect the issue. The Liberals, for instance, claimed that its effect would be the release of the artisan and labouring classes from the alleged oppressive influence and constraint of their employers, who were mainly Conservative, thus indicating a considerable increase to the Liberal poll.

At any rate, the doubt was enough to cause the Westminster Conservatives to hesitate to run more than one candidate for the two seats, on the theory that Smith, standing alone, might be reckoned fairly sure of being returned. Indeed, the Liberals made an approach for a tacit understanding that the representation should be divided by the unopposed return of Smith for the Conservatives and Sir Thomas Fowell Buxton[1] for the Liberals. But Smith refused to consider any such compromise. He wrote to Emily (January 26th):

> I have my agents at work and all the preliminary arrangements well forward and only Buxton is announced yet on the other side . . . to supply the vacancy caused by Grosvenor's retirement. Sir Richard Wallace[2] is not that I can hear coming forward with me.
> Lord Lascelles[3] . . . Lord Brabazon[4] . . . and Lord Charles Scott[5] are spoken of to come out with me, but nothing is settled or even that a second man will stand, until tomorrow at 4. . . .

But next day (January 27th): 'Well, it is all settled. I am to have a contest and Sir Charles Russell,[6] the good looking Guardsman who I introduced to you some time ago is to stand with me. . . .' And again next day (January 28th): '. . . Russell is a very good fellow and goes down very well. There was less opposition this time than ever before.' But, in view of Westminster's long Whig tradition, it was a bold and—as many thought—a hazardous enterprise to jeopardize the certainty of keeping one seat in order to have the chance of winning both.

This time Smith dropped all pretence of standing as a 'Liberal-Conservative' or of being independent of party allegiance and discipline. He now stood as an avowed member of the Conservative party and his election address contained some almost reactionary sentiments which might well have caused the author of the Second Reform Bill, Disraeli, to raise an eyebrow. Thus: '. . . There is, in my judgment, ample work for the energies of Parliament, without embarking upon great constitutional changes which are not desired by the people. . . .' His brother-in-law, Juland Danvers, wrote (January 29th): 'I thought your address very good. Gladstone does not like it and makes a mean attack upon you. However, you will be able to take your revenge.'

Despite Liberal hopes and Conservative doubts this first general election to be held under the Ballot Act surprised both sides by its

---

[1] 3rd Bart., M.P. (Lib.) Lyme Regis, 1865–8; Governor and C in C of South Australia, 1895–8.

[2] The great art connoisseur, whose collection was ultimately bequeathed to the nation by his widow as the 'Wallace Collection'; founder of the Hertford British Hospital in Paris; supposed natural son of the 3rd Marchioness of Hertford.

[3] Later 4th Earl of Harewood.

[4] Later 12th Earl of Meath.

[5] Lord Charles Montagu-Douglas-Scott, son of 5th Duke of Buccleuch; a very distinguished naval officer.

[6] Sir Charles Russell, V.C., 3rd Bart., of Swallowfield; M.P. (Cons.) Berks, 1865–8 and for Westminster, 1874–83. Died 1883.

results. A Conservative minority of 90 in the old Parliament was converted into a majority of 50 in the new one. But no more sensational was this reversal of affairs than in the metropolis, where, having formerly only been able to boast of two seats out of twenty, the Conservatives now equally divided its representation with the Liberals. And the most resounding of their victories was at Westminster. It was described in the following terms by the *Spectator* (February 7th, 1874), then a Whig weekly:

> The most tremendous of the Tory victories is that at Westminster, where the two Tory candidates, Mr. W. H. Smith and Sir Charles Russell, have been returned, the former by a vote of close upon two to one, and that over a candidate supported by the whole strength of the Licensed Victuallers and of the religious philanthropists, as well as of the Liberal Party in general—Sir Fowell Buxton. The return is as follows:—
>
> | | |
> |---|---|
> | Mr. W. H. Smith (C) | 9,371 |
> | Sir Charles Russell (C) | 8,681 |
> | Sir T. F. Buxton (L) | 4,749 |
> | General Codrington (L) | 3,435 |
>
> Now on the last occasion Mr. W. H. Smith polled only 7,648 votes, which is much fewer than Sir Charles Russell has polled on this occasion, while Captain Grosvenor polled 6,584 votes, nearly two thousand more than Sir Fowell Buxton polls now. This is Conservative reaction with a vengeance!

On receiving the news Smith wrote simply, 'My dearest wife, Is not this simply wonderful! Your very affectionate husband.' And this too was mainly the work of those artisans and other humble subjects when released by the Ballot Act from the 'oppression and dictation' of their employers.

Gladstone resigned on February 18th and the Queen sent for Disraeli. There had at first been some doubt as to the latter's ability to form a Government fully representative of all that was ablest and most experienced in his party, since two of this category, Lords Salisbury and Carnarvon, had seceded from his previous administration over the 'leap in the dark' of 1867 and, though he was recognized to be the only man on their side capable of confronting Gladstone, Disraeli was still not completely trusted by the squires of the old 'country party'.

However, these doubts were quickly dispelled by the unreserved acceptance of Lords Salisbury and Carnarvon to return to their old posts at the India Office and Colonial Office respectively—and doubtless the confidence thus evinced by these two great territorial magnates and eminent Conservatives reassured the Squirearchy. The next thing was to try to reassure also the middle and mercantile classes who were equally important as bulwarks of the party. With this end in view Disraeli made two striking appointments of men chosen from these classes—and not from the traditional ruling class. The first was that of Richard Assheton Cross[1] as Home Secretary and the second was that of W. H. Smith as Financial Secretary to the Treasury.

The London newspapers had from the first fixed upon Smith as one of the new men likely to be brought to the front; in fact several of them were for placing him straight away in the Cabinet as Vice-President of the Council on Education or President of the Local

SIR R. A. CROSS.

" VERY CROSS.'

Government Board, owing to his known interest in and knowledge of educational matters, poor law reform and so forth. Thus the Whig *Spectator* not only pressed his claims for such office, but even

[1] Richard Assheton Cross, M.P. South West Lancashire; Home Secretary, 1874–80 and 1885–6; Secretary for India, 1886–92, created Viscount Cross, 1886. Cross, who had been educated at Rugby and Trinity College, Cambridge, was about one 'up' on Smith as a member of an established, wealthy, middle-class family; but, a little later on, he was lumped together with Smith as the subject of Lord Randolph Churchill's sarcasms on 'bourgeois placemen' and the pair were dubbed by that aristocratic sansculotte as 'Marshall and Snelgrove'.

6. The Hon. Robert Grimston.

7.   W. H. Smith, *circa* 1870.

went out of its way to defend him against false allegations and generally to boost his merits.

> . . . Mr. W. H. Smith, though certain to rise some day, if not now into the Cabinet, has one extremely strong impediment in his way. He is the greatest news-agent in the world, and the public have a notion that he is always, and therefore, sure of newspaper support. There never was a greater delusion. What he is sure of is unnecessary neglect, a dead silence about his merits as a Member, lest those who praise him should be suspected of wanting his goodwill. He will find this a real obstacle in his career, a great impediment to becoming known and the fact may as well be stated plainly and at once. The truth about him as a politician, however, is that he was made for the Ministry of Education in a Conservative Ministry: that he, and he only of the party, except poor Sir John Pakington,[1] possesses the needful knowledge, firmness and moderation.

But Disraeli had other ideas. Whilst he appointed Lord Sandon as Vice-President of the Council on Education, it was the very fact of Smith being the head—and to a certain extent the creator—of this great business enterprise which made him choose the latter for another, fundamentally even more responsible post—that of Financial Secretary to the Treasury. Consequently the following exchange of letters took place.

Confidential   2, Whitehall Gardens, Feby. 19. 1874
Dear Mr. Smith,
    It would give me great pleasure &, I believe satisfaction to the country, were you to permit me to appoint you Secretary to the Treasury.

Yours very faithfully,
B. Disraeli.

W. H. Smith Esq., M.P.

2, Hyde Park Street, Feb 19, 1874

Dear Mr. Disraeli,
    I am exceedingly obliged to you for the expression of your good opinion, and for the offer you have made, which I gladly accept.

Believe me,
Yours very faithfully,
William H. Smith.

The Right Hon. B. Disraeli M.P.

Nevertheless, despite the 'good press' which he enjoyed—especially from his political adversaries—and his pre-eminent fitness for the post, it was a measure of the innovation made by his appointment

---

[1] M.P. for Droitwich since 1837, he lost his seat in the 1874 election. Was First Lord of Admiralty, 1858–9 and 1866, Secretary of State for War, 1867–8, created Baron Hampton, 1874.

and the still lingering mistrust of Disraeli among his own side that there were mutterings from the aristocratic and squirearchical portion of it about such preferential treatment of 'the Bookstall Man'—another 'interloper', like the leader himself, albeit of a rather different kind. By and large, however, the appointment was well received—especially by the middle class, at whom of course, the astute Disraeli had deliberately aimed it. In fact there can be little doubt that Smith's inclusion in this and subsequent Conservative administrations was of positive influence in attaching this class to the party.

On receiving congratulations from his old schoolfellow and friend, Canon Ince of Christ Church, Smith wrote one of his characteristically endearing letters:

> I am myself surprised at my position when I compare it with the time to which you refer when we were both young together, and yet I can say most confidently that I never set to work aiming at personal advancement in the slightest degree. One circumstance has led to another, and I have gradually found myself of more account in men's eyes, simply from doing the work of the day as it presented itself to me.[1]

Fifteen years later, near the end of his career, he was still expressing the same modest wonderment at the inscrutable ways of providence and still disclaiming, almost guiltily, any calculated intention of achieving eminence in the State.

This first governmental appointment was indeed a position of great responsibility and importance. For the Financial Secretary to the Treasury receives the Estimates from the various government departments and in consultation with the heads of these departments has to hammer out the final form of the Estimates before their presentation to the House. Likewise he has to advise the Chancellor of the Exchequer over the framing of the Budget and in fact is generally most intimately concerned with the whole financial policy of the Government. All this inevitably brings him into close contact with all leading members of the Cabinet and Government and thereby places him in a position of great influence—or at any rate of potential influence, for the degree of influence obviously depends upon the qualities of the holder of the office. Inside the House itself he bears, in conjunction and consultation with the Leader of the House and the Chief Whip, the responsibility for the arrangement of the order of business. Even to a man of Smith's capability and experience the

[1] Quoted in Maxwell, I, 258.

sudden assumption of such a role was at first a strain. Thus he wrote to his sister Gussie from the Treasury (March 13th):

> . . . I am now regularly at work here and I find it somewhat hard. It will probably come easier as soon as I know more of the papers and the system, but it is never a bad thing to have plenty to do.
>
> Emily and I have had to go to a Court at Buckingham Palace today and I was presented again on taking office. You would have laughed to have seen me in white Kersemere breeches and white silk stockings—shoes and gold buckles. It was a perfect triumph of the Tailor's art. . . .

On this same day, as it so happened, Gladstone wrote one of his most portentous letters to his colleague Lord Granville, which, stripped of its verbiage, boiled down to an announcement of his intention to retire from the leadership of the Liberal Party. Indeed, so deeply chagrined had he been by the dismal end of his ministry, after its promising beginnings, and his own narrow escape from defeat in his own seat at Greenwich, that he had told the Queen on tendering his resignation that he intended to quit politics altogether. This decision was of course ultimately revoked, though he did, a year later, hand over the Liberal leadership to Lord Hartington in the Commons and to Lord Granville in the Lords.

Smith, meanwhile, soon settled happily into his office at the Treasury, for he was fortunate in having as his immediate chief, the Chancellor of the Exchequer, a man in many ways of his own type—quiet, serious, conscientious and religious. Though Sir Stafford Northcote's extreme amiability was in later and rougher times to be held against him by his own party, he was none the less an extremely able and intelligent man with a rare capacity for the mastery of financial affairs. The combination of these personal qualities and intellectual gifts attracted these two men to one another so that a firm friendship rapidly grew up between them which ended only with Northcote's death.

One humiliation Smith did, however, suffer—on one unfortunate and isolated occasion—in his first year of office. One night in May, having put in his usual stint at the Treasury in the morning and a few hours at the House in the latter half of the day and seeing affairs to be apparently proceeding smoothly he went home to dinner, counting on the customary forbearance of the Opposition at that hour. But a snap division was taken and the Government were defeated. Next morning he received the following reproof:

> 10, Downing Street, Whitehall
> May 2. 1874
>
> Mr. Disraeli presents his compliments to Mr. W. H. Smith, and much regrets to observe that he was absent on the division which took

place last evening at eight o'clk., on the motion of Mr. Synan; on which occasion Her Majesty's Government was, by reason of the absence of its members, placed in a minority; and he would beg leave to point out how difficult it must become to carry on a Government which cannot reckon on the attendance and support of its members.

Smith was penitent and mortified and he replied:

I have only two words to say with reference to your note of Saturday, and which I own was both just and necessary. I was excessively annoyed at my absence from the Division and I can fully enter into your feelings of vexation.

If I had supposed it possible that a division could be taken, I should have been in my place; but I shall take very good care to avoid the recurrence of such a mortification so long as I remain a member of the Government.

On the last day of this year 1874 Smith was summoned to Bournemouth, where Disraeli had gone to recoup his already fast failing health, to consult about the business of the approaching session. Thence he wrote to Emily:

> Bath Hotel, Bournemouth
> 31st Dec. 1874

Everything was very comfortably arranged for me. I have a good fire in my bedroom and a good sittingroom which I share with Mr. Corry.[1]

Mr. Disraeli came in to see me for a few minutes to tell me there was another King in Europe—a King of Spain.[2] He was very pleasant and cheerful. We are all to dine together tonight, Disraeli, the Lord Chancellor[3] and Northcote who was not yet come having missed his train poor fellow.

Tomorrow I dine with Lord Cairns at his house—and on Saturday I am to dine with—Mrs. Smith. These are my enjoyments for this week.

And next day, January 1st, 1875, he wrote:

We had a pleasant party at dinner. Lord Cairns, Northcote, Dizzy and Corry—and I think the purpose for which I was asked to come will be attained.

At 11 when we parted Disraeli said—'Well, we have been holding a Cabinet Council—and we must meet again tomorrow morning . . .'.

On his return to London he wrote (January 12th):

I travelled up very comfortably and Guards and Station masters were all very civil to Mr. Smith, who seems to be too well known . . . At

---

[1] Montague Lowry Corry, Disraeli's Private Secretary; created Baron Rowton, 1880.

[2] Alfonso XII was proclaimed King of Spain on December 30th, 1874, after years of civil war and a brief spell of republicanism.

[3] Earl Cairns.

Bristol I found Northcote in the train. He was very cheery. Today I
have seen Disraeli and Hunt.[1] D. looks well and happy . . . I am, I
think, better—less stiff. Work agrees with me.

So Smith plodded cheerfully on and when Northcote introduced
his Budget on April 15th he went out of his way to pay a high compliment to the Financial Secretary, alluding to the energy and capacity
for business he had shown in the examination of estimates submitted
to the Treasury and acknowledging the care and ability with which
he had discharged his duties.

It was a time of imaginative and audacious financial schemes, as
was fitting for an age of unprecedented national wealth and prosperity. First Sir Stafford Northcote's institution of a Sinking Fund
for the gradual liquidation of the National Debt and secondly
Disraeli's great plan for the purchase by Britain of the Khedive of
Egypt's shares in the Suez Canal.

On the latter Smith was asked to give his opinion—from the
Treasury point of view. This he did in a succinct and well-reasoned
minute. Whilst entirely agreeing on the 'great political importance
to this country' of the proposal, he thought that 'if it were possible
for England to purchase the Canal outright it would . . . be a safer
financial and political operation than that which is now suggested'
because 'we should not be committed to an indefinite expenditure at
the will of a practically irresponsible Commission'. But he admitted
that 'international jealousies would prevent anything of the sort and
it is useless to entertain the idea'.

His chief Northcote, the Chancellor, was also really opposed to
the purchase of the shares; but Disraeli was set upon it and clinched
the transaction while the going was good. A Bill then had to be
introduced to sanction the raising of the money required—four
million pounds—and Northcote was made responsible for seeing it
through—in the teeth of strenuous opposition from two ex-Chan-
cellors, Gladstone and Lowe. 'I am sitting at the table of the House
listening to Northcote defending the Suez Canal Bill, keeping my
ears open and yet trying at the same time to write to you', wrote
Smith to his wife (August 8th, 1876).

He seemed to be at the top of his form at this time for he wrote
again next day (August 9th): 'There are all sorts of rumours about
me—that I shall be President of the Board of Trade or Postmaster
General—but they are all false. Still, it is amusing and in some senses
not unpleasant to be talked about'. And again the following day
(August 10th): 'Everything went on well yesterday at the Whitebait

---

[1] George Ward Hunt, First Lord of the Admiralty, whom Smith was to
succeed in that office in 1877.

Dinner; both Disraeli and the Lord Chancellor appeared and spoke. The evening was most lovely, and the lights very pretty on the river; no doubt you are better off at Greenlands, but happily we can enjoy things as they pass.'

Whether Disraeli already had in mind that Smith should succeed Ward Hunt whose health was precarious, at the Admiralty, it is hard to say; nevertheless, for some reason he was chosen to accompany the First Lord on a tour of naval ships and dockyards. From the Admiralty yacht *Enchantress* he wrote to Emily (September 25th):

> We have seen the unfortunate 'Thunderer' and the boiler which burst killing and scalding so many poor people and all because one valve was not turned by the man whose duty it was to go round and turn them all.
> The poor fellows in these Ships have to work by candlelight always. No daylight can by any means penetrate and in order that the engines may be safe from shot they are well below the water-line.

Next day (September 26th):

> We went to the Torpedo Ship and a fish torpedo was discharged from the Ship and travelled under water for several hundred yards straight at the object to which she was intended to go . . . again to another Torpedo Ship and saw many submarine explosions of a terrible character. If ever they come to be used in actual war it is difficult to understand how any ship or any seaman will escape . . . the discoveries going on all round make me tremble as to the offensive and destructive qualities of man.

Easy acceptance of the deference shown to a minister of the Crown still came hardly to him. 'We are received everywhere with great respect and I have to keep a grave face—with some difficulty', he wrote to Emily (September 30th). And again (October 2nd): 'It is very interesting although somewhat fatiguing; but I never dreamed of being one of a party to be received with a salute of 19 guns, and to have to touch my hat to the Colors and the Guard.'

Back in London he was soon overwhelmed with the work of his department and when in November the children's nannie suddenly died, he was full of remorse at having to leave Emily alone to cope (November 24th):

> I hope you have passed without mischief through this trying day. I was very sorry to be obliged to run away from you: it seemed so unhusbandlike to allow you to be alone in a time of trial; but I think it was my duty to come here and the moment I arrived Northcote sent for me and kept me discussing business for an hour. The Cabinet then met . . . so that if I had not been here I should have been wanting in some parts of my work.

As the session of 1876 drew to a close the Government began to run into rough weather through the pressure and agitation worked up by their opponents over the so-called 'Bulgarian Atrocities'—the savage repression by the Turks of an insurrection among their Bulgarian subjects. Conservative policy having long favoured the strengthening of Turkey as a bulwark against the southward advance of Russia, the logic of politics required that Conservatives should be blamed for their protégé's misbehaviour. Gladstone himself re-emerged and dashed into the fray with an inflammatory article in the *Contemporary Review* advocating the expulsion of the 'unspeakable Turk, bag and baggage' from Europe. It so happened that Disraeli's reply to an attack from a lesser Liberal opponent happened to be his last speech in the House of Commons, for his rapidly failing health and strength had decided him to accept the Queen's offer of a peerage.

On this occasion Smith wrote to him (September 8th) a friendly letter in which he referred to the seriousness of the anti-Turkish—and anti-Conservative—agitation and the difficulty in which members and supporters of the Government were placed, who were unversed in the intricacies of foreign affairs and foreign policy.

Dear Lord Beaconsfield,

I cannot help saying I am very sorry to have to address you in this way, but yet I am satisfied the step you have taken was absolutely right and necessary, if we were to retain your guidance and direction, for I am sure you could not have borne the strain of another session in the House of Commons.

We shall, however, miss you very much, and the night will be dull and triste without you.

To say this, however, was not my intention in writing. I was asked today to go to a meeting at Slough to support Mr. Fremantle, but I thought it better not to go, as in the present critical condition of affairs I could hardly have avoided reference to the East, and I do not feel I have either the information or authority to speak.

In the present excited state of the public mind, one might easily say too little to satisfy one's friends at home, and too much for the difficult work in which the Foreign Office is engaged.

It is very possible I may be asked again, but I shall refrain unless I have a hint from you. If at any time you wish to see me, I can easily drive across the country on receiving a note or a telegram . . . [i.e. from Greenlands to Hughenden].

However, despite some considerable effect upon public opinion from Gladstone's invective and the loss of several Conservative seats at by-elections, a motion of want of confidence in the Government tabled by Gladstone was rejected by a majority of 131 votes.

With the coming of the new year, 1877, Smith was taken up with the preparation, in conjunction with his friend the Chancellor,

Northcote, of the Budget. On April 5th he wrote to the Prime Minister:

> Dear Lord Beaconsfield,
> I hope you will be satisfied with our financial work.
> The Chancellor of the Exchequer will have a surplus of £440,000 on the past year, and a safe estimate of the revenue for the coming year will give a small surplus over the expenditure without any increase of taxation. As this result is not expected out of doors, it will, I think, be the more satisfying to our friends and to the country.

The Prime Minister's reply contained such unqualified praise and congratulations as must have warmed and encouraged Smith for many a day:

> Hughenden Manor, April 7, 77.
> My dear Mr. Smith,
> I thank you for your Budget Report, & heartily congratulate you & the country on the result. After forty years' experience of parliamentary life, I can sincerely say that I never knew the affairs of the Treasury conducted with more thorough sense & efficiency than while they have been under your management & control.

Meanwhile, this summer of 1877 saw the beginning and development of a new feature in the ceaseless war of Parliamentary parties which was to dominate British political life throughout the remainder of Smith's career—and even beyond—and which was to affect him personally to an almost incalculable extent. For some Irish Nationalist Members, in an effort to force attention to their demands, began a systematic campaign to disrupt the business and procedure of the House at every opportunity by the use of filibustering and other obstructive techniques. The man primarily responsible was Charles Stewart Parnell, who was soon after to become the leader of the Irish Party—though the nominal leader was still Isaac Butt, who disapproved of these methods. Butt, however, was overridden and in July 1877 there was a foretaste of things to come when the House met on Tuesday, July 31st at 4.0 p.m. and sat continuously till past 6.0 on the Wednesday evening—more than 26 hours.

V

THE ADMIRALTY

$\longrightarrow$ ✦✦✦ $\longleftarrow$

A NYONE who was anyone in those days went to Bad Homburg—
or Baden-Baden or Karlsbad or Aix or Vichy—for their health.
Most of a fashionable doctor's business consisted in deciding for his
rich patients whether their particular ailments would be cured or
alleviated by the waters of one or other of the great continental spas.

Emily Smith and her daughter Mary Auber had just arrived there
in the summer of 1877 when there arrived there also the gigantic
person of the First Lord of the Admiralty, George Ward Hunt.[1] A
very sick man, he had just managed to present his Naval Estimates to
Parliament, which had probably imposed upon him an exceptional
strain owing to the military preparations which the Cabinet felt
obliged to accelerate in case it were necessary for England to intervene in the war which had just broken out between Russia and
Turkey. But he had scarcely been at Homburg a month when he died
on July 29th.

A few days later Smith received the following letter from the
Prime Minister:

Confidential   2, Whitehall Gardens,
                                                                    S.W.
                                                          Aug. 3: 77
Dear Mr. Smith,
    If agreeable to yourself, it is my intention to submit your name to
the Queen, to fill the vacant office of First Ld. of ye Admiralty.
    If you accept the post, I doubt not you will fulfil its duties with the
same devotion and ability, which have distinguished your transaction

---

[1] Ward Hunt, on his earlier appointment as Chancellor of the Exchequer, had
been the subject of one of Disraeli's most audacious comments to the Queen in
which he had warned her of Hunt's huge physical dimensions, adding that 'he has
the sagacity of the elephant as well as its form'. See *Queen Victoria's Letters*,
Second Series, Vol. I, p. 507.

of affairs in the all-important Department to which you are now attached.

Believe me,

faithfully yours,

Beaconsfield

This letter Smith sent on to his wife at Homburg, telling her to keep it secret until he telegraphed further and adding, 'Lord Beaconsfield was extremely kind when I saw him this morning and said frankly that he thought me the most fit for the post. It had not been offered to anyone else'. Though Beaconsfield's motives in saying this were understandable it was by no means the truth. For he had in fact already offered the post to Lord Sandon, who had refused it. He thereupon recommended Smith to the Queen in the following terms (August 3rd): 'He has obtained a high character as a first rate man of business distinguished as much for his judgment as his capacity for labor. . . . He is purely a man of the middle class and the appointment wd. no doubt be popular.'[1] The Queen replied (August 4th) that she was prepared to agree if necessary but that she *'fears* it may *not please* the Navy in which Service so many of the *highest rank* serve, & who claim to be equal to the Army—if a man of the Middle Class is placed above them in that very high Post. . . .'[2] She suggested Lord John Manners[3] or Sir Michael Hicks Beach[4] instead.

Replying that he 'has given the gravest and deepest consideration to the matter', Beaconsfield pointed out that in the previous government neither Childers nor Goschen were socially superior to Smith—and they were nothing like as rich. Knowing that the Queen approved of Assheton Cross, the Home Secretary, he described Smith as being, 'of a character similar to Mr. Cross—in mind, manner, energy, but more weighty & with much repose' and that 'he has entirely gained the confidence of the House as Mr. Cross has'. At the same time he produced reasons against the appointment of the Queen's candidates. He also strongly emphasized the importance attached to having a 'City or Borough member in the Cabinet'. Finally, he declared that 'the condition of the Admiralty is not satisfactory. . . .

[1] Royal Archives, Windsor: E.53/37.

[2] Ibid., E.53/38.

[3] M.P. co. Leicester (Melton Div.); Postmaster General, 1874–80 and 1885–6; Chancellor of Duchy of Lancaster, 1886–92; succeeded brother as 7th Duke of Rutland, 1888.

[4] 9th Bart., M.P. East Gloucestershire; Chief Secretary for Ireland, 1874–8; Secretary for Colonies, 1878–80; Chancellor of Exchequer and Leader of House of Commons, 1885–6; Chief Secretary for Ireland, 1886–7; President of Board of Trade, 1888–92; Chancellor of Exchequer, 1895–1902; created Viscount (1906) and Earl (1915) St. Aldwyn.

The Admiralty requires a strong man & Mr. Smith is such; combinging vigilance & vigour with a perfect temper & conciliatory manners. . . .'[1]

Thereupon the Queen gave in to her Prime Minister's 'unanswerable' arguments; but she added an admonition that Smith must not 'lord it over the Navy (which almost every First Lord does) & be a little modest & not *act* the Lord High Admiral which is offensive to the Service. . . .'[2] Meanwhile, the subject of these anxious discussions was writing to his wife with characteristic humility (August 5th): 'Until now in graver matters I only advised. Now I must act on my own judgment and the sphere of that action concerns the Country's honour and its strength. I shall want all your strength, my darling, such help as you have ever given me since we were happily made one. . . . There is a heavy drawback to this new duty, Beach tells me the Cabinet have been warned that none of them must go out of reach of a sudden summons to a meeting . . . while Foreign affairs are in their present critical state.'

To his favourite sister, Augusta, he wrote the same day: 'I wish my Father had been alive. He certainly did not expect that at 52 I should be a Cabinet Minister and now I almost wish I had never entered public life for it seems impossible to stop or to refuse work accompanied with the intimation from one's associates in Government that it is one's *duty* to undertake it.' 'It is very sweet', she answered simply, 'to think how highly you are thought of.' But he remained oppressed. 'Don't you understand', he wrote vehemently to his old friend Miss Giberne, 'it is not matter for rejoicing with me, except it might be with a soldier charged with a great work. He may fail or he may fall, but his Country's welfare depends in a measure on his performance of duty.'

But even if Smith could not bring himself to rejoice, his friends and colleagues—and even his political opponents—must have alleviated his gloom by their genuine and spontaneous congratulations. Sir William Hart Dyke, Conservative Chief Whip and Joint Secretary of the Treasury, wrote:

I must write and tell you how unanimously your appointment has been received on both sides of the House—Harcourt,[3] Lawson,[4] Forster and everybody came and congratulated me on your success and old Seely[5] wished me most particularly to mention his name to

[1] Royal Archives: E.53/41.

[2] Ibid., E.53/43.

[3] Sir William Harcourt, Q.C.; M.P. (Lib.), Oxford; Solicitor-General, 1873–4; Home Secretary 1880–5; Chancellor of Exchequer, 1886 and 1892–5.

[4] Sir Wilfred Lawson, Bart.; M.P. (Lib.), Carlisle.

[5] Charles Seely; M.P. (Lib.), City of Lincoln.

you. Although I shall miss you terribly at the Treasury this has been a very pleasant day for me, and whatever the result may be, there is no one more deeply anxious for the success which I believe awaits you than—

Your old mate,
Billy Dyke

Harcourt himself, a thoroughly good-natured man underneath his arrogant exterior, wrote (August 8th):

I heard your writ moved today with great satisfaction and greeted it with an approving cheer. No one has better earned and deserved the great post which you have reached in a comparatively short Parliamentary career.

Your opponents no less than your friends sympathise in your well merited success—and none more amongst them than

Yours sincerely,
W. V. Harcourt

Even more significant were the words of William Cowen, the Radical M.P. for Newcastle, coal-owner, manufacturer and newspaper proprietor, who wrote (August 9th):

Will you allow a political opponent to congratulate you. You carry with you to your new office the good wishes and sympathy of the entire House of Commons . . . The large mercantile and trading classes will regard your appointment with especial satisfaction.

I never voted for a Conservative in my life. But if there should be a contest in Westminster (where I am an elector) you can calculate on at least one Radical recording his vote for you.

Soon after his appointment Smith had to make the pilgrimage to the Queen at Osborne to be sworn in as a Privy Councillor. To his wife at Homburg he described (August 13th) the journey by special train to Portsmouth 'with ceremony and honor' and how the very mixed party of about-to-be-honoured ones was divided up between two saloon cars. 'It was necessary to draw the line somewhere,' he wrote ironically, 'Bishops and P.C.s in esse or in posse could not travel with Admirals who were merely going to be Knights.'

We had to wait some time at the house [Osborne]. . . . At last Lord Hertford[1] called in Lord Coventry[2] and myself. The Queen was standing before a table. We knelt down rather by her side. The oath of allegiance was read over to us. We kissed the book on our knees and then kissed her hand and rose up. Then, standing, the Privy Councillor's Oath which is a very long one was read and we again kissed the book, and then I shook hands with all the Privy Councillors

[1] Francis, 5th Marquess. Lord Chamberlain, 1874–9.
[2] George, 9th Earl. Captain of Hon. Corps of Gentlemen-at-Arms, 1877–80.

present. . . . We then withdrew bowing as we withdrew with our faces to her, the Queen standing, but not saying a word.

But, in all these ceremonies and honours he badly missed the presence of his wife, to whom he wrote (August 16th):

> It is hard to have to go through all this without your comfort, for I really have wanted so much to lay my head on your shoulder and be petted just a little. So much kindness brings a sense of sadness with it—of weight and of fear lest failure should follow.
>
> My Patent has come today and I have taken my seat at the Board who address me as 'Sir' in every sentence. It is strange and makes me shy at first; and I have to do what I hardly like—to send for them—not to go to them, but I am told they expect me as their Chief to require respect and they would be disgusted if I did not.

At first Smith was strongly averse to the idea of actual residence at the Admiralty. Montague Corry, the Prime Minister's Private Secretary, whose father had been First Lord ten years before, warned him of its being unhygienic and Smith wrote to his wife (August 5th) that they would 'only use it for the official entertainments which *you* and I will have to give there'. His young daughter, Beatrice,[1] confirmed this view writing to her mother (September 20th): '. . . I don't think it would do for us for there are no bathrooms.' But later Smith told his wife (October 8th): 'Lady Lopes[2] says all other First Lords have gone into it and she should think we ought to do so'—as indeed they eventually appear to have done, at least for part of the time.

Within a few weeks the new First Lord was setting out upon his first tour of the naval stations and dockyards—perceptibly proud of his great office and zealous to see, to learn and to succeed, but always modest to the point of diffidence. From Portsmouth—he wrote to Emily (September 15th):

> The First Lord, although only making a private visit was received by the three admirals on the Station and men and boats waited upon him. It was rough and the wind very high. We had to jump from the boat on to the ladder of the Temeraire with the aid of ropes. It was perfectly safe but I was glad the boy [his son] was not with me. I had to fill my ears with cotton wool to prevent the firing from deafening me. The guns were of great size and the charge was 85 lb. of powder with a shot of 5 cwt. It was a great roar and vibration.

But a little later Freddie Smith was allowed to accompany his father on an *official* visit. The latter wrote to Emily (October 1st): '. . . As I stepped on board *Enchantress* the flag was hoisted and the

[1] Married 1885 Col. Alfred Dyke Acland.
[2] Wife of Sir Massey Lopes, Bart., M.P., a Lord Commissioner of the Admiralty.

same moment the "Duke of Wellington" saluted. I called to the boy to watch the flash of the guns.' Then again on October 4th:

> We have had another very busy day . . . going from ship to ship and from guns to torpedoes with firing at one time from heavy and at another from light guns, men shouting the word of command, the Captains raising their voices to explain what was going on and what they wished changed—and so on until one became weary and tired. I have smashed in my hat once or twice by crawling about engine rooms and I have descended right into the holds of ships to see what was to be seen where daylight never penetrates. It is curious work and leaves a somewhat confused medley in one's mind which requires sorting and sifting. . . .

It may be noted that the torpedo, though it had been used in certain crude forms in the American Civil War of the previous decade, was still in a rather embryonic stage. The type which was beginning to be adopted by the Royal Navy at this time was the Brennan torpedo, which was controlled by wires from the shore, which either conveyed electric power to an engine in the torpedo or operated the propellers by unwinding the wire off drums. But this was shortly to be superseded by the Whitehead automobile torpedo, which operated independently under its own power. Meanwhile the French had already conceived the idea of building small fast vessels to attack with torpedoes as a form of harbour defence and, within only a fortnight of Smith's appointment to the Admiralty, Sir Stafford Northcote, the Chancellor of the Exchequer, was writing to him (August 17th): '. . . I am glad you are looking into the question of Torpedo-boats. They may save us from a very formidable expenditure on harbour defences.' Indeed, later in this same year, 1877, Messrs. Thornycroft built the first torpedo-boat for the Royal Navy.

As regards the ships of the Navy at this time, though the fleets used in the Crimean War only twenty years earlier had differed little in appearance from those that fought at the Nile and Trafalgar, the coming of explosive projectiles had caused a revolution shortly afterwards and brought into existence the 'Ironclad' warship. The French *La Gloire* of 1859 was the prototype—a wooden ship protected above the water-line with a corselet of iron—but this was quickly eclipsed in the following year by the British *Warrior*—the first all-metal battleship, with an iron hull and a belt of iron armour thick enough to withstand contemporary shells.

But even the *Warrior*, though propelled by steam engines and screws, still carried masts and sails, and navy men still regarded the latter as the main equipment and the former as merely a useful adjunct. As regards armaments, muzzle-loading guns were still the order of the day in the Royal Navy, though France and other maritime powers had already adopted rifled breech-loading guns. However, under Smith's direction of the Navy the decision to remedy this omission was taken (1879), though it was not until after his term that the manufacture and installation of the new weapon fairly commenced.

The state of the Navy was of more than usual moment when Smith took over the Admiralty on account of the alarming developments of the Russo-Turkish War, in which England seemed likely to become involved if a serious threat to Constantinople developed. The Czar had declared war on the Sultan in April 1877 and during the first few months of the conflict his troops carried all before them, until they were checked by the great Turkish victories and successes at Batum, Sukhum Kalé, Kars, Plevna and the Shipka Pass.

'Public affairs give us all much anxiety,' wrote Smith to his sister (September 15th). 'The war is a most dreadful one. Nothing that has gone before has been so murderous and I fear from the weapons now in use all wars to come will be as dreadful in their effects.' And to his wife (September 16th): 'There is dreadful slaughter going on in Turkey and without much advantage to either side.' But soon after this the tide turned once more against the Turks with the fall of Kars, Erzerum and Plevna and the occupation of the Shipka Pass by the Russians. 'The Cabinet have decided to sit every day for the present,' wrote Smith to Emily (November 5th), '. . . My friends are all very cordial here and we have met as if it was a most delightful change and we were all weary of our wives and families and of the country— but it is not quite so really. . . .'

On December 1st Smith was entertained at a banquet in St. James's Hall given by the Westminster Conservative Association to celebrate his appointment as First Lord of the Admiralty. After a suitable eulogy from Sir Stafford Northcote, Smith addressed the five hundred constituents assembled in that direct and disarming manner, which, all artless as it was, in an age tending to pomposity and smugness never failed to touch the hearts of his hearers,

. . . When I reflect that it is only twelve years since I was invited to offer myself for the representation of the City of Westminster, and that I then failed, although not disastrously, and when I remember that in 1868 you were kind enough to entertain the proposal that I should be your member, I say it appears like a dream to me that I should occupy my present position, and I can hardly understand how it is that I am here today, not only wearing the blue riband of the representatives of the City of Westminster, but also standing as the Servant of the Crown and people. Frankly, I cannot tell you how it has come to pass, unless the sympathy and kindness of my friends have pushed me into a position which I should never have dared to seek for myself. . . .

The significance of the author of these words as a national and party figure was shrewdly assessed by a newspaper correspondent next day:

> . . . One of the chief reasons of the popularity the Ministry still enjoys, and of the confidence it still commands, is that it numbers so many men of the Liberal type, and of the special type to which Mr. Smith belongs. Sir Stafford Northcote, Mr. Cross and Mr. Smith are all men, who, without conspicuous oratorical power, or any claim to originality, have raised themselves to the front rank by moderation, honesty, skill in business, conciliatory manners and a broad and genial Liberalism. To Lord Beaconsfield much credit is due for having recognized the merits of men so totally unlike himself. . . . They import prudence and good sense into every Conservative gathering. They are always, as it were, brightening up the boots of the party and making it look tidy and respectable when it appears before the public.

Beaconsfield himself, too, was kind and considerate towards the man who helped so much to give his Ministry this 'new look'. When the Queen invited Smith to Windsor for the first time to dine and sleep, Beaconsfield wrote to him (December 16th): '. . . I am going there myself, and you can, if you like, accompany me; as it is sometimes awkward to be alone on the first occasion. With regard to costume: the usual evening dress, except you must wear breeches.' Arrived there, Smith wrote to Emily (December 18th):

> . . . I came down in the same carriage with Lord Beaconsfield who was very chatty. One of the Queen's carriages awaited us and he and I drove off, our Servants with luggage in another. I am seated in a nice old-fashioned sitting-room in the Lancaster Tower, the furniture at least fifty years old—but very comfortable. . . . My bedroom opens out of the sitting-room and there is a good fire in both. It is now just 6 and the Servant who speaks English with the Royal Accent is going to bring me a cup of tea and to come for this letter at ½ past 8 when I am to be summoned to dinner. . . .

And next day (December 19th):

> The Queen was very gracious to me yesterday and I am not disappointed at all. We did not dine until past 9. The dinner itself lasted about an hour and after one glass of wine at dessert the Queen rose and we all left the table standing round the room. H. M. approached Lord Hawarden[1] first and talked and laughed with him. Then she crossed the room and came straight to me, asked if we were in the Admiralty and after Mrs. Hunt,[2] talked about the Fleet, the 'Sultan' of which the Duke of Edinburgh is Captain, the House of Commons and one or two other things, chatting with the freedom of an ordinary

[1] Cornwallis, 4th Viscount. Lord in Waiting to Queen Victoria.
[2] Widow of Ward Hunt, Smith's predecessor at the Admiralty.

8   H.M.S. *Alexandra*, Flagship of Admiral Hornby (from *Illustrated London News*, 1878).

THE GODS COLLEGE. THE MAIN BUILDING.

lady, and then she passed on to Lady Biddulph[1] and presently bowed
and left the room. . . .

Emily Smith, with her retiring and rather nervous disposition, was
apt to feel a little frightened by the invitations from the highest in the
land which now began to reach them in ever-increasing number.
When Lady Salisbury invited them for a week-end at Hatfield, Smith
wrote to his wife (January 2nd, 1878): '. . . I think you should accept
as it it a cordial one and will put you on good terms with her.' After
further hesitation on her part he wrote again next day: '. . . I can
quite enter into your feelings about Hatfield but my own conviction
is that it will pass off well and that you will very fairly enjoy yourself
there.'

During the last days of December 1877 the Sultan of Turkey's
now desperate situation caused him to send a Circular Note to the
Powers appealing for their collective mediation with the Russians.
When this failed he made a special appeal to the Queen and her
Government begging for their good offices. The Sultan's desire for
an armistice was duly conveyed by Her Majesty's Government to the
Czar, who replied, confirming his desire to end the war and his readi-
ness to open negotiations. Nevertheless, the Russian armies continued
their advance for several weeks and not till they had captured
Adrianople did they consent to sign an armistice with the Turks
(January 31st, 1878).

Although a promise had earlier been obtained from the Czar not
to occupy Constantinople or the Dardanelles, the delay in the
armistice and the rapid Russian gains made in the interval violently
aroused again the fears and warlike reactions of the majority of the
people and Government of England, headed by the Queen herself,
who bombarded her Premier with demands for immediate war. But
there was not complete unanimity in Beaconsfield's Cabinet, Lord
Derby,[2] the Foreign Secretary, and Lord Carnarvon,[3] the Colonial
Secretary, being strongly opposed to intervention under all but the
most stringent circumstances. Derby's vacillations during this critical
period—he twice resigned and returned to office—not only maddened
the Queen but placed his colleagues in considerable embarrassment,
especially Smith, who was the Minister responsible for organizing
any demonstration of force which might be decided upon.

Derby was inclined to split hairs as to the permissible extent of
Russian encroachments and British counter-moves, but Smith's

---

[1] Wife of Col. Sir Thomas Biddulph, Privy Purse.
[2] Edward, 15th Earl, Foreign Secretary, 1866–8 and 1874–8; Colonial
Secretary, 1882–5.
[3] Henry Molyneux, 4th Earl. Colonial Secretary, 1867–8 and 1874–8; Lord
Lieutenant of Ireland, 1885–6.

views of the matter were firm, practical and clear-cut, as may be seen from the following letter from him to Northcote (January 12th):

> I wish you would see Lord Derby. I quite understood yesterday that he agreed to the occupation of Gallipoli in the sense you suggested, and although I have satisfied myself that the Fleet can anchor there without serious risk, it would be a more sensible operation to take possession of the lines.[1]
>
> You will remember, however, that the most formidable forts are at the entrance to the Black Sea, above Constantinople. If a foreign Power holds the City it holds also the key of the Black Sea.
>
> If we cannot come to an agreement on our policy on Monday in certain events, it is a question whether it would not be more patriotic to break up and resign now. It will not do to be fighting in the House with the Opposition, and in the Cabinet with each other.

But, unlike the Queen, Smith did not want to ignore or dispense with Derby, as witness this further note to Northcote on 15th: 'I hope the telegram will not be sent tonight if Lord Derby objects to it. The delay of a few hours is important, but the loss of Lord Derby would be a greater evil.'

Parliament had been specially summoned for January 17th and the Queen's Speech hinted at the possibility of the necessity for intervention and for a special vote of credit for an expedition. Indeed, on receipt of the news of the fall of Adrianople, on January 23rd, the Cabinet actually decided to send the Fleet to the Dardanelles. Whereupon Lord Carnarvon resigned office and Lord Derby was only persuaded to reconsider a similar decision by the receipt of a—in fact misleading—version of the Russian terms for the armistice, which induced Lord Beaconsfield to tell Smith to rescind the orders to the Fleet, at that moment on the point of entering the Dardanelles.

Nevertheless, a few days later, on January 28th, the Cabinet made plain the firmness of its intentions by giving notice in the House of Commons that a vote of credit for £6 million was to be moved for immediately. This did not of course pass unchallenged by the Opposition, and W. E. Forster moved a vote of censure on the Government. Smith contributed a spirited defence of the Government's proposal, ending with the time-honoured arguments—which in this case, as in most, proved to be entirely well-founded: 'We believe that the making of such preparations as we may deem to be necessary will be a security against war.'

The terms of the armistice entitled the Russians to advance their headquarters to within a few miles of Constantinople—though this was probably imperfectly understood at the time in England. At any

[1] Defensive lines of earthworks, made by British and French engineers during the Crimean War, at the narrow waist-line of the Gallipoli peninsula.

rate, when they actually proceeded to do this, tension mounted again in the country and Derby even withdrew his objection to the passage of the British Fleet through the Dardanelles. It reached breaking-point, however, on February 7th, when a telegram from the Ambassador in Constantinople alleged that the Russians had already occupied the city.

The effect upon Parliament and the country was electric. Forster withdrew his amendment to the motion for the Vote of Credit, which was carried next day (February 8th) by 295 votes to 96. Then the telegram turned out to be untrue—Layard, the Ambassador, having been deceived by the presence of a number of Russian officers and men on leave in the streets of Stamboul. But the Queen was nevertheless 'sure they were there or nearly so' and wrote no less than three violent letters on this day (February 7th) about Russia's 'monstrous treachery' and urging her Prime Minister to take 'strong measures' and even threatening 'to throw everything up and lay down the thorny crown'.[1]

But Beaconsfield himself needed no spur to action; the only brake upon him was the need for preserving the cohesion of his cabinet and for pursuing a consistent policy. 'It is not . . . Lord Derby, or even Lord Carnarvon,' as he told the Queen (February 10th), 'that has mainly brought about the present, no doubt lamentable state of affairs: it is the necessary consequence of a policy of neutrality.'[2] The Queen wrote back the same day, pointing out with considerable truth, that 'a policy of neutrality is fatal. . . . It has not kept the Russians in check, and yet we have offended and thwarted them, while we have estranged the Turks with whom we could have done anything, and have lost all power over them.'[3]

However, the Queen's arguments and exhortations, coupled with the now thoroughly aroused temper of the nation, probably considerably strengthened the Premier's hand when bringing his Cabinet up to the fence on February 8th; for on that day they agreed, without dissent, to the ordering of part of the British Fleet to the Dardanelles. To Smith fell the duty of placating his tormented Sovereign with the welcome details of the plan of action (February 8th): 'Orders have been sent to Admiral Hornby to proceed with Alexandra, Temeraire, Swiftsure and Achilles, Ironclads, and Ruby and Salamis, Wooden Ships, to Constantinople to protect life and property of British subjects.' This was the cloak for the real object which was of course to deter the Russians by a show of force from taking Constantinople.

[1] G. E. Buckle: *Life of Disraeli*, VI, 245.
[2] Ibid.
[3] Op. cit. 247.

The dramatic story of the next few months is vividly conveyed in the cables and letters, passing daily and even hourly between Smith, as First Lord, and Admiral Geoffrey Phipps Hornby, the Commander of the Mediterranean Squadron which had been despatched to the scene of trouble.[1] Smith was a most considerate and punctilious chief and made a practice of establishing good and confidential relations with his commanders, explaining as far as circumstances allowed the broad lines of Government policy and the reasons behind the orders he gave.

The first of these communications, sent by the First Lord to the Admiral, not only gives a very fair idea of Smith's clear style and pleasant touch, but also, in view of Hornby's subsequent complaints, demonstrates how unjustified these were.

Admiralty,
Whitehall.
February 9th, 1878

My dear Admiral,
Events have marched very quickly during the past fortnight and if we only hear in a day or two that you are safely anchored at Constantinople we shall begin to breathe a little more freely. It is only within the last 24 hours that we have become acquainted with the conditions of the Armistice [of Adrianople]—very possibly we do not know them all yet; but it appears clear that a large portion of the European side of the Sea of Marmora and the shore of the Aegean Sea from Makri to [?] in the Gulf of Xeros[2] are to remain in the hands of Russia. As the lines defending Constantinople were to be abandoned by the Turkish forces, it is clear that all possibility of defence has been taken away and the Government felt it necessary therefore to provide some security for the safety of British subjects and British property which might be seriously imperilled by a sudden panic or commotion.

It was under these circumstances that the decision was taken to send you up with a portion of the Fleet leaving the rest available for any other duty which may be required of it.

We are of course somewhat anxious about the security and safety of the Channel [Dardanelles] but Russia appears studiously to have avoided the appearance of controlling that by keeping clear of Bulair and Gallipoli and we have no wish by any other action of ours to imply more distrust than can be helped.

Our attitude as between Turkey and Russia is still one of complete neutrality and we are on friendly terms with both. While therefore keeping a very vigilant lookout at everything which could possibly be dangerous we are anxious to avoid any cause of offence to either side.

---

[1] Copies of both sides of this correspondence were happily preserved by Smith and are now among the Hambleden Papers. Oddly, however, some of the items quoted by Sir Herbert Maxwell in his 'Life' do not appear to be among the papers today. On the other hand, the majority of those quoted in the present work do not appear in Maxwell's book.

[2] Now usually written 'Saros'.

Very probably there will now be a lull and we shall await the terms of peace between Turkey and Russia and the labours of the Congress,[1] but I cannot help feeling that the situation is very grave and one which requires good judgment and good faith all round if Europe is to keep as I hope out of war. . . .

Public feeling here is running very high. . . .

You will have heard that we obtained our Vote of Credit last night in the Commons by a very large majority which was due very much to the strong expression of feeling out of doors.

I hope to hear that you have authority to proceed and are on your way to the Straits.

Yours sincerely,
W. H. Smith

But prior permission to pass the Straits had not been obtained from the Porte—and here the first snag arose. The Ambassador was instructed to obtain permission, but met with no response, the Sultan presumably being more frightened of provoking the Russians than of obstructing his would-be protectors. For Admiral Hornby telegraphed (February 10th): 'Governor of Dardanelles has not received instructions for ships to pass and protests against their doing so. Have anchored off entrance. . . . Am I to proceed by night with ships named or to force passage by day with whole squadron?'

Orders were evidently sent to force the passage by day, for Smith wrote Beaconsfield (February 14th) that 'the six armoured ships passed through yesterday at 3.0 p.m. into the Sea of Marmora, the Turkish authorities protesting but not resisting. . . .' But the situation which confronted the British Squadron after penetrating the Straits was alarming and difficult. Hornby telegraphed that the Russians were in force with an estimated 50,000 men near Bulair, just above the narrow waist-line at the Northern end of the Gallipoli peninsula, where the Turks held defensive lines of earthworks, and he added that they 'are believed to have a feasible plan to cross the Gulf of Xeros and land in the rear of Bulair lines, while they attack in front'.

The Admiral followed up his cable by a letter full of practical suggestions, some of which give a startling, but amusing insight into the condition of the Turkish body politic.

Private   H. M. S. Alexandra
                                                    Sea of Marmora.
Dear Mr. Smith,   February 14/78.
The news which I telegraphed to you today on Captain Fife's[2] authority of the concentration of Russian troops so near Bulair may

---

[1] The idea of submitting the final settlement after the war to a European Congress had been accepted by all the Powers, including Russia.

[2] British Naval Attaché at Constantinople.

have surprised you. I have no reason to doubt the accuracy of the report. . . .

If true it would appear that the Gallipoli peninsula, that is the Dardanelles, is almost as much at the disposal of Russia as Constantinople. If we are to take any steps to save it those I suggested for the co-operation of our ships is the very best we should adopt; and so far as offending Russian susceptibilities they have no right to object as much to our putting ships in the Gulf of Xeros, as I propose, as to keeping them at Gallipoli, but ships can afford more aid to the defence of the lines from the Gulf than from the Straits. It will always be a matter of regret to me that we did not occupy the lines last July. Now our chance of saving them, according to Captain Fife's idea, is small. He thinks we have two chances of seeing them given up to the Russians without struggle—1st By the possible treachery of the Sultan's ministers, who may order them to be surrendered as they did the lines of Buyub Tehrekmadjre—2nd thro' their being bought by the Russians from Suleiman Pasha who commands at Bulair.

His [Capt. Fife's] remedy is to buy Suleiman ourselves and his troops. The first by pay and promise of pension, the latter by taking them into our service. Provide with English officers and I have no doubt we should have 14,000 excellent troops much cheaper than by any other means. I do not offer any opinion as to buying the General because I don't know him. But I think it is a pity the power to do such a thing is not in the hands of someone on the spot—say the Ambassador, or Sir Coll. Dickson.[1] It might save us from a great disaster—which may occur while instructions are sought from home even by telegraph. It is a startling thing to think that the day after tomorrow the Russians may march through the Gallipoli lines!

. . . I have not heard what your project is. . . . But I do see that while we are at the East end [of Sea of Marmora] and Gallipoli not secured we run the risk of check which would be very discreditable to us. In fact I look on that peninsula and the Dardanelles as the key to the Naval position. If we hold those we can command the Turkish Fleet. If we lose it the Fleet would be of no use—and we should go as far west as Salonica to find a base, and that a less influential one for any military operations.

Yours very truly,
G. Phipps Hornby

On February 15th Smith sent the orders which Hornby was expecting:

All ships but one are to go from Besika Bay to Gulf of Xeros with orders to watch Russian troops and if they observe preparations for embarkation with a view to landing on the peninsula of Gallipoli, they are to warn Russian Commander they have orders to prevent such landing, and they are to oppose it by force if persevered in. . . .

[1] General Sir Collingwood Dickson, K.C.B., Inspector-General of Artillery, 1870-5. Military adviser to Turkish Government and military attaché to British Embassy at Constantinople.

and on the same day he received this cable from Rear-Admiral Commerell, Hornby's second-in-command:

I visited Gallipoli lines today with permission of Suleiman Pasha. Was not favourably impressed with state of defences. Advanced post of Russians at Kadikoi in sight of Bulair, from which place I am of opinion that determined attack in force would carry Turkish position. Am informed privately that large quantity of munitions are being collected at Kadikoi.

Commenting upon his orders in a cable to Smith of February 17th, Hornby reiterated his conviction that the Gallipoli peninsula was strategically vital, but declared that his squadron was not strong enough to defend it without active Turkish support and the latter being unlikely with the treacherous Suleiman Pasha in command, he again urged 'a speedy understanding with the Turkish Government'. Indeed, the continual necessity for bolstering the Turks, financially even more than militarily, is revealed by the following telegram of February 19th from the British Ambassador, Layard, to the Foreign Secretary, Derby (a copy of which was passed to Smith). It was in answer to Derby's inquiry as to the possibility of buying units of the Turkish Fleet.

... Porte has given instructions to Musurus Pasha to sell frigate to Her Majesty's Government on the terms mentioned by you. But the [Turkish] Prime Minister earnestly begs Her Majesty's Government to take measures to prevent money being stopped in England, and to have it remitted here at once as there is the most urgent need of it. Treasury is perfectly empty and a vast number of fugitives to feed besides the normal requirements.

Next day (February 20th) Beaconsfield was asking from the departments concerned: 'How many Turkish ships in course of building here have we bought, what are the prices, and when will they be ready to commission? I want to shew what we have been doing with our six million since we got it. . . .' The answers from the Admiralty and the Treasury, of which Smith kept copies, showed a total of £1,163,000—including two partially built corvettes at £240,000 and £126,000 respectively and a completed frigate at £443,000. Meanwhile, Beaconsfield had already told the Queen (February 16th) that 'the Cabinet discussed the Sultan's offer . . . and empowered Your Majesty's Ambassador to purchase, if possible, the chief ships of the Turkish fleet, promising their best offices to prevent the Russians entering Constantinople, and offering hospitality, if necessary, in Your Majesty's Fleet, to the Sultan'.[1]

[1] Buckle VI, 248.

But news now arrived which threatened to stultify these hopes and projects, for Hornby cabled (February 20th):

> Ambassador has informed me that the Russians have demanded peremptorily Turkish Fleet and to enter Constantinople with 30,000 men. Do my orders still hold not to interfere?. . . .

and again later the same day:

> . . . Russians reported to be advancing to M. San Stephano, thus turning will get in rear of the last line of defence Moukhtar Pasha was preparing for Constantinople. The city and Bosphorus will be at their mercy.

Next day (February 21st) he was a little more reassuring:

> Rear-Admiral Commerell reports good progress in strengthening Bulair lines, but the assistance of ships to cover flanks is indispensable. If he might co-operate he thinks Russia would not pass. This squadron might assist materially in preventing Russians entering Constantinople, as it could command the best road for guns on each flank. I think they could not enter if we assist Turks at once.

Since the crisis began Lord Derby, the Foreign Secretary, had tended more and more to assume an air of detachment rather than of active opposition and to take a back seat in the actual conduct of affairs, which he left almost entirely to the Prime Minister—and the latter, if he consulted anybody, inclined rather to consult Lord Salisbury, then Secretary of State for India, or Lord Cairns, the Lord Chancellor. Even Smith found it necessary to adopt quite a peremptory tone in keeping the Foreign Secretary up to the mark on his duties in regard to supplying foreign intelligence. 'We ought to be informed of the sailing of every ship and its destination and of the preparations going forward in every Dockyard and Arsenal', he wrote to Derby (February 27th). 'At the present moment we know very little indeed as to work which may be on hand in the Baltic or the Black Sea and still less as to the ships which may be found in the Amoor or at Vladivostock.'

But when it became known at about this time that the Czar was preparing to make his own peace with the Porte and Derby only sent a very mildly phrased request for information about it, there was even greater alarm and anger in the Cabinet. Beaconsfield wrote him a furious and sarcastic letter (February 28th): '. . . I don't think we are justified in the present crisis to be sending to Russia civil messages: "We shall be obliged to you, as soon as you have made your terms with Turkey, to know what they are . . .".'[1] Then Derby

[1] Buckle VI, 249.

nearly resigned a few days later over Cabinet proposals for the occupation of a 'place of arms' in the Levant—though he did not actually do so until a month later.

Meanwhile Smith continued to do his best to keep his Admiral 'in the picture'. 'Almost every day we have information more or less direct of the transmission of Torpedoes from the interior of Russia towards Turkey and Rodosto harbour stated to be their destination. I take it for granted you are kept informed by the Ambassador,' he wrote to Hornby (February 28th). 'The change in the [Turkish] Command at Gallipoli appears to be an improvement, but I cannot say I am easy as to the position. We can do nothing at present as we are equally bound with Russia not to put a man on the Peninsula. . . .' This referred to a sort of interim agreement concluded—in order to gain time—on February 19th between England and Russia, whereby the latter undertook not to occupy Gallipoli or the lines of Bulair in return for England not landing troops in Turkey.

'Have you trustworthy information as to the Black Sea?' Smith asked Hornby in conclusion. 'I see Russian papers say the Bosphorus forts are not strong enough to prevent a Fleet from pushing its way through.' Here Smith was sounding the Admiral in the direction in which the ideas of the Cabinet were now moving, viz., the possibility of forcing the passage of the Black Sea. But at first this was considered by Hornby's brother officers at the Admiralty to be an almost impossible and very unfair task to impose upon him, for Smith wrote to Beaconsfield (March 1st): 'My naval colleagues protest against Hornby being asked if he can go into the Black Sea on the assumption that the Bosphorus forts fall into the hands of Russia. They say that he has not strength enough to force his way back again—even if he could maintain the Fleet in the Black Sea in time of war. . . .'

On March 6th Beaconsfield wrote to the Queen, saying that he was much pleased with the First Lord of the Admiralty, 'who is both calm and energetic', and went on to reassure her that, though Derby was still in the Cabinet, he was of little account now and would probably soon resign for good and all.[1] In fact, on March 8th, he confessed that 'the Cabinet has taken the management of the F.O. into its own hands'. Rather surprisingly, however, in view of the Admiralty's doubts, he also informed her in this second letter that Hornby 'finds his position in the Sea of Marmora much more satisfactory than he contemplated', that 'he has reconnoitred the Bosphorus and is quite prepared to force it when necessary and to enter the Black Sea'. 'He is not panic-struck by Torpedoes at all,' the Premier continued; 'he seems to have no doubt of ample supplies and of fuel. . . . He could cut off the Russians from all their supplies,

[1] Ibid. 254.

via Black Sea. . . . This alters everything: we are in a commanding position.'[1]

Nevertheless, either Beaconsfield must have exaggerated Hornby's confidence in order to satisfy the Queen's thirst for action or else Hornby had second thoughts, for the latter's cable to Smith two days later (March 10th) sounded a very different note.

> . . . Bosphorus forts would probably not stop ironclads going into Black Sea, but would stop all supplies. If in Russian hands and strengthened by torpedoes, no squadron could pass without severe loss. If there is any idea of moving in that direction, no time should be lost in opening negotiations with the Turks. Without their help the Straits cannot be saved, and the Turks seem daily succumbing to Russian influence.

Meanwhile, Russia had forced Turkey to sign the Treaty of San Stefano by threats of occupying Constantinople. Though the Treaty was signed on March 3rd Russia had persistently refused to disclose the terms and, again by threats, compelled the Porte to refuse to disclose them also. The Treaty all but rubbed out the remnants of Turkey-in-Europe, created a huge Bulgaria (to be occupied by Russian troops and supervised by a Russian commissioner for a term of years) and provided for the complete independence of Rumania, Serbia and Montenegro. Though these terms inevitably began to leak out the British Government was not actually informed of them till March 23rd.

Beaconsfield's contention was that the terms should be submitted to a conference of the European Great Powers—ultimately to be magnified into a Congress at Berlin with Bismarck as self-styled 'honest broker'. But whilst Prince Gortchakoff, for Russia, hedged by suggesting it would be sufficient for the terms of the treaty to be 'communicated' to the Powers *before* the Congress, the British Cabinet continued to elaborate precautionary measures. As Beaconsfield wrote to the Queen (March 16th): 'They [the Cabinet] discussed *corps d'armée*, new Gibraltars and expeditions from India in great fulness, Lord Derby said nothing.'[2]

But on March 27th, Russia having rejected the British proposals, Beaconsfield (strong in the knowledge of the full support of Austria and at least of the tacit support of Germany) forced the pace by persuading the Cabinet to call up the reserves immediately and to summon to the Mediterranean a large body of Indian troops. This was too much for Derby, who now finally resigned and was succeeded

---

[1] Ibid., 255.
[2] Ibid., 259.

at the Foreign Office by Lord Salisbury. Salisbury's appointment was a turning point in the crisis, for he signalized his advent almost immediately by issuing to the Powers a most able Circular Note, which brought even Bismarck fully round to the idea of the 'unlimited conference', and brought the final and peaceful settlement of the crisis rapidly within sight.

Whilst, however, the whole matter still hung in the balance, strategic plans for forestalling any possible Russian move upon Constantinople or the Dardanelles still had to be elaborated or evaluated. Admirals Hornby and Commerell did not conceal their irritation and mistrust in regard to what seemed to them the Cabinet's involved policy and oblique methods and both harped continually on the necessity for an out-and-out alliance with the Turks and a clearer show of British intentions. It was the classic and perennial struggle between the professional man on the spot and his political chief at Whitehall. Smith patiently re-stated the Government case, trying at the same time not to damp too much the Admirals' initiative.

> . . . It practically amounts to this [he wrote to Hornby, March 23rd] that if we go to war with Russia we ought to have had previously an alliance with Turkey and you say now that such an arrangement should have been made so that we could have occupied Gallipoli and covered Constantinople.
>
> You are probably right if military considerations alone prevailed: but an alliance with Turkey against Russia has hitherto been impossible whatever may happen in the future.
>
> I understand you to hold now that if England goes to war with Russia now she [Russia] will at once seize the northern shores of the Bosphorus, and by planting them with Torpedoes render it impossible to force the passage without serious loss, but you advocate risking that loss, in order to cut the communications by sea between Odessa and other Russian Ports in the Black Sea and the new Bulgaria.
>
> It would be a bold course to take and if the Fleet . . . could maintain itself in an effective condition in the Black Sea for one campaign, I concur with you in thinking it would be worth the risk involved in the return—but to justify the operation it must be capable of holding the Sea after it has forced the Bosphorus, and I am not clear on that point.
>
> Commerell writes to say that Gallipoli can be held by the men now there if they were convinced we were in earnest. There can be no doubt upon this fact that we are quite in earnest that Gallipoli shall not fall into the hands of Russia so long as our Ships remain in Marmora. If the lines are attacked the ships on both sides [of the peninsula] would assist in their defence with their guns, and as it would be an act of war against England by Russia there would be no hesitation in finding money, food, and officers, if they were wanted for the troops holding

the lines; but this cannot be done in advance of war. To do it would be a hostile act on our part which might well be held to justify war on theirs.

We are still waiting for the reply of Russia as to the conditions on which alone we can go into Congress. . . . We shall probably go into Congress but I am not sanguine of a satisfactory result.

I told you . . . of the serious anger caused by the visit of Prince Alexander of Battenberg to the 'Sultan' [Duke of Edinburgh's ship]. I am pressed to make this the subject of censure upon the Captain [the Duke]. . . .

There is the greatest possible indisposition to allow the Duke to come home at all, and I am requested to send him to another and distant station.—My own purpose is to put him on half pay on paying off—and it will be for the Royal Family to arrange that he shall then go to Germany for a time. . . .

Prince Alfred, Duke of Edinburgh, the Queen's second son, who was said to have 'shewn much aptitude for his profession' and to be 'highly esteemed as a sailor by sailors, but thought to be rather overrated as a musician by musicians',[1] appears to have been a stubborn, egotistical and tactless man, singularly devoid of the charm of his brothers. Being married to the Czar's only daughter inevitably inclined him to lean rather towards the Russian than the Turkish side during the Eastern Crisis and it was possibly unwise, if not unfair, to put him in command of one of the ships designated for the anti-Russian demonstration at the Dardanelles.

The incident of his inviting Prince Alexander of Battenberg on board his ship was seen in the very worst light by his country and his mother, not only for the above reasons, but because Prince Alexander was a nephew of the Czar, aide-de-camp to the Russian commander-in-chief, the Grand Duke Nicholas, and was known to be the Russian candidate for the throne of the newly created Greater Bulgaria. Alexander was therefore presumed—though quite wrongly as events were soon to prove—to be an inveterate Russophile. The fact that his brother, Prince Louis,[2] was an officer in the British Navy, did little to mitigate this impression and merely tended to make matters more uncomfortable for the latter.

Apart from their annoyance at the Duke of Edinburgh's tactlessness, the one idea dominant in the minds of both the Queen and her Prime Minister seems to have been to prevent him from returning to England. For when the question of the Duke's promotion had come up a few weeks earlier and Smith had consulted Beaconsfield, the

[1] Sir George Arthur: *Concerning Queen Victoria and her Son*, p. 111. See also Arthur Ponsonby: *Henry Ponsonby: His Life from his Letters*, pp. 86–7.

[2] Commander-in-Chief Atlantic Fleet, 1908–10; First Sea Lord, 1912–14; relinquished German titles and created Marquess of Milford Haven, 1917.

latter had merely telegraphed (March 6th): 'You can do what you like *provided he does not come home.*' Again on March 19th: 'I have just heard from the Queen to beg that I would stop any proceedings about Alfred's return—even for a few weeks . . .'. The truth was that the Queen was terrified of his exerting a bad influence over his brothers—especially her favourite, Prince Arthur, Duke of Connaught.[1]

When the episode of Prince Alexander's visit to the Duke's ship occurred the Queen at once telegraphed to Smith to find out the truth of the story and the part played therein by Hornby. The Admiral was naturally in a quandary as to how to compromise between maintaining discipline and not displeasing his Sovereign; but that his efforts in the latter direction were sadly unsuccessful is shown by the Queen's confidential letter to Smith of March 31st:

> The Queen . . . will be most anxious to see the full report of the reasons wh. made Ad. Hornby send Pce. Alfred and Pce. Louis Battenberg away—if he says he cd. *not object* to the visit, wh. the Queen thinks in a private and friendly way he *might* have, even if he had not felt he cd. do so on public grounds. . . .
>
> . . . The Queen thinks that for some excuse or other he [Duke of Edinburgh] should *not* bring home his Ship—for the Queen is *positive* he *shd* NOT come home.
>
> If possible he shd. soon get another ship but be sent to some distant tho' healthy station.
>
> Unfortunately the Queen is the first to admit her son's great thoughtlessness and want of discretion and is not surprised if the Admiralty can have no confidence in him. She thinks however that for the future and when only surrounded by people in no way connected with foreign Sovereigns—he will act with prudence. . . .

Smith must have written to the Queen urging that the Prince should be allowed to come home, for Beaconsfield wrote to him (April 3rd): 'I have just heard from Windsor. Your letter has produced no effect. *The Gentleman must not* come home. You don't know him. . . .' And then later the same day, '*I must see you about Prince Alfred's* business before the Cabinet . . .'. On April 17th he wrote again that 'the Queen feels "aggrieved and amazed that the whole of this painful business is thrown upon Her". This Her Majesty seems to think is occasioned by Adl. Hornby not sending "the reprimands to the D. of Edinburgh as promised" etc. etc. . . .'

Smith took immense pains to placate the angry and agitated Queen by arranging for the Duke of Edinburgh to swap ships on the spot so that he would not have to come home when his ship, the *Sultan*,

[1] See Mary Howard McClintock: *The Queen Thanks Sir Howard*, pp. 30, 87, 95, 145.

had to come home for refitting; by posting Prince Louis of Battenberg to another ship so as to remove him from the Duke's influence. But it was all of no avail. The imbroglio as to who should give orders to or reprimand the Duke merely seemed to intensify. Thus Beaconsfield again wrote despairingly to Smith (May 29th):

> There is fresh trouble about P. Alfred. The Queen was promised that a letter of reprimand shd be sent to him by the Admiral, of which H.M. advised the Prince. No letter has been sent, 'the Queen has been left entirely unsupported', and now the Prince says he must 'demand a Court of Enquiry'.
> What am I to say?

In his reply of the same day Smith reminded Beaconsfield that at the time of the incident he had telegraphed to Hornby requesting the facts of the case and as to whether he (Hornby) had sanctioned the visit.

> . . . His answer came giving a different colour to the story. The Prince of Battenberg was in German and not in Russian uniform and the Admiral was invited to meet him at dinner and went, and he added that if his sanction had been asked it would have been given.
> It became therefore impossible to reprimand in a formal manner an officer who had committed no breach of duty: but I became aware privately of the fact that the Admiral had written a private and friendly letter to the Duke which any sensible man would thoroughly well understand.
> I thought I had explained this fully to Her Majesty and I deeply regret that I failed to make it clear and still more the pain and annoyance the affair has caused the Queen.

While the machinery for calling the Congress of Powers was still being set in motion the crisis at the Dardanelles continued unabated. On March 31st Hornby cabled Smith about reports that the Russians were preparing 'to make a dash on Gallipoli in the event of a war between England and Russia' and were 'collecting torpedoes at Rodosto'. He requested 'instructions for guidance in the event of war being imminent, observing that the ships cannot remain with safety in the Bosphorus at night whilst the north shore is in possession of an enemy provided with Whitehead torpedoes'.

On April 2nd Hornby wired again:

> Affairs at Constantinople said to be very critical. Grand Duke obtaining great influence with several military Pashas. Appointment of Ministry favourable to Russia thought probable. General Dickson[1] tells me he thinks Bulair lines could be held by troops now there if ordered to defend them, but recommends assistance of men and

[1] Gen. Sir Collingwood Dickson. See *ante*.

officers from the fleet in the event of attack to prove to the troops that we are in alliance with Turkey.

He fears orders would be given from Constantinople not to defend the lines. In that case he thinks we should defend the lines by taking General and troops into our pay. I concur with him, and submit that the Rear-Admiral should have authority to do so if the Russians prepare to attack.

Submit in future that Treaty should be made with Turkish Government to join us if we are forced into war with Russia. . . .

I cannot believe Turkey would defend Gallipoli for us unless we will do something for them as well as for ourselves. Time seems precious. . . .

This opinion was reinforced next day (April 3rd) by a cable from Hornby's second-in-command, Sir John Commerell: 'I think First Pasha at Bulair would hail with delight an order from Constantinople to surrender lines—Second Pasha is different man altogether. . . .' Then again on the following day: 'I am not sure about the money. If I see my way, what sum may I offer? It must be high to succeed.'

Meanwhile the idea of purchasing the Turkish Fleet appears to have been assiduously worked upon by certain agents of the British Government and was now within sight of practical achievement, to judge from the following letter received by Smith at this time.

Hotel Suisse,
Geneva.
6th April, 1878.

Capt. J. E.-F. Aylmer presents his compliments to the Rt. Honble the First Lord of the Admiralty and respectfully asks his attention to the following:

Capt. Aylmer's Agent in Geneva, M. Charles Kusel, whose integrity and discretion are known to H.R.H. the Prince of Wales and others in London, assures him that he is in a position through his intimate and confidential connection with the officials of the Turkish Court, to arrange in secret, the purchase for Her Majesty's Government of the whole or a portion of the Turkish Ironclads.

In making this communication to the First Lord, Capt. Aylmer feels that his well-known adherence to the Conservative Party and his position as Conservative Candidate for the representation of Maidstone will prevent his intention being misunderstood.

If Her Majesty's Government desires to make such an arrangement and to obtain from the Sultan an order for Hobart Pacha[1] to deliver up his fleet to our Admiral at any time he may demand same against payment of the agreed sum. Capt. Aylmer will be happy to accompany

[1] Augustus Charles Hobart-Hampden (1822–86), 3rd Son of 6th Earl of Buckinghamshire, former Captain R.N., took service under Sultan and was given command of Turkish Black Sea Fleet, 1878. Reinstated in Royal Navy as Vice-Admiral, 1885.

Mr. Kusel to Constantinople, and will answer for his trustworthiness and discretion.

But on the side of this remarkable communication Smith only wrote rather dampingly: '. . . Under present condition of affairs not prepared to entertain proposals—thank.'

The condition of affairs which caused the Government to feel less inclined than formerly to pursue this extreme—and expensive—course was that, with Salisbury's advent to the Foreign Office and his prompt issue of his Circular to the Powers, the war clouds had already begun to roll back. 'There has been no definite result yet,' as Smith wrote to Hornby, 'but there is a sensible relaxation of the tension here. . . .' Nevertheless, while insisting on the necessity for the Congress to be held, Salisbury was equally insistent upon the necessity for scrapping the Treaty of San Stefano as a basis for discussion. To this end he entered into secret negotiations with Count Shouvaloff, the Russian Ambassador in London, and by the end of May had signed a Convention with him covering most of the differences to be formally discussed at Berlin.

But, in the meantime, as an earnest of the Government's firmness and determination and to impress the other Powers with the magnitude of England's resources, Beaconsfield insisted on pressing on with the arrangements for the Indian expedition to the Mediterranean; so 7,000 Indian troops arrived at Malta before the end of May. Also Smith wrote to Hornby (April 20th): '. . . we are pressing forward the fitting out of another Fleet and I hope in less than a month to have a formidable force assembled . . . available either for service in the Mediterranean or the Baltic.' Equally the watch on Russian moves in any direction was zealously maintained. Thus Smith to the Under Secretary at the Home Office (April 9th): 'I have been recently employing some detectives from Scotland Yard to make certain enquiries on behalf of the Admiralty with regard to Russian orders for torpedoes and etc. in this country. . . .'

The First Lord had, too, a most alert, as well as humorous, intelligence officer in the Naval Attaché at Washington, Admiral Gore-Jones. The latter wrote to him on April 16th:

In consequence of telegrams from Foreign Office we are all on the look-out here for the passage of 600 Russian Seamen across the Continent—and the New York papers have now got hold of the Story and canvas the Russian intention to purchase Cruisers and if possible to get up Privateering. Mr. Bodisco, the Russian Consul-General assured me there was not a word of truth in the report of men being sent out, saying 'of course I would not tell you if it was so, but as it is not so I assure you it is all false'.

He went on to report that he had reliable information that the Russians were negotiating with a certain American shipping line to purchase two of their steamers 'in order to fit them out as Cruisers in the Pacific' and that the company would probably be glad to dispose of them as they had been badly constructed. He also reported that the Russians had ordered 100 torpedoes in the United States, 'but I do not think they will ever prove a very effective weapon of attack'.

In a later letter (April 29th) Gore-Jones sent Smith cuttings from American newspapers purporting to show that 'Russian agents have been sounding steam vessel proprietors everywhere', but admitting that 'I fail to discover any purchases actually made'. One cutting referred to the visit in the previous year to American waters of three Russian warships carrying the Czar's son and heir, the Grand Duke Alexis, and the latter's younger brother and described a grand ball given on board the flagship, when 'scarcely had the music died away before the British Legation began to intrigue to have the fleet ordered away'. It then described how Gore-Jones's 'corps of spies not proving sufficient, he hired Aimée's troupe of dancers, and singers to snare the Russian Officers and get their secrets'.

Of this Gore-Jones remarked in his letter that 'although ridiculously told, there is a strong substratum of truth, especially with regard to Mr. Evarts' [Secretary of State] being badgered into frightening away the Squadron from their waters'; and he added, 'one Ballet girl did give us a good deal of information'. In conclusion he observed that 'the tone of American Society is much more with us now than it was—but they would not be sorry to see a war as they fancy it would give them a chance to revive their commerce'.

Meanwhile the professional members of the Admiralty Board pressed strongly for 'immediate steps to commence fitting six fast merchant ships as cruisers . . . to prevent an enemy preying upon our trade'. But on May 4th Smith replied that 'the Cabinet decided today that the time had not arrived to take any such decision as this and I am of the same opinion'. However, the continuing disquiet on the subject was shown by a letter (May 11th) to Smith from the Admiral commanding a British squadron in those parts regarding the defenceless position of St. John's, Newfoundland.

The arrival of a German steamer with 60 Russian Officers and 600 seamen gives importance to this fact, for Sir John Glover [Governor] assured me that there was nothing to prevent an armed merchant vessel from entering the Port of St. John's and laying it under contribution to the extent of £150,000 in gold coin *alone*, to say nothing of the vessels in port. . . .

But Gore-Jones related (May 14th) that a Russian naval officer, interviewed by the *New York Herald* about the 600 men aforesaid, had 'hinted the men will go to the Pacific by the Panama route and stated distinctly that Russia is not going to use Privateers—but to purchase fast vessels and use them as men of war'. He added, 'It is said the United States Government do not altogether like the men being sent in this way and the matter is under consideration'.

However, there was an Achilles heel in a Great Power dependent on foreign experts, as Russia was. For at about this time Smith had a letter from the British Military Attaché at St. Petersburg introducing someone 'in order to put you in possession of all he knows concerning the Russian Navy, torpedo boats, etc. He is chief engineer at Mr. Baird's works here and is now building torpedo boats for the Russian Government. . . . I think it is also possible that through him we might be able to purchase the plans etc., of Cronstadt. . . .

VI

ROYAL IMBROGLIOS

————————◆┼◆————————

D ESPITE the now reasonable hopes of a Congress of Powers
being held and of peace being preserved, before Shouvaloff
returned to St. Petersburg—in the second week of May 1878—to
acquaint the Czar with the British terms, Beaconsfield had told him
'that it was only fair to state distinctly that we could not in the
slightest degree cease from our plans of preparation; and that they
must go on even if there were a Congress'.[1] As Salisbury wrote to
Smith (May 16th): '. . . time is really for the purposes of attack
much more valuable to us who are rich and unprepared than to
Russia exhausted and armed to the teeth. The truth is neither of us
believes in the peaceful intentions of the other: and therefore, each,
while negotiating is arming.'

During this difficult phase the First Lord did his best to keep his
admirals *au fait* with the changing situation. He wrote (May 29th)
to Lord John Hay,[2] commanding the Channel Fleet, that 'the Govt.
have found it necessary to send you with the Channel Fleet into the
Mediterranean and although there is every reason to hope that
England will go into Congress with the European Powers to discuss
the Treaty of San Stefano . . . we do not feel it would be safe to
lessen our force in Eastern Waters'. And on hearing from Hornby—
after the Congress had actually assembled—that he was preparing
to forestall a rumoured Russian landing on the Island of Marmora,
he hastened to warn him that this was an unlikely rumour, adding
'we have no wish to fire the first shot while the Congress is sitting
and I do not myself see what object the Russians would have in
going to Marmora'.

Nevertheless, despite his pains, both admirals complained of being
insufficiently informed as to their probable tasks and future move-

[1] Buckle VI, 292.
[2] 4th Son of 8th Marquess of Tweeddale; Admiral of the Fleet. A Lord of the
Admiralty, 1866, 1868–71, 1880–3 and 1886.

ments. Hornby complained bitterly (June 24th) that Hay 'finds himself at Suda Bay with the Country [Crete] much disturbed . . . while he has not one line to guide him . . . a position so unprecedented for an officer of his rank to be placed in, that I am obliged to bring it to your notice, as I cannot think it will work advantageously for the Country'.

In his reply (July 6th) Smith was patient but firm—though not without a hint of exasperation and even sarcasm here and there.

> . . . We do place the most complete trust in you but we cannot tell you what our whole policy is under any possible contingency that may arise in the present very complicated state of affairs. . . .
>
> You say Lord J. Hay does not know why he was sent to Suda Bay and what he has to do there. Lord J. Hay's squadron is in the Medn. because yours is shut up in the Sea of Marmora. He has no special orders as to Crete because he was only sent there as a convenient station to which to telegraph. I suppose it is not unusual for an Admiral to find himself at a Port in those waters where there is more or less disturbance—and without instructions, but neither you nor he would find any difficulty as to the course to be taken especially as the Ambassador [at Constantinople] is at one end of the wire and Whitehall at the other. . . .

The Treaty of Berlin was signed on July 13th, 1878, though everything had really been settled already by secret conventions concluded between the Powers beforehand. The 'Big Bulgaria', the main bone of contention, was broken up again, and, though Russia was allowed to make large strategic annexations at the south-east corner of the Black Sea, Turkey regained her Macedonian provinces and suzerainty over the self-governing province of Eastern Rumelia. She also received a guarantee by Britain of her Asiatic possessions in return for pledges of reform and safeguards for Christian subjects—and the cession to Britain of Cyprus.

This cession of Cyprus was of course one of the features which Smith had not been able to disclose hitherto to his admirals. As he wrote to Hornby (July 12th):

> . . . The news of the cession of Cyprus . . . came out on Monday and I hear from Lord John Hay he has assumed the Govt. of the Island without any difficulty.
>
> You are now no doubt fully aware of the conditions of the Treaty and of the circs. which prevented me from telling you what was in our minds.
>
> I am now very anxious to get you and Admiral Commerell out of the Marmora and the Dardanelles—the Treaty ought to be signed today and the retirement of the Russian troops should begin at once. I take it for granted they will observe the conditions made with Europe and that no attempt at evasion will be made. . . . However

we shall not move at all without being quite sure of our ground—and then only with the greatest discretion.

Hurried withdrawal could probably have an injurious effect: but there is no harm in telling you privately that I am most anxious to get you back into the Mediterranean and the Fleet reduced to its usual condition.

Lord John Hay must remain at Cyprus as interim Governor until Sir Garnet Wolseley[1] arrives with the Troops. . . .

Now that the end of the emergency appeared to be at hand, Smith, with magnanimous disregard for Hornby's recent cantankerous behaviour, and wishing to reward his undoubted courage, resource and shrewdness throughout his arduous and difficult mission, submitted the Admiral's name to the Queen for a K.C.B. But the Queen showing that petty and vindictive side of her character which sometimes marred her actions, jibbed at bestowing the honour, purely on account of Hornby's supposed mishandling of the affair of the Prince of Battenberg's visit to the Duke of Edinburgh's ship.

Smith was extremely upset and wrote a lengthy letter to Beaconsfield, going over the whole story of the visit again and emphasizing Hornby's blamelessness and the fact that he [Hornby] 'did privately advise H.R.H. to deprive the mischievous manufacturers of gossip of any foundation for the stories which were put into circulation as to the sympathies of H.R.H., in what appeared to be an impending struggle between England & Russia'.

. . . The services of the Fleet [Smith concluded] have been most trying & most severe: watch by night by row-boats to guard against surprise and against torpedoes—vigilance of every kind—preparedness for instant action. All this sailors are accustomed to preceding or succeeding an action, but the strain upon men who have maintained this for five months without committing one mistake does, I venture to think, entitle the service to the recognition wh. I ask for, not on Adml. Hornby's account personally, but as an honour to be bestowed on the C. in C. of a squadron wh. has certainly done its duty thoroughly.

Moved by this fervent and eloquent plea the Queen gave in and Beaconsfield was able to write (August 6th) that 'the Queen has been graciously pleased to confer a K.C.B. on Adml. Hornby'.

The affairs and problems of the Queen's large and difficult family continued to obtrude themselves and to absorb an astonishing amount of her Minister's time. The Queen herself would be at one moment attempting to bring their affairs under her personal control and issuing instructions to her Ministers to suit her own wishes and

[1] Later Field Marshal Viscount Wolseley; Commander in Chief of British Army, 1895-9.

the next she would be disclaiming any wish or right to interfere and even complaining of being involved at all. Thus on July 3rd she writes to the First Lord:

> . . . The Dcss. of Edinburgh has continually begged the Queen to let Pce. Alfred have leave to join her at Coburg . . . to be with her at her Confinement. The Queen telegraphed . . . to Alfred saying *she* authorised *him* to *apply* to the Admy. for 7 weeks at the end of Aug. to go to Coburg (*not* on any account to Russia) for this purpose. He has himself been twice unwell—a little change will do him good. But 3 or 4 weeks wd. be enough & the Admy. must *say* exactly what may be feasible. . . .

Not long afterwards the Queen was complaining about being prevented by the exigencies of their education from seeing anything of her grandsons—the two sons of the Prince of Wales:

> The Queen has not heard any particulars about the Examination of the young Princes for wh. she had to give up seeing them at Balmoral . . . The Queen fears else the children will become complete strangers to her. She has not seen them but for *one hour's visit since* the 15th of last October!!!
> Is not Pce. Louis Battenberg going to join his ship soon?
> His presence in London is hardly very desirable for long—now.

Considering his recent experiences in the matter it is surprising to find Smith now bringing fresh trouble on his own head by, of all things, suggesting the return of the Duke of Edinburgh: 'as there is no prospect of Active Service H.R.H. would now be glad to come on shore and unless Your Majesty sees reason to the contrary there would be no objection so far as the Admy. is concerned'. But the answer came swiftly through Beaconsfield (August 18th) that 'the Queen both for public and private reasons wishes that the Duke of Edinburgh shd not return until the Spring, and that some hard work, which H.R.H. likes, & does well, should be provided for him away from home'.

Despite all the earlier correspondence on the subject the question of the proper channel for making communications to a Royal Prince who was also a serving officer in the Navy seemed to be in a worse state of confusion than ever, and it is difficult to avoid the conclusion that the reason lay in the Queen's inability not to interfere with ordinary procedure—and even with special procedure which she had herself earlier endorsed. For not long afterwards Beaconsfield was writing to Smith again (September 4th):

> Things seem to be worse than ever about the D. of Edinburgh. He writes to the Queen that he has received a letter from the Private Secy. of the First Ld of ye Admy. informing him that Mr. Smith has referred

to the Queen as to what the movements of the 'Black Prince'[1] are to be. If the decision is with the Queen, the Duke requests his early return, as he wants to get settled at Eastwell[2] before Xmas.

The Queen says to me that the Amdy. throw the whole odium & responsy. on her shoulders, acting contrary to the agreement, that all these arrangements should be made, & made only, between H.R.H. & his Chief.

The Queen seems terribly annoyed. . . .

Again, a week later (September 12th) Beaconsfield wrote to say that 'Her Majesty commands me to express "her surprise & displeasure at the way in wh. everything is thrown upon *Her* by the Admiralty".' Smith replied (September 13th) expressing regret for having displeased the Queen and adding that he had 'given directions that no communications whatever shall be held with H.R.H. the Duke of Edinburgh excepting through the proper official channels, and with such communications H.M. shall be acquainted'.

But the Duke was by now in a thoroughly angry and obstinate mood and told his brother the Prince of Wales, who told the Queen, that he would resign his commission if not allowed to come home. The Queen asked if he could not 'be sent to some Mediterranean Station and come home later'. Beaconsfield's comment to Smith was '. . . I know of no small Med. Station that he can be sent to. Don't you think its better to terminate the affair & say so distinctly?' To which Smith replied (September 20th): '. . . I remain of the opinion that when peace is assured the Ship ought to come home and be paid off.'

Upon this gloomy impasse a faint ray of hope now appeared to shine. The Marquess of Lorne,[3] who had married the Queen's fourth daughter Princess Louise, having just been appointed Governor-General of Canada, wrote to the First Lord suggesting that in view of his wife's royal status 'it would look best that the landing [at Halifax, Nova Scotia] should be made from a Queen's ship'. The Queen naturally approved of such a suggestion and then the idea came to her that it could be felicitously combined with the solution of Alfred's problem. Beaconsfield wrote to Smith (September 22nd):

I think Her Majesty has now made up her mind that the Duke of Edinburgh will return & that it is vain to resist any longer. . . . The Queen, in a letter this morning, throws out this suggestion as a means of changing his thoughts a little after the disagreeable correspondence & softening the situation.

[1] The ship of which the Duke had been given command in place of the *Sultan*.
[2] Eastwell Park, near Ashford, Kent, the country home of the Duke and Duchess of Edinburgh.
[3] John Douglas Sutherland Campbell, later 9th Duke of Argyll.

'The Princess Louise would be pleased if her brother cd. command the escort to Canada.'

If it can't be say so distinctly to me. Is the 'Black Prince' fitted for crossing the Atlantic? . . .

Smith thought she was, but owing to the ship's very limited coal storage capacity recommended a route giving maximum opportunity for coaling and a time-schedule enabling the Duke to be awaiting his sister at Halifax. These orders he conveyed very tactfully to the Duke in a letter of September 28th, adding that 'the duty to be performed will be an interesting one & will probably have important political results while the complete change to the officers and crew cannot fail to have a beneficial effect upon their health, before they return to England to be paid off'.

At this juncture the owners of the passenger ship *Sarmatian* offered her to Lord Lorne for the voyage—in place of the cruiser *Northampton*, which had earlier been decided upon. Consulted by Lorne, Smith advised that the *Sarmatian* would be much more comfortable and Lorne therefore accepted. But neither of them apparently thought of informing the Queen, who read of the change in the newspapers and telegraphed indignantly from Balmoral to know 'the meaning of this report'. A ship of the Royal Navy was in her view the proper form of transport on such an occasion and so the new proposal was hurriedly dropped.

But there was to be still one final alarum before the plan could reach a happy conclusion. General Ponsonby[1] wrote from Balmoral (October 7th) that 'the Queen has been informed from various quarters that the "Black Prince" is not a fit ship to cross the Atlantic, especially at this season of the year' and requesting suitable assurances. Smith, however, with supreme tact replied (October 9th) that 'properly handled, as she certainly would be by H.R.H. the Duke of Edinburgh, she is a perfectly safe ship for the duty on which it is proposed to send her'. And so at last the matter was settled.

Meanwhile, despite the signing of the Treaty, the situation in the Near East was still fraught with anxiety. Referring in a letter to Hornby to the state of affairs at Constantinople, Smith wrote (August 22nd):

. . . We hear now that *the* great difficulty is entire absence of any money—anything on which to obtain money—and that order cannot be secured until by some means or other money is had to pay the public servants and especially the police.

I sent you out officially the correspondence with the F.O. as to the simultaneous withdrawal of the Russian Army and the [British] Fleet.

[1] General Sir Henry Ponsonby, Private Secretary to Queen Victoria.

I cannot say I am very sanguine that the Army will be withdrawn yet—for Russia probably sees all the unpleasant symptoms [at Constantinople] which you describe and she would not willingly be at a distance when a catastrophe occurred which she has so much to do with, so that I shall not be surprised if the Army remains on some pretext or other. . . .

At about this time the First Lord made a speech at the Mansion House in which he took the opportunity to 'give expression to the strong feeling I had of the Service rendered by the Officers and men of all ranks and of the strain upon them', as he wrote afterwards to Hornby (September 5th). But the latter, notwithstanding his K.C.B., was still inclined to be prickly and felt that more should have been said about his second-in-command, Admiral Sir John Commerell. Smith assured him that this could be done in due course and pointed out that to some of the Squadron's services 'it will not be possible to make allusion in a public paper, as it will not be at all desirable to place on record our knowledge of the weakness or treachery of the officers commanding the forces of our Turkish friends'.

Nevertheless, on the very same day, Smith wrote to Admiral Commerell 'to say how very much we feel . . . we are indebted to you for the tact, energy and skill you have shown in keeping things straight at Gallipoli. . . . I believe it was entirely due to your watchfulness that the lines were at last placed in a state of defence and that [Turkish] officers were appointed who were determined to hold them if they were attacked. . . . If you had not been at Gallipoli, I feel persuaded the Russians would have seized the Peninsula and the result would have been war.' But, in spite of this, Hornby still vented his spleen by sending in to the First Lord (September 18th) a shocking report of the condition of some of the ships of his squadron and adding sardonically: '. . . Probably you would not like to have to break them up at Malta & to show Foreign Governments with what rotten vessels we had been keeping up appearances lately.'

At the same time the Chancellor of the Exchequer, Sir Stafford Northcote, was worrying over the bill for the whole affair and wanted Smith to confer with his opposite number at the War Office[1] on the possibility of a systematic inquiry 'into our Naval and Military expenditure'. 'The prospects of the Revenue are, I am sorry to say,' he wrote on October 1st, 'most gloomy. . . . Something desperate must be done or we shall find ourselves landed in a big deficit.' Moreover, serious complications were threatening in Afghanistan through the high-handed action of the Viceroy of India in the face of Russian intrigues. Thus Northcote continued: 'I don't like Afghan

---

[1] Col. the Hon. F. R. Stanley, M.P. Northern Divn. Co. Lancs; later succeeded as 16th Earl of Derby.

matters at all. Lytton[1] has acted wholly against orders, and has placed us in a great dilemma. . . . I see no justification for going to war with the Ameer. On the other hand we can hardly leave matters as they are.'

Now at last Hornby reported that the Russians appeared to be beginning to withdraw from their advanced positions in European Turkey. 'He asks leave', Smith wrote Salisbury (October 7th), 'to withdraw the ships from Xeros and I am inclined to think they might come out of the Dardanelles unless you think it necessary to have at

STAFFORD NORTHCOTE.

hand protection for the Sultan against his own subjects. . . . I should withdraw the Channel Fleet from Cyprus, leaving perhaps a Dispatch boat and perhaps a gun vessel at the call of Sir Garnet Wolseley. . . . I do not propose to move more vessels until we see a little more into the future. . . .'

To this Salisbury replied (October 7th):

I have no objection to the withdrawal of the ships from Xeros—in fact, I think it would be in every way desirable. But please don't bring down the Marmora fleet through the Dardanelles till the Russians are well retired into Eastern Roumelia. We shall have great difficulty in getting them out of Adrianople: & the fact that our ships are still above the Straits will be a powerful reason.

[1] Edward, 1st Earl of Lytton, Viceroy of India, 1876–80.

The Fleet is probably not wanted at Cyprus except for sanitary purposes; but perhaps you had better communicate with Wolseley before withdrawing it.

Is it necessary to send the Fleet so far West as Gibraltar. Will not Malta be as good? There may very possibly be a war between Greece & the Porte within the next two months.

But, despite these hopeful arrangements, the end of the year still found the Russians lingering where they had no right to be and arguing about it as well.

Meanwhile, the First Lord of the Admiralty and the Secretary of State for War were planning a trip to Cyprus to try to ascertain at first hand the potentialities—naval and military—and the local feeling of Britain's latest possession. Before starting Smith consulted Salisbury as to the likely scope of his investigation. The latter replied (October 20th):

> I have been thinking a good deal about Cyprus; but I have really no special point to which I wish to direct your thoughts beyond the harbours and the barracks. . . . If we cannot get an ironclad harbour . . . we ought at least to have one in which transports can land & embark troops quickly. A more important matter still is to observe Wolseley's general tone & that of those about him—whether they are really hopeful & cordial in their work or not: whether they seem to hold the balance even between Turk and Greek. Layard, who is inclined to quarrel with Wolseley, thinks that he despises & puts aside the respectable Turks too much.
>
> Do not forget the function of roads & railways. . . .

The First Lord and the Secretary of War and their respective advisers and aides left England on October 21st. Smith's party included Admiral George Wellesley, First Naval Lord; Sir Massey Lopes, M.P., a Lord Commissioner of the Admiralty; Admiral Sir W. Houston Stewart, Controller of the Navy; The Hon. Algernon Egerton, M.P., Secretary to the Admiralty; Captain Codrington, private secretary to the First Lord. Smith kept a journal of the tour[1] and the first entry shows once more how much a parting from his family meant to him and how constant the warmth of his character had remained through the years.

> *Monday, Oct. 21st* 1878. Started from Greenlands for the 10.10 train. Did not 'light up' in the brougham as we had been accustomed to do. Neither of us cared for it. The two dear children had our last goodbye as we drove rapidly through the gate, and although we were not sad,

---

[1] This was evidently seen by his original biographer, Sir Herbert Maxwell, who quotes copious extracts from it [*Life*, I, 338 seqq], but it appears now to be missing from the Hambleden Papers. Such excerpts as I have quoted here are therefore taken from Maxwell's pages.

we were as once before, not talkative. The weather cleared up, and we cleared up too, and we began to say to each other, what a blessing it will be not to see a pouch for perhaps a month!

The Admiralty was a rush. I took leave of Admiral Hood,[1] and gave him parting directions. . . .

At the Charing Cross station a saloon was provided, and there we met Sir George Elliot,[2] who had come from Newcastle to join us.

Leave-taking again with Lethbridge, and, to my surprise, White, Sandifer and Taylor, old Strand faces, came to shake hands, and say, God bless you, Sir.

We were off, with a box of cigars with which Alpin MacGregor actually ran from the Admiralty to Charing Cross at the last moment, that we might not lack good tobacco on the road.

The party stopped at Paris, which was in the throes of the great industrial exhibition of that year. 'Our object was to see the naval models of ships and the specimens of iron and steel exhibited by France & England', wrote Smith (October 22nd). 'The Creuzot Exhibition was very interesting and might almost alarm one for the supremacy of our national industries in iron and steel.' He also called upon the Prince of Wales, who was staying at the Hotel Bristol, and who informed him—not much to his sorrow, one imagines—that he had only just missed the Duke of Edinburgh, who had passed through on his way to join his ship at Marseilles (to carry out the escort duty to Canada). Then 'up and down the Rue de la Paix, lingering at the jewellers' windows, admiring Sirandin's baskets and the nattily dressed girls who presided over the sweetie-shop; wondering whether the electric light really was so wonderful; thinking in between of home and of all that makes home lovely'.

From Paris on through France and Italy till the party reached Naples where they were to embark on H.M.S. *Himalaya* for the rest of the journey. Arriving late at night at Naples and searching along the water-front for the pinnace which was to take them out to the warship, they were accosted by three sinister local characters and thought they were about to be kidnapped. But at the crucial moment the British naval party turned up and took charge of them and 'the three men disappeared like evil spirits in the darkness'. Next morning, safely aboard the *Himalaya* and surveying the scene from her deck, Smith noted characteristically: 'The Bay of Naples is very lovely, but, if I dare say it, it wants the bright green of an English landscape.' While at Naples he also had the opportunity offered to him of being shown over the newest ship in the Italian Navy, the *Italia*, 'which is

[1] Admiral Sir Arthur W. Acland Hood (later Lord Hood of Avalon), 2nd Naval Lord of Admiralty.

[2] Admiral, Commander-in-Chief, Portsmouth; M.P. Chatham, 1874–5.

larger and will have more powerful engines than any ship in the English Navy'.

They left Naples and headed first for Crete and then for Cyprus. '. . . have kept my watch to "home" hours,' recorded Smith (October 28th), 'and it is very pleasant to turn to it and know perfectly what is doing at home. I see the boy [his son] running out for a rose, and I almost hear the gong, and I imagine the cold foggy mornings you have had, while we are inclined to be languid from heat. . . .'

The *Himalaya* dropped anchor at Larnaca, Cyprus, on the evening of October 28th. General Wolseley, the High Commissioner, came on board, accompanied by the two admirals, Hornby and Lord John Hay, and 'we had a friendly greeting', noted Smith, possibly antici-pating something different after his recent correspondence with the latter two. Within thirty-six hours, however (October 30th), 'Sir Garnet Wolseley, Stanley, and I, with attendants, started on ponies to make the round of Government stores, offices and hospitals. On our way we passed through Printing-house Square, and by the Beaconsfield Chambers, Anglo-Egyptian Street, and hosts of others newly named by the municipality. . . . It was curious to be saluted by Englishmen and recognized as one passed up and down, the pony threading its way over stones and through dust and dirt up and down steps.'

Conscientiously the party plodded their way round the island, visiting all the British units and installations, Smith closely observing and noting, as was his habit, the dazzling, sun-baked and rather ruinous scene with the brilliant and contrasting costumes of Turks, Greeks, Arabs and Negroes. On November 1st he wrote:

. . . We then started for General Payn's camp at Dali, and lunched there. It was a striking sight. The horses tethered under trees as their stables, and having no other shelter, the bed of the river below quite dry, and at the back of the tents, cotton plantations and trees and wells. As we were lunching a Bengal *syce*, used as a postman, passed in front, and with his copper-coloured face, black hair, and white turban and dress, he looked, as he was, a striking evidence of the variety of form England can bring to bear to discharge her duties in the world. After lunch I mounted a fresh horse, and rode home in the cool of the evening, passing few human habitations, but many evidences of past prosperity. Dinner in tent again and to bed.

At Famagusta (November 3rd) he was depressed by what he saw:

. . . Such desolation I had never before witnessed. Everything is a ruin, and much of the ruin is as if it had been accomplished only a few months, or at most years, ago. There are they say, remains of forty churches in the town, and not one perfect one remaining. The cathedral is turned into the one mosque in the town, disfigured and dirty, with tower and pinnacles gone. . . .

At Kyrenia (November 4th) they visited the camp of the Black Watch:

. . . The poor fellows were in a very depressed state, as they had had a good deal of fever and ague, which made them look washed out, and they had no games or amusements; but if all is well they will soon be moved. There is one lady, a wife of an officer, but there is only one other officer to call on her, so her life cannot be very cheerful.

Lastly at Limasol (November 5th):

. . . We landed at a little pier covered with myrtle and carpeted in honour of our arrival. . . . There was a crowd and a deputation. The municipality wished to present an address, which was read to us with great emphasis by a gentleman in black and a top-hat. When he finished there was 'Zeto!' or 'Long live the Queen!' 'Long live the Commissioner and the Ministers!' in good round cheers, and these were followed by 'God Save the Queen' in Greek, sung by the school-boys of the town. We hurried through the town, for time was precious, to the castle, the Kahn, and the jail; and coming out of that, we were met by another crowd and another address in Greek, to which we listened gravely, not understanding a word, and, all agreeing that Mr. Gladstone ought to be there to translate it.

This was the climax of the tour, for the same day the party embarked again on the *Himalaya* for the return journey via Port Said and Alexandria. 'Poor Sir Garnet felt our parting,' wrote Smith, 'but he said our visit had been a real comfort to him.' They were back in London by November 20th.

The Russian withdrawal from European Turkey, which had seemed to be under way six weeks earlier, was still hanging fire. A few days after Smith's return Salisbury wrote to him (November 25th):

'I have seen Shouvaloff this afternoon. He feels that the Russian Government are prepared to evacuate Turkey proper the moment the Turks evacuate Spuz & Podgoritza. I have telegraphed in this sense to Layard: & it is possible that the retirement of the Russians may not be long delayed. We are, as you doubtless will remember, under engagement to withdraw our fleet below the Straits as soon as the Russian army has crossed the Southern boundary of Eastern Roumelia.

Smith replied (November 28th):

From all that I can gather I should take a serious responsibility upon myself if I ordered Hornby to stay on at Artaki through the bad weather. I have told him he must stay there for the present, but Count

Shouvaloff should understand that it *may* be necessary to move the ships if the Russian army does not go soon.

The same day Smith wrote—a trifle apologetically—to Admiral Hornby the gist of Salisbury's letter and added:

... with his letter before me I had no alternatives but to telegraph to you to hold on for the present where you are. It is certain Russia does not want to see our ships back so near Constantinople as Ismedt but I shall not be averse personally to be the means of putting some pressure upon them if it is necessary to do so.—I take it for granted you *can* make arrangements to remain where you are if the Foreign Office desire it. . . .

But evidently Hornby became difficult again and probably uncooperative about the plan for moving in closer to Constantinople, for on December 24th Salisbury wrote to Smith: 'A month ago I told Shouvaloff you were going back to Ismid. The Russians have no sort of right to stay where they are: & there is no reason that you should be squeamish. . . .'

In fact Hornby had sent in to the Admiralty a new list of complaints about what he called 'a nasty system', of which Admiral Wellesley, the First Sea Lord, in a note to Smith (December 31st) remarked: 'If an officer holding the position he has during the critical events of the past year is not able to see the necessity of deviating in certain circumstances from the usual routine I do not think any reasoning would do any good. I confess I have a high opinion of Hornby's skill in manoeuvring but not quite so much in his judgment by common sense.'

Smith wrote a letter to his *enfant terrible* which was a model of firmness coupled with forbearance and magnanimity (January 1st, 1879):

... I am very sorry indeed that you should have failed to see the cordial intention expressed and implied in our acts—and I must say I think you have not been successful in placing the right interpretation upon them, but that will not prevent me from communicating as frankly in the future as in the past in order to secure the complete understanding which ought to exist between us. I will not pursue the subject further.

Meanwhile the First Lord was not to escape his seemingly endless troubles with the Queen and the Royal Family. First, on December 14th, 1878, Princess Alice of Hesse, the Queen's favourite daughter, died of diphtheria at Darmstadt, and Smith was informed by General Ponsonby that 'the Queen is a little distressed that the Admiralty with the best intentions should have sent out the melancholy news to the Duke of Edinburgh . . . as she wished to tell him first'. However, in the event it transpired that the letter which the Queen had sent by special messenger did reach the Duke before the Admiralty's message—so Smith was exonerated.

Barely a week later (December 20th) the Prime Minister was writing that the Queen was 'most anxious' to see the Duke of Edinburgh promoted to rear-admiral before his ship was paid off. Then, when Smith had hastened to prepare the necessary Order in Council, the Queen was asking that the Duke, as Admiral, should take precedence of the other officers to be promoted to that rank— and presumably her wishes were again respected. Hard on this again came worried communications from the Prince of Wales about the lack of progress of his two young sons, Prince Albert Victor[1] and Prince George,[2] who were undergoing naval training in the training-ship *Britannia* and were not expected to pass their examinations.

Then in February the First Lord had a lively discussion with the Queen on the subject of seamen's dress. British naval ratings were then wearing the round, broad-brimmed straw hats—usually placed well on the back of the head. Ponsonby told Smith (February 17th) that 'Her Majesty does not like the fashion of the seaman's White and Black Hats—the Brim which is intended to shade the face becomes more turned up every year and it is now worn in such a manner that it has ceased to be of use'. But when Smith suggested 'it would be a very popular thing in the Service if the Queen approved it, to do away with the hat altogether' and substitute a 'blue cap', he was told that 'Her Majesty does not like giving up the hat. She thinks a smaller brim might be preferable . . .'.

Early in the new year 1879, an event of great personal significance to Smith and his wife took place, when his stepdaughter, Mary Auber Leach, married his Private Secretary at the Admiralty, Captain Codrington. Smith was delighted as he both liked and respected Codrington and had always cherished Mary Auber as if she had been his own daughter. Unfortunately Codrington did not enjoy good health and the marriage was cut short by his death after ten years.

By March 1879 there were at last more positive signs of an end to the deadlock in the Near East, for on the tenth of that month Smith received the following from Salisbury:

The telegrams for which we were waiting have arrived from Dufferin[3]: and the fleet may now be withdrawn. I have spoken to the Prime

---

[1] Created Duke of Clarence, 1890. Died 1892.

[2] Later King George V.

[3] Earl (later Marquess) of Dufferin and Ava, British Ambassador to the Emperor of Russia.

Minister who fully agrees. We will send you an official instruction:
Dufferin will be instructed to inform Emperor tomorrow. The order,
therefore, should be given at once.

Soon after this it was learned that the Sultan had entertained the
Admiral and Captains of the British Fleet to a banquet at Constantinople—presumably to celebrate and give thanks to his protectors
for his deliverance from the Russian peril.

Yet, despite these signs and portents, even two months later the wily
Russians were still inclined to take any opportunity to protract the
process of evacuation, for Salisbury wrote again to Smith (May 12th):

> There is no doubt that Dufferin's threat that the Fleets would move if
> there was any attempt to return to E. Roumelia, or to prolong the
> occupation, had a powerful effect during the recent negotiations. If
> they should show signs of lagging the neighbourhood of the fleet
> might have a stimulating effect. Could you defer your cruising opera-
> tions till the end of June?

By August Beaconsfield was able to boast that 'not a single
Russian soldier remains in the Sultan's dominions';[1] but even after
yet another two months had elapsed the Government showed no
inclination to drop their guard, as is evident from the following from
Salisbury to Smith (October 29th):

> I think the arrangements you propose will quite suffice. There is no
> reason the 'Rupert' should *stay* at Alexandria: but it has decidedly a
> valuable effect if she can occasionally look in. I do not at present sus-
> pect any intention on the part of Russia of an attack on Constantinople.

But, while the major war-scare receded there grew a tendency to
inquire critically into the cost of the great defensive preparations
which it had necessitated—and particularly into the cost and conduct
of the other two minor wars in which the Government had become
involved against the Afghans and the Zulus. Northcote, Chancellor
of the Exchequer, whose friendship with Smith had become close and
who greatly respected the latter's business acumen, took him into
his confidence over his Budget proposals. The figures and calculations thus disclosed appear endearingly tame and neat beside those
of today. On March 26th, 1879, he wrote Smith:

> . . . I should like to know what you think of this scheme:
> Estimated Revenue (now) £83,000,000
> „ Expenditure (ordinary) £81,700,000
> _____
> Surplus £1,300,000
> Calculate on the Zulu War costing first and last, £3,000,000; of which

---

[1] Beaconsfield to Lord Lytton. August 14th, 1879. See Buckle VI, 475.

£1,500,000 has already been provided. Therefore £1,500,000 wanted for 1879/80; leaving us in a deficiency of £200,000. Raise this by readjusting the scale of the Probate duties so as to make them bear equally on small and large properties. . . .

Don't touch Succession Duty, House duty, Receipt stamps or any other. And don't raise tea duty. . . .

Smith's reply (March 29th) shows him as an accurate prophet as well as a very realistic businessman.

I should like more taxation and I am sorry our colleagues decline to face an increase in the Succession duties. It will come and be all the more severe in reaction from the comparative immunity which land now enjoys. However the decision is taken and there is no use going back upon it.

. . . there is very much to be said in favour of any arrangement which would give the Country breathing time just in the very crisis of its commercial existence.

Probate and Succession duties do not affect trade or at most very indirectly, but Customs, Excise and Stamps do, and it would be very valuable indeed to show that no change would be made and that none was necessary.

When the Budget was presented the Government came under heavy fire from the Liberal Opposition regarding the big increase in the national expenditure as being the direct outcome of their foreign policy. Goschen,[1] who had been First Lord of the Admiralty in Gladstone's preceding government and, incidentally, whose refusal to reduce estimates had been largely responsible for its dissolution in 1874, asked Smith for a 'return' of all naval ships built, building, commissioned or scrapped under his administration of the Admiralty and was rather offensive about the manner of the production of the document, complaining that '. . . Your advisers and servants are to draw up not only your brief but ours . . .'. This was the first of a number of brushes which the two men were to have: despite a superficial similarity of type there was some fundamental antipathy. Nevertheless, Smith replied suavely (April 7th): 'I cannot agree with you that the information we shall give will be vague. We shall answer the question "how disposed of" by showing in brief the history of *every* ship for the time and I think it can be done fairly and without immense labour.'

A Radical, Peter Rylands, M.P. for Burnley, had tabled a resolution 'that the taxes required to meet the present expenditure impede

---

[1] George Joachim Goschen (later 1st Viscount Goschen) became estranged from Gladstone and with Lord Hartington founded Liberal Unionist Party, 1886. Joined Salisbury's Unionist Government as Chancellor of Exchequer after fall of Lord R. Churchill in January 1887.

the operations of agriculture and manufactures, and diminish the funds for the employment of labour in all branches of productive industry, thereby tending to produce pauperism and crime and adding to the local and general burdens of the people'. But in his speech in the debate, Goschen assumed a more statesmanlike attitude and declared that 'he regretted the burdens that were imposed upon the people; but he did not feel clear that it would be wise on the part of the House in the face of Europe, which was watching how we bore our commercial depression and warlike enterprises, to put such a resolution on the journal of the House'. Smith, in defending the Government's policy said that 'every step that involved expense, every step through long-continued negotiations, had been taken with the firm object and the sole desire of securing an honorable peace'.

The Prince of Wales's anxiety about the lack of progress of his two young sons in their naval training now led him to consult the First Lord about a plan for sending them on a long cruise of several months in a ship of war. Smith put the proposal before the Cabinet— with dire results. He reported back to the Prince (May 2nd) that 'after grave consideration it was felt that there was very serious objection to the two Princes being at sea in the same ship, for a period of six or seven months'. The Prince was furious. '. . . I thought it was clearly understood', he wrote (May 3rd), 'that the matter would only be discussed confidentially with your Board—but never for one moment anticipated that you would bring the matter before the Cabinet which is greatly to be deplored—as I was naturally anxious to bring the matter first before the Queen and obtain her sanction—and also consult Lord Beaconsfield on the subject. I am now placed in a very awkward position. . . .'

Smith wrote off the same day apologizing profusely. '. . . It did not appear to me to be possible to take any step in so grave a matter without the knowledge of Lord Beaconsfield and the Cabinet. I trust Your Royal Highness will speak to Ld. Beaconsfield. He will, I am sure, satisfy you that no other course was open to me. . . .' And, sure enough, the Prime Minister loyally backed him up. But the Queen had consulted the young Princes' tutor, Mr. Dalton, whose opinion she respected, and he had persuaded her to disregard the Ministers' objections.[1] So when Beaconsfield returned to the charge (May 19th) repeating the obvious risks and objections connected with the plan, the Queen for once smartly snubbed her beloved Prime Minister, telegraphing back the same day: 'I entirely approve the plan for my Grandsons going, which ought never to have been brought before

[1] See *Letters of Queen Victoria*, 2nd Series, Vol. III, p. 22. Also Sir George Arthur: *Concerning Queen Victoria and Her Son*, p. 192.

the Cabinet. The Prince of Wales only mentioned it to Mr. Smith, and was with right extremely annoyed at his doing so. Such a thing was never done when the Prince of Wales and Prince Alfred went long voyages.'

Beaconsfield then quickly climbed down and to cover his confusion blamed the 'inexperience' of poor Smith (May 20th). 'He most deeply apologises. . . . The fact is, it was brought under his notice at the end of a long and exhausting Cabinet. . . . Had the matter been originally brought before his notice, he should, he hopes, have given it more thought, and acted with more discretion. He takes the whole blame upon himself and trusts your Majesty will not be angry with Mr. Smith, who is inexperienced and ought to have been better guided by Lord Beaconsfield. . . . Lord Beaconsfield will now withdraw the subject from the consideration of Ministers. It grieves him much', he concluded artfully, 'and yet he must congratulate the Empress of India on the triumphant conclusion of the Afghan war.'[1]

Meanwhile Ponsonby had written Smith to express the Queen's hope that the command of *Bacchante*, the ship chosen for the Princes' cruise, might be given to a certain naval officer. Smith replied rather wryly that he did not even know that the cruise had been decided on—'I am not aware what the result has been of the communications which have passed between the Queen and the Prince of Wales and the Prime Minister'; but added that it would be 'both my duty and my pleasure to give every effect to the Queen's wishes as far as it is possible to do so'.

A little later, the Duke of Cambridge,[2] who from now on, whenever Smith was in office, was to badger him for favours for his sons, was asking him to get the command of the *Bacchante* for his son, Commander FitzGeorge. But Smith was able to reply that the Prince of Wales had insisted on selecting the officers for the cruise and had given the command to Lord Charles Montagu-Douglas-Scott.[3] And at last, on August 3rd, he could write to the Prince of Wales that the two young Princes would be appointed as midshipmen to the *Bacchante*, that a compromise had been arranged regarding their exact placing in the Navy List, and that they had 'been awarded 3 months for seamanship and 3 months for conduct'. The Prince of Wales was delighted with this arrangement and wrote Smith a very gracious letter.

In the early autumn of 1879 the First Lord went on one of his periodic tours of naval dockyards and other establishments. To his

---

[1] *Letters of Queen Victoria*, 2nd Series, Vol. III, p. 25.
[2] George, 2nd Duke of Cambridge, Commander-in-Chief of Army, 1856–95.
[3] Captain, R.N.; son of 5th Duke of Buccleuch.

wife, as usual, he wrote daily, and especially on the occasion of her birthday his devotion shone out as brightly as ever (September 22nd):

My precious wife,
   Your birthday letter came on board last evening and I read it in the intervals of dinner with all the enjoyment which comes to snatches of pleasure. It is a blessing that we know we have each other's entire love. I wish I could have been at home to see the Children and the Children's presents. . . .

It was not, of course, to be expected that the Duke of Edinburgh would remain for long without bringing his affairs to the fore. Having become an Admiral, his current ambition was to have some kind of responsible office at the Admiralty or some place high up in the hierarchy on shore. Smith, as First Lord, suggested for him the post of Admiral Superintendent of Naval Reserves; but, before accepting it, and despite some strong advice to the contrary, the Duke took the extraordinary step of consulting a group of his brother officers as to his best future course. As a result of this he came to the conclusion that 'it would be impossible for me to undertake these duties as they stand at present without risk of failure', as he wrote to Beaconsfield (July 21st).

The Duke accordingly enclosed a proposal which really amounted to his being firmly propped up by a highly qualified deputy whose efficiency would obviate the much-feared 'risk of failure'. For Beaconsfield wrote to Smith that 'it appears to offer a solution of a painful difficulty. . . .Although myself entirely opposed to the Prince taking any office, a great part of which would be performed by deputy, I am still keenly alive to the importance of H.R.H., who is a competent & able officer, being actively employed in the public service. . . .'

Smith accordingly wrote to the Duke (October 27th) that, having obtained the Queen's approval and found a certain captain of 'very senior rank' to act as assistant to the Duke, nothing now stood in the way of the latter's appointment as Admiral Superintendent of Naval Reserves. Characteristically the Duke at first objected to the officer chosen—though he later acquiesced—and then claimed a 'house-allowance' of £200 per annum which had been granted to his predecessor or else a 'table allowance' for the whole year. He argued, perhaps a trifle disingenuously, that if he did not claim these he would be prejudicing 'the interests of my brother officers . . . who may succeed me'.

But Smith adroitly scotched this suggestion (November 13th):

I am sure everyone will appreciate the generous sentiments Y.R.H. entertains for the interests of the officers of the service, but is my duty to protect Y.R.H. from the misapprehension which would arise if any increase was made in the allowances of the Adml. Supt. during the time of Y.R.H.'s appt. . . . and it wd place Y.R.H. in a false position if, when it was explained that the whole time of the Adml. Supt. could not be devoted to the special duties of his command, any increase of table money was asked for.

The Government had been trying for a long time to reframe the law governing military discipline and finally, in this year 1879, introduced an Army Discipline Bill. Under pressure from the Radicals, led by Joseph Chamberlain, particular attention became focused on the question of flogging. Cardwell, the great military reformer of the previous government, had abolished flogging in the Army in peacetime, but not for offences on active service. The present Secretary for War, Col. Stanley, declared himself anxious to see it abolished altogether, but said he had been advised by military experts that discipline could not be maintained without it.

Smith's own views on this question are unfortunately not on record and in any case the Navy was not directly affected by the present Bill, but it is evident from an interesting letter to Smith from Colonel Stanley (July 5th) that it was regarded by his colleagues purely as a matter of party political expediency.

> . . . I have had a long & interesting talk with Lord B[eaconsfield] & since that have seen Salisbury & the Duke [of Cambridge] respectively.—The position is this.—Both Lord B. & Lord S. have no objection abstractedly to giving up corporal punishment, but they think that our giving way may break up the party.
>
> Lord B. is not strong on this point but thought that difficulties with the Duke would be insuperable.—Salisbury on the contrary cares little for the latter, but says that for party's sake, there must be no appearance of concession & is kind enough to advise that we should fight the bill through by physical force, which I only wish he had to do himself & I told him so.
>
> The Duke . . . says that as matters have gone so far he is quite willing to suggest to us to give up flogging altogether provided that we may use such means for enforcing discipline as exist in foreign armies. I think the solution is this, *if* the party & Cabinet will not give up flogging altogether—
>
> Restrict it for crimes for which death can now be awarded & when sentences pronounced allow death to be commuted for flogging if the officer thinks fit & if the man prefers it.
>
> For minor offences where we now flog on Service use the German putting in irons etc.
>
> How can 'humanitarians' object to this?—& yet does it not bear out my promise of a statement which should be satisfactory?

The Government, as is plain from the above, had not made their own views and intentions plain enough on introducing the Bill and

Stanley was consequently subjected to a considerable amount of browbeating by the Opposition. Battle raged round the number of lashes and the actual form of the 'cat'. Smith having said that there was a sealed pattern of the regulation 'cat' for the Navy deposited at the Admiralty, members demanded to see specimens of all 'cats' in use and eventually four were exhibited at the House—the 'approved Navy cat', the disused Navy 'cat', the Marine 'cat' and the Prisons 'cat'.

It was during the debate on this Bill that a section of the Irish members, at the instigation of their future leader Parnell, began those obstructionist tactics which were to be the bane of governments—both Conservative and Liberal—for the next decade. The Bill was not finally passed before it had occupied 23 sittings from the time of its passing into Committee and, when it was, despite all the sound and the fury, the lash was still retained.[1] But it is interesting to note from a newspaper clipping among Smith's papers that at this time a Captain Verney, Liberal candidate for Portsmouth, convened a meeting of seamen and petty officers to ask them their views on flogging and that after he had spoken in favour of abolition 'several seamen addressed the meeting, some in support and some against the continuation of flogging'.

Meanwhile, Northcote was getting worried again about his next Budget and hearing that—on top of the Duke of Edinburgh's expensive deputy—Smith was proposing to increase the establishment of Naval sub-lieutenants by 1,000, he wrote to expostulate, concluding '... I must tax somebody or something. As regards H.R.H. I suppose you could not help yourself'. Also Sir Ralph Lingen,[2] chairman of a Committee of Inquiry into Admiralty Reorganization, added his reproof about the Duke's '*extra* Captain' being 'not very defensible'. In addition to these pin-pricks, as the realization grew that the Committee's proposals would involve drastic reductions in staff, the First Lord began to be badgered by the influential friends of likely victims of the axe. Most of these importuners he turned firmly, but urbanely, away. On the other hand, when he became aware that one officer retired under the scheme was suffering acute hardship owing to delay on the Treasury's part in paying out his gratuity and pension, he immediately lent him £200 out of his own pocket.

His more general philanthropic instincts also remained as alive as ever. For at this time he gave £1,000 into the hands of the First Commissioner of Works 'towards laying out the vacant ground to the south of the New Palace of Westminster' as a public recreation

---

[1] Until its total abolition for the Army under the Army Discipline Act, 1881, and for the Navy under the Navy Discipline Act of 1884.

[2] Permanent Secretary to Treasury, 1869–85; created Lord Lingen, 1885.

ground. 'I acknowledge', he wrote, 'to a morbid desire to prevent open spaces being built upon in the vicinity of great public buildings and in a densely populated district.'

Smith had retired from active partnership in the running of the family business as soon as he entered the Cabinet in 1877 and he felt that others in that situation should do the same. Writing to Salisbury (November 29th) about such a case he was uncompromising:

> . . . I think a Civil Servant holding a very responsible position in the Public Service cannot also serve a Company or a body of Share-holders. I do not understand the difference between public and private time. If a man does not think of his work except when he is in his Office, he does not rise to my conception of what a good Public Servant should be.
>
> The attempt to serve two Masters must dilute the quality of the work given to both.

The fact that—quite apart from its waning popularity through its association in the public mind with dubious foreign wars and with the current economic depression—the Government was approaching the term of its natural life, caused the usual intensification of activity on the part of the Opposition. Gladstone, who, after his defeat in 1874, had given it to be understood that he had retired from politics, had recently re-emerged from the wings like a giant refreshed. Renouncing all intention of standing again for his former seat, Greenwich, he took the field against one of the doughtiest Tories of the North by contesting the seat of the Earl of Dalkeith, eldest son of the Duke of Buccleuch. In November 1879, therefore, he set out on the first of those electioneering exploits which came to be known as the Midlothian Campaigns.

Lady Dalkeith, who had written to thank Smith for a personal kindness, gives an amusing glimpse of the scene as the campaign opened (November 24th):

> . . . Gladstone arrives in Edinburgh this afternoon and drives in a carriage & four to Dalmeny where he remains as Lord Rosebery's guest during the whole of his stay in the County. On his way north he is to have his wardrobe replenished by various gifts of clothing of Scotch manufacture, but happily it is raining cats & dogs, so that a gift from the Clan Mackintosh would be the most appropriate present today. The Liberals are doing all in their power to organize great demonstrations wherever he appears, especially on the occasion of his visit to this town [Dalkeith] on Wednesday.

Meanwhile, the Afghan situation—which had taken a disastrous turn with the massacre of the British mission in September—having been got under control again by General Roberts,[1] Beaconsfield and Salisbury pressed on undeterred with their imperial schemes and the 'containment' of Russia. These involved a rather dubious bargain with the Shah of Persia which frightened even the Queen, not to mention the sedate Northcote, who, as Chancellor of the Exchequer, would be naturally disinclined anyway towards any increase of British responsibilities and liabilities, and who wrote to Smith (November 24th) about 'never having liked the "forward policy" '.

Nevertheless, Salisbury's vigilant eye roved over the remotest outposts of the world, where the Great Powers were beginning to jockey for position in the attempt to carve out spheres of influence for themselves, and never lost a moment in staking his own country's claims. Thus he wrote to Smith (December 30th):

> Munster[2] proposes that the three Powers Germany England and America should recognize Malietoa the de facto King of Samoa & protect him for the present with a man of war each. . . . It seems to me reasonable & as having the advantage of preventing isolated action on the part of the other Powers. If we refuse to act with them— it is obvious Germany will act alone. Have you a vessel in those parts to send? & do you see any objection to sending it?

Smith evidently did not share Northcote's dislike of the 'forward policy' for he replied promptly (December 31st): 'I do not anticipate any difficulty in sending a ship to Samoa within a few days and I quite concur with you as to the course you propose to take.'

Genuinely as Beaconsfield admired Smith's judgment and his handling of the Admiralty, he tended, as we have seen, when put under pressure by august or difficult people, to ascribe any *désagrément* they might have suffered at the First Lord's hands to the latter's 'inexperience'. Thus, when Smith passed over a certain Admiral Sir William Loring for a command and the latter wrote to complain to the Prime Minister, Beaconsfield wrote Smith one of his few unmitigatedly pompous and patronizing letters (January 6th, 1880) referring to his own greater experience of public life and warning him against the professional prejudices of his naval advisers. '. . . They are, themselves, too much, & too personally interested in such matters; & you are placed by the Queen in the position wh. you now fill to control the jealousies that are common to all professions, & from which, I regret to say, the Royal Navy is not exempt.'

But Smith was not the man to retreat from a conscientiously made decision—even when challenged by such a venerable chief—and he defended himself with spirit and refreshing simplicity:

[1] Later Field Marshal Earl Roberts of Kandahar, V.C., K.G., Commander-in-Chief of British Army, 1900–5.
[2] Count Munster, German Ambassador in London.

. . . Sir W. did not get a command from Mr. Goschen or Mr. Hunt and I have not met with a single officer who thinks he was improperly passed over. He has repeatedly applied to me and in making my refusal as little disagreeable as possible I have referred to my Naval advisers in the hope that he would see the opinion of the entire service was against him.

He complains that if he is not employed he will have to retire, but that is the principle and intention of the existing regulations. . . .

In February the Duke of Edinburgh was once again on the war-path, trying to get the Cork (Queenstown) Command for his relative the Prince of Leiningen,[1] who was also an officer in the Royal Navy. But Smith managed to persuade the Queen that there would be a public outcry if any more Home Commands were given to members of the Royal Family. Moreover, the Prince himself evinced less enthusiasm for the post when he learned that it would entail residence in Ireland for 46 weeks out of the 52—and possibly no leave owing to the unsettled state of that country.

Strangely enough, however, the sufferings of Ireland provided for a time a means of self-realization for the fretful Duke of Edinburgh and a harmonious rounding-off of the long and exasperating relations between him and Smith. For he was sent, shortly before the end of Smith's tenure of the Admiralty, to take charge of the organization of the transport of stores for the relief of distress on the West Coast of Ireland. Owing to the existence of many separate local relief committees, as well as American ones, it was a difficult assignment; but the Duke appears to have handled it with tact and aplomb. He wrote a full account of it in a private letter to Smith, which clearly reveals that the occasional tributes as to his professional competence were not merely formal ones. '. . . I have found myself gradually, by special requests on their part [i.e. the local committees], directing the whole relief on the West Coast. . . . The work is most interesting & instructive & I take great pleasure in it.' Smith wrote back warmly and generously—especially after receiving a special letter of congratulation on the Duke's work from the Viceroy, the Duke of Marlborough.[2]

Another who deserved the gratitude of the stricken Irish at this time was that remarkable woman, Baroness Burdett-Coutts,[3] whose

[1] Son of the Queen's half-brother. The first marriage of the Queen's mother, the Duchess of Kent, had been to a Prince of Leiningen.

[2] John Winston Spencer, 7th Duke of Marlborough. Viceroy of Ireland, 1876–80.

[3] Angela Georgina, daughter of Sir Francis Burdett, M.P. Westminster, 1807–37 early champion of parliamentary reform; granddaughter through her mother of Thomas Coutts, the banker. Created Baroness, 1871; married William Lehman Ashmead-Bartlett, 1881.

immense wealth and passionate desire to use it for the succour of suffering humanity both surpassed even Smith's. She had a great admiration for him, however, and though this was in great measure reciprocated by him, he found her lengthy letters and continual requests for advice on all subjects something of a trial. Now she came forward with a munificent scheme for the relief of Irish distress, which she asked him to put before the Cabinet. This, recapitulated by Smith in his reply (February 8th, 1880), was no less than 'a gift of a sum not to exceed £250,000 to be applied in the first instance to the purchase of seed for destitute tenants in the distressed districts of Ireland, and repayment being obtained after the harvest, to be then applied in relieving these poor people from the debts by which they are oppressed'.

As it happened, however, the Government were already in course of contemplating an exactly similar scheme, and so the Baroness's appears to have been shelved; though unfortunately and quite perversely all their relief measures were persistently obstructed in the House of Commons by the Parnellite members.[1]

With the final disappearance of the Russian threat Admiral Hornby relinquished the Mediterranean Command, and, despite their occasionally strained relations, Smith wrote with the utmost warmth and friendliness to the man with whom he had been in daily, even hourly contact at the height of the crisis two years earlier.

> Admiralty,
> Whitehall.
> March 6th 1880.

My dear Admiral,

I must say one word to you in parting from you in our official relationship—to say how much obliged I am for all the support and assistance you have given me. The times were very anxious and difficult and I had to make large demands on your patience in preparing for the unforeseen.

I cannot be too thankful that the actual strain of war did not break upon us, but neither the Government nor I had any concern that the best use would not be made of the forces at your command—if the storm broke. . . .

. . . And now I will say Goodbye—once more thanking you heartily for all the good work you have done and for the good understanding between us.

[1] Although in justice to the memory of Baroness Burdett-Coutts, it should be remembered that many of her schemes for the relief of Irish distress were fully realized. Since 1863 she had been paying for the passage of countless Irish emigrants to Canada. She also revived the fishing industry at Baltimore, Co. Cork, where she set up a fishery training school in 1887. This apart from her countless good works in England and elsewhere.

We shall be very glad to welcome you in England, but if you propose to stay with Lady Hornby in Italy, as I hear, the Election will be over and I may not be found in this place.

Yours very sincerely,
W. H. Smith

But perhaps the best memorial to Smith's administration of the Admiralty is to be found in a letter of his—written after he had left office (May 2nd, 1880)—to one Charles Kempe, an Admiralty clerk, who had written to him complaining of having been forced out of his job by the Reorganization Scheme and of having been shown scant gratitude for his long services. Despite the man's bitter tone of recrimination Smith took the pains to answer at considerable length and with a kindness and humility which, in the circumstances, can seldom have been equalled.

... I had no wish to give you pain, or any other of the principal clerks. ... I am sorry I did not see more of your work when I was at the Admiralty, but I was very fully employed and although I was always ready to see gentlemen who had anything to say to me, I never sent for them unless I wished for information.

If there has been any want of appreciation on my part either of your abilities or services or claims, I am very sorry for it indeed. .... For all that you did to help me and to discharge the duties of your post, I thank you very heartily.

I thought it my duty to act as I did—entirely ignoring all personal considerations and looking simply & solely to what appeared to me to be the good of the service. I have very likely been mistaken in some things. It is not given to man to be always right, but I have endeavoured to be so, as far as I could—very often at a great personal sacrifice of feeling.

VII

IN OPPOSITION: FIRST PHASE

————————◆╪◆————————

W HEN Parliament reassembled on February 5th, 1880, the
dominating topic of debate had been Ireland, where, at the
instigation of the recently founded Land League, the recent bad
harvests had been made the pretext for the withholding of rent, and a
great intensification of the agitation for Home Rule had begun. Even
the Government's relief measures were being impeded, as already
noted. They had proposed advancing money on easy terms out of the
Irish Church temporalities through various local authorities to enable
the latter to employ the distressed and needy. But their proposal
had been violently attacked by the Home Rulers as being an indirect
method of favouring the landowners.

In the Debate on the Address, Smith strongly defended the
Government's proposals and reiterated the view which he had so
often expressed in regard to the evil effects of indiscriminate outdoor
relief, whether in Ireland or elsewhere. 'We are here in presence of a
much more serious matter than anything which can happen to a
political party,' he said, '. . . and that is to care for those poor people
in the manner which will afford relief with the least demoralizing
effects to those distressed fellow-subjects. . . .'

But, despite the ominous outlook in Ireland and the persistent
obstruction of the Home Rulers at Westminster, the Government
were not at this juncture by any means disheartened about their
prospects in the approaching general election. On the contrary, two
resounding victories in by-elections at Liverpool and Southwark
inclined them to feel that they could take their time for going to the
country—and that when they did the issue would be in little doubt.
Nevertheless, on account of the obstruction in Parliament and the
urgent need to strengthen the Speaker's hands to deal with it, if
various important measures were ever to be carried, the Government
became more and more inclined in the ensuing weeks to lose no time
in seeking a fresh mandate from the electorate.

Thus it was that the announcement, on March 8th, that Parliament was to be dissolved forthwith, appeared to the general public to come with disturbing suddenness. Moreover, the method employed was unusual, for the news was contained in a manifesto, which in turn was in the form of a letter from the Prime Minister to the Viceroy of Ireland, laying very heavy—and, many thought, exaggerated—stress on the gravity of the Irish situation and on the threat which this held for the integrity of the United Kingdom and the Empire. A part of it which was particularly resented and ridiculed by those affected was that which hinted at complicity between the Liberal leaders and the Home Rulers.

However, that optimism was still high in Government circles is evidenced by Smith writing to his sister Augusta (March 12th): 'I think we shall do pretty well at the Elections and if we do not I shall have rest which will go a long way towards compensating for defeat.' Meanwhile he busied himself with his electoral address to his constituents, but with his usual diffidence he sent it for approval to his colleague, Richard Assheton Cross, the Home Secretary. 'Will you criticise and correct this draft. I never felt so much difficulty; but I never wrote before as a member of the Government. . . .' Cross replied: 'I did not look at your address till I had written my own, which I will shew you tonight. I see no objection to yours.'

But, on the eve of battle, the outlook began to darken for the Conservatives. Lord Derby, who, though he had openly dissented from the Government's foreign policy for some time past, was still reckoned one of the leading and most influential Conservatives, now finally broke his connection with them and went over to the Liberals. Coming at this moment this was a heavy blow to the party and to his former colleagues—and a particularly bitter one to Beaconsfield, who from the beginning had been the mentor of his old colleague's son.

Fortified by this unexpected accession of strength, Gladstone now set forth upon his second Midlothian Campaign and, amid tumultuous scenes of enthusiasm, represented the election as a great state trial at which the electors would have to bring in verdicts of 'Guilty' against Beaconsfield and his late Government. Meanwhile Beaconsfield waited disconsolately at Hatfield, which Salisbury had put at his disposal for the election period, whilst Salisbury himself recuperated from a recent illness in the South of France. The fact that both these great party leaders were precluded, through being peers, from speaking and participating in the campaign increased the sense of doom and impotence.

General elections were spread over a couple of weeks in those days; but with the results of the first few days the outcome was clearly foreseeable. Northcote wrote to Smith (April 4th):

The state of affairs is gloomy enough and I don't feel sure we have seen the worst yet. . . . I don't feel cast down. We have been over-whelmed before and have recovered from it; and there will be plenty of work for us in Opposition. But I am very sorry for the Chief. There is much to mortify him in this personal triumph of Gladstone's at what he must feel to be the end of his political career. He may count, I think, on a reaction in his favour; but he will hardly again take office. . . .

Smith's solicitor and friend, William Ford, wrote (April 16th) that: '. . . It is marvellous the influence the name of that man [Gladstone] has had as a popular word in every City and Borough. Even in Conservative meetings the mention of his name elicited cheers not faint but loud and deep. I was struck with this when Sir Chas. Russell was with ill-judged persistency reiterating the name. . . .' Sir Charles Russell was, as already noted, Smith's col-league as second Conservative candidate for the representation of Westminster. Despite his alleged lack of discretion, both he and Smith were returned by sizeable majorities over their Liberal op-ponents, John Morley[1] and Sir Arthur Hobhouse.[2] Nevertheless, the prevailing Liberal reaction reduced Smith's original majority, in 1874, of 5,522 to 2,529.

But, hard upon this success, poor Smith found himself picked by the Prime Minister to go at once to Baden Baden to attend the Queen who had gone thither for the confirmation of her two mother-less grandchildren and who had demanded the instant despatch of a Cabinet Minister to keep her in touch with current affairs. To his wife he wrote (April 1st):

Is not this dreadful? It is nearly the last straw. I suppose it is very kind of the Queen, but I don't quite feel it under present circumstances. I have however sent down to Corry to know if an ornamental Peer cannot be sent in my place and pleading how hard it is to be chivvied away in this manner.

. . . I have received some very pleasant congratulations as far as I am personally concerned but there are terrible regrets all round at the slaughter of our friends and the probable consequent fall of the Government.

He was spared the Baden Baden assignment. 'I hope the Queen herself is not aware I was asked to go and begged off', he wrote nervously to his wife (April 2nd). 'The Elections are all going against us . . . it is just like a tidal wave, appears to be rising higher and

[1] The prominent Liberal Statesman and author of the *Life of Gladstone*. Created Viscount Morley, 1908.
[2] Q.C., K.C.S.I.; Law Member of Council of Viceroy of India, 1872–7. Created Lord Hobhouse, 1885.

sweeping everything before it'. but added philosophically, 'there is great compensation in the hope of seeing more of one's wife and children than has lately been possible.'

Everyone seemed dumbfounded by the Election result. Admiral Wellesley wrote (April 29th):

> ... the past month seems like a strange dream and one is almost tempted to rub one's eyes to feel sure that this strange bouleversement is a real fact. I suppose the old proverb that if dirt enough is thrown some of it is bound to stick has been the principal cause of mischief, but I am afraid it does not say much for the intelligence of the masses that they should have been so easily led astray and if we are to have the County franchise lowered I do not see how the Conservatives are ever to come into power again. . . .

More perceptively, Sir Edward Clarke—who had been the victor in the Southwark by-election in January and who now found himself defeated—wrote (April 7th) that 'the Liberal majority of 1880 has been got together by its leaders deliberately setting aside all questions of policy and confining their programme to the overthrow of a Ministry' and that 'when the object of its construction has been effected, the inevitable process of disintegration must begin'.

This compares with a conversation at this time (recorded by Sir Herbert Maxwell[1]) between Beaconsfield and Smith in which the former forecast the difficulties in store for the victorious Liberals. He thought, rightly, that they would first try hard to avoid coercion for Ireland, but would soon be forced in self-defence to adopt it—'in which case the Irish party and the extreme Radicals will coalesce and form a strong split. That will be the beginning of the disintegration of parties, and of course it will become the duty of Conservatives to support the Government in any moderate measure . . .'.

In making these prophecies Beaconsfield was assuming that Hartington[2] would become the new Premier, and, indeed, on his advice, the Queen did send for Hartington. However, under pressure from both the latter and Lord Granville[3] she finally and reluctantly agreed to send for Gladstone, who became Prime Minister for the second time. For the old and ailing 'Dizzy' it was the end of his career, as Northcote had remarked. But for Smith it was only the end of a chapter, upon which he looked back with mingled feelings of regret and satisfaction. To Admiral Sir Beauchamp Seymour, who

[1] Maxwell, II, 31–2.

[2] Spencer Compton, Marquess of Hartington (later 8th Duke of Devonshire); Secretary of State for India, 1880–2 and for War, 1882–5; Lord President of the Council, 1895–1903.

[3] Granville George, 2nd Earl Granville; Secretary of State for Foreign Affairs 1870–4 and 1880–5; Lord Warden of Cinque Ports.

had just taken over the Mediterranean Command from Hornby, he wrote:

> ... In a few days I shall have to make way for a successor at the Admiralty and I hope I am not expressing too great confidence in our Administration in saying we leave the Navy a great deal stronger than we found it. I shall be sorry to go because I really like the Service very much indeed, and it is a pleasure to work with men, who, taking them all round, have generally had one object in view, and that is their duty.

On April 29th, 1880, he formally handed over his office to the new First Lord, Lord Northbrook.[1]

From the very first day the new Government and the new Parliament ran into difficulties which seemed to justify the prophecies, already noted, regarding an 'inevitable process of disintegration'. Charles Bradlaugh,[2] self-professed atheist and republican, who refused to take the oath on taking his seat in Parliament, typified the extremist elements with whom Gladstone had obliged the moderate Liberals and aristocratic Whigs to make common cause to bring down Beaconsfield's 'Jingoes'. In fact Gladstone's Cabinet was hamstrung from the first through the inability of Whigs and Radicals to work together and through the revulsion of the former against the measures which Gladstone thought fit to introduce for the pacification of Ireland.

For the Queen's Speech at the opening of the new Parliament had announced that the Coercion statute passed by the Conservatives would not be renewed and that the Liberal Government hoped to govern Ireland by the ordinary law (just as Beaconsfield had predicted). But if there was to be any hope of this, the first and most pressing task was to relieve the terrible distress arising from the wholesale eviction of tenants who had been unable through the crop failures to pay their rent. Yet, only after the Irish Party had attemped to introduce a Bill to give the evicted tenants compensation did the Government introduce a similar measure of their own.

This Land Bill, which sought to compel Irish landlords to compensate evicted tenants, naturally horrified the Whig section of the Liberal party, which comprised many Irish landowners in both Houses. In the Commons 20 Liberals voted against and many more abstained—though the Bill was forced through by 299 votes to 217.

---

[1] Thomas George Baring, 1st Earl of (2nd Baron) Northbrook; Viceroy of India, 1872–6.

[2] Elected M.P. for Northampton 1880; unseated, but re-elected 1881; expelled and re-elected 1882 and again in 1883 and 1884. Finally allowed to take his seat in 1886, remaining M.P. for Northampton till his death in 1891.

But the Lords, as expected, threw the Bill out and, moreover, Lord Lansdowne,[1] mighty Anglo-Irish magnate, resigned in protest from his office of Under-Secretary of State for India. Consequently, the distress remained unalleviated and things went from bad to worse in Ireland—'boycotting', 'moonlighting', burning ricks and maiming cattle, and finally the atrocious murder of Lord Mountmorres in County Galway (September 25th).

At Westminster the counterpart to these activities was an even more ruthless and persistent obstruction of procedure by Parnell and his confederates than had bedevilled the life of the previous Government and Parliament. The situation is vividly evoked in a letter from Smith to his wife (August 28th):

> We have had a curious life today. It has been two days in one or one day prolonged into another.
>
> I went home last night shortly after 1.0 knowing that the Irish were going to keep it up all night; and at ½ past 6 they sent for me to say that the House was still sitting and would I come down? So I got up and had my breakfast and went down and sat in the House until ½ past 11 when I went to a meeting at Seamore Place to see the Peers. They talked for two hours and on my return to the House I found the Thursday sitting had been ended and we had got into Friday. The poor Ministers look fearfully fagged and they will have another bad night again but it is very much their own fault as they never lose an opportunity of truckling to the rebels. . . .

If the domestic life of the Government was full of stresses and strains, that of the Opposition was not much happier. The leadership of the Tories in the House of Commons had devolved upon Sir Stafford Northcote, who was of a far too amiable and retiring disposition for such a post at such a time and who, having once been Gladstone's Private Secretary, was patently in awe of the Grand Old Man. This aroused much scorn and irritation among some of the livelier spirits in his party—notably, Lord Randolph Churchill, Sir Henry Drummond Wolff, John Gorst, and for a time, Arthur Balfour—who formed themselves into a sort of Tory ginger-group— the 'Fourth Party'—attacking their own leader with as much audacity and irresponsibility as they attacked Gladstone.

Smith and Cross also both came in for a great deal of the Fourth Party's attacks and taunts, both being known to be close friends of Northcote and both therefore being arbitrarily considered staid and timorous. In the case of Smith, at any rate, this was a gross misapprehension, as Lord Randolph was to discover a few years later; but for the time being he would be sure of raising a laugh at their

---

[1] Henry, 5th Marquess; Viceroy of India, 1888–94; Secretary of State for War, 1895–1900 and for Foreign Affairs, 1900–5.

expense by referring to them as 'Marshall & Snelgrove' and on a celebrated occasion (in 1884) when Smith expressed a doubt about the eligibility for the vote of Irish peasants living in 'mud-cabins' he was scathingly classed by Lord Randolph as one of the 'lords of suburban villas . . . of pineries and vineries'. But Smith had the rare good sense not to allow this treatment to affect his judgment of Lord Randolph, for whom, despite later provocations, he came to have a high regard and even a certain affection.

Meanwhile, in private life, his great wealth and renowned business flair caused him to be continually in demand either for assistance or

| LORD R. CHURCHILL. | SIR J. E. GORST. | SIR H. D. WOLFF. |

"ONE OF US."

FIRST APPEARANCE OF SIR J. E. GORST AS SOLICITOR-GENERAL

advice. The two aspects of this demand are reflected in a resigned letter to his wife (August 20th): 'Lady Burdett-Coutts took up nearly two hours of my time this morning. She had a great deal to say and wanted me to see Mr. Money and the Bank people on her behalf, but I asked what I was to say, and what I could do, and she was obliged to admit I could do nothing. . . . The Princess Mary's[1] letter . . . asks me to become joint security with some other men for a debt on her Houses. . . .'

[1] Mary Adelaide, Duchess of Teck; daughter of 1st Duke of Cambridge and mother of Queen Mary. She was perennially in debt.

His public conscience and sense of duty were, at the same time, so highly developed that they were bound sometimes to involve him in the suspicion of being devoid of feeling. But the truth was that his human feelings were so warm and strong than he often feared their deflecting him from his public duty and accordingly would go out of his way to assume a sterner mask than was really his. When through this his actions came to be misinterpreted his distress was acute.

Thus, when he was Financial Secretary to the Treasury some years earlier he was called upon to adjudicate in the matter of a financial award to Sir William Palliser, the inventor of 'Palliser shot' and other techniques relating to guns and rifles. An unidentified friend of his and of the Pallisers seems to have reproached him for his meanness some time after Palliser's death in 1882, when Lady Palliser and her daughters were evidently in financial straits. The very fact that Smith was always particularly moved by the spectacle of impoverished widows and daughters of distinguished men and that he often, as in this case, tried to give tactful private assistance made the attack all the more unbearable.

> I have had some trials in my life but the most painful are when one's motives are entirely misunderstood by one's oldest friends, and this penalty is inflicted on one in the discharge of duties which are distasteful—which have never been sought in any way—and which have only been undertaken as they appeared to be a duty. . . .
> In telling me that 'my heart is dead' you cut me to the very quick. . . . I have always felt I was bound to be liberal with my own money but to be just in dispensing the money of the people so far as my voice may affect it. . . . If your judgment of me is just I have a great sorrow added to the trials of a public position wh. has been forced upon me, and it is clear that the sooner I escape from it the better for the Country and for my own peace of mind. . . .

He then declared that he was 'prepared myself to subscribe liberally' to any privately organized fund to help the family.

This sense of being 'trapped' ever since accepting office under the Crown was an ever more frequently recurring theme in Smith's more private communications and marks him off from the ordinary run of politician of any epoch. For his only spur was duty and being totally devoid of ambition made it harder for him to take the knocks which the ordinary politician accepts as the price of his rewards.

But as soon as the Session was brought to its weary close on September 7th Smith seized the opportunity to give himself a long and thorough holiday with his family. He had always been fond of the sea and his recent connection with the Navy had increased its attraction for him; so he bought the steam yacht *Pandora* (500 tons) from a Mr. Penn, who had fitted her with powerful engines after taking her over from the Duke of Hamilton. From now on the *Pandora* was to play a great part in Smith's life—and also in the lives of his friends, for he was extremely hospitable in inviting them to share his cruises and also frequently lent her altogether, complete with crew, to special friends like Sir Stafford Northcote and Baroness Burdett-Coutts.

For his first cruise Smith chose the Mediterranean and the *Pandora* was sent to Venice, where, on September 10th, he and his party joined her. A letter to his sister, Gussie, written from Gravosa, gives a good idea of the pattern and texture of life on such a cruise.

We have been here since Saturday morning with the ships of all Nations under the chief command of Sir F. Beauchamp Seymour. The harbour is a very beautiful one sheltered on all sides by high strong hills like the Calabrian hills beyond Naples and it is a very pretty sight to see a dozen large ships at anchor with their different colours flying and boats passing to and fro between them and the shore.

The Admiral is an old Navy friend of mine:—in fact I gave him the command and several of the officers are friends of ours also so that we have received a hearty welcome. The Admiral came to call upon us in his steam pinnace almost before we had dropped anchor—he came to take us to Church on Sunday morning on board his ship and he has done everything he could to make us comfortable. We shall probably stay until Thursday and then go on to Corfu and from there to Zante and Crete.

We have had a very pleasant trip so far and although there has been some little rocking and knocking about there has been exceedingly little discomfort. Indeed, I think Ship life and its quiet and freedom grow upon us and it is wonderful how soon one gets reconciled to the absence for days together of letters and newspapers. The girls were charmed with Venice and although it was very warm there they did not suffer as I had expected. We were laying out opposite the public gardens, five minutes off the Doge's Palace and therefore away from the stinks, which in the town were certainly very bad. . . .

While he was away a big reorganization and expansion of his private life and arrangements was being undertaken for him. Towards the end of the previous year, with the prospects of having to entertain on an ever-increasing scale—and also of very soon not having the Admiralty in which to do it—he had decided it was time to get himself a bigger house than the comparatively modest one at 1, Hyde Park Street, which they had had since their marriage. He accordingly bought one of the huge mansions (No. 3) at the Hyde Park Corner end of Grosvenor Place and set about redecorating and furnishing it with great magnificence, but also with his usual care and attention to detail and comfort. He also began to enlarge and develop the house and estate at Greenlands, near Henley-on-Thames, which he had bought from Sir Dudley Marjoribanks in 1871, and which had become his cherished country retreat and the rearing place of his children.

The man upon whom devolved the responsibility for these arrangements—as well as for the general supervision of all Smith's interests and private affairs—was Jacob Luard Pattisson, whom he had first met on his North American tour when Pattisson was acting as private secretary to Lord Dufferin, the Governor-General of Canada. The latter was so impressed with Pattisson's qualities that he also entrusted him with the management of his estates in Ireland. However, when Pattisson's wife's health prevented her staying either in Canada or Ireland, he came to Smith with the request for a job. Strangely enough, William Lethbridge, Smith's life-long friend and business partner, had once been tutor to Pattisson and so was able to endorse Dufferin's high opinion of him. At any rate, in January 1880, after a certain amount of negotiation, Smith drew up a formal document proposing that 'Mr. Pattisson should place his services entirely at his disposal as a Commissioner or Agent in Chief and General Private Secretary, including management of his landed Property and financial interests . . . at £800 per annum'.

So, while Smith took his well-earned leisure in that September of 1880, Pattisson was coping with remarkable efficiency with a multitude of various affairs on his master's behalf. The day after Smith left England (September 11th) he wrote a detailed account of the proposed furnishings of 3, Grosvenor Place:

> Mr. Cubitt Nicholls [architect] and myself have arranged to buy on your behalf from Sinclair the Diana Classical Chimney Piece . . . for the Front Drawing Room, and the Chesterfield with Sienna marble (less the ornamentation scroll in Frieze) for the Dining Room at £450 for the two. This is £100 less than he first asked.
>
> We propose to recommend to you that we should buy the second White Marble from Sinclair with the Figures of Boys playing, for the Back Drawing Room. . . . For the Boudoir we propose the white with a medallion head in the centre of the Frieze, the other ornamentations being vine leaves & grapes. There are no Bacchanalian scenes in this. . . .

A week later (September 18th) he announces that 'we have bought 60 Hampshire & 40 Scotch sheep for Greenlands & 8 Highland Steers'; and on the 26th that 'Veitch's man was there to examine the vines. He says that they are in bad order owing to deficient drainage from the Bed outside. But he is to render a written report.' Then back to Grosvenor Place (October 2nd): '. . . the Gilding of the Front drawing Room ceiling is nearly finished and looks very well. Two of the Mantel Pieces are fixed and a third in place. The one in the Dining Room (from Chesterfield House) looks very well & is much improved by the objectionable scroll work on the frieze being cleared away. . . .' Then on October 8th: '. . . your telegram announcing that the *Pandora* had run aground but was safely off was forwarded to me at Clandeboye. . . . I find that the first part of the news was in the Times yesterday—but not saying that she was afloat again, so I am sending a little paragraph to the papers to reassure your friends. . . .'

Pattisson's reports on these domestic matters were freely interspersed with political news, presented in a racy and vivid manner, which gives an excellent picture of the times. Thus on October 9th, he wrote:

. . . I am sorry that the newspapers have not reached you . . . They are full of the Turkish and Irish questions. Even those that support the Government begin to admit the awkward position Mr. Gladstone is in, while the cartoons in the comic papers are as usual very telling. . . . Ireland too grows from worse to worse. Outrages are literally of more than daily occurrence. A very strong deputation of Landlords & others waited this week on the Lord Lieutenant[1] & Mr. Forster.[2] The Lord Lieutenant's reply was almost whining—asking for sympathy in his difficult position & saying he was not the Cabinet—while Mr. Forster simply said 'we have done all that is in our power—what do you suggest?'

The loyal Irish are very indignant and the North are getting religiously excited over it, and this will be another complication which will not tend to improve matters. But at the same time the doctrines of 'hold the harvest & pay no rent' are spreading to the Ulster tenants. Even while I was in Down, Lord Annesley 'ran' in a most undignified manner, leaving his wife behind—because he had one or two threatening letters. He is very unpopular. . . .

In the next letter (October 19th) he returns to the reorganization at Greenlands and the furnishing of Grosvenor Place:

. . . The Establishment [i.e. Greenlands] generally is working quite smoothly . . . some of the hands did not like Brown's stricter discipline, but now so far as I can see he is better understood. He thinks the men are somewhat overpaid and that there are too many foremen. He would prefer to have put two viz. Claydon for everything relating to the Flowers and Boxall for the Fruit and Vegetable Gardens. . . . In the last week's packet I enclosed Veitch's report on the Vines. We have begun to remedy the drainage & propose to remedy the other

---

[1] Francis, 7th Earl Cowper.
[2] W. E. Forster; Chief Secretary for Ireland.

defects by gradual renewal of the Vines, working a few pot vines every year to keep the supply from falling off. . . .

I have had a long talk with Mr. Smith of Kew, and he has cordially accepted an invitation to spend a day & night at Greenlands. I submitted to him some planting which I proposed to do this month. . . . In the Remenham meadows we propose to put in such trees as white poplars, red & golden willows, alders, dogwood, Lombardy poplars, etc . . . and further back beyond the Floods some Maples, Planes. On the sloping ground we thought of putting in a clump here & there of Scotch & Austrian Pines, Birch etc. . . .

The additional room to the Keeper's House is now nearly complete & is an improvement both externally & internally. In the alteration I have also arranged a small fire for cooking his Pheasant food, as we had no place before. . . .

3, *Grosvenor Place*

The works here are going on satisfactorily & coming out well. The white tiles downstairs are a vast improvement. Mr. Nicholls and I are today going to choose the fire grates for the downstairs rooms. Mr. Nicholls is testing all the drains. . . .

The Bill for the Venetian Goods has been presented and paid. . . .

I do not think I have mentioned that the Flowers & etc. have been gratefully acknowledged by the Hospitals. The Hampers to Mrs. Danvers and Mrs. Codrington also are regularly sent and I believe give satisfaction. . . .

Since 1877 Smith had also been acquiring property in Suffolk at Thurlow and Hundon and in Devonshire at Rewe and Silverton, near Exeter.[1] On October 28th Pattisson sent on a report from the bailiff of his Suffolk estates giving details of further parcels of land and of houses and cottages which could be purchased around Thurlow and Hundon. The houses and cottages mostly appear to have been in a very dilapidated state, but this appealed to Smith's philanthropic instincts in enabling him to demolish them and rebuild decent habitations for the tillers of the soil. But it was evident from one letter of Pattisson's that some people were not above trying to take advantage of him. 'When I was last at Hundon', he wrote (October 30th), 'the Clergyman was very eager to commence to make some alterations to his church, hoping that you would bear the expense. . . . They were not extravagant or out of the way, but this notion of spending £50 or £60 and sending the Bill in was amusing.'

Even at this early stage Pattisson was already finding his multifarious duties almost too much for him and he suggested (November 4th) that '. . . a good clerk from a Surveyor's or Estate Office, who could keep the Books and do the routine office work would be almost a

---

[1] Sir Herbert Maxwell says he had 'invested upwards of £450,000' in these properties.

necessity if I myself were to keep a proper supervision over all your interests, independently of any political or secretarial assistance that you might also expect from me'. He added: '. . . your investments alone require an amount of attention & watching which can hardly be measured by time . . .'. But even with an assistant, after three years the weight upon his shoulders had grown so unbearable that he asked to be relieved of the management of the landed property. 'I doubt, Sir,' he wrote rather reproachfully, 'whether you altogether realize the amount of office work my duties entail or of the high pressure at which Durnford & myself are kept to cope with it.' Shortly afterwards he was ordered complete rest by his doctor and Smith had to relent. But after this crisis their relationship seems to have been one of complete mutual confidence and affection to the last day of Smith's life.

Meanwhile, the *Pandora* sailed on her way round the Mediterranean, up the Aegean and through the Dardanelles—so lately and for so long the centre of all Smith's thoughts, fears and preoccupations—and dropped anchor at Constantinople. From here he wrote to Pattison (November 16th) a lively account of a dinner with Sultan Abdul Hamid II. The mention of Goschen is explained by the fact that the latter was on a special mission to Constantinople to try to bring pressure to bear on the Sultan to carry out the stipulations of the Treaty of Berlin:

The delay here has been caused by the Sultan's invitation to dinner which as it included my wife and my two daughters I had no wish to escape from. The dinner was in State, the Sultan and most of his officers being in uniform. My Wife was placed on his left, Mrs. Goschen on his right, the Prime Minister sitting next and Goschen as Ambassador next to my wife, then came Osman Pasha[1] and my daughter Emily. The dinner was a good one from the European point of view, and there were some Turkish dishes thrown in.

The Sultan received us first—i.e. the Goschens, my wife and myself in his Cabinet and took pains to make himself very agreeable to all of us. His little sons dined with us and they are to come on board directly to see the Yacht, after which I am to go to the Palace to take leave.

I pity the poor fellow [The Sultan] very much indeed. He is described by all as a very intelligent and kindly man, but he is in fear of everybody and he trusts none but his personal attendants in the Palace—a few Albanians, some Circassians and a battalion of blacks who are quartered within the precincts of the Palace. There are many very good-looking and intelligent Pashas whose countenances would

[1] The outstanding Turkish commander who had been responsible for the great Turkish victories at the beginning of the Russo-Turkish war.

lead one to suppose that they possessed both ability and honesty: but Said the Prime Minister is the most servile looking and repulsive creature I have ever seen.

In a memorandum[1] kept by Smith of his interview with the Sultan he says that the latter wished to confer a decoration upon him, but that he declined on the grounds that 'it would be misunderstood in England and that it would embarrass us in speaking as plainly as I should wish on my return of Turkish affairs'. He asked instead for a signed photograph of the Sultan; but he was also given a watch worn by him. Both the Sultan and his Prime Minister complained bitterly of Gladstone's attitude to Turkey and expressed fervent prayers for the return of the Tories; but Smith stoutly refused to be drawn into any recriminations regarding English politics and instead admonished his hosts to keep faith over the Treaty of Berlin. 'I said, "Carry out your engagements, and the old feeling in favour of Turkey will return and even Mr. Gladstone will not be able to go against it".'

After leaving Beirut, on the way home to England, the *Pandora* encountered terrible weather and the British Consul at that place wrote to Smith (December 16th): 'We were exceedingly anxious about you after you left as the storm here was fearful, and our forebodings became still more gloomy when on Monday a report spread through the town that the yacht was seen to founder off Cyprus, and only one person was saved. . . .'

The fact was that Smith braved the gale, which had begun to blow before he left Beirut, because he was anxious to hasten his return, having heard that Parliament had been summoned to meet in January instead of February. On his way back he received an account from Northcote of the state of affairs at home (December 21st):

There is a complete breakdown of all law and order in Ireland, except of the Land League Law, which is fully in force, and implicitly obeyed. But the English public are not half so excited about it as they were about the Bulgarian Atrocities or the Slave Circular.

The Fourth Party are pretty friendly with me, but there is agreed diversity between them and the Irish Landlord section of our party, and we shall have some delicate steering. . . .

Pattisson, too, added his bulletin (December 7th):

The Govt. seem quite to have lost their reason about Ireland. Outrages of all kinds, short of actual murder, are reported daily. 'Boycotting' is practised everywhere, and arms are found to be imported whole-sale. . . .

---

[1] Reproduced in full by Sir H. Maxwell (Vol. II, pp. 99–101) but not found among the Hambleden Papers by the present writer.

I have little doubt myself that the attitude of the Govt. on the Land Question in Ireland is very closely watched by the Farmers & Chambers of Agriculture in England and that agitation in England for similar concessions is likely to follow. I heard in Suffolk beyond doubt that Farmers are giving notices of quitting simply to make new terms with their landlords. . . .

On the strength of this Pattisson went on to urge Smith to grant his tenants a ten per cent abatement on the half year's rent, as other landlords in Suffolk were doing, to mitigate the effect of the bad harvest and to forestall the farmers from forcing it out of them. Smith evidently agreed to the proposal, for in a further letter Pattisson wrote that the ten per cent abatement was 'thankfully received', but that 'there is an uncertain tone among the tenants, partly disaffection and partly distress, which is not encouraging'.

As Smith neared home the preparations at Grosvenor Place were reaching their climax. Thus Pattisson (December 22nd):

Mrs. Swinburne [housekeeper] and her legions will take up their new quarters on Tuesday week. . . . The last workmen are not quite out of the place—but we are driving them before us. The carpets are made & ready to go down. . . .

Before leaving the year 1880 a word must be said about the domestic affairs of the Conservative Party at this stage and about the part played therein by Smith. Since the General Election it had been widely recognized among Conservatives that a neglect and mismanagement of party interests in the Beaconsfield Ministry's last years lay as much at the root of their crushing defeat at the polls as the economic depression and Gladstone's eloquent denigration of their foreign policy. Yet, at the beginning of their term of power, the Conservative organization had been far superior to that of their opponents—and this had been largely due to the energy and organizing capacity of one man. This was John Eldon Gorst, an able young barrister, whom Disraeli had appointed—though only on a part-time basis—as Principal Party Agent in 1870. Gorst, in fact, had been largely responsible for the great Conservative victory in 1874.

Though he was made a Q.C. in 1875 Gorst nevertheless appeared to feel that his services had not been sufficiently rewarded and consequently became embittered and difficult. He quarrelled with Hart Dyke, the Chief Whip and Patronage Secretary, over their respective spheres of influence and function and because Dyke was inclined to manage electioneering from the Treasury and to regard Gorst as his employee. So in 1877 Gorst was removed and replaced by W. B. Skene, though not without writing a solemn warning to Beaconsfield about the dangers of 'managing elections at the

Treasury' (i.e. by the Chief Whip instead of the Principal Agent of the Party, who was outside Parliament) and forecasting that at the next General Election 'our organization . . . will be as inferior to that of our opponents as it had been superior in 1874'.[1]

Gorst's forebodings were justified, as, under Skene, matters deteriorated further and the Whips ruled the Party from the Treasury till the end of 1879, when the system disintegrated through Dyke falling ill from overwork. This went far to explain the fiasco a few months later when the General Election came. As a result of the

SIR J. E. GORST.

" THINKING OF THE BO'SUN."

general recriminations arising from the defeat, Rowland Winn[2] became Chief Whip in place of Dyke; Skene was removed from the post of Chief Party Agent and Gorst was recalled to take charge again of the Conservative Central Office. Meanwhile, a special Committee, which came to be known as the 'Central Committee', was appointed by Beaconsfield, as party leader, to consider ways and means of improving the party organization, with Smith as chairman,

[1] Buckle VI, 519–20. I am also indebted in this account of central party organization to H. J. Hanham's *Elections & Party Management: Politics in the time of Disraeli & Gladstone*, p. 356 seq.
[2] M.P. N. Lincoln, created Lord St. Oswald, 1885.

Edward Stanhope[1] as vice-chairman and Lord Percy as representative of the National Union of Conservative Associations.

The Central Committee took charge of all questions of organization outside the House of Commons and Gorst acted as its exectuive officer, which implied that his original contention had been respected and that the Whips were again to be confined to their House of Commons work. Nobody liked Gorst much, whereas everybody seemed to like 'Billy' Dyke and there were some heart-searchings before sacrificing the latter and saddling themselves with Gorst again. Thus Northcote to Smith (May 15th, 1880):

> ... I return Gorst's curious, and as you say, prophetic letter ... I see the difficulty about Dyke, and we do not clearly see how to deal with it. We must not hurt his feelings, but he certainly cannot manage the whole business himself. I fancy we shall be obliged to make some experimental arrangement in the first instance, and not to commit ourselves to any one till we have tried him. ...

Finally, in July 1880, an interview took place between Smith, Northcote and Gorst, of which Smith kept a note, from which it appears they promised Gorst, in return for reorganizing the party organization and winning the next election, 'the offer of office for which he might be eligible'. Gorst replied sourly that a similar promise had been made to him before 1874, but 'the only offer he got was an Under-Secretaryship with the Chief in the Commons, thus practically shelving him', and insisted that next time 'it shd be one wh' wd. not silence him in the House or deny him the chance of showing his own ability and claims for further political promotion'.

At a further meeting terms were thrashed out in which Gorst strove his utmost to see that he was master in his own house. Thus, the clause: 'Mr. Gorst to be charged with the primary responsibility of securing candidates for Seats, but not to be at liberty to promise any party money' had to be softened by Smith to 'shd. in all cases initiate proposals to spend money tho' he shd. have no power to do this without the sanction of the Committee'. Another clause became: 'Mr. G. or some one member of the Committee shd. be head of the office & the Secs. & clerks shd. take orders from him only.'

Once in the saddle again Gorst began to throw his weight about. He was as suspicious and contemptuous of the new Chief Whip, Rowland Winn, as he had been of his predecessor, Hart Dyke. But it is to his credit that he had more conscience in the matter of electoral corruption than had a number of local party agents and even certain of the Whips. Thus, in a forthright letter to Smith (September 8th),

[1] Hon. Edward Stanhope, 2nd son of 5th Earl Stanhope; President of Board of Trade 1885–6; Colonial Secretary, 1886–7; Secretary for War, 1887–92.

he objected to the Conservative agent at Sheffield, T. C. Shaw, who was a protégé of Winn, on these grounds:

> . . . I will do my best to 'ménager' Winn & his protégé Shaw. My objection to the latter is more complex than the former supposes. Chiefly he is prone to corrupt practices, which accounts for his being in such demand in corrupt constituencies. What Winn's phrases about not appreciating the money & etc. spent by Birmingham come to is that I won't fight corruption by corruption. To this I plead guilty: it is our policy to force the Government to pass an Act that will stop as much corruption as possible, and if Harry Thynne[1] & his friends will have corrupt practices on our side they must have them locally, not fostered & organized from headquarters by Mr. Shaw or anybody else. Armit & the sugar people are an example of how we become the prey of dupes when we seek to influence elections by questionable means. . . . I am quite in favour of treating Winn & the old identity with consideration, but they can hardly expect us to take their modus operandi as our model or accept Dyke's judgment of character as infallible.

In this matter of corruption Gorst certainly had the leaders of the party with him. On the other hand, a circumstance which did not endear him to them was the fact that he had allied himself with Lord Randolph Churchill, Drummond Wolff and Balfour in the Fourth Party, whose avowed object was to make things hot for the said leaders. In this same letter to Smith, therefore, we find Gorst uttering open threats against the official leadership and, strangely at this early date, proposing that Smith should take it over.

> There is a regular intrigue going on on the part of Bourke[2] & others against Ld. R. Churchill, Wolff & myself. They tried to detach Balfour from us but failed. We mean to stick together & we shall be loyal to Northcote if he is loyal to us. But self-preservation is the first law of politics as well as of nature and contingencies may happen which will end in your being obliged to take the place of leader in the Commons whether you like it or not.

This, in its rather brutal fashion, may have been a sort of compliment to Smith personally; but the situation where the principal executive of the party organization was so openly critical of the party leaders as a whole, and, owing to his allegiance to a ginger-group, often in open opposition to them in the House of Commons, was obviously an impossible one. So, at the beginning of the next year, Smith seems to have appealed to Balfour, as being the soberest and

[1] Lord Henry Thynne; 2nd son of 3rd Marquess of Bath; M.P. South Wilts; Assistant Whip.

[2] Hon. Robert; son of 5th Earl of Mayo; Foreign Under Secretary, 1874–80 and 1885–6. Created Baron Connemara, 1887.

least committed of Churchill's followers, for help in the predicament, for Balfour wrote to him (January 25th, 1881): '. . . I shall be most happy to do anything in my power to diminish any friction there may be in working what the Americans call "the machine".'

But Gorst himself did not seem to be any more happy than anyone else, for he wrote to Smith (March 23rd):

> I have gone down home and shall probably not appear again for a few days. I am not exactly ill, but the difficulties political & personal with which I am surrounded so prey upon my mind that I want rest & repose to fit me to continue my encounter with them. I am beginning to think that I am growing too old for the task I have undertaken & that it won't be long before I break down altogether. . . .

Gorst was only 45 years old; but with equal despondency he wrote again a month later (April 20th):

> . . . I will have the work we are doing in stimulating local effort pushed on. I don't however expect much practical result. Political activity seems to me to depend on causes too wide & deep to be controlled. A gardener might as well try to stimulate the rising of sap in the spring. . . .

The question of recompense for his services then arose again and further beclouded relations. At first—perhaps feeling it might prejudice reward in the form of office—he seemed to reject the idea of a money payment. Thus to Smith (May 27th):

> . . . Our conversation yesterday has confirmed a growing apprehension that I have this year put myself into an equally false position by intimating a willingness to accept pecuniary recompense. I wish therefore to withdraw that intimation & I beg that it may be considered as not having been made.

Nevertheless, a month later, he wrote to Smith (June 23rd):

> I am willing to continue to conduct the business of the Central Committee . . . until June 21st 1882 and to accept the sum named as a sufficient & satisfactory remuneration. . . . It is of course meant that the sum you name has reference to the services of next year only and that I am entitled to a like sum in respect of the services of the year that is past.

Smith thereupon appears to have sent him a cheque for 500 guineas—instead of the 1,000 which Gorst expected. Referring to 'our unpleasant pecuniary affairs', Gorst then asked Smith (July 11th) to 'confirm in writing that the cheque is for one year's services only', i.e. that more was due to him. To this Smith replied (July 16th) with studied vagueness:

I ask your acceptance of 500 gns in no sense as a payment for services rendered to the party or in discharge of any claim you may feel you have upon the leaders. . . . We are not paying a debt for which we expect to receive a receipt in full of all demands, but we are in some degree recognizing recent work done and we remain conscious of obligations for time and ability devoted to the service of the Party in the past. . . .

This is so unlike Smith's own straightforward style that it is obviously the result of overmuch deliberation by cautious colleagues—Northcote probably predominating. At any rate, Gorst continued to argue the point in further letters until, meeting Smith in the House one day, he declared it was impossible to come to any understanding and that he abandoned any further claim. After this he seemed to have felt himself absolved from taking his duties too seriously and to have gone off on a holiday without telling anyone. This lapse elicited from Smith the following stern rebuke (August 17th):

My dear Gorst,

You have made a serious mistake in going away without a previous understanding with your colleagues at St. Stephen's. Neither you nor I in the position we occupy are at liberty to do just what would be most agreeable at any given moment. We are bound to consider the claims of the Party and of our friends.

. . . I confess I was both surprised and disappointed at your absence from the Committee . . . your advice was really wanted and we looked for a plan and policy from you.

Your absence from the House last week was a serious defection . . . although all has ended well, it would not have been so if men who were not at all more bound to come than you were, had stayed away for their personal convenience.

I speak plainly because it would be most unfriendly not to do so. You and I have accepted responsibility in common with Stanhope, Percy & Winn in the care of the affairs of the Party and we are not at liberty to do what we like just when & where we please. . . .

When I came back to town there was not a soul at the office capable of giving an order and no one knew where you were. . . .

I think I have a right to speak to you as a friend, from all that has passed, and I am bound to tell you that for your own sake you must control yourself and avoid erratic conduct of this sort.

You can yet attain any position you please if you will be guided by common sense, but you disappoint & distress yr. friends by these eccentricities.

Yours very truly,
W. H. Smith

However, even after this, matters limped on somehow for another year. Meanwhile an Organization Committee was formed, to keep in closer touch with the constituencies and to arrange meetings and lectures, which Smith invited Balfour to join, writing (October 5th, 1881): '. . . I want as much youthful energy as I can get, and therefore it is that I ask you to join us'. Then on July 10th, 1882, we find him asking Balfour to see that 'Gorst's cheque is drawn and paid over to him', continuing: '. . . Randolph dropped to me a remark that Gorst had said to him that his engagement had come to an end. I said quite unconcernedly that it was a mistake and that nothing had occurred to alter our arrangements with him and I let the matter drop. It may have been only a suggestion of mischief for the love of it.'[1] Nevertheless, a few months later we find Smith writing to Sandon (November 17th, 1882): '. . . Northcote has written to Gorst telling him of the feeling expressed by many of our friends as to his conduct and the result is that he has written resigning the Agency of the Party. I shall take the opportunity of resigning too and Edward Stanhope will I hope take my place. . . .'[2]

In the midst of these efforts to put its house in order the Conservative Party suffered a great blow to its morale in the death of its great leader and regenerator, Lord Beaconsfield, on April 19th, 1881. 'It is a great loss to the nation and to the Queen and to our party', wrote Cross to Smith (April 20th), 'How and when his successor will be chosen it is not easy to see.' And Smith's fellow member Sir Charles Russell, wrote (April 24th): 'Poor Dizzy! I really believe he is much regretted even by ultra radicals. I have met two already who said they considered him an honour to any country.' To Emily, Smith wrote (April 21st):

> Lord Beaconsfield will be buried at Hughenden on Tuesday morning and we shall all go down to his funeral. I have seen him for the last time and he looked better in death than in life, but there was a sort of evidence of struggle on his face which had ended.
>
> Already men are asking who is to be the future Chief, and I am afraid that question will have to be settled.

Gladstone had already incurred the odium of his old adversary's admirers by not attending his funeral, when he made matters worse by deputing his Chief Whip, Lord Richard Grosvenor, to move a resolution that a national memorial to Beaconsfield should be erected in Westminster Abbey. The temper of the Tory opposition is reflected in this letter from Russell to Smith (April 26th):

> . . . The scene in the H. of C. last night is too disgraceful & I hope we have not heard the last of it yet. Gladstone having purposely missed the train & dressed himself in mourning clothes to give the trick greater effect, put up R. Grosvenor to make the bare-faced

[1] Balfour Papers.   [2] Harrowby Papers.

notice of motion & so get the Land Bill on. . . . I do hope that some notice will be taken of the way in which upon the death of one of the greatest of Parliamentary memories, that memory was despised by the Prime Minister at the time being.

Gladstone himself made up for this to some extent by delivering a nobly-phrased eulogy on his late rival a fortnight later; but one of his Radical followers—Henry Labouchere, the editor and proprietor of *Truth*—had proposed an amendment to the memorial motion protesting against 'public money being voted to commemorate a party leader'. However, he was supported by only 54 out of a House of 434 members.

Smith, meanwhile in his capacity as chairman of the Central Committee, had been corresponding with an experienced journalist named Maclean[1] with a view to having some vigorous anti-Government tracts produced. Maclean very sensibly wrote (May 8th) urging him to 'seize upon the subject which happens to be most talked about', this being 'the boorish opposition' to the proposed monument. 'The bad taste of the Radicals . . . might, I think, be turned to excellent account. . . .'

The chaotic state of Ireland had meanwhile compelled Gladstone, under pressure from the Viceroy, Lord Cowper, and the Chief Secretary, Forster to yield to the introduction of a new Coercion Bill (again as Beaconsfield had foretold). Introduced in the Commons by Forster on January 24th, 1881, it met with an orgy of obstruction and only passed after Gladstone had moved a closure resolution—the first of several attempts on the part of Liberal and Conservative Governments to tighten Parliamentary procedure in order to thwart the Irish tactics. The closure resolution itself was only carried after most of the Irish members had been suspended. Thus armed, Gladstone introduced a further Land Bill (April 17th), which purported to give Irish tenants the 'Three Fs'—Fixity of tenure, Fair rents and Free sale.

The Whigs were again horrified at this threat to the sanctity of property and the Duke of Argyll resigned from the Government (April 13th). Even Parnell—who had not been consulted over the measure—refused to be appeased, calculating that, having got this much, further concessions could be wrung from the Government. The battle for the Land Bill was a protracted and bitter one—it occupied 58 sittings—and was waged almost single-handed by Gladstone, who became more Olympian every day. Countless amendments were tabled by the Opposition and some of them came from Smith, to whom the Prime Minister was good enough to write

---

[1] James Mackenzie Maclean, former leader-writer of *Manchester Guardian;* Editor and Proprietor of *Bombay Gazette;* M.P. (Cons.) Oldham, 1885–92.

(July 2nd) that 'I recognize & share the spirit in which I believe you to be acting'.

But Irish obstruction affected both Government and Opposition alike. 'Those dreadful men have broken out again,' Smith wrote to Emily (July 28th), 'and I must wait for my amendment which may come on at any time. . . .' And on August 9th: 'The Government appears to be disposed to conciliate us but all sorts of rumours were in circulation last night and I thought Gladstone at Grillions,[1] where I dined, was particularly serious & quiet.' Again on August 12th: 'It is very anxious work just now as men's tempers are warm and concession which might reasonably be made is refused: but I hope all will come right.' It did, in so far as the Land Bill was finally passed on August 22nd.

As soon as Parliament rose Smith was off for a cruise round the coast of Ireland in the *Pandora*, which now and for all his remaining years was to be his great joy and solace. He loved the sea and these days of the early eighties, when his health was still good, his family still young and the cares of office were temporarily off his shoulders, were perhaps among the happiest of his life. This letter to his wife from the yacht at Queenstown (September 1st) conveys something of his happy mood.

. . . We left Swansea at about 1.0 with a fresh easterly breeze, but as we were sheltered a good deal by the land it was not too much for us. When however we were fairly out at sea we found a good deal of swell and we were all glad to turn in early. We were off the harbour before daylight and came in just as the sun had risen, taking up the buoy which Codrington knows just ahead of the Flagship. The Officer of the Watch came on board to see that we did not require any help and the Admiral has sent to say he will pay his respects to us at 10 o'clock. We shall I suppose go up the river to Cork in the course of the morning, but all that will be arranged when the great man comes on board.

The wind has dropped and the sun is shining out splendidly. It looks as if it was at last going to be settled and I am sure I hope it may be.

The Girls are very happy and well and so is the boy who is certainly a very good traveller and companion. He and I were both a little upset last night after dinner but it only lasted a moment with me, and he went to bed without dinner: making up for it however with sandwiches at daylight this morning. . . .

Next day he describes a visit to Blarney Castle—'where the famous Blarney Stone exists'—

Lady Colthurst[2] received and her daughters showed us over the old castle with a great deal of kindness—but they tell a terrible tale of the

---

[1] A very select dining club.
[2] Wife of Sir George St. John Colthurst, 6th Bart.

state of the Country and the mischief caused by the Land League and the weakness of the Govt. It is very shocking and everyone says that not even a firm and good Govt. now would bring things round. . . .

Indeed, certain Irish Conservatives were at this time urging their party leaders to exploit the Government's feeble handling of Parnell and from a Liberal came even the first tentative suggestion for a Conservative-Liberal alliance 'against the common enemy, viz: the Land League'. But Sir Dunbar Plunket Barton, who reported this to Smith (October 1st), considered that 'if there were to be a union of

"MR. G."

parties to support a Conservative, it might be acceptable to us, but . . . it would be monstrous to suggest that we should join in supporting a Gladstonian at the present moment'. He added that Parnell was 'King of Ireland' now, that the Govt. had 'virtually abdicated' and were even releasing suspects whom they had earlier arrested.

However, within a few days of this damaging assessment, Gladstone, goaded by Parnell's incitements to wreck his Land Act, delivered a clear warning to him in a speech at Leeds (October 11th) that force would be met with force in Ireland and that 'the resources of civilisation were not yet exhausted'. When Parnell remained defiant these resources were invoked by the Government and Parnell and several of his followers were arrested under the Coercion Act and imprisoned in Kilmainham Goal. Thereupon the Land League declared a rent-strike and was proscribed by the Government, its leaders also being arrested and imprisoned.

Despite these stern measures matters continued to deteriorate and, bent on at least curbing the obstruction of the Irish in Parliament, Gladstone declared in a public speech just before the reassembly of Parliament in the new year that there must be a further reform of the Rules of Procedure. Smith made reply to this in a speech to his constituents on January 30th, 1882, saying that he and his colleagues would consent to any reasonable change in the rules—though they objected to closure by a bare majority. This was ironical in the light of later events, when Smith himself, as Leader of the House in 1887, struggled with might and main to secure the passage of a rule to establish closure by a bare majority.

At about this time, Smith's colleague in the representation of Westminster, Sir Charles Russell, became hopelessly ill and had to resign his seat. Smith had earlier approached Lord Algernon Percy[1] with a view to his standing for Russell's seat when the time came and it is proof of the remarkable influence which Smith had established over this former Liberal stronghold that Percy was returned unopposed by the electors of Westminster in February 1882.

Parnell, meanwhile, was anxious to get out of prison, partly fearing that his authority might be usurped by certain extremist sections in Ireland and partly because he wanted to get back to his mistress, Mrs. O'Shea, whose child by him was dying. Ironically it was through the 'good offices' of the latter's husband, Captain O'Shea (whose motives were purely selfish) that negotiations were opened with Joseph Chamberlain, on behalf of Gladstone, resulting in a pact or bargain, known as the Kilmainham Treaty, under which the Government should bring in an Arrears Bill, to help the Irish tenants pay off arrears of rent, and Parnell should support the Land Act and use his influence to end crime and disorder.

Accordingly Parnell and his friends were released on May 4th. Forster thereupon resigned from the Irish Office in protest and the Viceroy, Lord Cowper, resigned at the same time.

[1] 2nd son of 6th Duke of Northumberland.

VIII

IN OPPOSITION: SECOND PHASE

⋙━◆━◆━⋘

W ISHING to press further some of the investigations into Irish conditions which he had begun on his brief tour of the previous autumn, Smith set out in April 1882 on another and more extended cruise in his yacht round the coast of Ireland.

He had always been friendly towards Forster and had sympathized with some of his aspirations—such as his Education Act of 1870—and he felt deeply for him as the crisis over Parnell's release approached. On his arrival at Dublin he was therefore tempted to call on the Chief Secretary. But he wrote to Emily (April 9th):

> Poor Forster! I wrote to him saying I thought it better I should not call on him as everything would be known and get into the papers and be misrepresented and you see he agrees with me, but I thought it only right to tell him that I was not deficient in regard for the Chief Secy. He has very serious and difficult work and not of a kind to suit his temperament, but I am very thankful I have no such responsibility.
>
> I have had a very quiet Sunday . . . and went again to the Mariners' Church where there was a very good service. . . . I could not help thinking of you all with great thankfulness and the reports you sent me from Eton made me still more so.
>
> I almost tremble when I think of the blessings we enjoy and my eyes filled this morning when I read the good accounts all round which Frederick's Masters give of him.

Forster had been appreciative of Smith's sympathy. 'Thank you much for your kind note', he had written (April 9th), 'I believe you are right & that we cannot meet without misconstruction, but I am sorry for it, as I think we could have helped one another by a quiet private talk.'

On his return home Smith wrote to his friend and solicitor, William Ford (April 13th):

> I returned last night from Ireland after a most interesting week but one which fills me with anxiety as to the future.

170

I spent the greater part of Saturday in Westmeath where Mrs. Smythe was murdered and I saw Mr. Smythe for whom the fatal shots were intended. I was greatly struck with his resemblance in eyes, forehead, complexion and lips to my father and his temperament is much the same. It is a curious fancy but I could not get it out of my head as I sat looking at him while he was talking excitedly to Mr. Gibson.[1] He was born in 1809 and for curiosity's sake which I have not mentioned to a single soul, I should very much like to find out whether there was ever a missing link in his Ancestors' family and who they were. . . .

Intermittently throughout his life Smith showed great interest in trying to trace his family's origins. In 1884 he approached the then Rouge Dragon, Scott-Gatty, as to the possibility and cost of having a pedigree worked out by the College of Heralds. Scott-Gatty replied that there was a danger of the unfortunate genealogist going mad if confronted for years with the name of 'Smith'. Smith nevertheless commissioned the work, but sharply rebuked the flippant Dragon for his 'joke in poor taste'.

Referring again to Smythe in a letter to his wife (April 7th) Smith wrote:

. . . It is hardly possible to imagine a more indulgent landlord or a more religious man, but he is deeply moved by the ingratitude of his tenants almost all of whom have shown either indifference to the wicked murder or to the fact that it was intended to kill him. The people are sullen and during the entire drive out and back there was not a single salute of any kind—a smile or a salutation from any one of them. We were in no danger as we were strangers, but we were offered an armed Constable to go with us if we had wished it. There is no doubt it was the act of Ribbonmen, but they have no evidence at present to fix anyone with the crime, although many people must know who did it.

Smith was deeply interested in the Irish land question and as a result of his own investigations and information received from knowledgeable people in Ireland,[2] he became strongly in favour of the establishment of a peasant proprietary in that country as the only lasting means of allaying the chronic agrarian and political disturbances. This was particularly remarkable having regard to his lifelong aversion to any interference with the rights of property or with the ordinary laws of free contract and supply and demand. The means to the desired end he saw in a plan of land purchase with money advanced to the tenants by the State.

[1] Edward Gibson, M.P. (Cons.) Dublin University; Irish Attorney-General, 1877–80; created Lord Ashbourne, 1885; Lord Chancellor of Ireland, 1885, 1886–92, 1895–1905.

[2] In particular a lengthy memorandum drawn up for him by Judge Longfield, Chief Judge of the Irish Landed Estates Court. See Maxwell, II, Appendix.

Immediately on his return to London he lost no time in pressing this course (which ultimately found expression in Lord Ashbourne's Land Purchase Act of 1885) and gave notice of a Resolution to this effect which he proposed to move in the House of Commons. In this connection Northcote wrote to him (April 17th):

> When can you and I and Gibson have a quiet talk over the Irish question, and especially over the details of your motion? It is very important that we should be prepared; and I confess to sad unpreparedness at present. . . . Particularly we must consider what are the prominent objections to the scheme and the answer to them.
>
> Observe that Redmond[1] and Healy's[2] bill stands first for 2nd Reading on the 26th,[3] and that Gladstone is not unlikely to take the opportunity of forcing on a discussion of your scheme, and damaging it beforehand.

Meanwhile Smith had been trying to ascertain the likely reception of such a scheme by the Irish themselves. An informant, A. J. Hamilton-Smythe, wrote from Athlone (April 30th):

> . . . The temper of the people has perhaps somewhat improved quite recently, as they think they perceive a disposition on the part of the Govt. to meet their wishes by adopting the scheme, ascribed to you, for purchasing the landlord's interests and reselling them to the tenants on repayment by instalments spread over a number of years. . . .
>
> I gather there is no doubt the people expect further legislation in their favor, and that they will remain dissatisfied without it; but I also gather that most of the farming class being very much oppressed by the unsettled state of the country, are so tired of agitation that they are much more disposed to accept a system of peasant proprietary as a final settlement than they might have been a year ago.

These comments reveal the factors which were already re-shaping Conservative policy towards Ireland and that the form which that policy took when the party came back to power in 1885 was not merely the almost involuntary outcome of Randolph Churchill's and Carnarvon's secret contacts with Parnell. That they were largely factors of simple expediency goes without saying under a party system. The irony of the Liberal Government's present position, after coming to power only two years earlier loudly denouncing the Coercion policy of their Tory predecessors, was too rich not to be exploited by the latter, just as it was inevitable, when Parnell and his

[1] John Redmond, M.P. (Irish Nationalist) New Ross, Co. Wexford; leader of Parnellite group after death of Parnell in 1891; became leader of re-united Irish Party, 1900.

[2] Timothy Healy, Irish Nationalist Leader and M.P. Wexford; became first Governor-General of Irish Free State, 1922.

[3] Bill to amend Gladstone's Land Act, of 1881.

friends were gaoled, that they should protest at 'certain of H.M's. Irish subjects being imprisoned without cause assigned and without trial'. Though it must be said for Smith that he always tried to take a higher view. Of a speech he made at Coventry at this time he wrote to his wife (May 7th): '. . . It was my aim to bring people to think rather of what was right as distinguished from that which might be at the present moment most conducive apparently to party interest.'

But even the rank and file of the Tories knew in their hearts that the Liberals' vacillations between coercion and appeasement in Ireland, though providing excellent ammunition for the time being, were unlikely to benefit any succeeding Government. After the 'Kilmainham Treaty' had set Parnell free again, Hamilton-Smythe wrote again to Smith (May 6th) that the Irish people saw in this 'recent triumph of the Land League and surrender of the Govt. . . . a prospect of a speedy practical separation from England, which they did not previously think likely' and that 'the belief of the rank & file of the executive in the stability of the English Government in Ireland has been so shaken that the difficulty of carrying out any repressive measures . . . will be greatly increased'. He also thought that it was 'now generally believed by the people that the present government will yield legislative independence to Ireland before long' and that 'the tenants may well think that they might get rid of their landlords on easier terms under an Irish popular government, by waiting a little & keeping up an effective pressure, than by accepting any terms offered to them by the Imperial Parliament'.

Any chances the Liberal appeasement policy might have had, however, were wrecked on the very day this letter was written (May 6th) by the atrocious murder of Lord Frederick Cavendish,[1] the new Chief Secretary, and of T. H. Burke, the Under-Secretary, in Dublin's Phoenix Park, within a few hours of the former's arrival in Ireland. Parnell was the first to realize the fearful damage that the crime could inflict upon the prestige of his movement, apart from its effect upon the recent pact with Gladstone, and, with Michael Davitt,[2] issued a manifesto condemning the deed. But the attitude of the Irish people at large was more ambiguous. Hamilton-Smythe reported to Smith (May 10th):

. . . The people were greatly impressed at first by the daring nature of the murders, & by the unusual use of the knife, but from all I

[1] 2nd son of 7th Duke of Devonshire and brother of Lord Hartington; M.P. (Lib.) for the North West Riding of Yorkshire.
[2] With Parnell one of the founders of the Land League; served several prison sentences for treason and sedition. Elected M.P. for County Meath while a prisoner, February 1882.

gather I am sure that the predominant feeling was simple curiosity as to the political result. It was only when the Parnell-Davitt manifesto appeared that the people seemed to acknowledge that the murders were blows aimed as much at the Land League party as at the government with which it had temporarily coalesced, & to affect to resent them, but I fear that they really feel very little concern about the matter, especially since they have found that the government policy as to arrears etc., will be very little affected by what has occurred.

It is now believed . . . that the murders were committed by the Fenians for the purpose of showing the country that there is a living power distinct from the Land League which is ready & willing to push forward if the Land League halts, & to which irreconcilable separatists can attach themselves without fear of being drawn into any compromise with an English Government. . . .

He went on to refer to the diminished zeal of the police 'owing to their growing dread of making themselves personally obnoxious to members of a rising power in the State' and that their officers and the resident magistrates 'are inclined to bring themselves into as little prominence as possible by official activity—until they can see what their superiors really want of them'. The Recorder of Londonderry, R. W. A. Holmes, also told Smith (May 12th) that 'we all believe that the sympathies of the mass of the people are with the murderers. . . . Moreover if poor Tom Burke had been the only victim I don't believe they would have even pretended grief. . . . In their manifesto . . . Parnell & Co. do not refer to Burke, nor does Davitt in his letter to the "Standard" '. The last observation is interesting in the light of later developments when Parnell was accused in the forged letters of saying that 'Burke got no more than his deserts'.[1]

As a result of the murders and in deference to public opinion in England, Gladstone was compelled to introduce an even more drastic Coercion Bill; but, at the same time, to offset this, he also introduced (May 15th) an Arrears Bill, as promised to Parnell under the 'Kilmainham Treaty'. The effect of this was to cancel arrears of rent in cases where tenants occupying land worth less than £30 a year were unable to pay. The Tory Opposition was somewhat divided in its reaction to the Bill—but Smith's instincts as a man of business were outraged. So Northcote begged Smith (May 21st) to stand by in the debate on the Second Reading 'so that in case of their forcing a division your description of the Bill may go forth to the country for consideration before the next stage'. He thought that 'we should denounce the Bill not only on account of its intrinsic demerits, but because it damages or destroys the chance of a much more hopeful settlement, including aid to purchase and aid to emigration'.

[1] See below, p. 250.

Smith duly rose to the occasion and made one of his calm, considered, but forceful speeches. He pointed out that the Arrears Bill would be of no benefit at all to those tenants who were really destitute as well as heavily in debt—as so many were—and that an emigration clause, as an alternative to the government proposal, would be far more effective and helpful to these cases; also that this would give those who remained behind a much better chance of making a livelihood. 'I have seen with my own eyes that, under present circumstances, it is impossible for thousands of human beings to find a livelihood among the stones and bogs of districts like Connemara.' He concluded by saying: 'For my own part, I am certainly unwilling to vote for a Bill which appears to me unsound in principle, likely to perpetuate most grave evils, and offering a distinct premium on dishonesty.'

The Bill passed through the Commons and went to the Lords who amended it to such an extent that the Government merely restored it to its original form and returned it. For a while there seemed some danger of a constitutional crisis and Smith wrote to his wife (August 9th), 'Salisbury was very grave and very seriously concerned at the aspect of affairs and at the want of courage amongst his friends in the House [Commons]. I confess I sympathize very much with him although I wish very much to avoid a crisis now and I believe we should do much better for the party and for the Country if the election took place a year hence rather than at the present time.' But next day he could write: 'Well we are let off and the crisis is at an end. Salisbury himself was for standing out but the Peers as a body said at their meeting today that they wished to accept the Bill as it stands.'

As a further consequence of the Phoenix Park murders Cabinet Ministers now received special protection during their daily movements from armed detectives. Indeed, threatening letters to Ministers and others had become a commonplace. When Salisbury received from the Chief Constable of Hertfordshire one such letter 'threatening to take your life and that of Mr. W. H. Smith on Monday', he sent it on to Smith (August 6th) with the remark: 'My dear Smith, the enclosed may interest you. I am afraid I am in point of superficies the biggest mark of the two.'

Meanwhile Conservative policy towards Ireland was still in a fluid state and largely dependent for its course upon the actions of the Government, as is shown by this letter from Northcote (September 21st):

. . . I shall have the chance of talking over our Irish policy with some of our friends before I deliver my sentiments in public. Very much too will depend on the line Gladstone may take upon Irish questions next month. I am myself very suspicious of mischief lurking under his 'devolution and delegation' rules of procedure, and think they will cover a good deal of Home Rule. We must watch this. The question you raise as to putting forward Conservative candidates in constituencies where the fight is between Liberals and Home Rulers will turn very much on the attitude now taken up by the Government.

Then there was the situation in Egypt, where, owing to the revolt of Arabi Pasha and the threat to the safety and interests of the European colony, Gladstone had been reluctantly induced by the French Government to intervene. Alexandria had been bombarded by the British Fleet (July 11th) and an army landed under Sir Garnet Wolseley, which had overwhelmed Arabi's army at Tel-el-Kebir (September 13th). The French having withdrawn from active participation in these steps at the last moment, the British were left to 'carry the baby', though declaring they would withdraw as soon as the Khedive's authority had been restored. Therefore, Northcote's letter had continued:

> . . . We must also ask for a statement as to Egypt. There is a great deal for the Govt. to explain, and to defend: but what is still more important is that they should tell us what we are to expect. However complete Wolseley's success may have been, we are not where we were before we came to blows. Neither in Egypt, nor before Europe, do we occupy the same position. We may have got a better one, or it may be a worse one, but it is a different one, and we ought to know what it is, and how the Govt. mean to turn it to account. . . .

The Opposition—and particularly their ineffably diffident Leader—were in a quandary as to what attitude to take towards these curious events. On September 28th Northcote asked Smith if he could have a word with him 'as I am feeling nervous about my utterances. . . . I cannot avoid saying something about the position in Egypt, and it will not do either to appear to carp at our success, or on the other hand to make much of it without qualifying the congratulations with some serious words of warning!'

Lord Charles Beresford,[1] dashing sailor and equally dashing politician, who as commander of the gunboat *Condor* had performed feats of valour at the bombardment of Alexandria, wrote in much the same vein to Smith (November 7th):

> . . . I do hope the party will say as little as possible about Egypt, until the bill comes in, or until chaos commences there, as it

[1] Captain, later Admiral: created Baron Beresford, 1916. 2nd son of 4th Marquess of Waterford; M.P. Co. Waterford, 1874–80; E. Marylebone, 1885–9. Fourth Sea Lord, 1886–8; M.P. York, 1897–1900; Woolwich, 1902–3; C. in C. Mediterranean, 1905; C. in C. Channel Fleet, 1907–9; M.P. Portsmouth, 1910–16.

undoubtedly will, if they do not soon organize a strong police. I am sure if we begin now it is too soon as the country has not yet got over the natural burst of delight at the return of the victorious troops and it will look as if we were jealous of the success attained in Egypt. . . .

Northcote's feelings of uncertainty about his role as leader of the Opposition in the Commons were fully echoed by the rank and file of the party, who tended more and more to look to Randolph Churchill and his spirited little band for some kind of lead that was at least vigorous even if it was also crude and irresponsible at times. Even Smith, despite his great respect and affection for Northcote, was often foremost among their colleagues in trying to keep him up to the proper mark of combativeness. But when he saw that his friend was becoming ill from strain and worry he hastened to persuade him to take the *Pandora* for a recuperative cruise.

Before Northcote went, however, he took the opportunity to ask him to relieve him of the chairmanship of the Central Committee of the party. 'I have done my best', he wrote (November 17th), 'to forward the interests of the Party, since I was asked by Lord Beaconsfield to undertake the duty, but I do not feel able to continue the work as I am conscious that it requires more attention and time than I have been or shall be able to give to it.' But the truth was he knew that relations between him and Gorst had little hope of improving unless one or the other were content to knuckle under—which, given their respective characters was improbable—and felt the party was deriving more harm than benefit from existing arrangements.

Smith's second daughter, Helen,[1] who was also convalescing from an illness, was sent along to take command of the *Pandora* and to act as hostess to the Northcotes. Through her Smith kept the Leader in touch with events at Westminster—and sometimes exerted mild pressure on him. On November 29th he wrote to her:

. . . You can tell Sir Stafford that we are getting on very slowly indeed in the House and some of us are getting angry. The Govt. don't like to be fired on from behind and many of their own friends today show impatience at their proposals. There is almost a panic about Ireland. The Conspiracy there is stated to be vast in proportions and Trevelyan[2] shows signs of real alarm.

Healy has been making an incendiary Speech at Carlow and it looks very much as if a fresh agitation was springing up which will be most dangerous now that the dark nights are approaching. . . .

[1] Married 1896 Henry Sydney Seymour, kinsman of Duke of Somerset. She died 1944.

[2] Sir George Otto Trevelyan 2nd Bart., M.P. (Lib.) Border (Hawick) Burghs, Parlty. Sec. to Admiralty, 1881. Appointed Chief Secretary for Ireland, 1882, on resignation of Forster.

And on December 1st:

> . . . I think the House will be wound up this week. The Govt. are very anxious to get rid of us as the state of affairs in Ireland is serious and the Irishmen in the House are becoming aggressive. . . .

And on January 10th:

> Gladstone is said to be seedy and shirks the renewal of a Midlothian Campaign, but some people think it is a family plot to prevent him from exhausting himself. It would not be anything remarkable if a man of his age did knock-up. . . .

Meanwhile, to Sandon (who had just succeeded his father as Earl of Harrowby) he had written (November 28th, 1882):

> The House will be up this week. I never knew it so weary and so entirely indifferent to everything. If Gladstone proposed the abolition of the Constitution in Church and State, members would not come to debate the question and his majority would vote that or anything else. . . .

And to the same on January 17th, 1883:

> . . . I wish I could see my way to leave the arena of politics and be at rest, but I am afraid the inclination is cowardly. . . .
>
> One cannot help feeling there is a good deal of disquiet and insubordination all round. Liverpool and Preston [by-elections] prove that men care more than we had supposed possible for themselves rather than for principle and very much for the action of the 4th Party and the Review and Newspaper articles are prompted by a resolve to push personal interest at all hazards. Who is to lead if Northcote fails. . . . There would be attempts below the gangway at rival leadership. I suppose these things must always happen when a party is in the position we occupy. For my part I will gladly follow anyone. . . .[1]

By the New Year, 1883, it is clear that Smith considered Northcote ought really to get back to his duties. For he wrote to Helen (January 13th) that he had written to Northcote, offering the yacht until Easter 'if he should think it right to stay away till then in order more thoroughly to recruit himself'. But, he added, 'one cannot help feeling that if he is well enough to come, it wd. be right for him to be here at the opening of Parlt.—but it wd not be right if he ran any risk of relapse and being put on one side'.

Helen, for her part, was obviously thoroughly bored with the Northcotes by this time and when Sir Stafford finally decided to come back overland from the Riviera, she could hardly wait to get home. Her father wrote to her (February 1st): '. . . It will hardly do

---

[1] Harrowby Papers.

I think for you to leave Paris a day in advance of the Northcotes. We should be delighted to have you, but it would look as if you were so tired of them that you seized the very first chance you had of running away.' When she acquiesced he wrote again (February 6th): 'I am very glad you have arranged to come over with the Northcotes. I am sure they will like it better and it looks like a fitting wind-up to the excursion, although we lose you for a day longer.'

It is worth noting here that, devoted as he was to his daughters, he was curiously and unnecessarily modest in his ideas about their marriage prospects. Thus, in the previous October, 1882, when some suitor for one of them had presented himself, he had written to Emily:

> I don't at all wish or suggest that any one of the girls should accept a proposal if there is no affection and no fitness—but our girls will not marry above the class to which Arthur C.—belongs. They must not look higher or they will remain unmarried. Don't mention this to them, but it is matter for consideration for you and for me and it must influence us in any advice we may have to give them.

During this year Smith decided to withdraw himself still more from that close attention to the family business which he had formerly given and to delegate his authority to an even greater extent. Thereupon he received from Charles Eason, the manager of the 'Dublin House', a *cri de coeur*, which, though he admonished the writer for being 'morbid', was nevertheless a well-merited tribute to the tremendous affection and respect which he had earned among his employees. Eason wrote (October 22nd, 1883):

> The relation in which the trusted servants of your firm stand to you goes beyond any Technical form of service.
> The dry hard facts of which Mr. Lethbridge spoke are all contained in the above [business reports] but we have a relation beyond all this which this cannot describe and which has existed all along to yourself personally. That relation has a more human side.
> If I might be permitted to speak for my fellows, it began to be a force when we felt the influence of your character in our work and we have been willing to spend our lives in your service not alone for the material coins you have paid us but for the love and honour in which you have been personally held by us.
> Are things to be changed?

Lord Randolph Churchill had in the meantime pushed his ambitions a good deal further than his early comparatively harmless one of mere leading a band of skirmishers in the House of Commons and was now set upon overturning the Tory party leadership and capturing control of the party organization. To this end he first succeeded in getting himself elected to the Council of the National Union of Conservative Associations and then proceeded to try to gain power for that body, which had hitherto counted for little, by wresting it from the Central Committee of the party, where, as things then stood, it wholly resided. In the light of this it is interesting to hear an estimate of him and of his future from a local Conservative party leader in Birmingham. Thomas Treadwell, the writer of this letter to Smith (July 13th, 1883) appears to have been a well-to-do manufacturer of working-class origin—of just that class which was so susceptible to the magnetism of Churchill and which found even his cruder and perverser diatribes if not exactly to their taste, at least more warming than the sedater strictures of the official leaders.

> The election of Lord Randolph Churchill to a seat on the Council of the Conservative Union is an event which I think it possible you may like to know the effect of amongst the Conservatives of this town.
>
> The general impression is that his position and talent justify it, and the hope is expressed that recent mournful events[1] may soften down to a great extent his impetuosity and ill-timed utterances: he is without doubt accepted as a force that must be recognized and utilized by any future Conservative Administration and the opinion is pretty generally held that the present leaders will wisely act in adopting a tone of forbearance with, and toleration of his eccentricities. . . .
>
> I don't think his election will be at all detrimental to Conservatism in the provinces. Many of the rank and file are determined and strongly outspoken men, but the unity of the Party is complete, and any differences that may exist between present leaders and the 'fourth party' will not affect the Constituencies at the poll. . . .

This letter goes far to explain Churchill's confidence in challenging the leaders and also his perennial preoccupation with gaining for himself the representation of one of the Birmingham seats. The leaders meanwhile watched rather helplessly as Churchill made one move after another, but not daring to show their mistrust too openly for fear of drawing the wrath of the usurper or his followers upon themselves. Thus Northcote wrote to Smith from the *Pandora*, which had again been lent to him after further illness (September 26th):

> . . . I have had a letter from a friend who desires his name may not be mentioned, telling me that Randolph Churchill, Gorst & two others have sent a 'Confidential' circular to the members of the National Union who are expected to attend as delegates at the Birmingham Conference, forwarding a list of names for the Council of the Union and requesting that they may be voted for. My friend says the object is to form a Council which will give the Fourth Party an assured

[1] His father, the Duke of Marlborough, had died suddenly on July 4th.

10. The Third Earl of Harrowby.

11. W. H. Smith as Leader of the House
(from the *Spy* cartoon).

majority, and then to use it as a piece of machinery for promoting their views. They will, he says, begin by 'choosing a leader'; claiming for themselves the right to be considered a representative body and to speak in the name of the whole party. I do not see that we can do anything in the matter, but it is as well to have some friend at Birmingham who can watch the turn of affairs and report to us. Do you know anyone who is going?

During the summer recess of 1883 Smith and part of his family went on a Baltic cruise in the *Pandora*, visiting Copenhagen and then Kronstadt, whence they went overland to St. Petersburg, as the yacht could not cross the bar at the mouth of the Neva. Of the Russian capital he wrote the following description to his sister Augusta (August 26th):

. . . The streets are wide but the paving execrable so that while you race with another droshky you bound from stone to stone and from hole to hole in a manner which adds excitement to the pleasure of a drive. Every driver in St. Petersburg would be prosecuted by the London Police in a week, but as the distances are great in St. Petersburg it is well to get over the ground quickly.

If I were to describe the City I should say it consisted of Palaces, which abound, of huge public offices, of barracks, and of three good streets of shops—but it is interesting chiefly as the people themselves are so obviously [?different] from any other Europeans one has met with. You feel you are on the confines of another Continent and are in the midst of another set of races, stolid, strong and quite confident in themselves. . . .

From St. Petersburg they went by train to Moscow and from here Smith wrote again to Augusta:

In Moscow you are in Russia. It is a semi-eastern, wholly Slav city . . . with numberless Churches of poor exterior, but barbaric in gilding, colours and jewels inside. To all appearance the Eastern Church is as much inferior as a religion to the Roman as *we* think the Roman is to the English church.

At Moscow there is a holy picture over the gate of the Kremlin, and every man passing through the Gate takes off his hat to it and crosses himself. I saw another—the Iberian Icon—going about Moscow in a carriage with six horses, the picture occupying the seat of honour facing the horses and two Priests inside, in charge, like the personal attendants of Royalty—and everyone as it passed . . . took off his hat & crossed himself. This is faith.

It is tempting to conjecture what his feelings would have been—had he lived on another fifty years—to see the children and grandchildren of these Muscovites filing with equal fervour past the embalmed body of Lenin in its glass case in Red Square.

Just before Parliament reassembled in the New Year 1884 Smith made a tour of the British Isles for the purpose of delivering a few party platform speeches. On January 18th, at Exeter, where he was the guest of Northcote at his nearby family home, Pynes, he attacked the Government's Egyptian policy and ridiculed their talk of conferring a representative constitution on Egypt. 'I value free institutions . . . but to talk about a free representative system in Egypt is about as wise as to talk about a free representative system further on in the middle of Africa.'

Afterwards he was a witness of the affection and esteem in which the kindly Northcote was always held on his home ground. To Emily he wrote (January 18th):

The Meeting is over and I have left Sir Stafford and the family receiving an ovation at the New London Inn to which the carriage was drawn by enthusiastic supporters. There were great numbers present and very great enthusiasm. It has certainly gone off well, and personally I was very kindly received. I hope it will do good . . . but the people are very hearty and kind and there is a great deal of real friendship and homeliness about them which one likes.

On January 28th he spoke at an immense meeting in Dublin, and courageously stated his objection to the extension of household suffrage to Irish counties, which formed part of the Government's Reform Bill. This was the celebrated 'mud-cabin' speech so scornfully derided by Randolph Churchill.

. . . I find at present there are in Ireland 228,000 county electors, and it is now proposed that every inhabitant of a house shall be a voter. The census gives the number of good farmhouses at 422,241, out of which come the 228,000 electors; but it also gives, I grieve from the bottom of my heart to say, 425,140 mud cabins, so that if the mud cabins are enfranchised, the mud cabins will be the majority of the electorate of Ireland. . . . And not only so, but in many counties the majority of the electors will be of that class which are perfectly illiterate. This is the proposal which is deliberately made with the view of assuaging popular discontent, and preventing those who are supposed to support Mr. Parnell from having another victory.

But this extension of the household suffrage to the Irish Counties— which trebled the Irish vote at a stroke—was at the best a two-edged affair from the Government's point of view. As a Conservative Central Office official wrote to Smith at this time: 'It is evident that the extension of the franchise to Ireland will split up the Cabinet. . . . The Government are in this dilemma—if they grant the franchise to the Irish the franchise will be used merely to emphasize the demand for Home Rule & Separation. If they refuse they will work a revolutionary agitation on the pretext that their rights are refused. . . .'

Although Gladstone's Reform Bill was merely a logical extension of Disraeli's Reform Bill of 1867, in that it proposed to confer upon the country householders the rights of suffrage already granted by Disraeli to the town householders, it would probably be fair to say that most Conservatives considered the franchise already quite low and wide enough. However, since their own great leader had sponsored the last Reform and since it was inexpedient and impolitic to alienate the masses upon whose favours they would themselves soon depend, they could not say so. Instead they took the line that no such extension of the franchise should take place without the electoral map of Britain being re-drawn. Therefore, when the Bill, having passed the Commons, reached the Lords, the latter refused to pass it unless and until a Redistribution clause were incorporated with it.[1] A grave constitutional crisis threatened, which was only resolved after several months by the personal intervention of the Queen, who brought the leaders of the two parties together to effect a compromise.

The great stumbling-block lay obviously in each party's suspicions of the other's trying to gain unfair advantage for their party in the working out of the redistribution scheme. Thus the Conservative proposal that two-member constituencies should be split, while it undoubtedly had little effect upon the chances of a homogeneous party like their own, which put up two Conservatives for such a constituency, was full of significance for the Liberals, who had been used to running a Whig and a Radical in double harness—to suit all tastes, as it were. For, with the growing predominance of the Radical wing this would accelerate the eclipse of the Whigs.

Smith, to whom the recent tendency towards a hardening of party lines between widely separated extremes was distasteful, alluded to this aspect in a memorandum which he had printed for circulation among the leaders of both parties (November 6th). Commenting on a recent speech by Sir Charles Dilke,[2] he wrote that 'it may fairly be assumed that it is not intended to maintain the existing very limited representation of minorities by means of the three-cornered constituencies or provide in any other way for the expression of the views of those who are not included in the majority'. Then, voicing his own strong feelings, he concluded: '. . . So long as majorities in the

[1] Upon this Harrowby, in a letter to Smith (June 13th, 1884), made the following pungent and probably quite valid comment: '. . . I hope that all our friends will remember that, though "re-distribution" is well understood by politicians, the Country is extraordinarily ignorant on these matters. . . . The vocabulary of the masses is so limited that half of *our* best speeches are absolutely Greek to them. . . .' (Harrowby Papers.)

[2] Sir Charles Dilke, 2nd Bart.; M.P. (Lib.) Forest of Dean; Under-Secretary to Foreign Office, 1880–2; President of Local Govt. Board, 1882–5.

population can be persuaded they have something to gain by the action of a political party, there will be a tendency to vote "solid" for the party ticket . . . but . . . there is a strong desire felt by men who are not fanatically attached to one side or the other in politics that means may be found to secure that the House of Commons for the time being shall not represent a Party, but the Nation. . . .'

The crisis over the Reform Bill, as well as the unremitting Irish obstruction, kept Smith long hours at the House and generally very busy. It was the last year of his short spell in opposition and out of office and, if he was beginning to feel the weight of his years, he was still well and happy and capable of extracting much enjoyment from life.

In the summer of 1884 he entertained the tenants on his Devonshire estate on the occasion of a political meeting at Rewe, addressed by his neighbour Sir Stafford Northcote. Afterwards he wrote to Emily (June 5th):

Dinner is waiting and we have only just got back from the excited crowd at Rewe. Everything has gone off well. Flags, triumphal arches, mottoes and all. There was a band to meet us when we drove into the village, men and women and children cheering and every little place and cottage showed some sign of pleasure.

The bells rung and the flags flew from the towers of Rewe and Silverton Churches and everyone seemed pleased and happy. There was an enormous tea drinking, beef ham and cake, bread cream and butter. People followed people in the seats at the tables, but they were all very orderly, very hungry and very happy. At last we came away and the day has ended with very warm feelings on both sides.

It is astonishing how far a little kindness goes down here. . . .

And writing to thank his sister Gussie for her wishes on his 59th birthday (June 24th):

. . . It is very pleasant to know that I have the warm affection and that I am in the minds of my sisters. But I am getting older and I am also getting tired: but I have wonderful health considering the small amount of sleep I get. I am at work with very little rest all day and my day begins at 9 or 10 and goes on until ½ past two or three in the morning.

This morning I got into my bed at ½ past three and got up again at nine. . . .

And again to Gussie at Christmas the same year:

. . . As I get older and I am sensible I *am* getting older it is useful to take account of time and compare season with season and year with year. I remember when we were children together and how we talked in your bedroom over our projects and wishes, our hopes and our sorrows. It seems a short time ago—but there have been great changes since then: and my children are now doing what we did together.

Mabel,[1] the last of the girls, 'comes out' this year and Frederick has grown to be taller and promises to be bigger than any of us. I have a very good account of him from the Masters at Eton which I will send you. . . .

Smith's interest in the Navy had not waned with his relinquishment of the Admiralty and for some time past he had been laboriously collecting evidence, with the aid of some of his former naval colleagues, for mounting a big attack on the Liberal Government's naval policy. He confided his plans to Northcote, but that supremely uncombative leader was not at all enthusiastic. He wrote back: '. . . I suppose we cannot help criticising the condition of the Navy; but I should be extremely sorry to find ourselves pledged to large increases in the Estimates. . . .' Undismayed by this reception, Smith wrote in February 1884 to his successor as First Lord, Lord Northbrook, that he proposed to ask a question regarding the present state of readiness of the Navy—with particular reference to the defence of military ports. Owing to the latter aspect of the question Northbrook passed it to Lord Hartington, the Secretary for War, who replied to Smith that he would be 'glad to give you some information confidentially', but that it was 'not desirable to make the matter the subject of debate or question in the House'.

Smith was irritated by Hartington's evasion of the issue under pretext of security and wrote to him bluntly (February 8th, 1884):

Dear Lord Hartington,

Shortly before I went to the Admiralty there was an agreement between the War Office and the Admiralty that the War Department should undertake forthwith the protection of the Military Ports by Submarine Mines and Torpedoes on a plan which was to be communicated to and approved by the Naval Commander in Chief at each Port. During my tenure of office I urged that the work should be proceeded with, and considerable progress was made, but the system was not perfected.

I am under the impression that it is still incomplete and that the Naval Commanders in Chief are ignorant of the plan of operations.

I held and hold that we ought to be in a position to bring all those defences to bear at a few days notice.

I know the Germans are ready and I believe the French are also: and as we are nearer to a War by four years than we were in 1880 we run therefore very serious risk indeed if we are not also ready.

If you can tell me that the Ports will be adequately protected in the course of this spring to the satisfaction of the Naval Officers

[1] Married 1887 Lord Sandon (later 5th Earl of Harrowby).

Commanding I will say nothing about it in the House: but if not I must bring it seriously before Parliament.

Hartington replied (March 2nd), enclosing letters from Sir Andrew Clarke, Inspector General of Fortifications, to the effect that these plans had been worked out 'in the minutest detail', approved and signed by the Naval Officers Commanding and were 'in boxes of which only Commanders-in-Chief respectively have keys'. It was admitted however that there were some deficiences in the matter of trained personnel in certain cases—a fact of which Smith was soon to receive ample evidence from his old naval friends and colleagues, who set to work with gusto to probe the true state of affairs. Thus Admiral Houston Stewart, Controller of the Navy under Smith's administration, reported (November 15th) that at Devonport 'the Torpedoes, Stores and appliances are quite incomplete & that it will take 12 *months* to carry out the plan as contemplated'. Whilst Admiral Hornby wrote on the same date unfavourably comparing the German torpedo defences at Kiel ten years earlier with the present British ones.

To cap it all the boisterous and outspoken Lord Charles Beresford wrote from Wadi Halfa (October 20th) a general and hair-raising assessment of the Navy, declaring that 'nearly all if not all of the officers of H.M. Navy view with grave concern the misplaced confidence the British Public have in the power of the Navy'; that 'the British Navy could barely defend itself and our great arsenals at home & abroad' and that 'England has no stores of modern war materials whatever . . .' and so on in the denigrating style habitual to British serving officers of any time or period.

Indeed, many of the criticisms and suggestions which Smith received from former naval colleagues and subordinates, whilst flattering to his own self-esteem, were foolish and unrealistic. One such officer, who wrote that 'I think the Country looks (*I am sure the Service does*) to *you* in this matter', wanted him to 'demand' from the present First Lord, Lord Northbrook, the reinstatement of a certain very capable senior officer of Smith's time. Smith naturally replied that this was quite impossible, 'for he *must* refuse to act on the suggestion. . . . If he did not . . . he must admit that he and his Board were incapable of managing the affairs of the Admiralty, and however true a man might feel that to be, he would sooner resign than acknowledge it in that way'.

Nevertheless, under the exaggerations Smith knew there was a core of truth—and accordingly he gave notice once again to Hartington that he intended to raise the matter in Parliament. Hartington again replied (January 19th, 1885) that he thought it undesirable to discuss the details of the defence measures, but assured him that things were better than he thought and that considerable progress had been made since 1880. But Smith remained unsatisfied—especially after receiving from Admiral Codrington, his former Private Secretary at the Admiralty and his step-daughter's husband, the following forthright letter (January 30th):

> I don't suppose you wish to press Lord Hartington to 'discuss the details' of the Torpedo Defence of our ports—but only to press him to state in public that all the material, the scheme and appliances as well as the men to do the work are ready and fit for immediate action. . . . I venture to say that he could not say Yes to any of these questions and I think you might boldly assert in the House that such is the case and leave him to reply. . . .
>
> Until . . . the whole Torpedo defence of the military ports [is] handed over to the Navy . . . the ports will be left in an unsafe condition . . . for I for one do not place the least confidence in the capacity of the Engineers to manage it.
>
> [As to] the experiments with a new locomotive Torpedoe . . . I have seen them and the whole affair is in its infancy . . . Lord Hartington's concluding remark that 'the progress made in the development of submarine defence has been satisfactory' is absurd—considering that foreigners have had for years their ports protected by some plan of torpedo whilst we have none and seem to be waiting until a perfect system is devised. . . .

The letter reveals the basic trouble as being due to lack of co-ordination, under this system of dual control, between the Army and Navy, and lack of confidence in and jealousy of each other. The same theme runs through a score of other letters received by Smith. Thus Admiral Hornby (February 19th): 'You are aware that the laying of torpedo defences for this Port [Portsmouth] rests entirely with the Royal Engineers—but . . . any supervision of their practice by the Navy is regarded with some jealousy. . . .' And Admiral Phillimore (February 19th): 'The Submarine defences are entirely in the hands of the Royal Engineers and the Commander-in-Chief has nothing to do with them. . . . At present there are no preparations. . . .' This jealousy was enormously aggravated by the astonishing fact that at this period—and until 1886—the Navy was dependent upon the War Office for guns and war-materials and stores.

Profoundly disturbed by the weight of evidence Smith finally raised the whole matter in the House of Commons in the debate on the Army Estimates (March 19th):

> . . . I shall be told that we have gone on for several years and that there has been no danger. My answer is, why have we forts or other means of defence unless there is danger? . . . Perhaps I shall be told that I am doing injury to the public interests by what I am about to say. . . . I do not agree in that view of the case. If there is sufficient

defence the country ought to know it. If the defence is insufficient the country ought to know it too, because it is absurd to suppose that those abroad who take an interest in the matter are unacquainted with the facts.

But he said he would 'so far respect the position maintained for a great many years as not to state precisely what I know of the weakness and strength of particular ports. . . . I will call them A, B and C.' He revealed that he had accumulated a considerable amount of information 'which any man or newspaper may get that chooses to take the trouble, and that without any breach of confidence or betrayal of trust by those whose duty it is to take charge of such places.' He then retailed some of the detailed information quoted above, without mentioning names. 'There is no cause for alarm,' he concluded, 'but it is to be regretted that schemes that have been on paper for years should never get beyond paper. We cannot afford to be less than ready with our materials for warfare.'

Hartington again gave a disarming reply and the question was soon swamped by other more sensational developments both on the national and international planes. Indeed, already in February everything had been overshadowed by the terrible fiasco in the Sudan, which had resulted in the death of General Gordon at the hands of the Dervishes.

Gordon had been sent out a year earlier, after the Government had decided upon abandoning the Sudan, with orders to conduct the orderly evacuation of the various Egyptian garrisons at Khartoum and other points in the Sudan. Instead, he tore up these instructions, declared himself resolved upon 'smashing the Mahdi' and wrote home for armed assistance. For several months the Government hesitated whether to ignore or acquiesce in his demand until Gordon became cut off by the Mahdi's forces. When at last the Government decided to send a relief expedition under Wolseley, Gordon's situation was already desperate and eventually the advance column of the relief arrived two days too late. Khartoum had fallen to the Mahdi and Gordon had been killed on January 26th, 1885.

The news only reached London on February 5th. For many weeks fears for Gordon and hostility towards Gladstone and his Government had been growing in intensity among the general public and the Opposition had been bombarding them with demands for information and pledges. But Gladstone had given bland assurances that there was 'no reason to apprehend danger', that 'the time had not come' and that 'the Government fully recognized their responsibility for General Gordon'. Even after the disaster ('leaving Downing Street amid a storm of hisses and groans from the mob')[1] on the day

[1] Mary Gladstone: *Diaries and Letters*, p. 344.

of Parliament's reassembly (February 19th), Gladstone attempted to palliate the disgrace of the Government by declaring that 'General Gordon contentedly forbore—indeed more than contentedly, he determinedly forbore—to make use of the means of personal safety which were at all times open to him'. The displeasure of the House at these words was so intense that Gladstone was obliged to withdraw them.

Smith was never lacking in primary sources for his information. Through the contacts and acquaintances which he had always been at pains to cultivate while at the Admiralty and on his travels, he had virtually built up his own intelligence service. Thus, through the Governor of Malta, Field Marshal Sir John Simmons, he received the following account of the tragedy from a British officer serving in Egypt.[1]

What can I write about this terrible news from Khartoum. We are in a kind of helpless rage at the Ministry at home. Week after week the General[2] here urged and pressed last summer to be allowed to do something. The precious days passed—they said they were waiting for cooler weather. All the time we had regiments up the Nile broiling in tents, who might just as well have been on the march. They said they were waiting for the river to rise. I was asked about it more than once. The river had begun to *fall* before Wolseley left England! I look upon it that Gordon's captivity, far too likely his death, has been brought about absolutely and entirely by Gladstone's deliberately *refusing* to see what he did not choose to see. . . .

The belated relief expedition involved the deaths of two other distinguished general officers: General Sir Herbert Stewart was killed in a skirmish the day after winning the battle of Abu Klea (January 1st) and Major General William Earle at the battle of Kirbeken (February 10th). That Gladstone was regarded to all intents and purposes as little less than their murderer is evident from this letter of Smith's to his wife (February 18th):

. . . From all accounts Mr. Gladstone must be off his head. Mrs. Gladstone went to call on Mrs. Earle who of course would not see her. Lady Codrington[3] came down and saw her; and she gave her a bit of her mind. Mrs. Gladstone saying that they did not allow William to see the papers. Lady C. then said other blood will be on the heads of the Govt. besides that of Genl. Earle's if they will not read or know what is going on, or something to that effect—and Mrs. Gladstone left in a huff. It is dreadful.

[1] Col. Sir Colin Scott Moncrieff, adviser on irrigation to the Egyptian Government.
[2] Gen. Sir Frederick Stephenson, commanding British occupation forces.
[3] Wife of Sir William Codrington of Dodington, 5th Bart.

Next day (February 19th):

> ... Hobart Pasha[1] whom I met in the street is all for a Turkish Alliance of course and he says Gladstone in a long conversation told him that he (G.) had always been friendly to the Turk!!

And the day after (February 20th):

> Poor Stewart's death is very sad. How many widows have been made by the folly and obstinacy of Gladstone.

But fortunately for Gladstone a first-class war scare supervened shortly afterwards, which caused these bitter recriminations over Gordon to recede more rapidly into the past than would otherwise have been the case. For, whilst a Russo-British commission was still at work marking out the frontier between Russia and Afghanistan (and despite the Czar's earlier promises to avoid conflict) Russian troops came into contact with, and defeated, Afghan troops at Penjdeh (March 30th). The two Great Powers once more seemed on the brink of war. Smith wrote to Emily (April 19th):

> The news this afternoon is very serious indeed—much more so than any I have heard for a long time. It looks very much as if Russia had played a deliberately treacherous part and in a contemptuous, defiant manner.
> I am afraid we have embarked on a very serious war which will tax all the resources of the Country.

But it was not to be; for this time Gladstone's reaction was prompt and resolute. He immediately proposed a vote of credit of £11 millions to cover the expenses of military preparations to meet the threat and earned the applause of both sides of the House for the vigour and determination of his speech on the occasion. The Russians drew back at once and agreed to submit the incident to arbitration. The alarm subsided almost as rapidly as it had risen and a great deal of the edge of the Tory party cry that Gladstone was indifferent to the honour of the Empire was blunted—despite the fact that he had simultaneously announced that the Sudan was now to be abandoned to the Mahdi.

Nevertheless, the ever present shadow of Ireland soon darkened the horizon anew when the question arose of renewing or not renewing the Coercion Act, which was due to expire in August. Chamberlain and Dilke, with Gladstone's approval, sponsored a scheme of local self-government as a more constructive means of conciliating Irish opinion. But they were outvoted in the Cabinet (May 9th) and when Gladstone announced the intention of partially renewing the Coercion Act, they both resigned from the Government.

[1] See ante, p. 115.

Shortly after this the Government was unexpectedly defeated on the Budget (June 8th) by a combination of Conservatives and Irish Nationalists—a combination betokening the ostensibly new attitude of the Tory party towards Ireland, heralded by Randolph Churchill's recent public speeches and his and others' secret interviews with Parnell. Gladstone resigned the next day.

IX

THE HOME RULE STRUGGLE

I T was not possible on this occasion to hold a general election to give one party or the other a fresh mandate to carry on the Government, as the new register of voters under the recent Reform Bill was not yet ready. But the Queen having sent for Lord Salisbury, the latter consented to form a minority 'Caretaker Ministry' in the existing Parliament till the end of the session, with an informal understanding that the Liberal majority would not obstruct the necessary routine of business.

'The new Government have indeed an arduous task before them both as regards home, foreign and colonial affairs and deserve well of the country for stepping into the gap, which certainly you would not have done if you had consulted your own convenience', wrote Sir John Simmons to Smith (June 19th). This was more than true, for the crisis found the Tory party in a state of exceptional disarray as the result, mainly, of division of opinion over Irish policy and of the revolt, led by Randolph Churchill and now joined by the influential Hicks Beach, against Northcote's leadership. As Salisbury frankly admitted some months later: '. . . we took office under many and great disadvantages. No one who is at all conversant with party tactics would doubt for a moment that it was a great misfortune to us. . . .'[1]

At any rate, in forming his Government, he capitulated to the rebels in his party, after Churchill had virtually blackmailed him into doing so, by sending Northcote to the Lords, giving Churchill the India Office and Beach the Exchequer with the leadership of the House of Commons—as well as by giving minor office to Churchill's henchmen Wolff and Gorst.

Smith—despite his erstwhile identification with Northcote and the 'Old Gang'—received the office of Secretary of State for War. But

---

[1] Speech at Newport, Monmouthshire, October 7th, 1885.

with his habitual modesty and self-effacement he had been quite
prepared to be left out. To Emily he had written (June 16th): '. . . I
am still very uncertain if I shall have office at all, although many
people say I shall, but I shall not be at all sorry to be left out. . . . A
position of greater freedom and less responsibility will be very far
from disagreeable to me. . . .' His old post at the Admiralty was
given to Lord George Hamilton. 'My office is nominally superior to
the Admiralty, but I should have preferred the old post', he wrote to
Miss Giberne. 'I have taken however that which the Chief thought
best for me and for the Government.'

" FANCY GERMAN PORTRAIT OF GENERAL SIR SMITH,
THE BRITISH SECRETARY OF STATE FOR WAR."

His new post brought him into direct and frequent official contact
with the Commander in Chief of the Army, the Duke of Cambridge.
This much-maligned and much ridiculed prince had already developed a great regard and affection for Smith, which, despite some
natural exasperation from time to time on the latter's part, was
genuinely reciprocated—as is clearly to be seen from their correspondence. For the Duke was an exceptionally kindly man and,
though inclined to be hidebound in professional matters, had such a

fine sense of duty and loyalty that his frequent importunities on behalf of his morganatic children[1] could be readily forgiven.

As soon as Smith was installed at the War Office the Duke endeavoured to persuade him to take his third son, Major Augustus FitzGeorge, as his personal assistant. But Smith, in a most tactful letter, pointed out that 'in the present state of public feeling' such an appointment would invite damaging criticism. '. . . I wish if I may be allowed to say so,' he concluded, 'to respect and maintain Your Royal Highness's authority and position; and in refraining myself of Major FitzGeorge's personal assistance . . . I have a strong belief that I am really serving both Your Royal Highness and your Son.'

The palatial house in Grosvenor Place now came into its own with the frequent entertaining inseparable from high office. Even making allowance for the very different circumstances of those times one cannot help pondering on the diffident Emily Smith's feelings on receiving in quick succession on the same day (July 14th) the following two notes from her husband:

My dearest wife,
Lord and Lady Wolseley will dine with us this evening at 8 and perhaps one or two others of my colleagues.
The ordinary dinner will do,

Yours very affec.
W. H. Smith

My dearest,
Salisbury, Beach and Lady Lucy [Beach] and Lord Randolph are coming to dine at 8 with the Wolseleys.
Don't make any bother or fuss,

Your loving,
W. H. S.

One of the foremost problems that Smith had to tackle on taking over his new department was the control of the British armies in Egypt and the Sudan. Moreover, it was necessary, though difficult at such a distance, to try to keep some sort of curb upon commanders on the spot—especially those of the independent type, like Kitchener, who, though still comparatively junior, was rapidly rising to fame and popularity. Thus Salisbury to Smith (September 11th):

My dear Smith,
I am afraid we cannot deny that a proclamation was issued offering a reward for [name illegible] dead or alive. But it is not true that Kitchener or any other officer had him killed or that he was killed in consequence of that proclamation. Is there no military rule about

[1] He married in 1840 an actress, Louisa Fairbrother, who was known as Mrs. FitzGeorge, their children likewise taking the name of FitzGeorge.

proclamations of this kind? I should have thought some solemnity or formal authorization was wanted before such an offer can be made. . . .

Accommodation for these armies was another pressing problem. The commander-in-chief in Egypt, Sir Frederick Stephenson, sent proposals for the construction of barracks at the squalid, but strategically vital, little Red Sea port of Suakim. Replying to him, Smith wrote (September 25th):

> . . . The fact is we are in the country and we cannot at present get away from it, the English garrison cannot be withdrawn but everyone must be anxious to lessen the number of our men who are exposed to all the dangers of inaction in a most exhausting and debilitating climate: whatever may be done to mitigate its effects on the constitutions of our men. . . .

THE REALITY—
" W. H. SMITH, ESQ., WAR OFFICE."

Also at this time Smith had to do a tour of duty as Minister in Attendance on the Queen at Balmoral. No minister ever relished this duty and Smith was no exception. Moreover, during his stay, the Queen was greatly exercised about the situation in Bulgaria, where the southern province (Eastern Rumelia) had revolted against the

Turkish rule under which it had been left by the Treaty of Berlin and wanted to join up with the northern half which already had its own ruler in the person of Prince Alexander of Battenberg. Though Alexander was ostensibly under Russian tutelage, he ignored all contrary commands from that quarter and enthusiastically responded to the invitation of the southern Bulgars to come to their aid and proclaimed a united Bulgaria under his own sceptre. The Queen was strongly in favour of this prince, whom she had once so much mistrusted, partly because of his defiance of the Russians and partly because he had paid court to her granddaughter.[1] This view she pressed strongly on Lord Salisbury with ultimate success, though the latter at first argued strongly that the terms of the Treaty of Berlin must be upheld—an aim which was difficult to reconcile with any gesture of approval towards Alexander.

Such was the background to the following correspondence during Smith's stay at Balmoral. On September 27th he described to Emily how, after church at Crathie, he went for a walk:

> . . . Soon there came messages from the Queen to me. She is greatly disturbed about the position of Prince Alexander and at her request I wrote a long memorandum on the subject. Then came a command to dine with the Queen . . . then another talk with the Queen after dinner and a command to telegraph to Salisbury and to write to him, and this I have done. I find that to be in attendance on the Queen is no fiction, and Ponsonby tells me that if Her Minister goes out walking without sending word She is pretty sure to see him somewhere about and to send for him on some business or other, just by way of reminding him of his duty.
>
> She is out now and so I am going to breathe the fresh air, as I have been writing all this morning.

To Smith the Queen indicated her wishes, with a hint as to the manner in which they might be satisfied: 'The Queen fears time is being lost. . . . She wishes that some sign should be given that while we cannot approve of the infraction of the Treaty of Berlin we are ready to accept the *fait accompli* and that we should support Prince Alexander in the difficult position in which he is placed.' Smith was naturally diffident about expressing an opinion on the conduct of foreign affairs, though he had a good grasp of them and knew the workings of Salisbury's mind: '. . . The only hope Mr. Smith would humbly submit is in Germany and that she might be appealed to in plain language to use her influence with Austria . . . but Mr. Smith has no doubt . . . that Lord Salisbury is using every means in his power to influence both Germany & Austria.'

[1] The daughter of her eldest daughter, the Crown Princess of Germany.

12. Viscountess Hambleden (Mrs. W. H. Smith) with, behind her,
her son-in-law, John, Fifth Earl of Harrowby and her daughter, Mabel,
Countess of Harrowby.

13. Lady Hambleden and grandchildren.

Though Salisbury, who was always glad to please the Queen, soon discovered that the great Bismarck could be squared over the union of the two halves of Bulgaria, providing a conference was held 'to drown the question in ink', the sight of his neighbour's aggrandizement was too much for King Milan of Serbia, who shortly made war on Alexander. In anticipation of this Salisbury wrote to Smith (September 29th):

> I have no doubt you had a difficult task in tranquillizing the Queen's mind—& that you gave her the best advice. . . .
>
> After my first effort to get immediate pressure—within twenty-four hours—put on Alexander I held my hand for a few days. My wish was to force Austria to show her game. There is something wrong there. However, matters are going better than I could have expected. Servia is the great difficulty. It is only Austria that can keep her in order: & if Austria is not playing true we may have trouble.
>
> It is clearly our policy to insist that Alexander shall not be dethroned.

Despite this and the fact that Salisbury had instructed the Ambassador at Constantinople, Sir William White, in the same sense, the Queen's fears for her protégé were unallayed, for Smith wrote to Salisbury (October 3rd): 'I am writing by the Queen's commands to say that she is anxious if the Ambassadors have not already met at Constantinople that they should assemble without any further delay; and that your instructions to Sir W. White . . . to refuse to admit any suggestion for the supersession of Prince Alexander, should be firmly adhered to. . . .' To Cranbrook[1] he wrote next day (October 4th): '. . . I have had rather a rough time of it here. The Queen is very anxious about affairs . . . and I am the buffer on which a good deal of this feeling is expended. I have done what I could to assure her that everything is being done that wisdom and prudence can suggest: but it ends with a Command to write a letter or send a telegram. . . .' And to Emily the same day: 'I am not sorry my stay here is coming to an end. It is not a life I should like to lead and I do pity the ladies much.'

However, on his last night, a more cheerful air prevailed. Thus, to Emily (October 5th): 'Last night there were only Lady Southampton[2] and Sir H. Ponsonby in addition to myself at dinner with the Royal Party and we laughed and chatted and talked mischief like old friends—the Queen taking her share in the gossip. . . .' And finally, on the last day:

[1] Gathorne Gathorne-Hardy, 1st Viscount (later Earl of) Cranbrook; Secretary of State for War, 1874–8; Secretary for India, 1878–80; Lord President of the Council, 1885–6 and 1886–92.

[2] Lady of the Bedchamber: widow of 3rd Baron Southampton.

... Today at 4 She suddenly sent for me for a talk—Ponsonby running into the room, saying 'Oh, you are not out. The Queen wants to see you directly' and I went up and had a 20 minutes talk with her as with any other Lady: and then a few minutes later follows this gift and note. I think you will be grateful to her, as I am, for the womanly return she makes for service honestly rendered. I do all I can to soothe and comfort her and I think she is grateful. And now goodbye, my darling, and remember that if I have a Queen to serve, I have but one love.

The General Election, based on the greatly extended register of the recent Reform Act and on the re-drawn constituencies of the Redistribution Act, came on in November of this year, 1885. On the 21st of this month a manifesto was issued by the Irish Nationalist leaders to 'the Irish electors in Great Britain' which denounced the Liberals, enumerated all their misdeeds, not only in Ireland but in Egypt, and advised Irishmen 'to place no confidence in the Liberal or Radical party and to prevent the government of the Empire falling into the hands of a party so perfidious, treacherous and incompetent' by voting against them, except in some few cases where there was 'proof of courageous fealty to the Irish cause in the last parliament'. There is a copy of the original manifesto among Smith's papers and it is worth noting that, contrary to the assertion of so many history books, the Irish electors were *not* ordered specifically to 'vote Conservative'.

Alongside this may be placed Smith's own private little manifesto, as expressed in a letter to his factotum, Pattisson (November 29th).

... make all our people [on his estate] understand that they are quite free to vote as they like, but that I shall support Mr. Paley and shall vote for him, because I am opposed to humbug and deception in politics as in private life: and I am confident every laborer who votes for the Liberal because he hopes to get something out of them will find that he has made a great mistake and has only been made a tool of—a mere footstool to be kicked away when he has served his purpose.

However, to offset the Irish defection from the Liberals, the latter gained the vote of these very agricultural labourers—notwithstanding Smith's views on the subject. Thus, though London and the towns generally turned against Gladstone and his party, the new electors in the counties repaid the party which had enfranchised them with their vote. In the result, therefore, the Liberals had a majority of 86 over the Conservatives in the new House. But, at the same time, the greatly extended franchise in Ireland had enabled Parnell to build up the strength of the Nationalists to exactly the same figure—and he therefore found himself, as he had long desired, holding the balance between the two English parties.

The Nationalists' sweeping success—they had conquered every seat in Ireland outside Ulster and the Protestant University in Dublin—had another great consequence, for it converted Gladstone finally and irrevocably to the cause of Home Rule. To him it seemed the incontrovertible verdict of a nation. But he was quite prepared at this stage to treat the issue on a bipartisan basis—even to allow the Conservatives, if they stayed in office, to take the initiative in drawing up a scheme for Irish self-government and then to collaborate with them. The Tories did in fact stay in office a little longer, since Salisbury decided not to resign but to meet Parliament in the New Year, and Gladstone did make overtures to them over the great question. Nevertheless, things were not to take the happy course he had anticipated, for the news of his 'conversion' leaked out prematurely, causing suspicion and dissension in his own party, hardening the attitude of the Conservatives and laying up incalculable trouble for the span of another generation.

Meanwhile, the election wrought certain changes for Smith personally. The Redistribution Act had abolished the double representation of Westminster and divided the constituency into three single seats—Westminster, St. George's and the Strand. The first was fought and won by Lord Algernon Percy, the second fought and won by Burdett-Coutts,[1] whilst Smith himself very appropriately carried his colours to the Strand, which he won easily against his Liberal opponent by a majority of 5,645 to 2,486. But he had not been too confident of the result beforehand, for he had written to Harrowby (November 19th, 1885):

> ... I am in rather low spirits about my own seat. I deliberately selected the least promising of the three—but I have two serious dangers to contend with—the first,—the universal belief of 'the Party' that I am safe, because everyone whom one meets in Pall Mall, Piccadilly and the Clubs is 'all right'; and therefore there is no need for any exertion: and the second is the extreme Radicalism of the working tailors, shoemakers and the like who swarm in St. James's and St. Anne's—but I am doing my best.[2]

The next few weeks were fraught with confusion, uncertainties and rumours. Though beaten, the Tories stayed on in office, awaiting the inevitable *coup de grâce* when Parliament should meet. Lord Randolph Churchill, in despondent mood, was pressing Lord Salisbury to make some kind of alliance with the moderate Liberals and

---

[1] William Lehman Ashmead-Bartlett-Burdett-Coutts, husband of Baroness Burdett-Coutts.
[2] Harrowby Papers.

Whigs. It was in these circumstances that Smith wrote to Balfour (December ?, 1885):

> . . . I do not agree that we *must* break up. We may be broken up, but it would be treason not to make efforts to give the Country a strong Government.
>
> An appeal has been made to Hartington. If he accepts it loyally, few of us will object—certainly neither you nor I—to the conditions he may make, and Salisbury recognizes that it would be possible under such circumstances to agree to legislation which would otherwise be impossible.
>
> If he will not take Office then we must go on bravely until we are beaten, and with those who beat us will rest the responsibility of preserving or destroying Parliamentary Government in England.[1]

But rumours of Gladstone's conversion to Home Rule were abroad—though they had been denied—and Salisbury felt that despite, or because of, his Government's impending demise it would be well for the Tory party to state its position once for all in regard to Ireland. Added urgency was given by the knowledge that Lord Carnarvon, the Viceroy, who had advocated Home Rule, was on the point of resignation owing to differences of opinion on this issue with the Cabinet. In these circumstances the framing of the Queen's Speech at the opening of the new Parliament was a matter of paramount importance—and over this there was discussion in the Cabinet. Salisbury wanted to include the announcement of a measure for the suppression of the Land League. But this was strongly resisted by Lord Randolph—supported by Beach—and Smith, Cranbrook and Cross, who had supported their Chief, had to effect a compromise. The result was unfortunate as it made the Government appear to be hesitant or to have no policy at all. Even Lord Iddesleigh (as Northcote had become) in a letter to Smith (December 27th), confessing he was 'very much in the dark as to what is contemplated about the Speech', thought that 'if we have a policy we ought to submit it to the House and to the Country'.

In the midst of these upheavals Smith had still to cope with the problems of his department, in the course of which he came under heavy pressure from the Duke of Cambridge, from Sir Frederick Stephenson, the Commander-in-Chief in Egypt, and from Sir Garnet Wolseley, the Adjutant-General, for a large increase in the size of the Army on account of the still critical aspect of affairs in the Balkans, Egypt and the Sudan. Smith was sympathetic, but refused to be stampeded and pleaded the difficulty of obtaining men; to which Wolseley replied bluntly that 'if more men are required in the interests of the nation, it is—if I may presume to say so—the duty

[1] Balfour Papers.

of the Govt. to find the men. Everything is to be had if you will pay the market price for it, and men are no exception to this rule—we continue to offer only boys' wages . . .'. He thought that to increase the private soldiers' pay to 1/6d a day 'would get us out of all our difficulties'! 'Party politics', he concluded, 'are gradually ruining our Army, as both sides shrink from facing the considerations of our military requirements . . . and our military strength is dwindling away before our eyes in consequence. . . .'

There was also adverse and unfair criticism of military policy in Egypt in the Press. Smith dealt with this pungently and at length in a letter to the Editor of the *Standard* (January 13th, 1886):

> I notice in the Standard an allusion to 'retreat in Egypt'. There has been no retreat. . . . If any advance is made beyond our present positions which we have held for six months we could not stop short of the reoccupation of the province of Dongola which would involve a great & costly expedition. . . .
>
> The late Government in their arrangement with the Powers bound themselves to protect the frontier of Egypt and deprived England of the power to obtain any compensation for the sacrifice she was called to make. . . .
>
> It is easy to say that the Soudan and Dongola are necessary to Egypt, but Egypt under the tutelage of England submitted to financial conditions imposed by the Powers in the interests of the Bondholders, which make it impossible for her to pay the charges of an army to reconquer the provinces or to hold them when reconquered and as I have said there is absolutely no compensation possible to England under her self-imposed denying ordinances for the sacrifices she has made and will yet have to make. . . .

Dissension was still raging in the Cabinet over the framing of the Queen's Speech and the degree, if any, of coercion for Ireland to be announced therein, when Lord Carnarvon's resignation as Viceroy was finally announced on January 16th, 1886. It was followed immediately by that of the Chief Secretary, Sir William Hart Dyke. The latter office had become within recent years almost the most responsible—and certainly the most onerous and thankless—within the Government and could no longer be filled by a Minister outside the Cabinet. It required patience, firmness, calmness and experience. One man at that moment seemed to have all the necessary qualifications as well as the standing—Salisbury accordingly wrote to Smith the kind of appeal which the latter's nature would never allow him to reject.

Confidential Hatfield House.
My dear Smith, Jan. 17. 86.
    As you know Cranbrook has refused the Lord Lieutenancy. But now comes a new complication. Last night Dyke came to Beach &

afterwards to me—& explained that he did not want to go on as Irish
Secretary—that Carnarvon had never let him know anything that
was going on—& that for that, & for other reasons more special to
himself he did not feel equal to doing the work in the House of
Commons. Now it is possible to go without a Viceroy by the help of
Lords Justices, but it is not possible to go without an Irish Secretary.
Are you disposed to take it?—supposing of course that we are not
immediately turned out. I need not tell you how much confidence
such an appointment would give to the party & the Country. It is not
a question whether the acceptance of this proposal would be an
advantage to the Country—of that there can be no doubt; but whether
you will take it. It is the post of difficulty now—& therefore the post
of honour. You would either have Lords Justices or a decorative
Lord Lieutenant if we could find one. There is, as you know, one
alternative: but we have discussed it together—& I still think the
drawbacks formidable. I am afraid you are the only person who can
avert them.

Ever yours very truly,
Salisbury

Thus appealed to, Smith did not, of course, refuse. Lord George
Hamilton wrote from the Admiralty to say 'how I admire your
patriotism, self-sacrifice and courage. . . . It is an act as gallant &
self-denying as any that has won the V.C. in action. . . . You have
extricated the Government from a really serious embarrassment.'
And Edward Stanhope, who was some months later to succeed him
at the War Office: 'If the news I see be true, all I can say is you are
the most public-spirited man in England. . . .' Carnarvon also wrote
commending his self-sacrifice and arranging to meet him to brief
him on the latest developments and on Dublin personalities.

Parliament met on January 21st—a few days after Smith's acceptance of this new office, but owing to the differences still prevailing
in the Cabinet the Queen's Speech did no more than hint haltingly
at the renewal of coercion in Ireland. It was not until three days
later—days fraught with hourly danger of defeat for the Government
before they could fire their parting shot—that Churchill and Beach,
under mounting pressure from the party, finally climbed down and
agreed to the announcement of a Coercion Bill. It was nearly too
late, for that very evening they did meet their defeat on Jesse Collings's
'Three Acres and a Cow' amendment to the Queen's Speech.

But before all this had happened Smith had already gone to
Ireland (January 23rd). He took with him a piece of paper on which
he had copied in his own hand—as a sort of guidance or reminder
as to what he was up against—the following report of a National
League meeting in Dublin a few days earlier, at which the Chairman
had said: 'The Irish Party were entering upon this session of Parlia-

ment with the utmost confidence as they knew they had a united, determined and organized people behind them and had every trust that their great leader who had been playing the two English parties against each other during the past few years, would be able to continue at the same little game, with the same success as in the past.'

From the foregoing account it will be seen that he had scarcely arrived in Dublin before Hicks Beach—the former recalcitrant—announced in the Commons, as Leader of the House, that the Chief Secretary would, *two days later*, move for leave to introduce a Bill for the purpose of suppressing the National League and other

W. H. SMITH.

"THE O'SMITH. BIG WITH FATE. THE START."

dangerous associations, for the prevention of intimidation and the protection of life, property, and public order in Ireland. In other words, as the Annual Register recorded sardonically: 'Scarcely eight-and-forty hours could have elapsed between Mr. W. H. Smith's arrival in Dublin and his arrival at the conviction that the re-establishment of some form of Coercion was absolutely necessary'.[1]

But the truth was not quite as absurd as this. For, as Salisbury told the Queen, the Coercion Bill was already prepared by the day of Parliament's reassembly and the lack of specific reference to it in the Queen's Speech was only 'to prevent the secession of the two leading Members of the House of Commons', i.e. Churchill and

[1] Annual Register, 1886, 25.

Beach, who had still not completely capitulated.[1] Therefore Smith had gone to Dublin with the knowledge that the Government—with these two exceptions—had made up its mind and was merely marking time to allow the latter to catch up with dignity. While it is true that during his brief sojourn in Dublin he was unaware of the full extent of the confusion at Westminster and also may not have been altogether unmoved by Carnarvon's—whose guest he was—pleas against coercion, there is still no reason to suppose that his report would not have been in line with the declared policy of the Government.

The Government had hoped to meet with their inevitable defeat on the issue of the Coercion Bill which they had announced and thus not only to be able to go out with the cry of 'Law and Order in Ireland', but also to show up in the course of such a debate the serious dissensions over Irish policy among the Liberals. But the Liberals—and the Irish too, since they now saw their only hope in the Liberals—seeing the advantage of the defeat taking place over Jesse Collings's amendment, which would free them from any need for showing their hand on Irish policy or exposing their own dissensions about it, pressed that this resolution should be dealt with first. Beach, as Leader of the House, concurred, thinking that the Coercion Bill could still be reached later. But it was not to be and the defeat took place on the first resolution. Nevertheless, Liberal disunity was all the same revealed, for Hartington, Goschen and Henry James were among sixteen Liberals who voted for the Government, whilst seventy-six others abstained.

While these dramatic events were going on Smith was still travelling back from Dublin to—as he supposed—move the Coercion measures. By the time he arrived in London the Government had already resigned (January 27th). A few days later he received a typically fatalistic sort of note from Carnarvon (January 29th):

My dear Smith,
    There is but one word and feeling for the events of Tuesday [26th] night—congratulations; and no one deserves it more than you do. You very gallantly undertook an impossible task; and, as you know, I could only foresee failure and sorrow. I cannot tell you how deeply I pity this unfortunate country—my sympathy being divided between the poor starving people and many of the hapless landlords. But the responsibilities at least are transferred to others, and I am satisfied that from every point of view it is better that it should be so. . . .

Smith himself, however, showed rather more of a continuing sense of responsibility. As he wrote to his sister Gussie (January 31st):

I took the Chief Secretaryship as a matter of duty and it will not be a sorrow to me to be relieved of it. I suppose we shall give up the Seals

[1] *Letters of Queen Victoria*, 3rd Series, Vol. I, p. 18.

of Office at the end of the week and then the troubles and sorrows of those who succeed us will begin.

It is a dark time for the Country but I should not at all fear for the issue if the people understood the questions on which the Government will have to decide. As it is I tremble sometimes lest in the mysterious providence of God blunders and trials and misfortunes are in store for us as a consequence of ignorant wilfulness.

Smith's brief tenure of the Irish Office had one important result affecting the structure of his business empire, for it caused him to dissociate W. H. Smith & Son henceforth completely from their 'Dublin House' and to transfer their Irish business absolutely to Charles Eason and his son, who had for so long faithfully managed it for him. Although it would in any case have been characteristic of him to have wished to avoid the suspicion of favouring his own firm through his position as a Minister of the Crown, the immediate reason for this drastic step is said to have been that owing to the excited state of public feeling in Ireland and the imminent introduction of a Coercion Bill, Eason feared that a business bearing the Chief Secretary's name might well be physically attacked and therefore suggested the instant transference of it to him and his son. At any rate, Smith at once agreed and, though he ceased to be Chief Secretary within a few days through the fall of the Government, he faithfully carried on with the transaction on what the younger Eason later described as 'most generous terms'.

As some compensation for their recent gruelling experiences and for her own chagrin at having to have Gladstone for her Prime Minister again, the Queen was anxious to bestow honours on her outgoing Ministers. To Salisbury she offered a Dukedom, which he gratefully declined 'as his fortune would not be equal to such a dignity and on Smith she wished to confer the Grand Cross of the Bath' But Smith too declined. As Salisbury explained to the Queen: '. . . he is of opinion that for the purpose of serving your majesty, in his peculiar position with respect to his extraction and the original avocation of his family, it would diminish his usefulness *at present* if he were to seem to the outside world to be too anxious for a decoration which, until recently at all events, has only been given to men of his social standing for very distinguished services. Lord Salisbury thinks Mr. Smith's scruple is exaggerated, but is deserving of respect; and there is no doubt that the kind of influence he enjoys is a very peculiar kind, and might be destroyed by any suspicion of self-seeking. . . .'[1]

There is little doubt that both Smith's instinct and Salisbury's assessment were shrewd and right. 'The Queen was very gracious to

---

[1] *Letters of Queen Victoria*, 3rd Series, Vol. I, pp. 17–18.

me on Saturday when I gave up the Seals,' wrote Smith to Gussie, 'but I am sure you will be glad to know I remain, by my own strong wish, plain Mr. Smith'. Gussie replied: '. . . I am very glad that for the present you wish to be plain Mr. Smith. . . .'

On February 8th, partly as a result of hardship through a protracted frost and partly as a challenge to an allegedly Radical Government, a meeting of unemployed in Trafalgar Square developed into a serious riot. A body calling itself the Revolutionary Social Democratic League incited the mob by inflammatory speeches and pamphlets to rush up Pall Mall and St. James's smashing windows, pillaging shops and private houses and robbing those they met. They were only finally checked and dispersed by police on reaching Oxford Street. Much of this occurring in Smith's constituency he was inundated with complaints and claims for damage; but he was more interested in setting up and obtaining subscriptions for a Relief Fund for the unemployed. The main fund was launched by the Lord Mayor and, despite the looting and damage suffered by the donors, quickly reached the sum of £78,000.

When Parliament met on February 18th, Gladstone, the new Prime Minister, announced that before the end of March he hoped to be able to lay before the House his proposals for the future government of Ireland. The Conservatives lost no time in mounting their campaign against Home Rule—and in the forefront, practically conducting a private campaign of his own, was Lord Randolph Churchill. Ever since the Liberal victory at the General Election he had been pressing Salisbury to try to liberalize Conservative policy enough to draw over the Whigs and Moderate Liberals. He also wanted to change the party's name and it was in fact he who presently coined the name 'Unionist' for the allied anti-Home Rule elements of all parties.

The following letter, dated February 5th, is indicative of this trend of thought on his part, but also reveals his best side and the good and easy relations subsisting between him and Smith.

My dear Smith,

I agree with your correspondent and the change of name may come if a Hartington-Salisbury Govt. is ever formed. I never thought Conservative an attractive designation and never use it myself.

If you are so patriotic as to dine the new members it will always be a great pleasure to me to assist in any way. I quite agree that it is most important, and that it should be done on method so as not to excite jealousies. At any rate I am as always at yr. orders.

Very sincerely yours,
Randolph S. Churchill

Shortly afterwards, on March 3rd, in a speech at Manchester, Lord Randolph did in fact make an eloquent appeal to Liberals to join with Conservatives in forming a new political party; to be called 'Unionist', to 'combine all that is best in the politics of Tory, Liberal and Whig'. But it scarcely needed his initiative, for, as already indicated by the Liberal defections in the division of January 26th, the process was accomplishing itself. Gladstone had kept his 'conversion' and his plans for Home Rule a close secret until the 'leak' occurred and this had not unnaturally angered his leading colleagues—Hartington, Chamberlain, Bright, Selborne and James. It was in regard to Chamberlain that he had committed the worst blunder, in that he had concealed from him what he had revealed to others. This was to prove fatal both to Gladstone and to Home Rule, not only because Chamberlain was already a figure of immense importance whose ill-will it was wise not to incur, but also because he had very strong views on the Irish question and a plan of his own for its solution.

Chamberlain had very doubtfully accepted office when Gladstone had formed his Government—whilst Hartington, Bright, Goschen and James had stood aside. But when Gladstone laid his plans for Home Rule before the Cabinet on March 26th Chamberlain and Trevelyan, the two leading Radicals, resigned. Thus it came about that when, on April 8th, in an atmosphere of unprecedented excitement, Gladstone introduced his Home Rule Bill in the House of Commons, the opposition to it was led by Lord Hartington, powerfully supported by Chamberlain and Goschen, as well as by Churchill, Hicks Beach and the Tories.

Smith spent the Easter recess in Italy at Cadenabbia, whence he wrote the following letter (April 27th) to his friend and fellow M.P. Penrose FitzGerald.[1] Even among the high feelings engendered by the Home Rule Bill among people of all sorts at this time Smith's violent reaction was quite startling for one usually so calm and philosophical.

> I have been studying the new Home Rule and the Land Purchase Bill in the quiet which is afforded by the Lake of Como, and if these bills pass I am very much inclined to clear out of the old country altogether, with such means as I can carry away with me, and find a home clear of the dishonour of English politics. But we are not beaten in the fight yet—only one's indignation grows.[2]

He then proceeded to a scathing analysis of the Land Bill, designed for buying out the landlords, which outraged both his business instincts and his sense of fair play, concluding: 'Better—more

[1] M.P. (Cons.) Cambridge.   [2] Maxwell, II, 172–3.

honest—bills would have been drawn by a college debating society.'

Meanwhile, on April 14th, the first manifestation of the Unionist Alliance had taken place when, amid tremendous enthusiasm, Salisbury, Hartington and Goschen had shared the platform at a public meeting to denounce the Bill held at Her Majesty's Theatre in the Haymarket. But shortly afterwards Hartington met with a more mixed reception at the hands of his own constituents in Lancashire. Thus Smith wrote to Pattisson, his pessimism unabated (May 2nd):

> ... You tell me of the failure of Hartington's meeting at Rossendale. I am very much afraid that reason and facts have very little influence with the democracy and that the Press and the Caucus will agree together upon a leader—an idol—who will be the Tyrant capable of taking the State whither he pleases, until it is too late to avert the tremendous consequences. ...

'The Caucus' was the name given to the Liberal Party organization or 'machine' which had been created by Chamberlain and there was a grim irony in the fact that owing to his present attitude on Home Rule, he had been repudiated by it—though still retaining the allegiance of his 'kingdom' of Birmingham. Supposing his present isolation to render him vulnerable, Gladstone made great efforts to win back Chamberlain and to detach him from his new allies, finally offering to drop the clause in the Bill—which he knew to be specially objectionable to Chamberlain—regarding the exclusion of Irish members from Westminster, before the Second Reading came on.

Consequently there were strong but entirely unjustified fears in the Unionist camp lest Chamberlain might succumb. Randolph Churchill in particular kept urging him to 'stick to his guns' and to Smith wrote excitedly (May 8th):

> My dear Smith,
>
> I am very anxious to see you tomorrow morning. Joe has been 'cornered'. Could you possibly come to Connaught Place in the morning.
>
> Yours ever
> Randolph S.C.

But Chamberlain soon discovered that Gladstone's offer was not a really firm one and that his sincerity 'varied in the ratio of [his] hopes and fears for the success of the Bill', as he put it.[1] Apart from that he had made up his mind on the whole issue and was completely prepared for a final breach with Gladstone. Nevertheless, there was much fencing and manoeuvring and tremendous suspense up to the

[1] Chamberlain's 'Memorandum', q. Garvin: *Life of Joseph Chamberlain, II*, 218.

last moment. The Second Reading of the Bill was moved on May 10th, but not until June 8th did the division take place, when it was defeated by 343 votes to 313. In the majority were no fewer than 93 Liberals, of whom 46 were reckoned to belong to the Chamberlain wing of a party now definitely organized as 'Liberal Unionists'.

Next day Gladstone, after a Cabinet council, advised the Queen that Parliament should be dissolved and that the opinion of the country should be taken on the great question. That same day (June 9th) Lord Randolph wrote to Smith from Ascot, where he was attending the races: '. . . I am sure that the G.O.M. like Ulysses will have many tricks and he has this enormous advantage that he is unscrupulous while his leading opponents affect scrupulousness. Betting 6–4 on G.O.M.' Indeed, Gladstone flung himself into the election campaign with a feverish energy, freely appealing to the wisdom of the 'masses' against the 'classes', who, he declared, were always in the wrong on every political question.

If the Conservatives now had the support of the dissentient Liberals, the Gladstonian Liberals now had that of the Parnellites, which the Conservatives had lost after their volte-face at the beginning of the year. To this Smith referred in his election manifesto to the Strand electors (June 17th):

> . . . It is but a few months ago that the Country was exhorted in passionate language, to return Liberals to Parliament in such numbers as to render the Party independent of the Irish Vote in the House of Commons, as it was pointed out that no Party could be safely entrusted with the duties of Government which was obliged to rely upon the Parnellites for support. Mr. Gladstone did not obtain the majority he asked for and he has secured the support for his new policy of the men he denounced six months ago, at the cost of the secession of most of his colleagues who had been associated with him in Liberal Governments during the last thirty years. . . .

What Smith did not and obviously could not allude to in the circumstances was the fact that the volte-face in Tory policy had not only permanently alienated Parnell and his party, but that it had also, not very surprisingly perhaps, led to their making awkward revelations or allegations about their recent friendly relationship with the Tories. In fact on the very night of the fateful division on the Home Rule Bill Parnell had 'charged us with being ready to grant Home Rule, for which of course there was no foundation', as Smith wrote in a note to his wife on that evening (June 7th). It was, of course, vigorously and immediately denied by Hicks Beach, for the Conservatives, and thus had little, if any effect on the division. But it led to Carnarvon having to make a statement in the Lords (June 10th) on his famous secret interview with Parnell, which was acutely embarrassing to Salisbury, and to further uncomfortably circumstantial accounts by Justin M'Carthy, Parnell's chief lieutenant, of bargains made with other representatives of the Tory party.[1]

The elections took place immediately after the dissolution of Parliament on June 25th—which was Smith's sixty-first birthday. To his sister Gussie, who had written to congratulate him, he replied (June 24th): '. . . I am getting older and more tired and I have a great deal of work to do—making me long for rest. I hope it will come—but I must not neglect work which comes as a duty.' He was not to have rest, however; only unremitting work and strain for the few remaining years of his life. In his own constituency, the Strand, he was returned by an overwhelming majority of 3,526, gaining 5,034 votes to his Liberal opponent's 1,508. Whilst on the national plane the verdict against Home Rule was also overwhelming, the Unionists gaining 394 seats (316 Conservatives plus 78 Liberal Unionists) and the Liberals and Irish Nationalists but 276 seats between them (191 Liberals and 85 Nationalists).

The election had revealed how surprisingly deep was the feeling against Home Rule in the country—much deeper even than in Parliament—and that Gladstone had alienated all sorts and conditions of men—life-long Radicals and colleagues like Bright and Chamberlain as much as Whigs like Hartington and Selborne or moderate Liberals like Goschen or Henry James. Nor were some of the radical or liberal-minded intellectuals unaffected. Thus Professor Goldwin Smith, former Regius Professor of Modern History at Oxford, who, though not a politician, had once been a fervent admirer of Gladstone and was a life-long Radical in outlook, felt so strongly that he was prepared to wield his pen against him.

To Smith he wrote (July 3rd):

> I am afraid you thought my telegram suggesting the circulation of some of my own Tracts rather egotistical. But I find the people possessed with the notion, instilled into them by the G.O.M., that some immense wrong has been done to Ireland, that some equally immense reparation is due and that the only way of making it is Gladstone's Bill. . . . I direct my efforts to making Liberals vote. It is hard to get Yellow to vote Blue. However it must be remembered that a good deal of the hard fighting has been done by Liberal Unionists.

At any rate, the verdict of the country was so conclusive that Gladstone resigned forthwith and the Queen sent for Salisbury, adjuring him to form as strong a Government as he could and, if possible, to include some of the Liberal Unionists. This advice was

---

[1] Speech by Justin M'Carthy at Hull, December 13th, 1887.

entirely in line with Salisbury's own feelings; in fact he went so far
as to appeal to Hartington to form a Government and offered to
serve under him. This proposal was regarded with distinctly mixed
feelings by most of Salisbury's colleagues and followers; but as
Hartington refused, he was compelled to form a purely Conservative
ministry. Hicks Beach, meanwhile, was not only very anxious to
secure Hartington's co-operation but was also insistent that Churchill
should lead the House as Chancellor of the Exchequer, the role which
he himself had filled in the last Conservative administration. He
ultimately offered himself for the more arduous and thankless Irish
office.

A letter from Akers-Douglas,[1] the Chief Conservative Whip, to
Smith (July 17th) conveys the atmosphere at the time; Akers-Douglas
had strong feelings of his own on the question of Salisbury ceding
the premiership to Hartington and when it arose again a few months
later he addressed a direct rebuke to the former.[2]

> I saw Beach again this morning [he wrote to Smith] and he seemed
> anxious that Randolph should be sent for—I saw Lady Randolph
> later on and she told me that he intended to start home on Tuesday
> so perhaps it may not be worth while sending a telegram to him.
>
> Beach tells me he found a strong feeling existing at the Carlton and
> among your old colleagues that Salisbury must again be Prime
> Minister and I am sure the Party in the Country would not stand
> Hartington though they would gladly see him working under
> Salisbury. . . .
>
> From all I can gather from the Whigs the question of a Coalition
> will be settled at once by Hartington's declining.
>
> If he shd decline I hope it can be made known that Lord S. wd have
> welcomed his assistance & that nothing was wanting on our part
> to show him every consideration. . . .

But even so the business of Cabinet-making was fraught with
difficulties, discussions and mysterious comings and goings. Thus
Lord Cranborne,[3] the Prime Minister's son, to Smith (July 23rd):

> My father . . . would like it very much if you could manage to come to
> Arlington Street at 10.30 this evening—He does not want to see many
> people because he will be rather tired, but I am to give the same
> message to Sir Michael Hicks Beach & Douglas (Lord Randolph also,
> only he is away) and *nobody* else need know anything about it.

[1] M.P. East Kent, Chief Whip, 1885–6 and 1886–92; Chief Commissioner of
Works, 1895–1902; Home Secretary, 1902–5; created Viscount Chilston, 1911.

[2] See Viscount Chilston: *Chief Whip: The Political Life & Times of Aretas
Akers-Douglas, 1st Viscount Chilston*, p. 102.

[3] M.P. (Cons.) Darwen Division, 1885–92; Rochester, 1893–1903; succeeded
father as 4th Marquess of Salisbury, 1903.

Smith wrote to Emily on the same day:

Beach and Douglas came to see me today . . . Beach is very anxious Hartington should join and very indisposed to take office if he does not but he cannot stand out about this. He must go on with us if Salisbury decides on forming a Government. . . .

You see Dilke is cast in all the issues and is therefore declared by the Jury to be a perjured liar as well as an adulterer. It is an awful business.[1]

Read the letter in the Times signed M.P. today, I wrote it, but nobody is to know it but you and the two girls. . . .

But on July 25th he received a distressed note from Beach saying, 'Hartington will have nothing to say to it'. Evidently Beach had continued to hope long after the Chief Whip's prognostication, not realizing that Hartington would not come over without Chamberlain and that Salisbury had told the former it would be 'too sharp a curve' for him to sit in the same Cabinet with the latter.

Next day, July 26th, Smith told Emily:

I called on Randolph as he had asked me to do, and we again discussed the situation. From him at his suggestion I went on to Beach's but he was out and I could not wait as I thought it possible there might be something here from Salisbury.

I found Lord Cranborne had written asking me to go to Arlington Street: but to enter by the garden so as to avoid observation by the Reporters.

Just as I was starting Beach drove up in a Cab and I got into it with him, and we stopped in it with the glass down just at the end of the Green Park in Piccadilly while we finished our conversation. I then got out, walked by the Park path to the garden gate and let myself in— and saw Salisbury. Our talk lasted half an hour and I went out the same way. All this was done to escape observation and I was tracked from this door, our conversation in the cab remarked upon and my visit to Lord Salisbury are noted and reported in this evening's papers! It is really quite intolerable. These vermin are omnipresent and it is hopeless to attempt to escape observation.

Hy. Northcote[2] asked me to dine with him this evening but Beach has also asked me and I thought it better to go to him. It is probable I shall have a late visit from Randolph as Joe Chamberlain is dining with him alone, and he is anxious to tell me everything 'Joe' has to say.

---

[1] Sir Charles Dilke, the Liberal politician (q.v. *ante*) was co-respondent in the divorce suit (*Crawford v. Crawford and Dilke*) which ruined his extremely promising career.

[2] Henry Stafford Northcote, younger son of Lord Iddesleigh (Sir Stafford Northcote) M.P. (Cons.) Exeter, 1880–99; Financial Secretary to War Office 1885–6: Surveyor General of Ordnance, 1886–7; Governor-General of Australia 1903–7, Created Baron Northcote, 1900.

I think most of the Cabinet appointments will be made today or tomorrow provisionally at least, and that by tomorrow night it will be settled whether Beach or Randolph or I go there [i.e. to Ireland].

But next day, July 27th, he could only write:

We had a long talk at Salisbury's today . . . and although nothing is settled yet, I think I shall not have to go to Ireland. There is a little difficulty in securing an Irishman as Lord Lieutenant without which Beach will not go. . . .

And on July 28th:

We are getting on with our work slowly, but oh! the difficulties which personal questions place in the way of a Prime Minister. No one can appreciate them but those who have had to do with the work. . . . I again offered Salisbury to make way altogether, but he would not hear of it and so I stay to do anything he wishes; but as an Irish Lord Lieutenant has been found in the Marquis of Londonderry the condition Beach insisted upon is met, and he will go to Ireland.

Stanley comes to me at 6 to tell me his decision on the offer Salisbury commissioned me to make to him, and after that I am to see Cross and George Hamilton! So I have my work cut out for tonight.

Next day, July 29th:

I could not go down tonight to Greenlands because my work is not done, and you can imagine what it is when I tell you that at 10 o'clock this morning when it was arranged that Stanley should call on me to talk over the proposals I had conveyed to him, Cross was announced, and instantly after Salisbury also and the three men met in the Morning Room; and I saw Salisbury first, then Stanley and then Cross. I met Randolph at Arlington Street by the back door at 12 went home with him to luncheon and met Beach at his house. Drove down to the Holborn Estate Schools in Houghton Street Clare Market and gave away the prizes, returned to the Carlton and there saw Cross again and told him *not* to go back to Lancashire as he had intended and arranged, that he should come and dine with me tonight at the Wellington instead. There is a great hubbub of course about the men who are to be left out and I shall be most thankful when it is all over and we are quietly at work.

The climax was reached only four days later, August 2nd; when, as Smith told Emily: 'I found more letters here urging the writers' claims to office and I had to see Salisbury in the afternoon. He is sick to death of the whole business but he told me he hoped to finish practically this evening. I saw Iddesleigh walking up to Arlington Street and looking ill and old but quite happy. . . .' Next day the finally completed Cabinet was bundled off post haste to Osborne to

213

kiss hands. '. . . On our arrival off Cowes . . . we found the outgoing Ministers had not left the Pier and we had to go on a little to wait until they got away. . . . The Queen looked radiant and seemed quite glad to see us all again!'

From all the above it is quite clear that Smith's counsel and experience were already highly valued and that he was relied upon to a singular extent by all his colleagues—from the selfless Salisbury to the self-seeking Churchill—as a combination of go-between and father-confessor. Indeed, Salisbury, owing to his aloof and unsociable nature, had more need than most Prime Ministers of loyal and reliable liaison officers to keep him in touch with the feelings of less intimate colleagues as well as of wider circles in the party and the constituencies. Smith's business experience, commonsense and absolute integrity, added to the wider views and contacts afforded by the fact of his being a 'self-made man', together rendered him the ideal person for liaison within the Cabinet. Outside the Cabinet, for keeping him informed of the trends of feeling in the party and in the constituencies, Salisbury was equally ideally served by Akers-Douglas, the Chief Whip, and Middleton, the Chief Party Agent.

The final outcome of all these protracted negotiations over the formation of the new Government should perhaps be clarified. Lord Salisbury decided not to repeat the experiment of combining the Premiership with the Foreign Office, so, after two others had refused, it was given as a tardy reparation to Lord Iddesleigh—which was presumably why he was looking 'happy' that day, though 'ill and old'. Cross—another 'drag' on the party's Front Bench in the Commons—was sent to join him in the Lords, and solaced with the India Office, the most controversial and sensational appointment was, of course, that of Lord Randolph Churchill to be Leader of the House as well as Chancellor of the Exchequer—and he, moreover, had also insisted on Cross's place at the Home Office being given to a protégé of his, Henry Matthews, a clever lawyer, but, as it turned out, a most inept parliamentarian and administrator. For the rest, Beach went to the Irish Office, Stanley to the Board of Trade, Hamilton to the Admiralty and Smith, once again, to the War Office. The above quoted letters revealed how Smith, in addition to his other diplomatic roles, became the repository of all the complaints of the disappointed and disgruntled. Churchill's meteoric rise—over and above the heads of steady and experienced plodders—naturally aroused in the latter an especial degree of bitterness. Thus Robert Bourke, who had served as Under-Secretary of State for Foreign Affairs throughout Beaconsfield's late ministry and again in Salisbury's 'Caretaker' ministry, wrote to Smith complaining bitterly of being left out, recalling his past services and concluding:

. . . I hear that all who are not personae gratissimae to Ld Randolph Churchill may in future look forward to nothing but political efface-ment so long as they belong to the Conservative Party.

If this is so, the sooner we place ourselves under the allegiance of some other leader in the House of Commons, the better for our self-respect and consistency.

In his reply (August 1st) Smith expressed his distress at Bourke's upset feelings and more or less implied he thought him lucky to have been left out. This attitude of Smith's, genuine as it was in his own case, must often have struck his colleagues as incredible or possibly hypocritical. 'I do not myself know anything about it. I asked to be left out myself but Salisbury would not have it and shall therefore serve as well as I am able . . . from what I have seen during the last few days I should say the most difficult and detestable position in life is having to form a Government. . . .'

After Churchill's own appointment that of his creature, Matthews, aroused the most suspicion and resentment. For Matthews was a barrister and a Roman Catholic and had recently attracted con-siderable attention—not all of it well-disposed—for his ruthless cross-examination of the unfor-tunate Dilke. He had also sat, many years before, for a short time in Parliament for a small Irish borough as a Nationalist of a somewhat extreme type. He had now (1886) just been elected as a Conservative against a Glad-stonian Liberal in one of the divisions of Birmingham—and Churchill had had to use all his charm and persuasion on Chamberlain to win the latter's approval of such a candidate (for Chamberlain, apart from his proprietary feelings about Bir-mingham, had also been a close friend of Dilke). There were others in the Unionist camp be-sides Chamberlain, who not only

H. MATTHEWS.

"SAT SMILING."

remembered Matthew's political past, but were even prepared to produce embarrassing evidence of it. One such was George Pitt-Lewis, Q.C., Liberal Unionist member for North-West Devon, who wrote a letter of protest to Smith and sent telegrams to

215

Salisbury on the subject. In his reply (August 2nd) Smith, whilst disclaiming any real knowledge of the circumstances, showed some signs of embarrassment and ended on a note of quite disarming candour:

> . . . As I had nothing to do with the appointment of Mr. Matthews I am entirely unacquainted with the speeches to which you refer, but I hope it will turn out that they do not bear the character which your recollection attributes to them.
>
> Mr. Matthews is I believe a very able man, and I am not aware that he has done anything or said anything at all events for 15 or 18 years, which can be seriously called in question. . . .
>
> Akers-Douglas can give you a good deal of information about it [the appointment], and although it is I confess a startling experiment, we are now committed to it, and we must rely upon the help of our friends to assist in making the Government as a whole a successful one.

As the pother gradually subsided Smith took up the reins at the War Office once more: 'Here I am at work again in my old place and everybody seems well pleased to see me', he wrote to Emily (August 4th). '. . . I was beset this morning and the Duke of Cambridge added to my troubles by sending over to ask to me see him. He talked for an hour about everything and ended finally by virtually asking to go away on Monday to the Continent for a long holiday which I shall be glad for him to do.' Next day (August 5th): 'The Duke has been with me again today and has talked a good deal but he is very straight, taking him all round.'

When Parliament reassembled a fortnight later he wrote again (August 19th): 'We are going on all right, but both Salisbury and Randolph have colds and show already more or less signs of fatigue. The excitement for Randolph is considerable. It is a great epoch in his life and if he does his work well now, his position is positively secured.' Next day (August 20th): 'Well you see we passed through our first night pretty well and all our friends seem to be satisfied. Randolph spoke well, with great care, a great sense of responsibility and some nervousness, but he was withal clear and strong and the House generally was satisfied.'

A week later his tone was not quite so cheerful (August 26th):

> We have had a nasty night—not injurious to ourselves, but trouble-some, and I have had to sit almost constantly in the House. The heat has had something to do with it, I think, and I am beginning to have less hope of getting down early in September; but we must work on and do our best. The House is thoroughly factious—that is, the Opposition—and so we all get cross together, but I am keeping well.

A few days later, on August 30th, he reports: 'Very few members are here and it is difficult to believe that the Session can be greatly

prolonged with this temperature. Randolph said quite calmly—
"Well, if our Men won't come, we must be beaten and put up with
it. It makes no difference".' But September came—and was nearly
gone—and they were still at it. 'The Irish Members and some of the
English Radicals almost make one use bad language. They are nearly
intolerable', he told Emily (September 14th). And a week later
(September 22nd):

> It is simply beastly. Here I am at 6.45 writing to you instead of taking
> a quiet turn round the garden with you; and it has been talk, talk,
> and worry, worry all the afternoon, for no purpose whatever which
> can have any useful end, but as a member of the government I have
> been obliged to stay with the other members, or our supporters would
> have had a right to complain and would have gone away. . . .
> Although I am very much disappointed at not being with you,
> perhaps it is as well that I don't make a rush down and a rush back
> again tomorrow morning, for I am very tired.

But at last Parliament was prorogued on September 25th.

X

THE BATTLE WITH CHURCHILL

I F Lord Randolph Churchill was gaining the approbation of his
colleagues for the responsible and sober manner in which he
exercised the leadership of his party in the House of Commons, he
was also winning golden opinions for the assiduity and modesty with
which he applied himself to his work at the Treasury—where his
appointment as Chancellor had at first aroused feelings of the utmost
misgiving and even of panic. When the House rose for the autumn
recess he began to formulate the policy which was to inspire his
first Budget—and it soon became clear that the keynote of that policy
was to be retrenchment.

The main targets of his economy drive almost inevitably became
the Armed Services and as the size of these depended largely on the
course of foreign affairs and foreign policy, and as the international
scene was dark and tense and Churchill mistrusted its handling by
his old *bête-noire* Iddesleigh, serious clashes in the Cabinet soon
began to take place.

It is important at this stage to make clear Smith's personal position
in relation to these affairs, because various circumstances, including
the eventual denouement of the approaching crisis, might naturally
induce the notion that he was from start to finish the implacable
opponent of Churchill and of the latter's ideas. But we have seen
that, though he remained a close and loyal friend of Iddesleigh, he
was often out of sympathy with the latter's methods and policy and
also that, despite the affronts he had once shared with the old leader,
he had grown to like Churchill and to respect his views on many
things. Thus he had been among those who had endorsed his
appointment as Chancellor and Leader of the House and when, in
September, Churchill complained of Iddesleigh's handling of foreign
policy and of the tone of some of his telegrams, Smith joined
Lord George Hamilton in supporting the criticism. Again, when
Churchill delivered a highly controversial speech at Dartford on

October 2nd, covering such wide subjects as reform of Parliamentary procedure, Government economies, improvement of the lot of agricultural labourers and a major switch of foreign policy, Smith expressed approval in a letter to *The Times* (October 3rd), whereas the attitude of most of the party was one of hostility or at least acute embarrassment.

As regards Smith's attitude to the question of government economies there is evidence that, even in his own department, which was shortly to come so heavily under Churchill's fire, he was moving towards certain decisions which must have led to a substantial saving. In October he had evidently told Iddesleigh that he was proposing to reduce the size of the British forces in Egypt and Sudan, for Iddesleigh wrote the following letter (October 20th) which incidentally gives some idea of the disturbed state of the international scene:

I think the weight of the evidence is strongly in favour of an early reduction of the Egyptian contingent. . . .

But there are complications to be taken into account. The news from Bulgaria is alarming. . . . Russia looks like meaning to occupy, and if she does I should think Austria would move, and I fancy we should have at least to move our fleet. But Turkey is sadly in the hands of Russia; and France and Russia, if they pull together, will have a great influence over the Sultan's counsels. This they will exercise—are indeed now exercising—to attack our position in Egypt. . . . They are driving at . . . the substitution of an Egyptian for a British force, and at the advance of the frontier from Halfa to Dongola. . . .

I see no reason in all this against your policy of reduction; perhaps it strengthens the argument for it. But we must move cautiously. It would be possible for the French or the Russians to say a few words to some agent of the Dervishes which might bring them down on us. . . .

Paget[1] will tell you what is going on in Bulgaria. The story of the great plot is only too likely to be true. . . .

It was true; for a palace revolution forced Prince Alexander to abdicate and Bulgaria fell again under Russian influence. Here again Smith's divorce from Iddesleigh's views became apparent, for he again sided with Churchill and Hamilton against Iddesleigh's 'Disraelian' policy of opposing Russian interference in the Balkans.

Nevertheless, this did not alter the fact that Churchill was beginning to focus on the Service Departments as the main target of his retrenchment campaign. He began to bombard Smith with memoranda on the need for War Office economies, and the latter sought early on to reassure him and above all to prevent an open breach on the subject. Thus, just before Churchill was to address the conference of Conservative Associations at Bradford on October 26th, Smith

[1] Sir Augustus Paget, British Ambassador in Vienna.

wrote to him to forestall any attempt to force his (Smith's) hand. In this letter (October 24th), therefore, he begged Churchill 'not to indicate too precisely at Bradford the results you may anticipate from economies in army administration. I shall do everything I can in that direction. . . . I contemplate method, management, arrangement— rather than large present expenditure. . . .'[1] Moreover, the fact that his assurances were perfectly genuine is proved by a letter a month later (November 28th) to his Military Secretary, General Alderson, in which he discussed the impossibility of keeping pace with the present rate of artillery development, of the consequent great wastage in money and material and wondered 'whether a hand to mouth policy for land defences has not a great deal to be said for it'.

However, as time went on, Salisbury's extraordinary patience and apparent attempts to humour Randolph Churchill at any cost and the continual wrangles in Cabinet over every imaginable thing began at last to worry even those who had sympathized with Churchill. Thus Cranbrook in his diary for November 3rd:[2] 'Salisbury should lead more. I am thinking of writing to him. A conversation with Smith and J. Manners[3] separately, shows that distrust is entering minds besides my own.' Cranbrook did in fact write a forceful letter to Salisbury about what he called the latter's 'self-renunciation'; but Salisbury replied rather hopelessly that 'my self-renunciation is only an attempt—a vain attempt—to pour oil upon the creaking and groaning machine'.

Then the hysterical, obstinate and unreasonable tone of a letter (November 8th) which Smith received from Churchill made the former realize that the latter was turning rapidly from a somewhat eccentric progressive into a demoniac force which would wreck Government, party and everything—and he began to harden. The letter ran:

> . . . I am awfully worried and anxious about our legislation which I fear greatly will be of a kind, the responsibility for which I will not share. Anything more rotten than the Ld. Chancellor's Land Bill I never saw.
>
> Lord Salisbury's opposition to compulsion for allotment purposes makes legislation on that subject useless.
>
> While as for Local Govt. I can see ahead that a great comprehensive reform is utterly out of the question. Chaplin[4] will try and fight me on

[1] This letter is quoted in full in Winston S. Churchill: *Lord Randolph Churchill*, p. 566 (new edn. Odhams, 1951).

[2] *Gathorne Hardy, 1st Earl of Cranbrook: A Memoir*, II, p. 263.

[3] Lord John Manners, see *ante* p. 94.

[4] Henry Chaplin, M.P. (Cons.) Sleaford, Lincs. President of Board of Agriculture 1889–92; President of Local Govt. Board, 1895–1900; Created Viscount Chaplin, 1916.

the closure question, but he won't succeed for I shall not fight. I shall retire. I cannot get my ideas on foreign politics attended to. Iddesleigh is conducting himself like a child. No settled purpose or plan but fussy suggestions from day to day which make me cry with vexation when I read them. Oh! What an ass he is! . . .

Fancy Ld. I's last. He tells Lascelles[1] it would not do for England to take any part in putting forward a prince, but adds 'in yr. own name suggest one of the Swedish Princes'. Quel crétin!

Only the day before (November 7th) Smith had been writing to a friend a letter which throws into high relief the complete contrast in the attitudes of himself and Churchill towards their respective careers and in regard to ambition generally: 'Very, very often I tell myself I will throw it all up and go, but when I come to think quietly I feel I cannot—yet; for although I am not of much account in the House, still I feel I should damage the Government if I went out.'

Yet, for all this, there was never any lack of spirit in him. On the contrary, when roused or assailed in any way, he could be fiercely resolute and unyielding in defence of himself or his convictions. Thus it was when, later the same month, he received the following unnecessarily offensive letter from Churchill.

Carlton Club,
November 20 1886

My dear Smith,

I was flabbergasted this morning at learning that an intimation had been received at the Treasury from the W.O. that the latter would present a supplementary estimate of 560,000£! ! ! !

I never had the smallest idea you contemplated such expenditure, nor if I remember right did you give any notice in Parliament that the last year's estimates were so insufficient.

I cannot go on at this rate. Whether on foreign policy or home policy or expenditure I have no influence at all. Nothing which I say is listened to. The Govt. are proceeding headlong to a smash and I wont be connected with it; the worst feature of all is this frantic departmental extravagance.

Yours ever,
Randolph S.C.

Smith was naturally stung by this, but he answered with commendable restraint on the same day: 'This departmental extravagance is not mine, but my predecessor's and full *private* notice has been given repeatedly since August. I hope I may yet save something, but the cake was eaten before I got here. We will talk about it when we next meet.'[2] He was still frank and friendly, but perfectly firm,

---

[1] Sir Frank Lascelles, British Minister to Bulgaria.

[2] Winston Churchill: *Lord Randolph Churchill*, p. 567 (Odhams 1951 edition).

when he told Churchill finally on December 14th that he could not effect any further economies. 'My dear R.C.—I am very sorry to say that the first review of my figures affords no hope whatever of any reductions in W.O. estimates as compared with 1886–7. . . . I shall be able to give you a rough idea of the probable gross estimate on Thursday or Friday, but it will not be a pleasant one.'[1]

Lord George Hamilton, who, as First Lord of the Admiralty, was a fellow victim with Smith of Churchill's pressure, was able to give a sop to the fuming Chancellor of the Exchequer, as an arithmetical miscalculation made two years earlier enabled the Navy Estimates to be reduced without any sacrifice of defence interests. He was particularly glad to be able to do this as he regarded himself as the 'peacemaker between the different sections of the party', as he wrote to Churchill on November 25th. At the same time, of course, this appearance of complaisance provided Churchill with another stick to use on Smith. He therefore wrote the following furious reply to Smith's bland refusal to reduce the Army estimates, greatly exaggerating the importance of Hamilton's 'reduction'.

> Treasury Chambers,
> Whitehall, S.W.
> Dec. 15. 1886
>
> My dear Smith,
>
> Of course you know best what is wanted for the Army and on that ground I will not dispute with you. But I claim a right to my own opinion as to the amount of expenditure on armaments which will be tolerated by the people in time of peace, which being exceeded will ruin our party and consequently the State.
>
> I would not be acting rightly by you if I did not at once in reply to your letter tell you that I cannot continue to be responsible for the management of the finances unless the total expenditure shows a marked reduction, and unless in that reduction the War Office takes a considerable and marked share. On this my mind is fully made up and will not alter; I am too deeply pledged to reduction and economy to allow of my being the smallest use to a Govt. which does not aim honestly at these objects.
>
> George Hamilton has promised me a reduction in next year's Navy estimates of 700,000£. Under such circumstances is it likely or possible that I could consent to Army estimates which do not show a similar and proportionate economy?
>
> I own I do not look for much assistance in this matter from the Govt. generally or from the First Lord of the Treasury, but nothing will induce me to give way on this matter and if I cannot get my way I shall go.
>
> Yours ever,
> Randolph S.C.

[1] Winston Churchill: *Lord Randolph Churchill*, p. 569.

Smith's reply was again calm and adamant.

War Office,
Dec. 16 1886

My dear R.C.,

I have been thinking a good deal over your letter of yesterday.

I am as much committed to economy as you are but I cannot be the head of a great department in times like these and ask for less than the absolute minimum required for the safety of the Country.

I will go into figures with you if you like—but it is out of the question for you to talk of retiring. If one of us goes, I shall claim the privilege; and you may rest assured that if a man can be found to take my place, I shall be delighted to give all the help in my power to a successor brave enough to assume responsibility which I am not prepared to bear.

[Bear in mind that in the House I do not ask you to defend my estimates or to excuse them.][1]

Meanwhile, Salisbury had written to Churchill the day before (December 15th), very warily disclosing his own position in the dispute: '. . . The Cabinet, happily, not I, will have to decide the controversy between you and Smith. But it will be a serious responsibility to refuse the demands of a War Minister so little imaginative as Smith, especially at such a time. It is curious that two days ago I was listening here to the most indignant denunciations of Smith for his economy—from Wolseley. . . .'[2]

Lord Randolph revealed the details of his Budget proposals to the Cabinet on December 18th and, to his surprise, met with little immediate opposition. But Smith, who was unwell at the time, asked him for a printed memorandum of the Budget proposals, not only for himself, but because 'it would not be fair to you nor to your colleagues to decide upon them "across the table"'. This drew from Churchill the following extravagant and unpardonable reply:

Carlton Club,
Pall Mall, S.W.
Dec. 18, 1886.

My dear Smith,

Fancy! That d——d little Goat.[3] He met me today here & in a jaunty manner said, 'So you are coming over to *us* on Monday'. I replied I did not know what he meant, that I was going to see *you* on Monday afternoon, & left him squashed.

How can you be so unreasonable as to require me to write a 'short' memorandum on the Budget proposals? Changes so large cannot be

---

[1] This letter is taken from a copy kept by Smith. The actual letter received by Churchill is reproduced in Winston S. Churchill: *Lord Randolph Churchill*, p. 569, where the last sentence reads: '. . . I will speak to you after the Cabinet tomorrow . . .'

[2] Churchill; op. cit. p. 570.

[3] Churchill's nickname for Lord Iddesleigh.

set out in 'short' documents; they require a regular budget speech arranging all the arguments in favour, & I have neither time nor energy to do that until I [?find] it is absolutely necessary for H. of Cmns. purposes.

Really, considering your frightful extravagance at the War Office you might at least give one a free hand for 'ways & means'. If the Cabinet want further information on the proposed budget I am ready to be cross examined, but I could not possibly produce the document you demand. I assume for all practical purposes that the Cabinet have consented to the outline of the budget. The permanent officials are now hard at work on elaboration of details & I shall not trouble my head about it any more until a week or ten days before it is to be presented to Parliament.

Yours ever,
Randolph S.C.

Small wonder if the tone of this letter sufficed to alienate Smith, at least temporarily, from the man whose personality and whose ideas had hitherto obviously attracted him and to disincline him from any further attempts at conciliation. They met on the morning of December 20th and though there is no record of their conversation it is clear that neither budged an inch. Thus Smith to Emily December 20th): 'I have just had a two hours talk with Randolph Churchill which has pretty well tired me. He came here to go through my estimates and get me to make reductions, but I am afraid he was not well satisfied with the result.'

Later the same day (December 20th) Churchill travelled down to Windsor in the company of Hamilton, both men having been invited by the Queen to dine and spend the night. In the train he declared to Hamilton his intention to resign and, despite all the latter's remonstrations, wrote that night his famous letter to Lord Salisbury, threatening, at least in appearance, to resign if he did not get his way.

Back in London next morning Hamilton rushed to the War Office to tell Smith the news. In his memoirs Hamilton tells us that Smith 'was as much surprised as I was and could not understand it. . . . It was, in his mind, a gross dereliction of duty for Churchill under these circumstances to abandon his office . . . .'[1] Moreover, Smith was by now exasperated and indignant at the species of blackmail to which he and his colleagues were being subjected through Churchill's wilfulness and selfishness and he felt it was time to force the showdown. So he sat down the same day and wrote a letter to Salisbury upon the whole subject, in which he finally asked bluntly: 'It comes

[1] Lord George Hamilton: *Parliamentary Reminiscences & Reflections*, 1886–1906, p. 50.

to this—is he to be *the* Government? If you are willing that he should be, I shall be delighted, but I could not go on on such conditions.'[1] It was a sort of counter-ultimatum from a quarter from which the Prime Minister had perhaps been least expecting one and, although there is evidence that Salisbury's patience was already strained to the limit, it is likely that with this jab he made up his mind.

But Salisbury still acted with his customary caution and oblique-ness of approach, for he did not yet feel certain of his strength. He knew that, despite his recent behaviour, Churchill still had his admirers inside the Cabinet—as well as many thousands outside it—and that the most devoted of these was also a figure of great influence in the Cabinet, at least as much, and by some possibly more, respected than himself. Beach, who was this man, was in Ireland—and Salisbury wrote to him on this December 21st, even before he indited his reply to Churchill. This letter, which enclosed a copy of Churchill's letter, has been represented as a cunning manoeuvre on Salisbury's part, in that he did not—and did not want to—convey to Beach the urgency of the situation and the fact that he was likely to accept Churchill's apparent offer of resignation.[2] In other words, that Salisbury did not want Beach to 'save the situation' by exerting his influence over Churchill to remain. Indeed there is no doubt that, in his reply, Beach treated the matter as of no urgency, promising to talk round Churchill when the latter paid his customary Christmas visit to Ireland. It is also perhaps significant that Beach complained a few days later (December 26th) in a letter to Smith of having been kept in the dark about the crisis and of having been completely taken by surprise by the resignation.

Next day, December 22nd, while Churchill was still waiting for Salisbury's reply, he met Smith at lunch at the Carlton, who told him that Salisbury had intimated his intention to accept his resigna-tion. This was the first intimation Churchill had, that, far from being entreated to return, he was about to have the door closed against him. Confirmation of this dread news arrived the same evening, whilst he was dining with his friend Wolff, in the shape of Salisbury's long awaited letter. '. . . I have no choice', wrote the Prime Minister (December 22nd), 'but to express my full concurrence with the view of Hamilton and Smith, and my dissent from yours. . . . I should hesitate to refuse at this time any supplies which men so moderate in their demands as Smith and Hamilton declared to be necessary for the safety of the country. . . .'[3] Apart from this and from expressing

---

[1] Lady Gwendolen Cecil: *Life of Robert Marquis of Salisbury*, III, p. 331.
[2] See Robert Rhodes James: *Lord Randolph Churchill*, pp. 290–2.
[3] Cecil; op. cit. pp. 332–3.

his 'profound regret' Salisbury did not actually in so many words 'accept the resignation', but after what Smith had told him earlier in the day, Churchill took it in this sense and without delay penned an acknowledgement of the Premier's letter 'accepting my resignation'.

In expressing his regret at Churchill's attitude Lord Salisbury had said in his letter to him that '. . . no one knows better than you how injurious to the public interests at this juncture your withdrawal from

THE STUDENT.

LORD RANDOLPH CHURCHILL IS DELIGHTED AT BEING OUT OF OFFICE, AS HE WILL NOW HAVE LEISURE TO STUDY.

the Government may be'. Glad as some of his colleagues were to be freed from the continual strain and provocation of his presence, fear for the future of the Government without him was the dominating reaction among them when he was gone. Even Balfour whose voice had been the most insistent in urging the Premier to stand firm against Churchill's demands, wrote to Smith from Scotland as soon as he heard the news (December 22nd):

. . . I take a very dark view of our future. I think we *must* break up. How did your interview with Randolph go off on Monday? He explained his views of War Office Finance to me on Saturday. They were simple in the extreme. He knew (by intuition) that the War Estimates were too high by £500,000: therefore they must be cut down.—Yes, but if they were not too high?—But he was sure that they were.—If the Army could not be made efficient at a less cost?— Then we must go to war with an in-efficient army, in the full assurance that by the end of the third campaign it would become efficient!—&c &c.

Of all, Smith remained the calmest—firmly unrepentant about his own role in the affair and quite devoid of any animosity towards the man whom he had been forced to fight. Thus, in his reply to Balfour (December 23rd):

. . . I am very very sorry: but it is no use crying over spilt milk. I was quite ready to retire myself and have indeed been anxious to do so,— making it quite clear that in resigning I should support the Govt. with all my power, but Salisbury does not apparently desire this solution of the difficulty and Randolph will not hear of it.

I have no personal difference with him, but quite the reverse—my own belief is that our Estimates are the excuse and not the real cause of his retirement. Indeed, he admitted that if he had been in other respects in harmony with his colleagues he might have swallowed the Estimates.

I am very sorry indeed on many grounds. It is a great misfortune to the Country that it should not have a strong and united Govt. at this juncture.

Randolph outside cannot help being more or less in opposition. As regards his own position and his own future it is a great disappointment; to me it is clear that the real cause of his retirement is the simple fact that he cannot follow, and he can hardly be a colleague in the ordinary sense of the term.

If he is in a Government, he must be Chief, Supreme, a Bismarck. . . . Meanwhile there is Ireland to govern—and a great European War about to burst upon us. The outlook is not a cheerful one for those who are bound in honor not to desert the Ship.

Akers-Douglas, the Chief Whip, was also calm and did not share Salisbury's and Balfour's forebodings about the future. He was determined to try to prevent Salisbury from prematurely and, as he thought, unnecessarily truckling to Hartington and the Liberal Unionists. 'I find the greatest unanimity of feeling among our party', he wrote to Smith (December 24th), 'all are against R.C. . . . Many of his particular friends have told me they think his conduct insane. . . I have had heaps of letters today from M.P.'s regretting the present

crisis but all wishing me to assure the Govt. of their support. . . .'
Smith having written to him the same day saying that he was 'cordially
in favour of Salisbury's intention to work with Hartington', Akers-
Douglas replied pointedly (December 25th) '. . . Hartington's lead
in the H. of Commons wd. be followed by most of our men loyally—
provided he was Lord S's lieutenant, but I am not so certain as to
their approval in the event of his being 1st Ld. I am sure however
they wd prefer Beach or yourself. In any case and at all hazards a
general election *must* be avoided, as we should certainly lose *many*
seats. . . .'

Hard on this came the letter, already referred to from Hicks Beach,
from Ireland, presenting the opposite and much gloomier view:

Private

Glaslough House,
Glaslough,
Ireland
Dec. 26. 86.

My dear Smith,

I don't by any means regard you as the 'author of all evil' as you
seem to suppose. I know nothing, and will not therefore venture an
opinion, on the merits of the question at issue between you and R.C.
But I dare say I should agree with you if I did: and I fear (though the
announcement came absolutely without previous warning to me) that
other causes have been at work besides Army & Navy Estimates.

But the result is a grave disaster—and, by its unsettlement of the
future, it has gone far to undo any good I may have done here. I have
written fully to Salisbury, and will not trouble you with a repetition.
But my opinion is that we could *get* on with a new Unionist Government to be formed by Hartington including as many, or as few, of us
as he pleases: that we could *struggle* on, if he, or perhaps even
Goschen (though this I doubt) would join us; but that this is the
'irreducible minimum': & that without the real co-operation in the
Cabinet of moderate Liberal representatives, the story of last January
would be repeated, & therefore it would be better for everybody that
we should resign at once.

Yours sincerely,
M. E. Hicks Beach

All his colleagues were aware that, resolute as he had been at the
final showdown, Salisbury's self-confidence had been badly shaken
by the affair and that he was longing to pass the premiership on to
Hartington. Some, like Beach, thought his fears only too well
grounded; some, like Akers-Douglas, thought them exaggerated;
and some were just contemptuous, like Lord Beauchamp,[1] the Pay-
master General, who wrote to Smith (December 26th): '. . . I am
sorry Lord Salisbury has made such a fuss about Randolph Churchill.
He should have filled up the place at once. It is very foolish to go

[1] Frederick, 6th Earl; Paymaster-General, 1886–7.

again to Lord Hartington and to cry stinking fish. Lord R. Churchill carries no one with him and will not I think be able to do much harm in the country. Lord Salisbury is properly punished for having given Lord R. C. a post for which he was never fit and thereby dislocating the proper arrangements of the Party.'

But Lord Harris,[1] Smith's Under-Secretary in the War Office, wrote to him (December 27th), expressing his personal sorrow and disappointment at the fall of Churchill and adding '. . . But I don't think it would be wise to ignore that he had been a great power both in the House & the Country; and it remains to be seen whether the latter will forgive him . . .'. He then offered to give up his office, should Salisbury form a coalition government with Hartington, in order to make way for a Liberal Unionist. But Hartington, who had been abroad during these anxious days, scotched hopes and fears alike by immediately on his return seeing Salisbury (December 31st) and firmly refusing any form of co-operation on his own part. The telegram announcing the news to the Queen[2] would appear to have been composed between Salisbury and Smith, for there is a draft in Smith's writing among his papers. It represents Hartington as saying that 'he could not without losing all influence over the Liberals in the Country either join a Conservative Government or form a Coalition Government'. He might only do the latter if the Conservatives were 'unable to carry on Government'. This, Salisbury is supposed to have rejoined, would be 'a confession which would not be true and would be humiliating'. Nevertheless, despite Hartington's reference to 'Conservative unwillingness', he had still been pressed strongly to 'take the premiership' on account of the supposed benefits to Unionism as a whole.

The idea underlying this almost importunate approach to Hartington bade fair to throw away any advantages which might have accrued from the earlier policy of firmness—for it simply implied that the Government and Party felt they could not afford to alienate Randolph Churchill, but that he might be induced to come back to office under a Liberal-Unionist premier. Akers-Douglas, however, thought exactly the opposite and in a most forthright letter (December 30th), which Salisbury must have received on the day of his interview with Hartington, told the former that 'your resignation would be taken by large numbers of our party as an acknowledgement that you were afraid to go on though you had 320 followers and would magnify the position of Churchill. Such a Coalition as this with Hartington at its head would be a Liberal Coalition in the eyes of many and it would offend many who now say freely that by

[1] George, 4th Baron; Under Secretary for War, 1886–90.
[2] Given in extenso in *Letters of Queen Victoria*, 3rd Series, Vol. I, p. 240.

giving you the majority at the last Election they expressed their confidence in you which confidence you wd seem hardly to appreciate.'[1] Middleton, too, the extremely able Chief Party Agent, who had his finger on the pulse of the constituencies, had written the same day to Akers-Douglas: '. . . For goodness sake induce Ld Salisbury to fill the post allotted to him by the voice of the people at the late election—i.e. Prime Minister.'[2]

Meanwhile, *faute de mieux*, Salisbury had instructed Akers-Douglas to sound Goschen as to his willingness to join the Government. Owing to his outstanding financial ability the latter was an obvious choice to fill at least one of Churchill's late roles; but he hesitated much at first, fearing as a lone Liberal Unionist, to be isolated in an all-Tory Cabinet. Moreover, he also would have preferred Hartington to head a coalition Government with Salisbury and Churchill serving in it. However, though Hartington refused any co-operation on his own part, he raised no objection to Goschen joining a new government under Salisbury—and, at Salisbury's request, even urged him to do so.

'I understand Hartington to admit the possibility of Goschen's joining us and to have gone off to see him . . .', wrote Smith to Salisbury (January 1st, 1887), 'I think he ought to consent—unless he cares for his position in Hartington's party more than for the Country. As far as I am concerned he might have any post he liked. . . .'[3] But at least, of the two posts left vacant by Churchill, there was one which Goschen could not have. He insisted that if he joined at all he joined as a Liberal and as the Conservatives were the largest party in the House it was asking rather much of them to accept him as their leader there. But Smith—perhaps in his anxiety to avoid the post himself—did not seem to see any objection in this respect, for he wrote to Goschen (January 2nd):

My dear Goschen,
    I hear that Salisbury has asked you to be Chancr. of Exchqr. and leader of the House and I hope most sincerely that you will consent to become both the one and the other. I believe you will be supported in the Country and in the H. of C. in taking such a step. I should be glad to follow you loyally and to give you all the assistance in my power. There is very little difference of opinion between us—none that would prevent hearty co-operation in the effort to serve the Country in a time of trial and difficulty and I am sure you would find the same feeling in my colleagues on the bench with regard to whom there can be no sense of supersession, seeing that you are senior in Cabinet rank to every one of us with the exception of John Manners

[1] See Chilston papers and Chilston, op. cit., pp. 102–3.
[2] Ibid., p. 105.
[3] Salisbury Papers.

whose health would not allow him to lead. I was anxious that Hartington should come over on his own terms but he has possibly acted wisely in keeping his party together. If however he had seen his way there is no sacrifice of personal position or interest which we should not have made cheerfully under the circumstances in which the Country is placed.

There is among Smith's papers a memorandum prepared by Salisbury in his own hand (on January 18th) which was primarily written as a record of the events leading up to the death of Lord Iddesleigh, but which throws considerable light on the course of the negotiations with Goschen and on the nature of the various combinations proposed before Smith finally agreed to accept the leadership of the House of Commons. The following is an extract of Salisbury's memorandum:

> On Friday, Dec. 31 . . . I met Lord Hartington: and, failing to induce him to take office, I asked him to urge Goschen to join us. He objected to Goschen's taking the lead in the House of Commons: but when I pointed out that Goschen might become Ch. of Exchequer, and Mr. Smith might take the lead as First Lord of the Treasury, he consented to urge this course on Mr. Goschen. I mentioned that this arrangement necessarily involved my going back to the Foreign Office. On Monday Jan 3 I met Mr. Goschen who, after discussing public affairs, agreed to join. But he insisted that he should *not* be leader: & asked that two Liberal peers Lord Northbrook and Lord Lansdowne should be invited to join . . . I mentioned to him that to avoid disturbance as much as possible, I had tried to persuade Mr. Smith to try and work the Leadership of the House together with the War Office. Mr. Goschen demurred to this proposal. He had understood from Lord Hartington that I proposed to go back to the Foreign Office, leaving the Treasury to Mr. Smith: and he pressed very strongly that this arrangement should be adhered to. His ground was that he was strongly convinced . . . that Lord Iddesleigh . . . had not *now* the health requisite for the Foreign Office: and on public grounds he thought the change essential. . . . Seeing Mr. Smith immediately after, I found him deeply impressed with the impossibility of holding the Leadership & the War Office together. . . .

So the upshot of it was that on this day (January 3rd) Smith accepted the Leadership of the House of Commons on condition that he was relieved of the War Office and, since he had to be provided with a titular office in order to lead, Salisbury surrendered to him the First Lordship of the Treasury, Salisbury himself taking back the Foreign Office from Iddesleigh.

Next day the devoted Miss Giberne wrote ecstatically to Emily Smith: 'My dearest Emily, Isn't it beautiful! Isn't it lovely that Lord Salisbury has some sense in his head? To make just *the* right appointment. . . . Oh, won't a certain ex-leader grind his teeth (if he has any to grind at 77) and don't you think we did ought to send a vote of thanks to that little lord with the long moustaches for sweeping the path so cleverly. . . .'

Needless to say that this highly ingenuous view of the matter scarcely accorded with Smith's own. He was not only quite unelated by the high position and its responsibilities and extremely diffident about his powers of coping with them, but he was stricken with conscience about the feelings of his one obvious rival for the post— Hicks Beach. The latter had not only already held the position of leader with success in a former administration, but, as we have seen, held a very high place in the estimation of his colleagues. On the other hand, there is no doubt that his reserved and touchy disposition rendered him something less than ideal for a position requiring the qualities of patience, conciliation and persuasion. At any rate, Smith's first thought was to write to Beach to explain that he had only reluctantly accepted the leadership because he had understood Beach to have told Salisbury he would not take it on any terms. Beach replied, in kindly vein, but slightly cryptically, so that Smith sent on the letter to Akers-Douglas, for his opinion. '. . . With regard to the leadership', Beach wrote (January 4th), 'I did not go *quite* so far as to say that I would not take it on any terms or any considerations. I put most strongly before Salisbury my own reasons for objecting to take it in any shape: and I told him it was impossible for me to take it *with* Ireland. His reply was that he could replace me as leader, but felt it absolutely impossible to spare me here, and that Ireland must be the first consideration. . . . I am very glad that you are going to lead instead of me, anyhow: and need not say, will do anything I can to ease you in the work. . . .'[1]

The tone of the first part of this letter still left Smith feeling a little uneasy and he wrote anxiously to Akers-Douglas again the next day (January 5th): 'Is Beach at all huffed that he had not been pressed by Salisbury to take the lead?'[2] Then again on the day after that he returned to the subject in a letter (January 6th) full of doubts and anxious questions which he wanted to ask the Chief Whip—'. . . if my nomination goes on, but I suspect Beach does not really like it . . .'. One of these questions was: '. . . What is the form of invitation to the dinner given the night before the House meets? Is it the First Lord of the Treasury requests the honor etc. or simply Mr. W. H. Smith? I should prefer the simpler and plainer—but the cards will have to be printed—*if I go on*.'[3]

But of course he went on. 'It is not the first time that you have stood in the Breach', wrote his old Admiralty colleague, Sir Massey Lopes

[1] Chilston Papers. [2] Ibid. [3] Ibid.

(January 6th), '& I think it more than probable that you have only now been induced, by a feeling of Patriotism, to accept a Post which you would rather have *personally* declined. . . .' That was neither more nor less than the truth. Less charitably, Cecil Raikes, the Post-master-General, wrote to Akers-Douglas (January 10th): '. . . You will see that the attempt to conduct public business under Smith's leadership will prove a sad fiasco.'[1] But—apart, of course, from Lord Randolph—Raikes was in a minority as well as wrong: for, if Smith's colleagues knew his limitations as an orator or debater, they knew also that they had put themselves in the hands of a man with the highest standards of duty and integrity of perhaps any statesman of that age, whose well-known kindness and benevolence moreover did not preclude great resources of strength and firmness.

Meanwhile his going from the War Office drew the following lament from Lord Wolseley, Adjutant-General to the Forces. He wrote (January 9th):

> . . . I am in despair at your leaving us: for 15 years I have worked hard to bring about some definite army organization that would give the nation in return for the money voted for us yearly, something like an army that could be easily & quickly put in the field. I thought to see my hopes realised under you, and now they are all dashed to the ground. Even assuming that Stanhope will take the same view that you have done, he will require time to learn his lesson & to under-stand where it is, & how it is, the difficulty exists. The Head Quarter Staff who are now pretty much of my way of thinking regard your departure as a sort of national disaster.

Smith had a soft spot for the old Duke of Cambridge, despite the latter's obstinacy and importunities, so before leaving the War Office he wrote a minute recording his gratitude for kindness and co-operation shown to him by the Commander-in-Chief and his staff. The Duke wrote back (January 14th) warmly to say 'how much I appreciate this official record of your sentiments regarding myself & the other officers under my more immediate authority'. But not all his colleagues entertained such friendly feelings towards this extremely rigid old figurehead—especially Wolseley who had pro-gressive ideas about the Army and had already sent in his resignation as Adjutant-General, despairing of getting his way.[2] Thus he wrote to Smith the same day as the Duke:

[1] Chilston Papers.
[2] He remained Adjutant-General, however, until 1890 and although in that year a Royal Commission under Hartington recommended abolition of the post of Commander-in-Chief the Government did not adopt this course and the Duke continued to retain it till 1895, when he was succeeded in it by Wolseley. The post was not finally abolished until after the South African War and the Report of the Elgin Commission.

... Now that the month is not far off when H.R.H. is to be allowed his own way freed from my presence, I shall be glad to be rid of an office where under existing circumstances no practical progress or reforms can be effected. . . . As a taxpayer I feel it is monstrous to squander money as we do to satisfy the old-fashioned notions of H.R.H. and as a soldier employed in the administration of the Army, I feel it is culpable to join in hoodwinking poor deluded John Bull—I often feel inclined to 'chuck up' the whole business & tell the country the whole truth. . . .

When Salisbury took back the Foreign Office from Iddesleigh he was not only complying with one of Goschen's conditions for joining the Government, but also taking Iddesleigh at his own word, the latter in a letter of December 30th having placed his seat in the Cabinet at Salisbury's disposal. In view of his later reactions, however, it must be supposed that this was merely a formal gesture on Iddesleigh's part and that he did not expect to find himself, as he did in a cypher telegram from Salisbury on January 4th, excluded altogether without the offer of an alternative. Salisbury followed up the telegram with a letter (a copy of which is in Smith's papers) on the same day in which he expressed his regret, adding: '. . . The precise arrangement which has arisen out of this particular requirement of Goschen's is not likely in any case to last long & I hope that before much time has elapsed we shall be asking for your assistance again. Perhaps you will not be sorry for a little interval of rest. . . .'

There are different versions of the sequence of events in this unhappy affair, as well as of the motives and feelings attributed to the parties concerned, but the hitherto unpublished letter (January 10th) from Iddesleigh to Smith, reproduced below, not only clarifies the chronological side, but, despite its feignedly cheerful air, indicates the nature and extent of the hurt. It was in answer to one from Smith (January 9th) which shows that the latter, though he had certainly opposed Iddesleigh's appointment to the Colonial Office,[1] was anxious that his old friend should not think he had been hand in glove with Salisbury in the attempt to exclude him entirely. Smith had written:

I see by the 'Western Morning News' that there is some doubt whether you will remain in the Cabinet. As an old friend, will you let me say what pain it would give me if you went from us? I hold on, greatly against every personal feeling and inclination. I do not like the work I am called upon to do. I distrust my own powers to do it, and I remain and try, probably facing political death because I am told it is my duty. I do not attempt to use such language to you. I do not know, for Salisbury has not told me—having intentionally kept away while

[1] See *The Letters of Queen Victoria*, Third Series, Vol. I, p. 251.

all these changes have been going on—what he has said to you, but I am quite sure of this, that it would be a real sorrow to us all if we were not to meet you again in Cabinet.

It is possible to think the last sentence somewhat disingenuous, since Smith must have seen Salisbury only the day before about the Colonial Office proposal; but at any rate the present intention was sincere and kindly. Here is Iddesleigh's reply:

Confidential   Pynes
My dear Smith,   Jan. 10. 1887

Many thanks for your kind note, and let me add many more to you for your zeal and self-sacrifice in taking the arduous post which has been assigned to you. While I pity you, I also feel confident that you will meet with the success which you will deserve and will add enormously to the obligations which you have already conferred on the country.

My own position is very different from yours. When the attempt was made to introduce some of the Liberals into the Cabinet I told Salisbury that in case he wanted places, I should be only too glad to put my own at his disposal. I had thought there might be two or three such men as Northbrook or Landsowne, whom it might have been desirable to offer a Cabinet Office to.

When Goschen's appointment was alone in question I supposed all changes in the House of Lords were at an end; till, to my great surprise, I saw it announced in the newspapers that I had offered to resign in order to facilitate the arrangement and that my offer had been accepted. Some very uncomfortable hours were spent in trying to ward off questions in Exeter; but late in the afternoon the mystery was solved by Salisbury's telegram, describing the situation, and regretting that he must take advantage of my offer and ask me to give up the F.O. to him. He gave no hint of any exchange, and the language of his telegram seemed fully to imply a complete separation. Next morning I received a letter to the same effect. I therefore replied that, though I shall leave the F.O. with regret, I cheerfully acquiesced in his decision.

I regarded that as the close of my connection with the Cabinet: and when I afterwards received a telegram asking if I would take the P. Privy Council, I looked on that as a new departure, and thought myself at liberty to decline. He has since written to press me to reconsider the decision; but I can see no necessity, and I cannot but feel that I had better stand to the answer I have already given. I cannot help seeing that, if the P.C.O. is really vacant, Salisbury might himself have taken the office, retaining as P.M. his control over the F.O. and other departments, and that his preference for a course which will throw so much labour upon him is probably due to his dissatisfaction with my administration of the F.O. Anyhow it is clear that I am not really wanted, and I rejoice to look forward to a little freedom. I shall do my best to serve the Party, and to give my late colleagues and my chief the heartiest support.

Believe me,

Yours very faithfully,

Iddesleigh

It would certainly appear that Salisbury was intending to drop Iddesleigh out of the Cabinet altogether and that it was under the very considerable pressure which the Queen brought to bear[1] that he made the rather belated offer of the posts of Lord Privy Seal or Lord President of the Council. Also the Prime Minister did indicate in confidence to a section of the Press with which he was closely in touch his intention of taking back the Foreign Office; but this confidence was betrayed and the news prematurely leaked, with the result that poor Iddesleigh received the first definite intimation of his removal through a newspaper.

But probably the most light is shed upon this painful imbroglio by a letter (January 11th) from Iddesleigh's second son, Henry Stafford Northcote, who held minor office in the Government as Surveyor General of Ordnance, and who wrote to Smith 'to pour out my heart a little' and for advice about his own position, which he felt to be compromised by his father's refusal to be cajoled back into a sinecure. In this letter he told Smith that he had written to his father urging him to resume office: '. . . I thought patriotism should induce him to do so'. But:

> . . . When I got down, however, I found the state of affairs to be that personal annoyance was in the ascendant. Unluckily, down at Pynes amongst his own immediate relatives and neighbours the importance of the contretemps of the publication of the news got exaggerated; and oil instead of water thrown on the fire.
>
> It had got too high for me to extinguish—though had I been alone with my father, I think he would have listened to my arguments—but he was urged on by others. Unfortunately my eldest brother Lord St. Cyres is, I fear, more of a Liberal than anything else: and did harm.

Northcote then explains his own embarrassment in that he is ambitious, likes Lord Salisbury, does not agree with his father's reasons for refusing to return to the Government and therefore is loth to sacrifice his career out of feigned loyalty. On the other hand, 'some of my constituents, relatives, friends, enemies and outsiders will call me a shabby fellow for not resenting an affront to my father . . . of course I don't admit the existence of such an affront . . .'.

> . . . My father assures me he is not leaving in a 'huff'; and though privately I discount this—I do not think he will do or say anything to

[1] Op. cit., pp. 250–3.

embarrass the Govt. Of course I can't answer for angry remarks that may be made by other members of the family to persons of the Mrs. Jeune[1] type—nor how far this sort of tittle-tattle may get into the Society papers.

Of course much of the trouble has arisen from the fact that my father has grown old without appreciating that he has done so; and is therefore influenced to an undue extent by those immediately round him. Had he been in town when this occurred matters would have been settled quietly. I even think, now it is too late, he begins to waver. . . .

Smith evidently immediately communicated the substance of this to Salisbury, for the latter wrote to him (January 12th):

H. NORTHCOTE.

"BURNING QUESTIONS."

I would certainly earnestly advise Henry Northcote to go on with us—either in his present position or some other of equal weight. He has been very kind and loyal—& it would be very unpleasant to be put in a position of even momentary opposition to him. It would do harm both to us & to him. I regret more than I can say the indiscretion of somebody who let the matter out to the Press, during the short interval which necessarily occurred after our conversation, until I had consulted the Queen. But I think Iddesleigh has made too much of a mishap which I apologised for by telegraph as soon as I saw it, and to which, he must know, any public man is liable.

I can't help thinking Iddesleigh has forgotten, & his relations do not know, the language in which he wrote to me. The day on which I made my proposal to Goschen I received from Iddesleigh a letter in which he said 'if places are wanted for any combination, I am only too ready to give way'. I inferred that his inclination rather pointed to retirement: but even if that was a mistake, he can hardly treat my acting upon his words as an affront.

Smith passed both Northcote's and Salisbury's letters to Lord Cranbrook[2] with the remark: 'You should see these letters. Salisbury's is so genuine that one cannot help feeling the deepest regret Iddesleigh has allowed his feelings to get the better of him.' But later

[1] Celebrated political hostess; wife of Francis Jeune, Q.C. and Judge, who was created Baron St. Helier, 1900.
[2] See Cranbrook's own account of these events. Gathorne Hardy, op. cit., II, pp. 273–7.

that day the imbroglio turned to tragedy. Iddesleigh came up to town and went to call on the Prime Minister. The rest is related in a letter from Smith to Emily (January 12th):

> I hear that Lord Iddesleigh appeared at the Foreign Office to be in exceedingly good health and spirits, and he said goodbye to Sir James Fergusson[1] very cheerfully implying that it was only for a time and that he was coming back again to the Government.
>
> He then left the Foreign Office, crossed Downing Street to No. 10 and walked upstairs to the Vestibule of Lord Salisbury's room, was seen by Henry Manners[2] to stagger and was caught by him before he fell, and was placed on a sofa from which he never rose or spoke. He lived 20 minutes and in the time three doctors were brought to him, but they could do nothing and Dr. Granville his own attendant said he was not at all surprised, for he knew and the whole family knew that the end might come at any time in this way.
>
> Just before I heard of this I had a really touching letter from Salisbury on one I had sent him enclosing a letter from Harry Northcote.
>
> It will be of historical value as it will really prove conclusively how tenderly Salisbury wished to deal with his old friend and colleague.

Next day Smith wrote to Salisbury (January 13th): 'I hope you have in some measure recovered from the shock you had—in which we all shared yesterday. I would not come near you, because I could do nothing to help. . . .'[3] Randolph Churchill was also moved to write a letter of sympathy to Salisbury in which he expressed regret for his own part in bringing worry and vexation upon the dead man. In fact the shock seems to have sobered and softened him all round. He had been rude to Smith the day before—a scene described by the latter to his wife (January 13th): 'At the Carlton yesterday at luncheon I had a little scene with Randolph to whom I went up in a friendly way, by way of showing we were still friends—personally whatever may have separated us for a time: but he repelled me rather rudely, and this morning I have a letter from him apologising in very nice terms and this has given me the opportunity of rejoining in a cordial tone. I am very thankful for it.' This was Churchill's letter:

Private   2 Connaught Place, W.
                                                                Jan. 13. 1887

My dear Smith,
    I have been very much shocked by Lord Iddesleigh's death and new views on matters personal rather than political have come to my mind.

[1] 6th Bart., M.P. North East Manchester. Under Secretary of State Foreign Affairs, 1886–91.

[2] Lord Henry Manners, M.P. E. Leicestershire; Principal Private Secretary to Lord Salisbury; later succeeded as 8th Duke of Rutland.

[3] Salisbury Papers.

I am reproaching myself for having been rude & disagreeable yesterday at the Carlton when you spoke to me: so I write a line to say that in the event of your wishing to see me on any matter I am quite & always at your service. But I pray you not to imagine from this that I have in the smallest degree modified those views which caused me to leave the Govt. In spite of all the criticisms I am perfectly convinced that I did no wrong.

Occurrences such as that of yesterday however impress forcibly the duty of preventing political differences from embittering the relations between friends & I am very sorry if at times owing to irritation & anxiety I have allowed the importance of this duty to escape me.

Believe me to be
Yours very sincerely,
Randolph S.C.

Smith, in describing it to his wife, had not overrated the 'cordial tone' of his reply. It is a model of magnanimity.

Private   3 Grosvenor Place,
London, S.W.
13 Jan. 1887

My dear R.C.,

Iddesleigh's death has been a great shock to us all, and I agree with you that such an event does forcibly bring to one's mind other than mere political views and differences.

I am very glad you have written to me, because I wished to express to you yesterday my hope that nothing that has occurred between us as Ministers would prevent the continuance of the personal friendship which has grown up during the last few months.

You have a perfect right to hold the views you expressed to me in my room. I differed then and now from you, but it may turn out that you are right, and that I am wrong, and I shall accept the demonstration of that fact without any the very slightest personal annoyance.

But however that may be all that has happened is an incident in the career of a young politician of quite a temporary character, and unless my life is cut short as Northcote's has been I look forward with confidence to a future—and the sooner it comes the better—when I shall be in the retirement I long for, and you will be leading a great party with prudence and firmness and courage.

Believe me
Yours very sincerely
W. H. Smith

This was indeed a pleasant turn in the relations between the turbulent young 'tribune of the people' and his older, gentler, but still admiring colleague. But the fires caused by the Iddesleigh tragedy in the old statesman's home circle had still not died down. Lord St. Cyres, the eldest son, whom his brother had already described to Smith as having 'done harm', now wrote to Smith a rather ambiguous letter (January 16th), which began by praising Smith himself for having always been 'the kindest of the kind' towards his father and continued by saying that the latter 'felt not at all hurt that his resignation was accepted', that 'he was sincere in offering it' but that 'he did feel hurt that he was not told that it was accepted'—and then went into all the details again. 'My object in writing this', he concluded, 'is to put you in possession of what we do think—and then to assure you of the absolute horror with which we have seen the monstrous things that have been said of Lord Salisbury, for whom we feel deeply. . . .'

Forwarding this letter to Salisbury, Smith remarked: 'I am inclined to tell him frankly the story beginning with the conditions made by Goschen. What do you say?' Evidently Salisbury concurred, for, in his reply to St. Cyres (January 19th) Smith offered to show him Salisbury's memorandum on the whole episode, an extract from which has already been quoted. Meanwhile the chief circumstance which he deplored was 'that Lord Iddesleigh was not in town to be personally communicated with—if he had been there would have been friendly consultation and complete agreement'. He ended: 'I hope I have dispelled any feeling in your mind that there was slight or even carelessness. Nothing would pain me more than to think there was really ground for such an impression in the mind of my oldest and dearest political friend as against his still older friend and ally' (i.e. Salisbury).

But St. Cyres was not mollified—in fact his resentment, probably under the influence of the home circle, suddenly became more intense than before. In a further 'Most Private' letter to Smith (January 21st) he asked the latter 'to let me speak my mind'. 'It is impossible for us not to know that He [Iddesleigh] thought himself badly treated, for we saw him daily . . .', he wrote, proceeding then to some harsh recriminations about the conduct of Salisbury—with whom he had earlier expressed so much sympathy. He concluded menacingly that 'the real question is now to try to avoid the necessity of our having to express our own view of the case . . .'. Smith forwarded this letter to Salisbury, who simply replied that he did not think any reply would be useful.

The correspondence arising from this sad episode has been given at some length because it is singularly revealing of the characters of the protagonists—three of them important ones historically—and indeed of human nature generally. Of these three important men it could be said that each was kindly and well-intentioned though none comes out of it entirely irreproachably—even the one who might be termed the 'victim'. It might all be well summarized in Salisbury's

words in a letter to Churchill about the tragedy (January 14th):
'. . . As I looked upon the dead body stretched before me, I felt that
politics was a cursed profession.'[1]

[1] Churchill, op. cit., p. 607.

XI

LEADER OF THE HOUSE

PARLIAMENT reassembled after these disturbing events on January 27th, 1887, and one of the first items of business for which Smith, as leader, was responsible was the statement of his predecessor Randolph Churchill on his resignation. Churchill was still on his best behaviour—at any rate so far as Smith was concerned—and wrote two days before the reassembly (January 28th): 'Would it be agreeable to you to know beforehand the nature of the Statement which I desire to make on Thursday? If so drop me a line. I am anxious as far as possible . . . to say nothing which need lead to any immediate controversy.' Nevertheless the statement, when it came, presented a most welcome opportunity to the Opposition—who in any case were in high spirits over the recent upheavals in the Government.

That night Smith settled himself down to write, as custom demanded from the Leader of the House, his first report to the Queen of the day's transactions:

Mr. Smith presents his humble duty to Your Majesty & in venturing upon his first letter to Your Majesty from this House, he cannot refrain from saying how greatly he personally regrets the circumstances which have placed him in the position he occupies.

The House was full at the commencement of business and great interest was manifested in the anticipated statement of Lord Randolph Churchill but for more than an hour proceedings were delayed by a perfectly unprecedented number of motions for Bills. About 6 o'clock Lord Randolph made his statement which was received most sympathetically by the Opposition & particularly by Sir William Harcourt who in a sonorous voice cheered almost every sentence. . . .

After describing the tributes to Lord Iddesleigh and the moving of the Address, he continues:

. . . Mr. Gladstone immediately availed himself of the opportunity to praise Lord Randolph for the great sacrifice he had made on the altar of Economy and with great skill he invited the supporters of

Your Majesty's Government to assist Lord Randolph in his efforts
to bring about a reduction of armaments and of expenditure. . . .

This was an aspect of affairs about which Smith felt very
deeply concerned and which made him regret having been torn so
prematurely from the War Office, as much as Wolseley and the
progressive army faction deplored it also. As he wrote to his friend
Sir John Lintorn Simmons, Governor of Malta (January 30th):
'. . . Randolph's attacks on Army & Navy expenditure may have
very serious results. I cannot say we have full value for the money
we spend, but that fact is due to fads & systems—largely but not
wholly due to them—imposed by popular clamour and ignorance;
and in an infinitely smaller degree to the faulty constitution of Army
Government & control. I am very anxious by some means or another
to inform the public. We are governed by the Democracy and we
must somehow make these masses, these rulers of ours, know what
the Army is wanted for, what strength ought to be maintained and
what the Men, the Officers and the material really cost. . . .'

Three days after his Statement, in the Debate on the Address,
Churchill caused further embarrassment to his former colleagues by
belittling the role of the Liberal Unionists and at the same time
pouring scorn on Chamberlain for his eleventh hour attempt to
achieve Liberal reunion through the so-called Round Table Conference. Of this Smith wrote to the Queen (January 31st):

. . . A speech from Lord Randolph Churchill in which he sought to
clear himself from the charges brought against him by some of his
friends and with very great ability he suggested reasons for his
retirement which were intended to place him in a better position
before the country. But in the course of his speech he fell foul of the
Unionists who are Liberals and spoke of them as a 'crutch' which the
Conservative Party must learn to do without and he made fun of the
Round Table Conference insisting amidst cheers from the Cons.
benches that anything approaching to a Parliament in Dublin would
not & could not be entertained. . . .

The ordinary Irish members succeeded each other in dreary
succession. . . . Mr. George Curzon[1] then rose—speaking for the
first time but with a coolness and self-possession which was most
enviable. He referred lightly to Lord Randolph's speech & said he
had no intention of 'wrestling' with Lord R. as he knew his fate
would be that of Jacob when he wrestled with the Angel & one of
my colleagues remarks that it is the first time in his life that Lord R.
has been likened to an Angel!

[1] M.P. (Cons.) Southport Division of Lancashire; Viceroy of India, 1899–1905;
Lord Privy Seal, 1915; Leader of House of Lords and Lord President of Council,
1916–19; Foreign Secretary, 1919–24; created Earl, later Marquess Curzon of
Kedleston.

Smith had a veritable baptism of fire in his new position as Leader since the Debate on the Address dragged on until February 17th. He had to put up with lengthy diatribes from Labouchere[1] on the wickedness of the ownership of land and told the Queen that 'the prevalent view of highly instructed and advanced Liberals appears to be that property in land in a landlord is more or less criminal, while the property of the tenant in the land is absolutely sacred and that disregard or contempt or defiance of old-fashioned laws in defence of the tenant and defiance of the landlords is evidence of an enlightened mind & the highest Christian virtue . . .'. From the same irrepressible source came denunciations of Lord Salisbury as a 'warmonger', of Lord Hartington for his 'bad taste' in sitting on the Liberal Front Bench and of Chamberlain for his desertion of Gladstone and of 'true' Liberalism.

In reply to a sympathetic note from the Queen the harassed Leader wrote (February 7th) that 'Mr. Smith does not disguise the fact that patience is severely tried by the open & cynical waste of public time which is perpetrated for party purposes, but he is much more concerned for the danger to which it exposes Parliamentary institutions than for any personal inconvenience which may be inflicted upon the Servants of Your Majesty . . .'. Indeed, the very first business to be taken up, after the prolonged Debate on the Address had been finally terminated by the use of the closure, was a further reform of the Rules of Procedure.

The draft of the new rules which Smith as Leader of the House laid on the table was the fifth set to have been submitted since Gladstone in 1882 attempted to deal with the growing evil of obstruction. The most striking proof of the urgent need for further action was provided by the fact that the passage of the first rule, establishing closure by a bare majority (subject to the discretion of the Speaker) occupied no less than thirteen nights. Moreover, as a result of this slow progress, this first rule was the only one of the total of fifteen rules which was persisted with and carried. Thus Smith to the Queen (February 25th), referring to the spate of Opposition amendments:

> . . . Divisions were taken giving very large majorities against proposals which had a great family resemblance, but which yet the Speaker felt himself obliged to put to the House and the utmost Mr. Smith can hope is that after five nights debate the House will have affirmed one line of the first Rule. . . .
>
> (March 1st) . . . It will not surprise Your Majesty to hear that Mr. Smith has been charged in the course of the debate with tyranny

[1] M.P. (Lib.) Northampton; Proprietor and Editor of *Truth*.

and with want of nerve, with incapacity and stern unbending resolve and that indeed Mr. Smith is in the opinion of the Irish Party quite unfit for the office he holds. . . .

(March 2nd) . . . Mr. Smith had to begin and Mr. Gladstone answered and in answering bestowed lofty pity on Mr. Smith. . . .

(March 10) The Motion is still being debated with an obstructive ingenuity which would be entertaining if the interests at stake were less than those of the possibility of the continuance of Parliamentary Government in the country. . . .

These comments betray that sensitiveness which even twenty years of political life never blunted, but which was in keeping with his other fine qualities—his patriotism, his passionate sincerity and sense of duty—which were outraged by the cynicism and opportunism of some of his contemporaries. Therefore his office was a continual and very real ordeal for him. The Queen felt deeply for him; but her notions of comforting him were sometimes comically naïve and misplaced. After Goschen—who had had no seat on joining the Government—had, after a disaster at Liverpool, finally got a seat through the self-sacrifice of Lord Algernon Percy, the Queen wrote to Smith (February 17th): '. . . The Queen rejoices to think that Mr. Smith will soon have Mr. Goschen at his side who will be very useful.' Always a friend and admirer of Goschen, it never occurred to her that many of his colleagues—and Smith in particular—found him intensely irritating. She also added: 'Doubtless the Irish & other extreme Radicals who have no gentlemanly feelings will attack him a good deal at first.'

Meanwhile, it was at first thought that the Government had sustained another blow when on March 3rd, Sir Michael Hicks Beach resigned from the Irish Secretaryship on account of incipient blindness. Smith at once wrote to Salisbury: 'I think you should send for Lord John Manners & have a talk with him about Irish Office before you decide definitely on any appointment.'[1] But Salisbury seems to have almost immediately made up his mind that the man for the job was his nephew, Arthur Balfour. The choice caused astonishment and consternation among many who had been led by Balfour's delicate and languid exterior to underestimate his resources: though evidently the Queen was not one of these, for she wrote to Smith that 'she feels deeply for Sir M. H. Beach, but thinks Mr. Balfour will prove a very able successor to him'.

A special reason for anxiety about the appointment lay in the fact that the Government was on the point of introducing a new Coercion or 'Crimes' Bill for the pacification of Ireland and the gruelling task of doing this and of steering it through the Commons in the teeth of

[1] Salisbury Papers.

rabid Irish and Radical opposition would fall on the new Chief Secretary. Almost immediately after Balfour's appointment, Smith, who probably still underestimated his energy, wrote urging him to make up his mind whether he was really resolved to introduce the Crimes Bill without delay (March 5th). '. . . It is possible we may be upon it much sooner than we expect. We have said repeatedly that Irish legislation would be taken as soon as we obtained the [Procedure] Rules—and seeing our difficulties and for very mischief, the Irish are quite capable of changing front now—of letting the Rules through—and then mocking us'.[1] Indeed, when the day came on March 28th, Smith told the Queen: 'Mr. Gladstone & the Front Opposition bench appeared to be furious at the Bill and it will evidently be most strenuously opposed. . . . The Irish Members generally have been excessively disorderly, interrupting Mr. Balfour and anyone with whom they disagreed incessantly.'

But Balfour proved fully equal to the great responsibility and strain so suddenly thrust upon him—in fact the challenge brought into being almost a new and hitherto unknown man, apparently thriving on and delighting in the embittered skirmishes with the Irish members at Westminster, whilst pursuing a resolute and highly successful policy of Government in Ireland. Smith proved equally resolute in his determination to get the Crimes Bill through, for he told his Chief Whip, Akers-Douglas, to tell the Opposition Whips 'that the Government were determined to get the Second Reading of the Crimes Bill before the adjournment for the Easter vacation even though in order to do so it were necessary to sit through the whole of the Easter week'. He added blandly that he was anxious to consult the convenience of the Opposition leaders and that he said it 'in no wise as a threat'. As a result, the First Reading having been carried through Balfour's brilliance in debate, and Smith's determination in applying the closure, on April 1st, the Second Reading was able to be moved on April 5th and eventually carried on April 18th. But thereafter progress was slower, for, in addition to the Crimes Bill, the Government was carrying a new Irish Land Bill, a Coal Mines Bill and, inevitably at this season, the Budget. Moreover, the publication by *The Times* on April 18th of the famous 'Parnell Letter' set off the long train of repercussions leading to the fateful Parnell Commission and the imbecile intervention in the matter of two Unionist M.P.s, a row involving the suspension of the Irish leader Healy and finally the ceremonies and festivities connected with the Queen's Jubilee all combined to make of this Session, which was destined to last from January to the end of September, one of the severest endurance tests known to Members of Parliament.

[1] Balfour Papers.

'Smith led us admirably;' wrote Lord George Hamilton in later years,[1] 'he was absolutely unfailing in his touch of the pulse of the House. His "pounce" for closure was never refused, and though he was howled at by the extremists, the great mass of the House knew that the use he made of the powers of terminating debate were reasonable and just.' To this may be added the tribute of a well-known veteran M.P., Sir Walter Barttelot,[2] who wrote to him (April 4th), after the successful carrying of the First Reading of the Crimes Bill: '. . . No man could have led the House with greater firmness & dignity than you did . . . that courteousness with that English pluck which you have shown ever since you have led the House will carry us successfully through this all-important struggle. May you have health & strength to carry your good work to that conclusion—which alone can save the country from a great calamity. . . .'

A contrast to these views is to be found, perhaps not very surprisingly, in those of his predecessor. Immediately after making his Statement on his resignation, Lord Randolph had gone abroad on a prolonged holiday. From Palermo he had already written to his wife (March 2nd): 'I own W. H. Smith has done better than I expected for I expected a complete breakdown; but having made that admission, his Speeches read to me most commonplace, and I think before long the House and the Party will get much bored with him. . . .'[3] A little later, on his return to London, he was lecturing Smith on his duties and responsibilities as Leader of the House. The occasion for this arose out of a scene in the House on April 15th when a Conservative member, Colonel Saunderson, asserted that the Executive Committee of the Irish Land League, of which Parnell was the head, included both murderers and persons guilty of treason and that Parnell must be aware of this. Thereupon Healy, the latter's foremost lieutenant, called Saunderson a 'liar' and after refusing to

T. HEALY.

HERE'S TIMOTHY HEALY,
WHO SPOKE TOO FREELY.

[1] Hamilton, op. cit., p. 68.
[2] Sir Walter Barttelot-Barttelot, 1st Bart.; M.P. N.W. Div. Sussex, 1860–93.
[3] Churchill, op. cit., pp. 617–18.

247

withdraw was named and suspended. The Speaker was anxious to have the suspension rescinded as quickly as possible and Smith, perhaps anxious not to make a martyr for the Irish, was inclined to fall in with the idea. At any rate, Churchill got wind of this and immediately wrote off to the latter the following insufferable homily:

Private & Confidential   Carlton Club,
                                                          April 16. 1887
My dear Smith,
    The 'Scene' in the House last night was unfortunate. I should not however trouble you about it had I not understood from Plunkett[1] this morning that there was a possibility that the Speaker and you as Leader of H. of Cms. might be disposed to take a favourable view of some motion to be made on Monday to rescind the suspension of Healy.
    Against such a course much may be urged. In the 1st place I don't see how the motion can come on without a most unusual departure from the rules of ordinary procedure.
    A motion to rescind a decision of the House must be made after due notice and has no claim to precedence.
    I suppose that by the general consent of the House the Leader of the House might make a motion of the above kind without notice and before the commencement of public business, but even this is most doubtful and sets up an evil precedent.
    However, assuming that in some way or other the motion comes on I hope the Govt. will resist it. The authority of the Chair and the rules of orderly debate are in grave danger just now and any appearance of weakness on the part of the Speaker or the Leader of the House may entail consequences of which you cannot foresee the limit.
    I see no hope of ultimate safety and success except in this, that the Chair on points of order must consider itself as infallible and the Leader of the House must take the same view . . . [follows a lengthy examination of the incident in question]. . . . Please let me urge this. You have to fight two battles—one in Ireland against crime, the other in Parliament against disorder. You must win both. The loss of one entails the loss of the other. As you are firm with respect to matters in Ireland, so you should be equally firm with respect to the rigid preservation of order in the House of Commons. The return triumphant of Healy, after having called a member a liar and defied the Chair, under the pretext that Saunderson's conduct justified his conduct, would be ruinous to your position as the defender and guardian of parliamentary order. I quite understand the immense inconvenience which may result from any course which may lead to a postponement of the division on the second reading of the Crimes Bill. In a choice of evils it is best to choose the least and the greatest evil without doubt would be the selection of a course which establishes

[1] Though misspelt presumably Hon. David Plunket, M.P. Dublin University; created Lord Rathmore.

precedents of the worst kind and prepares the way for irretrievable disorder in the H. of Cms.

Excuse this lengthy letter. It deals with a general matter on which I feel much anxiety and greatly prefer communicating with you beforehand to expressing any difference of opinion with you in the House itself.

Yours very sincerely,
Randolph S. C.

In spite of this awful warning the matter was cleared up—and Healy's suspension rescinded—through Saunderson being induced by the Speaker to climb down.

Meanwhile, however, Smith could count on a constant supply of encouragement from the Queen who, with unashamed and truly feminine partisanship, would contrast his strength, nobility and courage with the baseness and wickedness of the Opposition generally and of Gladstone in particular. Thus, from Aix les Bains she wrote on April 11th, 1887, referring to the excited scenes when Smith applied the closure to secure the carrying of the First Reading of the Crimes Bill and Gladstone and the Irish tried to resist him:

The Queen thanks Mr. Smith for his full & interesting accounts of his successful defeat of that shameful conduct of the Opposition—especially of Mr. Gladstone! It is very shocking & very sad to see a man of his position, age & reputation heading an Opposition to the efforts of the Govt. under great difficulties to restore law & order & thereby *tranquillity* to a poor misguided Country, or portion of it, wh. *he* has done *more than anyone* to excite & encourage in its illegitimate aspirations & wild & misplaced expectations. His letter to the N. E. Daily Gazette of the 8th is perfectly monstrous & *very* wicked. But fortunately he injures himself—& shows *what* he is aiming at. This letter & his abuse of the Speaker show real aberration of mind.

The Queen hopes Mr. Smith's health & that of his colleagues in the House of Commons is *not* suffering from the fearful strain & fatigue of this great struggle? . . .

After the Bill passed its Second Reading and the publication by *The Times* of the 'Parnell Letter' and the series of articles on 'Parnellism and Crime' the Queen wrote again (April 20th):

The Queen thanks Mr. Smith for his letters—& is greatly rejoiced at the decisive majority on the 2nd Reading of the Crimes Bill.

She sees Mr. Parnell denies the letter, but the Queen hopes the subject will not be allowed to rest there.—She sends an Article in the Times wh. has struck her as full of truth. She has marked the passages to wh. she wd. wish to draw Mr. Smith's attention as well as Ld. Salisbury's & Mr. Goschen's!

Is this, for the honour of the British Parlt. & the British nation & for their *name* to be *allowed* to *go on*, unnoticed & unchecked? . . .

Mr. Gladstone & his unworthy coadjutor Sir W. Harcourt are completely unmasked & their position is really a terrible one, linked to rebels & traitors! . . .

Most unfortunately for the Government the Queen's hope that the subject of the Parnell Letter would not be allowed to rest was amply fulfilled, for the letter—in which Parnell appeared to condone the Phoenix Park Murders of 1882, at least in so far as Burke was concerned—turned out to be a forgery. But this was not to come to light until both *The Times* and the Government had virtually staked their reputations on its authenticity.

Meanwhile the situation was greatly aggravated by the already mentioned imbecile intervention at this stage of two Unionist M.P.s. These two members—Sir Charles Lewis[1] and Stavely Hill[2]—concocted, over a rather too good dinner, a scheme of summoning the editor of *The Times* to the bar of the House of Commons as guilty of an infraction of Parliamentary privilege, calculating that in self-defence he would produce some proof of Parnell's guilt and thereby benefit the Unionist cause. They even went so far as to send Dillon, the prominent Irish Nationalist, formal notice of the step. Smith knew nothing of this plan till an hour before the meeting of the House and though he angrily pointed out that the only issue which could be debated would be the guilt or otherwise of *The Times*, it was too late to withdraw the motion. However, he managed to adjourn the debate after a short, inconclusive discussion of the motion and next day the Solicitor General was put up to show, by citing precedents, that there was no case of breach of privilege to answer. Nevertheless, the impression of discord and confusion in the Unionist ranks did not enhance the party's image in the country. Lord George Hamilton wrote later: 'If it had not been for this clumsy and uncalled for interference by two private members in a matter which they did not understand, I do not think the Government would have been compelled next year to set up the Parnell Commission. I never saw Smith so put out as he was by this unwarrantable interference with his duties as Leader of the House, upon a matter which from its novelty and prominence required careful and prescient handling!'[3]

Despite the Queen's encouragement and the loyal support of his colleagues and followers in the House, Smith found the going very hard and as spring turned to summer and still the final struggle for the Crimes Bill continued, he became increasingly weary and despon-

[1] 1st Bart, M.P. Londonderry.

[2] A. Stavely Hill, K.C.; M.P. (Cons.) Staffordshire Kingswinford; Counsel to Admiralty and Judge Advocate of Fleet, 1874–80 and 1895–1905.

[3] Hamilton, op. cit., pp. 72–4.

dent. The following extract from his letters to Emily at this time poignantly convey the mood of these political doldrums.

(May 10) We had a rough night last night. I put the Closure on two or three times and only reported progress in Committee at ½ past 4, getting into bed at ½ past 5. Tonight things have been quiet, but quite as obstructive as ever, and we shall have to do something more yet to get the Bill through. . . .
(May 11) We have had another dreary day, 5½ hours in Committee and we have hardly advanced as many words in the Bill, but I used the Closure again and got majorities of 100. It is very sickening work and if it were not duty I should throw it up—but the people behind me are very warm and very good. . . .

Just at this time the Lord Chancellor made a generous allusion in a speech to Smith's Leadership. The devoted Miss Giberne immediately seized her pen—

. . . on arriving at the Ld. Chancellor's concluding sentence I jumped up & says I. 'I must'. Don't you see, dear friend, what I mean? how God *has* already answered prayer? The very things you asked us to pray for, were strength, grace, courage, wisdom—& what does the Ld. Chancellor say: 'On one point we shall I am sure be agreed, that his guidance of the deliberations of the H of C has been *firm, gracious, courageous & wise*. Here then is the very answer to what we asked! . . .

Though he may sometimes have smiled a little at these rather naïve effusions, Smith was too kind and too loyal and, above all, too humble to scorn such sincerity of intention and he answered gravely (May 11th):

You cannot tell what doubts & anxieties overtake one from time to time, as to whether on this or on that question to be decided suddenly, one is right. It is however a great comfort and a great support to feel that unseen help is coming to me. . . .

Then he resumed his reports to his wife, who had gone to Aix les Bains, where he was to join her for a brief respite during the Whitsun recess.

(May 13) . . . I am still in a very anxious state as to the condition of public business. The obstruction of the two Oppositions [Gladstonian and Parnellite] now united in one is beyond anything that has been seen in this House, and unless it gives way under the pressure of public opinion, very drastic measures will have to be taken. . . .
(May 17) . . . Here I am again droning on while the Irish and their allies spit and splutter and obstruct. It is desperate work, unmitigated obstruction utterly regardless of all consequences to Parliament or the Country.

We have now been eight days over one Clause and we have not finished it yet. The Country is getting very angry, and is beginning to say that the Government is 'deplorably weak' in not insisting on faster procedure.
(May 18) I am writing on the bench listening to tedious speakers whose only object is to delay business and worry the Government. I sat on this bench until 3.30 this morning and I was down again at 12. Our Men are very angry and some of them inclined to be a little unreasonable, but their great weariness is a complete excuse.

However, the brunt of coping with 'Our Men'—the Tory rank and file in the House—fortunately fell on the extremely capable shoulders of Akers-Douglas, the Chief Whip. He and his lieutenants had to keep a majority in the House at all times against the snap division and, moreover, now they had never to let the number drop below 200, lest it be necessary to apply the closure, which required this minimum of votes to carry it. This feat he scarcely ever failed to achieve, exercising a happy blend of tact, persuasion and firmness. Smith relied on him and there was happily too a complete understanding and a mutual liking and respect between the two men. The Leader set the example to his followers by never leaving the House during the evening, having dinner served in his private room, where he would usually invite one or two of his cabinet colleagues, Akers-Douglas and his private secretaries. After dinner, if no urgent debate was in progress, he would begin his daily despatch to the Queen, which had to go off at midnight, and also settle the order of business for the following day with the Whip.

As regards the attitude of the Government's Liberal-Unionist allies to the Crimes Bill there was more uncertainty. Nevertheless, after receiving warnings from Chamberlain and Hartington that their men could not support certain sections of it, Salisbury wrote resolutely to Smith (May 22nd): '. . . I quite think the best course is not to change our front. If we are beaten: & the bill works well nevertheless, the matter will be forgotten. If, as is quite possible, we have some bad murders & fail to get convictions, we shall be in a very good position—& shall have made the task of legislating for Ireland easier for others. If on the other hand we change front, we shall have whatever odium may attach to the original proposal, plus the odium of all the evils that may be imputed to the abandonment of it.'[1]

By the time the Whitsun recess came Smith was nearly at the end of his tether—and hardening perceptibly.

(May 23) My last letter to you before I start for Aix! I am tired,—very tired,—but the thought of rest and of joining you refreshes me.

[1] Balfour Papers.

I have been a little brutal tonight. The House does not want to meet tomorrow, but the Opposition wishes to advance business as little as possible, and I have put it to them gently—pass the Clause and I will move the adjournment this evening. Don't pass it, and I won't—and I think we shall get it for we have made very fair progress taking everything into account. . . .

But he had to put the screw on a great deal harder than this— and in so doing became the initiator of a procedure as yet without precedent. For, by June 10th, still only four clauses of the Bill had been passed and so, on that day, Smith moved a resolution that if the Bill were not reported by 10 o'clock on the 17th, the Chairman would proceed to put the remaining clauses without debate. Gladstone opposed the resolution though he was not prepared to go into the Lobby to vote against it, in fact he advised the Parnellites to clear the Bill out of the way so as to get to the Land Bill, which had come down from the House of Lords: but what actually happened in the end was that the Parnellites ignored his advice, whilst his own followers for the most part followed it, thus resulting in Smith carrying his motion by 245 votes to 93. 'I *was* tired this evening', he wrote to Emily (June 11th), 'and I had to sit on the bench without moving until 8.20 watching and waiting to bark and bite—but in the end I got my motion by a large majority. There was however some very hard hitting all round and we came off like a pack of schoolboys who had had a real row.' And to Salisbury the same night: 'We have had a lucky escape from an all-night sitting. The Irish were as nasty as they could be, and after trying for a Saturday sitting for the Crimes Bill they resisted the adjournment of the House. The Speaker nearly lost his temper. There will be hot work yet.'[1]

When the appointed hour arrived on the 17th, the Committee were discussing the 6th Clause of the Bill; Sir Charles Russell[2] was speaking against it; the Chairman interrupted him, rose and put the clause, and, after a single division, the indignant Opposition, Gladstonian and Parnellite, rose and marched out of the House. The remaining fourteen clauses were then put, and agreed to without further debate or division. Thus was born the instrument which came to be known as the 'Guillotine' or 'Gag'.

On June 30th Smith adopted the same procedure for closing the Report stage on the Crimes Bill. 'It was opposed vehemently by Mr. Dillon', he told the Queen (June 30th), 'who said the Irish Members would protest and debate until the Guillotine descended on them. . . .' There were also protests about 'stifling discussion' and

---

[1] Salisbury Papers.
[2] Not Smith's fellow member for Westminster, but the famous Q.C., who was Liberal M.P. for South Hackney and was later created Lord Russell of Killowen.

oppression from Labouchere and the Radicals. Nevertheless the division was taken and the motion carried, 'no member of the front Opposition bench being present'. 'The Irish members did not return to the House', Smith's report continued 'and greatly to the astonishment of everyone not in the secret the Members who had amendments on the paper did not answer to their names and none were discussed at all, so that the Bill passed through the Report Stage shortly after 8—instead of the hour fixed by Mr. Smith—7 on Monday evening.'

From this triumph Smith moved to another one only a few days later. On July 4th he moved to obtain all the time of the House for

W. H. CROMWELL SMITH.

the Government's business, for obstruction had caused much delay in this as well as the passing over of private members' motions and Bills. Smith told the Queen that Gladstone had 'attributed this degradation of Parliament to the mismanagement of the Government' and that he had replied that 'all their evils were due to the excesses and unparalleled obstruction of the Crimes Bill'. 'This astounded Mr. Gladstone and Mr. Morley got up to prove that in the past the Conservatives had been much worse than the Irish Members', but finally 'Mr. Smith carried this Motion after 3 divisions by a huge majority and the Govt. have now the entire time of the House at their disposal for the rest of the Session'.

But meanwhile there were worries caused by the failings of some of their own side—in particular Matthews, the barrister whom Churchill had foisted on Salisbury and who had been made Home Secretary—as is revealed in the following letters from Smith to his wife.

(July 5) We have been defeated by 5 on a Motion for adjourning the House which was directed against the Secretary of State—Matthews, because he failed sufficiently to sympathize with a poor girl who had been arrested by a Policeman and was taken before a Magistrate a few days ago.[1]

[1] Miss Cass, a very young dressmaker, arrested on a charge of solicitation. Despite her employer's testimony in her favour, the magistrate had accepted the policeman's evidence, whilst dismissing her with a caution.

I am going to dine with Salisbury very shortly to talk over the business and the course to be adopted with regard to it; but it cannot fail to give us trouble and to make the difficulties of our work greater. (Later same day) Matthews has shown great want of tact, and the worst of it is he does not himself seem to be aware of his failing, but this is not wonderful. Anyhow Salisbury is clear that we must not show the white feather and I agree with him.

(July 7) . . . Gladstone made a speech like a young man against the Crimes Bill and Balfour answered him very well indeed . . . but I am threatened with some trouble later as Colonel Saunderson the Irish Conservative Member threatens to make a speech containing statements which the Speaker will call on him to withdraw and if he does not withdraw I shall have to move his Suspension!

How I hate the work.

(July 8) . . . everyone is tired and the heat is very great indeed. It is knocking up some of our men, and one is wicked enough to hope it may have an equal effect on the other side. . . .

Even the Prime Minister himself appears on one occasion to have been the cause of some alarm and we find Smith, who albeit liked and admired him, speaking out manfully in the role of interpreter of the feeling of the party rank and file. The Local Government Bill which was the subject of this letter, was part of the Salisbury Government's programme of progressive or reformist legislation, designed to keep the Tory Party image bright and up-to-date and also to conciliate their Liberal Unionist allies. Smith wrote to Salisbury (July 6th):

My colleagues are a little alarmed at the scope of your suggestions as to County advances and the Local Govt. machinery to be used, especially as we have in view a L. G. Bill which would supersede a Vestry. Is it impossible for you, to meet the present pressing necessity, to deal with allotments alone, with legislative protection as you have indicated. . . .

Our men are quite prepared to stand or fall with you. They are absolutely loyal as a body—but they would consider that a fall just now on this question would be disastrous in the present condition of affairs in England . . . I am bound to tell you these things, but it is excessively disagreeable to me to do so.[1]

Salisbury was at first opposed in this measure by the leading element in his own party, namely, the country gentry, who envisaged the material foundations of their local prestige and influence in the Counties being undermined, even destroyed. Salisbury was inclined to be scornful and sarcastic about their fears, but Smith, though not by origin a member of their class, was broadminded enough to see

[1] Salisbury Papers.

their viewpoint and, above all, anxious to ward off any threat to the cohesion of the party.

Lord George Hamilton, who, with Smith, was accounted one of the more liberal spirits in the Government, gives in his memoirs a good picture of the immense value to the Tory Party of what might be termed the Salisbury–Smith axis. 'The combination between Salisbury and Smith was a happy mixture of the most worthy influences of Toryism', he writes.[1] Though he attributes to Salisbury 'the best qualities of the governing aristocrat', he adds: '. . . but he did not know or come sufficiently into contact with influences, movements and aspirations of classes other than his own. Smith admirably supplied this deficiency . . . he knew, felt and assimilated all that was best in the progressive movements of the day. His common sense and perception (amounting to genius) rarely, if ever, failed him in his diagnosis of the agitation of the moment. . . .'

He had always had the faculty of gaining people's confidence so that they wrote and spoke frankly and fearlessly to him about problems of mutual—and national—interest. A letter written after the Government had suffered an unexpected defeat in a by-election at Spalding, which in this case, reached him through an intermediary, illustrates the point. John Cropley, the writer, was a working-class member of the Council of the National Union of Conservative Associations and he wrote (July 6th) that in his opinion 'we lost the Spalding Election thro' over-confidence, no organization and also the fact that our party do not use working men speakers sufficiently, whereas our opponents do'. He also accused the Government of doing nothing for 'the chronic and acute agricultural depression' or about the question of 'Fair Trade'. 'If the Government continue to ignore the trade question we are done, for it is positively no good going to talk to working men, either about the Church, Queen or Lords if they are out of work.' He added that the Government were 'making a great mistake in supposing they got in altogether on Home Rule, as proved in the case of Spalding' (where a Gladstonian Liberal captured the seat from the Tories by 1,000 votes).

Again, studies of Lord Salisbury usually emphasize his almost exclusive preoccupation with and possessive attitude towards the conduct of foreign and imperial affairs. Yet there is ample evidence that Smith not only had his own strong views on these affairs, but also that he was not in the least afraid to voice them or to proffer advice on them from his own great store of common sense and knowledge. An instance is provided by some correspondence to be found among the Salisbury Papers. In January 1887 Sir Henry Drummond Wolff, who was a professional diplomat as well as a

[1] Hamilton, op. cit., pp. 252–3.

politician, was sent to Constantinople to try to negotiate an 'Ulterior Convention' with the Sultan to regulate the whole of the Egyptian Question. Echoes of his dealings reached home and caused anxiety and dissatisfaction in some quarters. His Fourth Party crony, Gorst, sprang to his defence. Smith wrote to Salisbury (February 15th):

> Gorst is very anxious to send this letter *anonymously* to the Times in defence of Wolff.
>
> It is not the sort of letter I should write, but I am not Gorst. Do you object to its going, and if you do will you send for Gorst.
>
> The argument would imply the necessity for the continued main-tenance of the two officers in Egypt—Home & Foreign Secretaries—and it hardly chimes in with our serious proposal to constitute a local Govt. which is to be strong enough to stand alone 5 years hence.[1]

And again some weeks later (April 6th):

> I am getting uneasy about Wolff and his negotiations. He telegraphs from day to day at absurd length and at great expense, saying the same things in successive telegrams. His doings get out and the Opposition want to know all about them. Some of our friends are suspicious and they don't like to be called upon to vote the heavy expenses his mission involves. I should not be a bit surprised if even Randolph objected to them as an ardent economist. I am sure it would be wise to urge him and the Turk to bring the business to an issue. The scheme is a very good one as it stands, and would be taken well in the country if it was properly explained, but that should be done while Parlt. is sitting and it can be stated clearly by yourself in the H. of L.
>
> It would be a different matter if it was first of all crabbed by newspaper writers in a recess and a prejudice created which no statements afterwards would remove.[2]

Again on May 24th:

> Now that you have got all you want out of the Turk, would it not be wise to advise moderation in Crete. If there is trouble there we shall be asked if we have used our good offices to avert bloodshed or to put a stop to it and it will make our path less difficult here if we can say we have done our best.
>
> Sorry Wolff won't go to Hong Kong.
>
> Randolph is very angry with me and is I think inclined for war.[3]

Smith's reputation as an ultra-religious man and loyal churchman also made him the obvious channel through which to apply pressure when legislation affecting the Church or the Clergy was afoot. The great issue in this connection at this time was the Tithe Question—on which Salisbury too, as another good churchman, had strong

[1] Salisbury Papers. [2] Ibid. [3] Ibid.

feelings. Indeed, there were several aspects to this question, which taken severally or added together, rendered some reform of the existing position of the utmost urgency. Lord Salisbury's Government had already tinkered with it in the previous year, but it was now brought home to them by ominous signs of unrest and revolt, that a general reform, transferring the responsibility for the payment of tithes from the occupier to the owner of the land, was essential Here again, however, there was some opposition from the country gentry element in the Tory Party.

But the object of the Government's proposals was not only to ease the burdens of agricultural tenants as a class at the expense of their landlords during the present agricultural depression, but also to ease the position of the clergy *vis-à-vis* their parishioners, especially in those cases where the former were themselves the tithe-owners. Then again there were the nonconformists to be conciliated to whom tithes were simply contributions to a Church to which they did not belong.

The Archbishop of Canterbury, Dr. E. W. Benson, was tireless in his efforts to expedite the Tithe Bill by prodding the Government and seeking the cooperation of the Liberals. He wrote to Smith on July 20th that Gladstone had told him he considered it 'a very proper measure', adding 'what will be the effect of next winter if no remedial legislation is attempted, and the present state of things continues, I do not like to think'. When Smith replied that, owing to Irish obstruction and consequent lack of time, the Bill might have to be dropped, the Archbishop sent him letters from desperate clergymen in Wales, where resistance to tithe payment was strongest, containing such phrases as: 'Government cannot possibly be aware of the state of things in N. Wales or they would not hesitate to push the Bill. Another declared that 'I have at this moment before me the "Plan of Campaign" for Wales, where Mr. Michael Davitt[1] is about to stir up my excitable countrymen by a series of his fiery addresses—The Welsh mind is even now seething with those pernicious principles which have had such a terrible outcome in Ireland—I therefore beseech your Grace to use your influence . . . to induce the Govt to push forward a measure on which much more than the mere question of tithes depends.'

Consequently the Government felt they must introduce even a temporary measure so long as they could obtain for it a modicum of agreement and support. Smith therefore wrote to Lord Hartington the Liberal Unionist leader (August 7th):

> I am pressed very strongly to do something with the Tithe Bill before the Session closes by many of our friends who are apprehensive of

[1] See *ante* p. 173.

very serious mischief during the coming winter if an attempt is not made to deal with the evil.

It is suggested that the Bill should be limited to effect the transfer of the incidence of the charge from the occupier to the owner. . . . The Bill to be for two years only and a Royal Commission to be appointed to enquire into the operation of the Tithe Commutation Act of 1836 generally.

Would you and your men support a proposal of this kind. It would cut the Bill down very much, and it would be in the nature of a truce rather than a settlement: but breathing time is required.

Salisbury, meanwhile, as in the case of the Local Government Bill, was becoming exasperated again with the attitude of the squirearchy towards the Tithes question. 'The landlords had better not talk about revaluation: honesty is their best game just now', he wrote to Smith (August 9th). 'It is evident the people are putting about that we are giving up the Tithes Bill—not on account of the difficulty of time—but because some of our landowners oppose it. It would be very desirable if possible to dissipate this error.'

But once again Smith diverted his Chief's wrath by impressing upon him the paramount necessity of achieving a temporary solution that would expedite a necessary reform without endangering party unity. In a letter to Salisbury of August 24th (in which he told him that he had been ordered by his doctor to take a holiday abroad as soon as the Session ended) he wrote:

Will you consider whether anything should be done as to a Commission on the Tithe Rent Charge question. It may not be necessary to decide it at once, but if we intend to do anything it should not be postponed until November. There is pressure for it from the Squires on both sides, and I understand the representatives of the Church to support the proposal if they could get a temporary Bill. But if the question once is opened there will be a great effort to show that the tithe now levied is out of proportion to the profits of cultivation on the poor lands. Revaluation is the object the Squires have in view— supported by the Farmers. Will *you* open the door even to the consideration of the question.

I think it will be opened soon by somebody if prices do not improve; and it has to be decided whether it would be wiser for you to take it in hand proving the reference so as to preserve or to recognize existing legal rights and settlements; or whether you will leave it to our successors to treat the subject as they please.

For the moment it would I think be popular with Squires and Farmers that a Commission should be appointed, but I am not certain that the popularity would survive the report.[1]

[1] Salisbury Papers.

Nevertheless, partly owing to the factious opposition of their own die-hards and partly to the general obstruction of all Parliamentary business by the Irish Members, no headway was made in this important matter and no Bill was able to be passed till 1891.

There comes at this point in the story a very touching letter from Smith to his wife, which, though we do not know the exact circumstances that evoked it, perfectly reveals the serenity of his inner life that was, of course, the source of his strength and calmness amid the hurly-burly and rough and tumble of politics. It provides the answer, for instance, to a letter from the Queen at this time (August 24th) in which 'she fears he must be very, very tired and wonders how his temper & patience *bear* the outrageous behaviour of the Irish & their worthy Allies . . .'.

House of Commons
My darling Wife, 22 August 87.
I must send a line to you of comfort and trust—for when you are in trouble and sorrow I am.

We cannot help being in sorrow, for that is almost the condition of our life from day to day, but years seem to me to have the effect of chastening and softening it. I do not think I feel less affection for those who may be passing away, but as I grow older I realise that I am getting nearer to the end myself and while the close of life loses any terror it once had, the duty of being useful to all around me—of so using my powers and my life as to do every day the very best I can under the circumstances in which I find myself, comes home to me *every* day with greater strength. So I must not disable myself by fretting or so entirely turn my thoughts in one direction as to find myself diverted from the daily work of life. Be careful of yourself my darling and help me as you do I know in prayer, and be assured that for me and for others whom you love, you have the petitions which you make to Him who is all Wise as well as all Good.

My love and my prayers go out to and for you. *He* will bless and keep all we love in all that is *really* good for them.

Ever your loving husband,
W. H. Smith

It is not surprising to find that not all the rank and file of the party possessed the fortitude, faith and patience of their leader. 'We had a bad night last night with the Amendments to the Irish Land Bill,' he wrote to Salisbury (August 19th), 'and only scraped through at last by throwing over your two amendments at the end which our Law Officers agreed were not vital. It was impossible to hold our men together any longer and there was really no other course open to us. You really must not let the Bill come down to us again under any circumstances.'[1] But though the strain fell upon him more than upon

[1] Salisbury Papers.

260

anyone else and he might well have felt impatient of the ordinary member who weakened and slackened in his attendance, Smith remained courteous and indulgent towards such, as may be seen by the circular letter which he sent to the Government's supporters while the struggle to secure the passage of the Irish Land Bill was on.

19 August 1887

My dear Sir,

I am exceedingly reluctant at this period of the Session and after the prolonged and incessant attendance of Members to make any further request to supporters of the Government which in the slightest degree interferes with the rest to which they are so fully entitled, but in the face of the opposition which the Government must encounter before the Session is brought to a close it is absolutely necessary that in addition to the ordinary working majority from day to day the Government shall be able to rely upon the attendance of at least 200 Members on any occasion at 48 hours notice to carry a motion for closure.

I have therefore to beg you most earnestly in any arrangements you may make, to retain absolute liberty to attend the House to vote on a Motion for Closure up to the end of the Session, and not to conclude any Pair which would interfere with your complete freedom to support Her Majesty's Government in this most vital matter.

I am, my dear Sir,
Yours very faithfully,
W. H. Smith

Another occasion on which we find Smith in the role of inter-mediary and 'smoother of paths' between the Prime Minister and his colleagues or allies arose when Chamberlain, who had given the Government a nasty jolt by voting against them on the 'proclamation' of the Irish National League as a 'dangerous association',[1] and who was generally pressing for a more 'constructive' policy towards Ireland, was hurriedly invited to go to the United States as Chief Commissioner for Britain to settle the current Fishery Dispute. It is a further tribute to Smith's tact and diplomacy to find Hartington confiding in him about his own relationship with Chamberlain. Thus Smith to Salisbury (August 28th):

Chamberlain told me on Friday night that he should consult with Hartington as to the expediency of going to the States to deal with the Fisheries, and Hartington came to me to speak about it yesterday afternoon. He said he felt a little delicacy in giving advice as it might be said he wanted to get him (Chamberlain) out of the way for a time!

[1] It is interesting to note that Smith himself wrote a memorandum for the Cabinet (now in the Balfour Papers) on the 'Proclamation' of the League' in which he declared himself to be 'very uneasy' about it since 'no facts whatever which would justify the proclamation are forthcoming'.

Hartington referred to the conversation Chamberlain had had with me and he said that he adhered to the view he had expressed that it would be inopportune to present a scheme of local self-govt. for Ireland simply to force Gladstone's hands—but that Chamberlain was restless—was of opinion that the Unionists must come to grief unless something was done, and he wanted to do that 'something'. But, said Hartington 'I don't want him to suppose I wish to get him out of the way which he may do if I tell him to go'.

I said I was convinced he wished to go himself—that he was flattered by the offer and that it opened out possibilities of influence in a new line which was attractive to Chamberlain and further that I thought he would do the work well.

The result was he said he would advise him to accept and just as the House rose Chamberlain came to me and said he should be glad to go. Holland & Goschen are both very well content.[1]

Next day Smith wrote off to Chamberlain saying, 'I have told Salisbury you accept the presidency of the Commission and he regards the question as settled . . .'.[2] But then, knowing Chamberlain's sensitiveness and his Chief's failings where the human touch was concerned, he quickly wrote to the latter (August 30th):

> I think it would be well (if you will forgive me for saying so) if you wrote to Chamberlain with the Fisheries papers expressing your personal satisfaction at his acceptance of the post of President. You have not had any direct communications with him hitherto and as you are going away you may not have the opportunity for some time to come.
>
> He is a very sensitive individual and easily influenced by attentions paid to him in an easy and natural sort of way.[3]

The interminable session was at last drawing to a close, but the Irish Nationalist Members kept up their gruelling tactics to the last. 'The Irish broke out again this evening and have been as nasty as they could be', Smith wrote to Emily (September 1st). And again next day: 'We had a bad night and excessive annoyance from the Irish . . . it is very galling to have to endure insult and provocation from these men and to be quite unable to cast it back again, except at the cost of prolonging our suffering.' Unfortunately, a few days later, an incident occurred in Ireland which roused the Nationalists to even greater paroxysms of fury. For on September 9th, at the opening of a prosecution (the first under the new Crimes Act) of the Irish leader O'Brien at Mitchelstown, County Cork, a crowd of about 8,000, incited by Dillon, attacked the police, who, driven back by weight of numbers to their barracks, opened fire, killing one man

[1] Salisbury Papers.
[2] Chamberlain Papers.
[3] Salisbury Papers.

and mortally wounding two others. Though a coroner's jury found wilful murder against the county inspector and five constables no one was brought to trial and later the Queen's Bench in Dublin quashed the verdict on technical grounds. Gladstone thereupon coined a new war-cry for the Home Rulers: 'Remember Mitchelstown!' The day after the incident Smith wrote to Salisbury (September 10th):

> We are going through our last Sat. of agony and although we are making good progress it is quite uncertain whether the few Irishmen who remain will keep us here until 7 or until 12 o'clock.
>
> The affair at Mitchelstown has been an unfortunate one for so far as we know at present no one seems to have been in command when the incident occurred, and from the telegrams received there appears to be a general desire to escape from individual responsibility for what has happened. The Irishmen are going to raise the question on the Appropriation Bill this afternoon and it will add strength to Harcourt's attack on Monday, but by that time we shall I hope have conclusive evidence that the affair commenced by a violent attack on the police in which many of them received severe injuries.—Since I wrote this Sexton has made a truculent attack accusing the Police of provoking the people and Balfour has answered very well indeed with great firmness and effect and carrying the charge of provocation home to the Irish Party.
>
> I do not think the debate will last long. . . .[1]

Parliament was prorogued at last on September 16th and, with this temporary truce in the parliamentary battle, Salisbury and Smith began to take stock of their men and of the respective performances of these. It seemed to Smith an opportune moment to get rid of Matthews, who by his ineptness as Home Secretary had begun to annoy his colleagues, and to bring back that tried veteran Hicks Beach, whose sight appeared to be recovering. Thus Smith to Salisbury (September 14th):

> Will you consider if we hold on whether in the event of Matthews becoming Judge, Holland[2] might not go to the Home Office and Beach if he is well enough come back to the Colonies. Such an arrangement would evade the difficulties of promotion which are very great so far H of C members of the Govt. are concerned.
>
> There would be great jealousy and heart burning at any choice you might make from among the Under Secs or from outside.
>
> I hear Beach is better and probably fit for work and he was very happy in the Colonies.

[1] Salisbury Papers.
[2] Sir Henry Holland, 2nd Bart.; M.P. (Cons.) Hampstead; Secretary of State for the Colonies, 1887–92; created Viscount Knutsford, 1888.

Arthur Balfour has greatly improved his reputation during the Session now closed. He has done his Parlty. work admirably. It could not have been done better.[1]

But Salisbury held different views on Beach and Matthews: though, being in the House of Lords, he was obviously not so well qualified as Smith to judge of the performance of these House of Commons men. He wrote back to Smith from Royat in France (September 19th):

> . . . Holland makes a very good & Popular Colonial Secretary—& I should be sorry to have to move him. I doubt his making a good Home Secretary. He is so amiable, he would hang nobody. On the other hand Beach was not a very good Colonial Secretary. His one fault is his manner—& that is an office where manner is specially important: & his record as Colonial Secretary is not quite irreproachable. On the other hand he would make a very good Home Secretary, & would hang everybody.
>
> If he is strong enough to take a Secretaryship of State at all—& there is a vacancy at the Home Office, I strongly incline to think he ought to go there. If he is *not* strong enough to take such a post—my idea was—Plunket to the Home Office, Gorst to the Works—& either Bartlett[2] or Worms[3] to India Office. But there is always the doubt whether Gorst's seat could be safely vacated.
>
> But are not we selling the bearskin while the bear is alive & kicking? Have you any ground for believing that there will be a vacancy at the Home Office? Matthews has not given us the help we hoped to get from him: but he has been unjustly run down.
>
> I am very glad to hear of Arthur's success—especially as his appointment was something of a venture.
>
> How heartily glad you must be of the opportunity of reposing upon your laurels—& the Pandora. Considering that we have no majority of our own, I think the Session has been a great success—but for the trip Chamberlain gave us [over proclamation of National League] an unqualified success. But you will have to tighten your rules for next year.

Smith had indeed not lost a moment after the Session ended in joining his yacht in the Mediterranean so that Salisbury's letter only caught up with him at Algiers, from which place he replied (September 29th):

> . . . I am sorry I bothered you about the Home Office. You are right about Holland. He would find great difficulty in hanging murderers

[1] Salisbury Papers.

[2] Ellis Ashmead Bartlett; M.P. (Cons.) Eccleshall; Civil Lord of the Admiralty, 1885–92; knighted, 1892.

[3] Baron Henry de Worms; M.P. (Cons.) Greenwich, 1880–5; Toxteth, 1885–95; Under Secretary for Colonies, 1888–92. Created Baron Pirbright, 1895.

and he is undoubtedly very popular in the Colonies—but when we walked away together from the House on the day of the Prorogation he told me he did not think he could stand another Session in the *Commons*. All this however may be changed if the majority will permit us to pass a Midnight Closing Rule. Matthews will be an anxiety if we and he hold on through another Session. He did not gain in Parlty tact and although he worked most laboriously at his Bills he frequently failed to secure a point he had almost committed himself to with his friends from want of suppleness and quickness in dealing with the forms of the House, but anything like a sacrifice is out of the question and it would injure us far more to throw him over than to bear with his mistakes; but if he has meant what he has said he is not willing to go through another Session on our bench.

I should be afraid Plunket has hardly strength enough for the place. I frequently urged him to speak in the Irish debates, offering him his own time, but he always failed me and I think he has less command over himself than formerly, but he is a favourite with the House and often meets a nasty question with a genuine piece of Irish wit to which no rejoinder is possible at the moment. I hear that Gorst's seat is not safe.

Beach would fret himself ill again at the Home Office. The condition of his eyes was due not to cataract but to his state of health—to worry. . . .[1]

But probably the most gratifying—and certainly well-merited— letter to reach him on his cruise was one from his oldest friend, Lord Harrowby, who wrote (September 16th):

I must send you one line of hearty congratulation at the successful end of this most eventful & historical session. I cannot say how deeply I feel that the Country is indebted to you for having steered the House of Commons through one of the most dangerous periods which it has had to pass through & for having maintained so nobly the dignity of its leadership & the honor of the Conservative cause. As one of your most attached friends you must let me tell you what a constant pleasure it is giving me to hear how warmly & widely all the best opinion of the nation appreciates your great services to the State. God grant that your health may not suffer! . . .

[1] Salisbury Papers. In fact in the following year Smith advised Beach to apply for a Political Pension owing to his reduced circumstances which made him unable to afford to live in London during sessions of Parliament, when out of office. In a note to Salisbury (March 12th, 1888) Smith wrote: '. . . I think it would go a long way towards softening and contenting him'. Eventually it was decided he should take over the First Class Political Pension left by Iddesleigh, worth £2,000 p.a., Salisbury commenting: 'If anybody deserves it, it is a man who has nearly sacrificed his eyesight in the public service'. (Balfour Papers).

XII

THE PARNELL COMMISSION

THE autumn of 1887 was marked by a series of grave riots in
London, allegedly to air the grievances of the 'unemployed',
but actually fermented by socialist, radical and Irish agitators. These
culminated in a particularly savage outburst on November 13th—
known as 'Bloody Sunday'—ostensibly to demand the release of the
Irish Nationalist O'Brien, when serious fights with the police
(resulting in about 100 casualties on both sides) took place in all the
approaches to Trafalgar Square and Foot Guards and Life Guards,
accompanied by magistrates, had to be called. A large number of
arrests were made, including the well-known radicals John Burns
and R. B. Cunninghame Graham. Once again Matthews, as Home
Secretary, came under heavy criticism for his fumbling manner of
coping with these riots—as did also the Chief Commissioner of
Police, Sir Charles Warren. Even in the riots leading up to 'Bloody
Sunday', Salisbury—who not long before had defended Matthews,
as we have seen—was becoming restive about him. He wrote to
Smith (October 24th):

> I pressed Matthews strongly both as to the reinforcement of the
> Police: & as to the prosecution of any attempts to incite people to
> break the law. . . . He was apprehensive of swearing in special
> constables on account of the alarm it would cause. . . . We discussed
> the question of railing in Trafalgar Square. I am in favour of it—with
> gates of course—: but I thought it had better be decided by a Cabinet.
> Arthur [Balfour] has written to me to ask that in case a priest brings
> himself clearly within the Crimes Act—should he write to the Bishop
> first to know what notice the ecclasiastical superior intends to take of
> it. I am inclined to answer 'Yes'. It is not theoretically correct: but it
> will place us in a much stronger position for the putting the priest on
> a plank bed.

Smith's reply to the latter part of the above reveals not only his
own strong Protestantism and mistrust of 'Rome', but also reminds

266

us how the feelings of all his generation towards Roman Catholics were coloured by their experience of them in Ireland in connection with the Home Rule issue, even if they did not nourish particularly strong doctrinal objections.

> As to the suggestion of Balfour's to write to the Bishop first before prosecuting a Priest—I should say 'Yes', decidedly, if you could trust the Bishop to deal fairly by you; but will not the Bishop in every case be against you? Perhaps even then it may be right to give him the opportunity of acting before you take civil proceedings. I am afraid it must be assumed that every Priest in Ireland is hostile to any English Government either from prejudice or self-interest and that nothing but a conviction that rebellion must fail will bring them round.
> Some of our supporters would be alarmed at the apparent recognition of the Bishop's jurisdiction in regard to civil offences, but that would not matter if it was successful. Of that I have doubt.[1]

In view of these strictures it is all the more impressive, if somewhat ironical, to compare the Irish Catholic Hierarchy's opinion of Smith himself, as expressed by its head, Archbishop Walsh, Primate of Ireland. A correspondent of Smith's in Dublin wrote to him about this time (November 1887) of a conversation with the Archbishop in which the latter had described Smith as 'practical-minded, kind, sound of judgement and completely to be trusted'. His correspondent added that, 'as I can read matters, any bill promoted by you personally is more likely to be accepted over here than if promoted by anyone else'.

We have already seen that Hicks Beach's sudden recovery had been noted by the party leaders and that various suggestions for fitting him into the Government again had been discussed between Salisbury and Smith. It now appeared that they had not been prompt enough in implementing this intention, for Beach now suddenly stepped forward in a rather menacing way and *demanded* office—and, what was worse, made it plain that he had been conspiring with Lord Randolph Churchill to bring them both back into positions of power. Much as his colleagues would have welcomed back Beach, it was felt to be more than a little early for the return triumphant of Churchill. On the other hand, the thought of the combined talents of these two men below the gangway as critics of the Government was perhaps even more alarming. Beach delivered his ultimatum when staying with Smith at Greenlands and the latter immediately wrote off (October 28th) to Akers-Douglas to get the Whip's reactions to this situation even before putting it to Salisbury.

[1] Salisbury Papers.

My dear Douglas,

Beach has been staying with me for two nights and this morning before he went away he showed me a letter he had written to Lord Salisbury declining to remain in the Cabinet without office[1] but expressing his willingness to come back and take any office that may become vacant and that may be offered to him. He thinks Salisbury does not himself care to have him back, or that he could get John Manners to give up in his favor; and he is a little hurt at the coldness or indifference which has—as he thinks—been shown to him.

It came out afterwards that he (Beach) had been in correspondence with Randolph and that Randolph wants to come back and to have the War Office: and Beach suggests that, as Holland[2] threatens to give up Stanhope[3] might go back to the Colonies.

I expressed doubts of the possibility of Randolph and Salisbury sitting in the same Cabinet. Beach said he was sure he could and would, as Randolph would be quite a different man at the War Office from what he was as Chancr. of the Excheqr. and leader. 'He would not give Salisbury any trouble' and 'he is sure he would get on very well with Goschen'

I begged Beach not to allow any public notification of his retirement from the Cabinet to appear, and he said that for his own part he should publish nothing, but that when he spoke at Bristol next month it must be either as a Minister in Office or as an independent member.

It is clear therefore that if Beach is not on our bench he will sit beside Randolph and the two will work together availing themselves of any opportunity to make their power felt.

Salisbury in speaking of Randolph's speeches to me the other day said that he wanted to come back, and I thought Salisbury was not so strong against it as he had been.

The great question is what is best for the Union and for the Party. I told Beach it would be infinitely more agreeable to me to give up than to go on, but he did not encourage that view, he did not deny however that the position of leader would be very far indeed from being a pleasant one.

Beach spoke of the strong personal antipathy Randolph has for Stanhope and that is of course a difficulty—if there was no other, in bringing him back. Holland would like to keep the Colonies and go to the Lords, but if he cannot have both, he would prefer a Peerage to remaining in the Commons with office. He said so plainly on Wednesday.

I must talk over these things with Salisbury early next week and tell him what I think. I wish I could have a chat with you first. . . .

My aim will be to carry our own friends with us solidly and to

[1] He had remained in the Cabinet when he resigned his office.
[2] Sir Henry Holland; Colonial Secretary, 1887–92.
[3] Hon. Edward Stanhope; Colonial Secretary, 1886–7; Secretary for War, 1887–92.

present as strong a Government as possible to our opponents.

Does the Party wish to have Randolph back? Will Salisbury accept him?

Yours sincerely,

W. H. Smith[1]

To Salisbury, next day (October 29th) he wrote: '. . . Beach has been with me for a day. I hope his retirement from the Cabinet will not be publicly announced. I did my best to dissuade him, but poverty to such a man as Beach is painful & irritating'.[2] But the only office which Salisbury was at that time in a position to offer Beach was the Board of Trade—and this, a little later, he did offer him. But, despite his declared readiness to take any office offered to him, Beach would not commit himself and kept the others on tenterhooks by continuing to conspire with Churchill. He proposed to the latter 'that they should both sit together and work together for the rest of the Parliament'. Churchill, however, 'would not countenance this generous attempt to relieve the isolation of his position', we are told by his son and biographer, and urged Beach to join the Government. 'They need you, and besides I shall like to feel I have one friend there,'[3] Beach finally accepted the Presidency of the Board of Trade in March 1888 and remained in that office for the rest of the Government's term.

Smith was always first and foremost the conscientious public servant rather than the militant partisan. He tended to fight shy of anything savouring of party tub-thumping and in his own speeches preferred to appeal to the reason and commonsense of his hearers rather than to their passions and prejudices. This attitude is perceptible in his reaction to a question at this time from the Chief Whip—who was and had to be a party man through and through.

'Douglas has asked me', he wrote to Salisbury (November 7th), 'if he is to stimulate or get up meetings throughout the Country. I told him I thought he might allow a little breathing time—that there was danger of a surfeit and nausea, and that of course if constituencies and organizations would have meetings to keep their own spirits up, they must, but that I thought we might rather follow the demand & satisfy it, rather than create it. Do you agree? . . .'[4]

The same attitude is apparent in a speech which he made at a big Conservative Meeting at Doncaster on December 5th. 'Now I have not come down to you to make a great speech', he told them, '—it is not in my line. . . . I claim to be a man of business—it is as a man of business that I have taken part in the conduct of affairs in Her

---

[1] Chilston Papers. [2] Salisbury Papers. [3] Churchill, op. cit., 766.
[4] Salisbury Paper

Majesty's Government. . . . I am not one of those who say that everything that the Government does is and must be right. It only rests with people who are a great deal wiser in their own judgment to make a statement of that kind. . . .'

In this same speech, however, he was able to relieve his feelings about Obstruction, answering John Morley, who in a recent speech had denied that obstruction had impeded legislation, with a minute and crushing analysis of the late session.

> . . . It is best to call things by their proper names. I say there was obstruction, obstruction of a most determined and persistent character, and I will give you one or two figures by way of showing that my statement is accurate. . . . Now we sat for 160 days and nights . . . for the usual hour for going home was 4 o'clock in the morning . . . and during that time I will just give you the number of hours we sat. It was 1,453, and the number of speeches made by the Radicals and the Parnellites was 7,368, an average of 42 speeches for each Parnellite and 19 for every Gladstonian Liberal. There were 3,590 Conservative speeches and 552 Liberal Unionist speeches. That is to say, the Opposition spoke 7,368 times, while the Ministerial party who had to answer them only spoke 4,100 times. . . . In other words, the average number of speeches of each member of the Opposition was 29, including Gladstonians and Liberals, while the average speeches for the Government side of the House were 10. . . .
>
> And now let me tell you what I believe to be the duty of the House of Commons. It is to attend to the business of the country. It is not to forward the interest of a faction. It is not because there is a faction determinedly bent on impeding a particular course of business that that faction should succeed. . . . Now how many times do you suppose the Opposition were called to order during the last session of Parliament? They were called to order 612 times. They broke the rules and regulations under which the House of Commons is conducted 612 times. I will be quite fair and tell you that on 64 occasions . . . those who supported the Government were called to order. . . .

Later in the same speech he denounced the proprietor of the Nationalist newspaper *Irish World*, Patrick Ford, who had written that 'Mr. Gladstone's Home Rule plan was but a small instalment of justice to Ireland' and that the Home Rule plan and the Land Acts were 'only stepping-stones to obtain that complete independence and separation which we aim at'. He also denounced Michael Davitt for having said that 'none of the safeguards [for the minority in Ireland] could be looked at for a single moment'. The latter denunciation involved him in some correspondence with Davitt, who denied the words bore the meaning attributed to them and even challenged Smith to prove when or where he had said them. Smith produced chapter and verse—and date—and added: 'I did not attribute to you a statement that the Home Rule scheme was "a stepping-stone towards complete separation", but I have not disguised my belief that if Mr. Gladstone's proposals are adopted complete separation or civil war are inevitable.'

With others, however, who were less obviously involved than Davitt and his like, the Doncaster Speech enhanced his already considerable reputation as a forthright and courageous statesman—and even as an eloquent one. Thus the Rev. Sir Emilius Laurie, Vicar of St. John's, Paddington, in a letter to him (December 7th): '. . . I only differ from you in one point, viz: in your disavowal of speaking gifts & power. Nothing can be more to the point, more telling or better put together than the speeches which from time to time you favour us with—and I am sure that their transparent honesty & straightforwardness give them great weight with all classes. . . . At all events, you carry with you the confidence of all, or nearly all, sensible men, & have behind you a vast reserve of power & good will. . . .' But Smith's own view of his political activities was, as always, an austere and sombre one. For, to Emily Giberne he wrote only a few weeks later (January 16th, 1888): '. . . All I say is God help me to do my work;—and take me out of it when I am no longer fit for it.'

When he wrote these words Smith was spending what was evidently quite a happy holiday, during the Christmas recess, with his family at Pau in the South of France. Here too he received one of Arthur Balfour's rather racy and cynical accounts of current affairs, written from the Chief Secretary's Office at Dublin Castle (January 6th):

> . . . The Old Man [Gladstone] is getting a more accomplished liar every day! If Providence spares him much longer Baron Munchausen will be a mere teller of white lies by comparison!
>
> Things are going on pretty well here I think: notwithstanding, the usual risks & bumps from the usual causes—viz. the slackness or inefficiency of our instruments. . . .
>
> I am a little anxious about Blunt's[1] case. We have the best of the Law & the argument: but this (in Ireland) does not secure a verdict. A somewhat disquieting telegram has just been received.
>
> I hope you are receiving much benefit from Pau:—and are prepared to meet the enemy in Feb. with good health & good spirits. I wish I was with you!

[1] Wilfrid Scawen Blunt, traveller, politician and poet, had taken up the Irish cause with fervour. Having stood for Parliament as a Tory Home Ruler in 1885 and as a Liberal Home Ruler in 1886 and lost both elections, he went to Ireland as an agitator in the cause, was arrested in October 1887 and served a term of two months imprisonment.

Hicks Beach was still havering at this time about his return to office as President of the Board of Trade and Smith, in his reply to the above, asked Balfour what he felt about it. The latter replied (January 25th):

> . . . As regards Beach I have no objection to his return to Office; I cannot imagine why he left it!—I do not think his presence will render Cabinets more agreeable socially, nor his absence materially increase the dangers of the Govt. in the House. He has not behaved so well as H. Chaplin;[1]—but I suppose he has stronger claims on the party.
>
> I hope in spite of yr. natural dislike of the Session, you are feeling well & happy. I have a sort of idea that our difficulties will not be so formidable as some persons suppose. . . . I am afraid that the Irish legislation is doomed to add to them; for cut down our proposals to the utmost we must have *four* and we ought to have *five* very controversial measures. . . .

Indeed, after Parliament had reassembled on February 9th, the debate on the Address turned chiefly on an amendment moved by Parnell directed against the alleged harsh administration of the Crimes Act. The division on this amendment was anticipated with some apprehension by Ministerialists owing to the recent efforts of Sir George Trevelyan to detach Liberal-Unionists from their support of the Government. However, in the result, only three of the Liberal-Unionists seceded to Home Rule—and, perhaps more seriously, one Conservative[2]—leaving a majority of 88 for the Government.

After this, whilst the horrors of the 'Jubilee Session' were still fresh in the minds of members, the most pressing task was to try to introduce a yet further tightening of the Rules of Procedure. Not for the first time Smith's reputation for correctitude and guilelessness enabled him to take his opponents completely by surprise—but after his experience of the last Session he was become a desperate man and was in a sense literally fighting for his life on this issue. Choosing the dinner hour, with a rather sparse and somnolent House, he launched his bomb-shell. In the words of Sir Henry Lucy: 'On Thursday night Mr. Smith, whose freshness and daring originality are the amazement of his most intimate friends, blandly proposed that the House should proceed to discuss in detail the Procedure Rules without the time-honoured ceremony of preliminary general debate.'[3]

---

[1] Henry Chaplin (created Viscount Chaplin, 1916); M.P. Sleaford Division Lincolnshire, 1868–1906; was Chancellor of Duchy of Lancaster in Caretaker Govt., 1885–6, but, disagreeing strongly with Churchill, declined office in 2nd Salisbury Govt. and stayed out until made President of Board of Agriculture in 1889.

[2] W. J. Evelyn, M.P. Deptford.

[3] Henry W. Lucy: *A Diary of the Salisbury Parliament, 1886–92*, 32.

Gladstone's deep-rooted respect for precedent was naturally deeply shocked; but, as Lucy expresses it, 'his fighting propensities were subdued by the influence of the hour'. He duly protested, but spoke only for a few minutes, concluding by expressing general approval of the proposal, and then left the House. This unexpected act of surrender completely unnerved the Irish members and though Healy rose, he too expressed general approval of the proposal. Thereupon Smith moved that a standing order be introduced that the sittings of the House should in future close at midnight and this, after some discussion on points of detail, was agreed to. Thus, says

"OLD MORALITY."

Lucy, 'in a single sitting of moderate length, a complete revolution in Parliamentary Procedure had been quietly accomplished'. He goes on to analyse Smith's achievement: 'The attitude of the opposition greatly simplified matters, but the happy result was in no small degree due to the management of Mr. W. H. Smith. As Leader of the House he is naturally gifted with two marvellous accomplishments. He knows how to sit through long spaces of time without saying anything, and when he does interpose he says so very little that no opportunity is furnished for controversy. A fussier or more ambitious Leader might tonight have spoiled the game. Mr. Smith, the Brer Rabbit of House of Commons Leaders, "lay low and said nuffin". He has his reward in the bloodless victory by which has been established a momentous change, the effect of which will extend

273

beyond narrow Parliamentary circles to the whole social fabric of London.'[1]

The relief afforded by the adoption of this rule was, needless to say, tremendous, but, whilst it did not materially interfere with the adequate discussion of measures and votes, it did undoubtedly demand an extra vigilance, and sense of judgment on the part of the Leader, as well as imposing an added responsibility on the Chair, by making necessary the more frequent application of the closure.

Since arranging the highly successful appointment of Chamberlain to head the mission to America in the previous year, Smith had always been on the look out for further opportunities to conciliate this rather wayward ally and bind him more strongly to the Government's side. Thus on March 24th he wrote to Chamberlain: 'Will you be at the House on Monday? I want to have 3 words as to some more work which I think you can do for the Country—if you are disposed.'[2] Chamberlain jibbed at the proposition and Smith wrote again (April 17th):

> You did not give me a positive answer as to the chairmanship of the Royal Commission on the system, organization and administration of the defensive forces of the Country and I have not pressed you as the subject is a large one.
>
> It is necessary however that we should now come to some decision and I hope most sincerely you will see your way to accept.
>
> *We* think you are eminently fitted for the work and the fact that you have not hitherto taken any part in the administration of these forces is by no means a disqualification.
>
> I hope you will assent.[3]

But Chamberlain still demurred and finally the desire to defer to Liberal-Unionist opinion was met by appointing Hartington. Smith himself was to be on the Commission. '. . . I have been *obliged* to accept an appointment on a Royal Commission on the Administration of the Army and Navy, with Hartington in the chair', he wrote to Emily (May 7th). 'Salisbury thought there was no one else to do it from amongst us, and as I can only be at work all day, I may as well do one thing as another. And it is all work in the highest sense of the word, the discharge of duty, and that gives me strength.'

Smith's tactful handling of Chamberlain was rewarded by some useful intelligence on the state of feeling among those electors with whom Chamberlain, with his mercantile and Non-conformist background, was most in touch—and also by the unusually friendly tone with which it was imparted: for Chamberlain was apt to adopt a

---

[1] Ibid., 34–5. [2] Chamberlain Papers. [3] Ibid.

rather harsh tone in writing to his other Tory allies. Thus Chamberlain to Smith (June 27th):

> In the great pressure upon your time I do not suppose that your attention has been specially called to the Technical Instruction Bill and I should like therefore to signalise to you the danger to the interests of the Unionist Party which it involves.
>
> I am afraid that the agitation on the licensing Clauses—with which as you know I do not sympathise—has set the great bulk of the Temperance people against us.
>
> Goschen's Van and Wheel Tax has disquieted and irritated a very large number of small tradesmen, many of them active politicians. Now this Technical Instruction Bill will drive to arms the whole force of aggressive nonconformity besides many of the most active educationalists in the country. . . .
>
> Is it worth while to proceed with it under these circumstances and in a session like the present? Should it not be withdrawn & reconsidered? . . .
>
> P.S. What an admirable speech Balfour made last night! In my opinion it was nearly perfect.[1]

Smith, as we have already seen, usually tended to be out of sympathy with Goschen and his ideas, but he had some special reasons for agreeing with Chamberlain in regarding the Chancellor's proposed Wheel and Van Tax with disfavour. Goschen's excuse for this and one or two other rather irritating tax proposals was that he felt he ought to reduce the income tax from sevenpence to sixpence and must therefore recoup his Budget in some way. Smith exposed his reasons in a letter to Salisbury (July 29th):

> Goschen suspects me of a desire to evade a debate on the Wheel Tax and he thinks I want to manoeuvre him out of his opportunity. He is quite right in his conjecture and I have two reasons for wishing that his Bill should not be brought on:—the first is that I fear we shall be beaten on a division and I don't want to give the Gladstonians a victory,—and the second is that I am convinced it will be impossible to deal with the Wheel Tax *and* the Tithe Bills before the adjournment.
>
> One will shoulder out the other; and even if it were possible, it would damage the Tithe Bills to be taken after a Wheel Tax defeat.
>
> But Goschen feels very keenly about his Bill. He wants to make his speech and it will be a very good one indeed—very conclusive as a good piece of reasoning, but however valuable from an educational point of view it won't turn a vote in the H. of C.
>
> It is for you to consider as Chief whether you should express any wish or whether the subject should be raised at Cabinet on Tuesday; and perhaps you would send for Douglas and ascertain what he thinks about the business.

[1] Chamberlain Papers.

275

For my own part I put the Tithe Bills before the Wheel Tax in importance to the Country and to the Government. . . .

Don't suppose I want to thwart or annoy Goschen. Very much the contrary, but we must weigh consequences whatever general feelings may be involved.[1]

The delicate question of the 'Appanages' of the Royal Family had come up at the beginning of the Session owing to the tabling of a question by a Radical M.P. and Smith, who always had a chivalrous regard for the Queen's feelings, as well as being a staunch supporter of the Throne, wrote to her then (February 11th) to warn her and suggest a course of action. He told her that he had privately asked Gladstone for his co-operation in this matter and that the latter had called in Childers, his former Chancellor of the Exchequer. These two Liberal statesmen recommended an enquiry by a Committee of the House of Commons; but Smith wanted the enquiry to be conducted by a Committee of persons appointed by the Queen. Such a committee, he told the Queen, might be able to 'recommend economies which, without interfering with Your Majesty's personal comfort, state, or dignity, might . . . be made available as a fund out of which provision could be made either wholly or in part for the Young Members of the Royal Family'. This might avert the necessity for a Parliamentary Committee 'from which Mr. Smith candidly avows that he shrinks', or at least might forestall some of the recommendations likely to be made by a Parliamentary Committee.

But the Queen did not smile upon the idea of creating a fund out of economies won at her own expense, so to speak—by whomsoever they might be recommended. The Prince of Wales on the other hand, writing to Smith (July 9th), perhaps not unnaturally concurred in the proposal to create a Crown Appanage Fund to provide for his younger children and thought the 'terms offered are liberal'. The Queen gave vent to her feelings in a letter (August 16th) to Lord Salisbury, which the latter passed to Smith, in whose papers it is, and in which she complained that it was 'most unjust that *she*, in her old age, with endless expenses—shd. be asked to contribute so largely to this appanage & considers herself very shamefully used in having no real assistance for the enormous expense of entertaining that immense number of Sovereigns & Princes last year [for the Golden Jubilee]. This was originally promised & the promise was not kept.' At the same time, unlike her son, she thought the sum proposed for her grandsons 'too small' and spoke of the dangers of Royal Princes getting into debt, 'as the Queen's dear Father & Uncles did'.

In a postscript written next day the Queen burst out again, declaring that 'the constant dread of the House of Commons is a

[1] Salisbury Papers.

bugbear.—Whatever is done you *will not* & *cannot* conciliate a *certain* set of fools & wicked people who will attack *whatever* is done & though it is better to ask for what is really *just & fair* than out of dread to appear weak & ask for too little money to please those will will *not* be satisfied with anything.'[1]

However, owing to other more pressing business, the matter was shelved for the present Session, coming up again in the following year. The only interim comment being from Smith in a letter to Salisbury (December 17th, 1888): '. . . My own impression is very strong that many of our men—all the Radical Unionists and the entire Opposition would vote against any attempt to provide out of public funds for grandchildren of the Sovereign other than the children of the heir to the Throne.'[2]

The special position enjoyed by Smith in the estimation of members of the Royal Family was emphasized again at this time when he was consulted confidentially by the Queen's third daughter, Princess Christian.[3] The Emperor Frederick of Germany had recently died and his son, the new Emperor William II, was being disagreeable to his mother, who was the Queen's eldest daughter. The Queen was very upset on her daughter's behalf. 'Trust that we shall be *very cool*, though civil, in our communications with my grandson and Prince Bismarck, who are bent on a return to the oldest times of government', she had telegraphed to Salisbury (July 7th).[4] Princess Christian had evidently spoken to Smith, hoping that he might influence the Government to underline the Queen's feelings in their policy. Smith was alarmed and, knowing the Princess was about to go to Germany, sought at once to correct any such fancy, writing to her (July 14th):

I have been treated by Your Royal Highness with so much confidence that I venture to take the liberty of addressing you with reference to your approaching visit to Germany.

I am aware that Your Royal Highness spoke to me on Wednesday with a complete absence of reserve and in absolute reliance on my personal devotion to the Queen and the Royal Family and I am emboldened therefore to write with great frankness although I may be taking a great liberty in doing so.

I do not for a single moment question that all the expressions of indignation at the past and the present, and of apprehension as to the future are entirely justified, and that ordinary flesh and blood must feel as warmly as Your Royal Highness does; but I have present to my mind this one overwhelming fact that a good understanding

[1] This letter is quoted in *Queen Victoria's Letters*, Third Series, Vol. I, 435; but without the postscript.
[2] Salisbury Papers.
[3] Helena Augusta Victoria, married Prince Christian of Schleswig Holstein.
[4] *Queen Victoria's Letters*, Third Series, Vol. I, 429.

between England and Germany is the only hope for the peace of Europe. So long as that exists there will be no war—and if there is war no living being is wise enough to foretell what the results may be to countless affected by it or to their Institutions. . . .

He went on to remind the Princess that 'in Germany the Sovereign is identified with the Government', so that Germans would naturally tend to regard any utterances of the English Royal Family as official expressions of English Government policy, and further that in England this would provide welcome ammunition for those anti-monarchists who liked to represent the Throne as an enemy of democracy. On the other hand, if the Princess could bring about 'a reconciliation of the jarring elements' [i.e. between the Emperor and Bismarck on the one side and the Dowager Empress and her mother, Queen Victoria, on the other] she would have done a great service, albeit unrecognized, to her country and humanity.

This wise and fatherly counsel was not wasted, for the Princess wrote back:

Private　　　　　　　　　　　　　　　　　Cumberland Lodge,
　　　　　　　　　　　　　　　　　　　　　Windsor Park.
　　　　　　　　　　　　　　　　　　　　　July 15. 1888

Dear Mr. Smith,

I am *most* grateful to you for your kind letter and for writing to me as you have done. It is only another proof to me of what a true friend you are to me. I so entirely agree & share the opinion expressed in your letter, & look at the subject in the same light. When I spoke to you as I did . . . it was as a friend to a friend and therefore I expressed *unreservedly* what I felt in my inmost heart—because I knew that it would go no further & that what I said to *you* wd be looked on as confidential. Even towards my own Mother I have *not* said half *what* I felt for I knew the importance, the vital importance of smoothing over differences when it is possible. My one object whilst under my Sister's roof will be to try to soothe & soften where I can, abstaining from giving *any* opinion & remaining perfectly neutral. I have been too often & too much at Berlin not to know that one cannot be *too* cautious in every respect. I cannot help hoping that when the Mackenzie[1] episode has blown over things will settle down & many differences disappear. . . .

I shall be very glad to have an answer to this, that I may know that your mind is quite at rest on the subject.

Wd you burn this when read. I cannot thank you sufficiently for having written to me as you have done.

　　　　　　　　　　　　　　　　　　　　　Yrs always most truly
　　　　　　　　　　　　　　　　　　　　　　　　Helena

---

[1] Sir Morell Mackenzie, was the doctor called in by the Empress Frederick to treat her dying husband and was strongly criticized and opposed by the Crown Prince and the German medical profession.

Meanwhile, the affair of the Parnell Letter and *The Times* articles on 'Parnellism and Crime', which had blown up in the previous year and had appeared to subside when the Government had refused Gladstone's demand for a Select Committee to inquire into the matter, now suddenly revived. For, an action for libel was entered against *The Times* by one O'Donnell, a former member of the Irish Parliamentary Party, on the grounds that he was one of the persons affected by the imputations of the articles.[1] The Attorney-General, Sir Richard Webster, appeared as counsel for *The Times* and, despite the fact that he was *not* appearing as a Law Officer of the Crown, practically converted his defence of his clients into an indictment of Parnell and his party by reading about a dozen more alleged and incriminating letters of the Irish leader.

A verdict was given in favour of *The Times* on July 5th. The following day Parnell rose in the House to contradict the charges made against him by the Attorney-General and to repudiate again the original letter which had been reproduced by *The Times*. When *The Times* retorted that they were prepared to prove the authenticity of the letter, Parnell asked the Government for a Select Committee. But Smith, in the name of the Government, refused a Select Committee, on the grounds that such a body, being necessarily partisan,[2] was unfitted to judge matters of such gravity and *offered* instead to introduce a Bill appointing a Commission with full power to inquire into the allegations.

Nevertheless, by July 16th notice for leave to introduce such a Bill was already on the Order Paper and, although Smith declared that it was open to Parnell to accept or decline the Bill, the new note of determination was still more apparent when he said that if accepted it would immediately be read a first time and printed, but that no provison would be made for debating the measure. Parnell was, not unnaturally, angered by these terms and declared that if the Leader of the House and the Attorney-General knew the allegations against him were true 'instead of attempting to make bargains with him they ought to indict him'. However, he said he would offer no opposition

---

[1] Of F. H. O'Donnell, who later became one of Parnell's bitterest critics, T. M. Healy has written: 'To bring a libel action against *The Times* required means, and O'Donnell had none. The reader must, therefore, make up his mind as to whether, in provoking this bogus trial under the pretence that he had been attacked, O'Donnell was merely being spiteful, or was an agent for (or in collusion with) an undisclosed principal'. (See T. M. Healy: *Letters and Leaders of My Day*, I, 279.)

[2] Select Committees are usually constituted on a party basis, the various parties being represented on the Committee in proportion to their strength in the House.

to the introduction of the Bill, but in Committee would claim the right to 'take the judgment of the House on any of its details'.

The hardening of the Government's attitude to the question is reflected in a letter of Smith to Salisbury (July 21st): 'Specific charges are to be insisted upon—and we cannot alter our Bill, therefore our Bill is to be opposed in Committee.'[1] But of course it was this air of desperate resolve which brought the Cabinet under suspicion of wishing to make political capital out of the charges against their opponents. Belatedly sensing this, Smith attempted to justify the Government's shift of stance, when he moved the Second Reading of the Bill on July 23rd. Thus: '. . . the charges and allegations have been made now in a formal and distinct manner in a court of Justice and they have therefore advanced from the position they occupied last year, indeed they are now in a totally different position.' Also that 'we are of opinion that if the enquiry be entered upon, it must be a complete and searching enquiry and must finally dispose of the charges which have been made wholly or partly upon hon. gentlemen opposite'.

Parnell retorted that the measure had been brought forward 'for the purposes of casting discredit on the great Irish movement . . . and to contrive a means of escape for his [Smith's] confederates from the breakdown of charges which he and the hon. and learned Attorney-General sitting beside him, knew full well would break down . . .'. He also very pertinently asked the Attorney-General: 'Did he ever learn from *The Times* the source from which they got these letters before he, the legal adviser of the Government, consented to link his fortunes and those of his party and the Government in these infamous productions?'[2]

Furthermore, while the Bill was in Committee, Smith was taxed by Harcourt with receiving John Walter, the proprietor of *The Times*, whilst the matter was under consideration of the Cabinet and with being 'in collusion' with the proprietor of *The Times*. Smith, describing the charge as contemptible, denied it vehemently. 'I say I deny absolutely that I have had any negotiation, any arrangement whatever, with Mr. Walter with reference to this Bill—Mr. Walter has called upon me, as it has been his practice to do, as an old friend —but we have made no arrangement whatever of any kind. He never saw the Reference—he never saw the Bill. I never had any sort of plan, or scheme or contrivance with Mr. Walter in regard to this Bill.'

But Harcourt, backed by Gladstone, persisted and refused to withdraw his allegation about 'collusion', saying: 'I think it is

[1] Salisbury Papers.
[2] Hansard, Vol. 329, 208 seq.

extremely improper, that in a matter of this kind, the Government should have communication with one party, and not with the other. The fact stands and the Government now admit it . . .'. Smith, reiterating his denial of the accusation, replied: '. . . If I had kept back the fact that he had called at my house once since the Bill has been in print, I should have been unworthy the belief which I trust the House will always have in any statement I make.'[1] A couple of days later (August 2nd) he was attacked by Healy who put down a question asking if the First Lord of the Treasury had had a visit from Buckle, the editor of *The Times*, with reference to the Commission Bill. Smith, being absent from the House, Goschen answered for him that he had 'had no communication with Mr. Buckle at all on this question—he has not seen him and has not been called upon by him'.[2]

The reason for Smith's absence from the House on this latter occasion was that he was attending the funeral of his step-daughter's husband, Admiral Codrington, to whom he had been deeply attached since the time when the latter served as his private secretary at the Admiralty. Codrington's long illness and the beloved Mary Auber's ordeal had therefore greatly added to the strain of the Session. Two months earlier he had written to Miss Giberne (June 3rd):

Emily went down to Tunbridge Wells yesterday to see Mary and Willie Codrington, and she came back in very great sadness at the great progress decay had made in Willie and the apparent imminence of his death. . . .

It is a mysterious thing here. There is a new and apparently a vigorous life begun in Emmie's[3] boy, who is doing well, and the mother also. She, bright and happy and thankful, and a little way off her own very dear sister is watching by the dying bed of her husband. And of course while this is going on we have to go through our duties.

I had to give a birthday dinner to Prince Albert Victor and a number of Peers and Privy Councillors last night. There was the trooping of the colours in the Park in the morning . . . and a great party at the Foreign Office in the evening.

But all these things, as the world is constituted, are matters of duty from which we must not withdraw ourselves in contemplation of bereavement to come. There are also great anxieties in Government—great responsibilities, and I tremble for myself and for my wife and my children lest any of us should fail to live up to our duty, and to the right use of the talents intrusted to us. . . . All I say is, God help me to do my work, and take me out of it when I am no longer fit for it.[4]

[1] Ibid., 1012–5. [2] Ibid., 1248–9.

[3] Smith's daughter who had married William Dyke Acland in 1887. He later became an admiral and also succeeded his father as 2nd Baronet.

[4] q. Maxwell, II, 223–4.

Two days after this family bereavement Smith was back at the House—though remaining in the background—to see his Commission Bill[1] pass its Second Reading. From there he wrote to Emily next day (August 3rd):

Here I am sitting on the Bench listening to Arthur Balfour who is answering Mr. John Morley and I have ears for him and thoughts for you and my very dear ones at home, at the same time. . . .

I did not come on to the Front Bench last night as my Colleagues did not think it necessary and I was not in a humour to take part in the fray which was hot and furious. I divided three times and arranged a great deal of business in my room and today I am thankful to say the atmosphere is certainly quieter and we have some hope of winding up . . . but it is well not to be too sanguine. . . .

When Parliament was adjourned for the summer recess his physician and great friend Henry Wentworth Acland wrote to him (August 11th):

Now the great strain of the week is over I venture to write to you, to you both, to say how grieved I was that your home sorrow came at last in the midst of the wild clatter of the Opposition attacks. But you never fail in the quietness and the confidence which is your strength—and the good & the evil of each day seem to bring to you their gain & their reward.

May you now have rest & peace. . . .

The signs of strain had not escaped the notice of his colleagues either, for Lord George Hamilton wrote also (August 15th):

Now that the Session is practically over I do hope that you will spare yourself, & get some thorough rest. You are considerate to everybody except yourself, & this all your colleagues feel & regret. You have had a most trying session with a lot of disagreeable work at the end & you have steered us through all the difficulties with wisdom & without mishap. So go away & put all work on one side for some time to come.

Smith duly went away to join his wife at Aix-les-Bains, where she had preceded him in her own search for better health, but the airy advice to put all work on one side was not so easily followed. Although the Government's line in insisting on the 'Parnell Commission' appeared to be generally endorsed by the rank and file of the Unionist Party, there were grave doubts about its wisdom in at least one important quarter. Lord Randolph Churchill, for instance, had conveyed his own reasons for disliking the whole procedure to Smith in a very ably drawn memorandum as early as July 18th. This lengthy document may be roughly summarized by three extracts. The opening alone was startling enough:

[1] Properly called the 'Charges and Allegations Bill'.

It may be assumed that the Tory party are under an imperative obligation to avoid seeking escape from political difficulties by extra-constitutional methods. The above is a general rule. The exception to it can scarcely be conceived. The whole course of proceedings, if the character of the allegations is remembered, will, when carefully considered, be found to be utterly repugnant to our English idea of legal justice, and wholly unconstitutional. It is hardly exaggerating to describe the Commission contemplated as 'a revolutionary tribunal' for the trial of political offenders. If there is any truth in the above, or colour for such a statement, can a Tory Government safely or honourably suggest and carry through such a proposal? . . .

I do not examine the party aspects of the matter; I only remark that the fate of the Union may be determined by the abnormal proceedings of an abnormal tribunal. Prudent po-liticians would hesitate to go out of their way to play such high stakes as these.[1]

THE ATTORNEY-GENERAL.

There were indeed two aspects of the affair which considerably reinforced the suspicion that the Government was out to make political capital out of it. One was the breadth of the terms of reference of the Commission, which, instead of being confined to establishing the authenticity or falsity of the letters, author-ized it to inquire generally into the charges and allegations made in *The Times* articles against Members of Parliament and 'other persons'. The other was the fact that the Attorney-General, Sir Richard Webster, whose duty it was to give legal advice to the Government, had also been counsel for *The Times* in the recent libel action. For, according to the custom of the time,[2] the Law Officers of the Crown were free to take private work and therefore Webster's Government colleagues had not been consulted or in-formed about the line which he had taken in this civil action.

As a result of this duality of status—his official status as a public

[1] This document is not now to be found among the Hambleden Papers, so that the quotations have been taken from Maxwell, II, 227–31.

[2] The law was amended in this respect in 1895.

servant and his private status as a fee'd laywer—Webster's position, once the Commission had been set up, was singularly delicate. Moreover Webster, to do him justice, was the first to recognize this. He wrote to Smith soon after the adjournment to say that he had 'come to the distinct conclusion that I ought not and must not appear before the Commission' owing to the very wide scope of the enquiry. Further, as he felt sure that the ultimate Report of the Commission would be the subject of debate in the Commons, he thought that 'the Govt. ought not to be deprived of any help which I can give them. If I am Counsel upon the enquiry my mouth will be closed in any debate'. From Aix, where he already was, Smith immediately telegraphed this news to Salisbury, who was taking a different kind of water at Royat, also in France. Sending on a copy of Webster's letter, he wrote (August 29th):

> . . . It came upon me as a great surprise as although I have not spoken to him on the subject since the Bill was brought into our House, I understood to the very last that he had got up the case and was going to take the whole direction of the affair for the Times.
>
> I do not see that we have any right to interfere in the matter at all, and certainly not to put pressure upon him to do what he considers he ought not to do. He felt the embarrassment of his position in the debate on the Bill, but I never expressed words I believe which showed any annoyance to him. I am very sorry both on his own account and for the sake of the Times that he did not come to the conclusion sooner which he has now announced to us.
>
> I confess I think that from the point of view of the Govt. alone the decision will be a relief to us:—our hands will be much more free to deal with the results of this great State Trial and to watch it while it is in progress now that our Chief Law Officer is not to appear as an Advocate for one of the Parties. . . .[1]

Smith therefore told Salisbury that he had advised Webster that he 'must act on his own sense of duty to his client and the Govt.'. But Salisbury's reactions to the news were quite different from Smith's. In an undated letter to the latter he wrote:

> . . . I am very much disgusted at Webster's view. My special reason for that feeling is this, Sir H. James[2] is here and informed me yesterday that he contemplated getting out of this case chiefly for the same reason as Webster—that it silenced him in the H. of C. Now the simultaneous refusal of these two men to go on will have the worst possible effect. There will be no persuading the outside world that they have not run away from the case because on scrutinising the

[1] Salisbury Papers.
[2] See *ante*. He had appeared with Webster for *The Times* in the O'Donnell libel action.

evidence they satisfied themselves that the case was bad. The effect of this impression which will be of course heightened by Parnell's scribes will be disastrous upon all the Irish witnesses. They will be convinced that [Parnell]'s is the winning end and they will forswear themselves like men. Again—where is the Times to supply the place of these two men? There is very little time left: men have made their engagements. This is a case which will require the devotion of all a man's time. There is a great danger that owing to this surprise the Times will have to put up with a some younger and inferior man. And this is a case in which everything depends upon examination of the Irish witnesses who are too much frightened to speak out—and the real truth will never be got out of them except by the screw of examination. What is there on the other side? No doubt the A.G. is of great value in debate—but there at least his place can be filled. All the debating power the Govt. has is available for a case of this kind. I do not of course wish you to alter your advice if you are still convinced of the soundness of it. But I should like Webster to know my view also. If I could have foreseen that this change of intention would take place at this time I think I should have somewhat modified my advice to the Cabinet on the subject.

Smith appears to have been impressed by these arguments for he wrote to Akers-Douglas (September 6th): '. . . I have told Webster that if Salisbury's fears are realised it will be a very serious matter indeed. . . . James is unfortunately at Royat and Salisbury has been talking very freely to him; all of which James has written to Hartington who has been here with the Duchess of Manchester;[1] and therefore everybody knows Salisbury's anxieties and fears which is unfortunate. . . . Hartington . . . thinks James and Webster are best out of it. I was careful to avoid hinting at Webster's retirement, but he told it to me as news. . . .'[2]

Webster himself, however, although he was intensely annoyed by James's threatened withdrawal, appeared unmoved by Salisbury's arguments. '. . . It is clear that his own view remains unchanged,' Smith wrote Salisbury (September 10th), 'but he gives no information as to the method by which the interests of his Client are to be protected, while, however, he says distinctly that he does not anticipate that the witnesses will be influenced by his withdrawal as you appeared to think they would be.'[3] Nevertheless, Smith evidently set to work to influence Webster to reverse his decision and the latter must have likewise influenced James, for in the end both gave in and consented to represent *The Times* before the Commission. 'The

[1] Hartington's mistress, whom he married in 1892. She was born Countess von Alten.
[2] Chilston Papers.
[3] Salisbury Papers.

question is settled as you will see from Webster's letter,' wrote Smith to his Chief (September 15th) '. . . and I am content with the arrangements which have been made'.[1]

Salisbury's anxiety as to the importance of keeping in the two counsel who had won the earlier case for *The Times* is, on the face of it, perfectly understandable. But what seems strange is that he should not have sensed that he might be putting his Government in a highly dangerous position by committing it so unhesitatingly to a line considered fit in an ordinary libel action. For, in the latter, Webster, acting as an ordinary advocate, had been satisfied to accept the authenticity of the 'Parnell Letters' simply and solely on the authority of his brief from *The Times* and had proceeded from there to indict Parnell as a traitor and criminal in a fashion which many had considered improper and irresponsible even in those circumstances. Now he would presumably proceed along the same lines— with no more guarantees or safeguards than before—before a tribunal set up by the Government of which he happened to be the Chief Law Officer. The respective sides of his dual status were now virtually impossible to differentiate convincingly. But then Parnell's personality was so generally considered odious (even most of his own side agreed on that) and his record of subversive activities so venerable that perhaps the details of certain charges hardly seemed worth testing more seriously when such a chance offered itself of completely exposing, discrediting and ridding themselves for ever of such an incubus. Churchill had called the Commission of Inquiry 'a revolutionary tribunal'; but even Smith had referred to it quite casually as 'this great State Trial'—so that was evidently what they meant to have. Of course, such was the prestige of *The Times* in those days, that none of them dreamt that the letters which had fired off the whole affair could be forgeries.

Whilst these worried exchanges were going on about the impending Commission, Smith, as the obvious target in Church matters, was being needled again by the Archbishop of Canterbury about the Tithes and Clergy Discipline Bills. '. . . The Church has really relied on this Government to "support the Church" as we were assured', he wrote (August 17th), 'and above all asks to be supported in getting rid of evils within. You recognize, I am sure, what constant postponements have attended the really vital Church measures. . . .' Smith of course treated this plea with the deference due to its author, but he was evidently a trifle nettled by the Archbishop's implied reproaches. For the latter in thanking him (August 26th) for 'the very warm tone in which you write about helping the Church', added: '. . . I feel sure that nothing in my letter could have even

[1] Ibid.

seemed to imply the least doubt on this point, for I have always known that the work of the Church enters not only into your political sympathies, but is among your inner personal anxieties. . . .' Nevertheless, a month later (September 27th) Smith wrote to Salisbury saying that he had told the Archbishop that though they would try their best to avoid postponing the Tithe Bill, it would very likely be impossible to deal with the Clergy Discipline Bill that session. But, alas, owing to Irish obstruction both measures, like so many others, had to wait more than another two years—that is until after the O'Shea divorce case had broken the Irish obstructive power—before they could be introduced.

With all these worries it is not surprising if Smith returned from Aix in late September not much the better for his holiday. 'I am unhappy at thinking that you have not profited much by yr trip abroad', wrote Balfour to him (September 28th), 'I do most earnestly hope on every ground public and private, that yr native air will set you up . . .'. Nevertheless, though strongly advised against it by two doctors, he insisted on undertaking his full share of platform speeches all over the country during the remainder of the recess. That he had some doubts about this himself, however, is proved by a passage in a letter to his friend Penrose Fitzgerald:[1] '. . . I have been sent by the Whips to Gloucester, and I am going for the same purpose to Salford. . . . My present impression is that I ought not to speak anywhere at all: old Jenner[2] is very strong against it. . . .'[3]

His speech at Gloucester on October 9th gave rise to an amusing incident. The *Birmingham Daily Post* (October 10th) commented upon a discrepancy between the report of his speech as given in *The Times* and as given in other papers, whereby an inference was drawn which proved to be quite unfounded, i.e. 'whether Mr. Smith did not put the probabilities of an early Coalition Government rather more strongly . . . than he had intended doing when he rose'. What he actually said was that 'he himself should be glad to give place to a Liberal-Unionist; but what the country had got to see was that, by some means or other, a Unionist Government was maintained in power'. But in *The Times* the second half of the sentence was missing and the paper went on to surmise that 'Mr. Smith, according to custom gave the manuscript of his address to *The Times* representative beforehand', and that 'he was so affected by his feelings of gratitude towards the Liberal Unionists' that he improvised. *The Times* then expatiated on the danger of a political leader not only

[1] See *ante*, p. 207.
[2] Sir William Jenner, the celebrated physician.
[3] Maxwell, II, 234.

writing out his speech but handing it to reporters before he had delivered it. Smith effectively put the snuffer on this homily by the terse comment, written in the margin of the cutting: 'Amusing. I never wrote out a speech in my life and could not do it. W.H.S.'

But, as a matter of fact, appeasement and conciliation of the Liberal Unionists was a matter requiring constant attention in those days, and Smith, unlike some of his colleagues, was acutely aware of it. He appreciated that their hypersensitiveness had its roots partly in their small size as a party and partly in their guilt-complex regarding their defection from the main Liberal Party. We have already noted his hint to Salisbury about making a friendly gesture towards Chamberlain in the previous year: now he passed on some Liberal Unionist complaints and again rubbed in the vital importance of keeping the alliance in being. Thus he wrote to Salisbury (October 18th):

> I had a wail from Goschen last night as to the treatment the L.U's receive in Edinburgh in the matter of legal patronage and generally in the distribution of loaves and fishes. He sent me a paper he had received expressing alarm as to the seat for the University and I sent that on at once to Douglas.
>
> I do not know whether you can suggest to Lothian[1] to give them some portion of the spoils.
>
> They are hungry and it is important to keep them with us heartily; as it is certain that without their votes the Unionist Govt. must fall, & although they would themselves be impotent. . . .

The importance attached to not offending Chamberlain—even at the price of other inconveniences to the Government—was revealed in another matter at this time. There had been, as already noted above, some disquiet and dissatisfaction among members and supporters of the Government (particularly Smith) over the inadequate performance of Henry Matthews as Home Secretary. He could only decently be ousted from that post by making him either a Judge or a Peer; but either of these steps would entail creating a vacancy in his Parliamentary seat of East Birmingham. Chamberlain had, as the uncrowned king of Birmingham, been consulted by Akers-Douglas on the subject in the previous year and had replied that as things then stood it was 'most undesirable that any vacancy should be created if this can in any way be avoided', because the seat would 'almost certainly be lost'.[2] This advice was duly respected; but a year later the urge to be rid of Matthews waxed strong again. How-

[1] Schomberg Henry, 9th Marquess of Lothian; Lord Keeper of Privy Seal of Scotland; Lord Rector of Edinburgh University, 1887–90.
[2] Chilston Papers.

288

ever, it was significant of the value attached to Chamberlain's good opinion that it was decided to take no action till his return from America, whither he had gone to marry his second wife, the former Miss Endicott. Even Salisbury, who was apt to be impatient over Chamberlain's pretensions as an ally, wrote to Smith (November 8th): 'I quite agree that we ought not if possible to make a vacancy at Birmingham in Chamberlain's absence. But as I see he is to be home by Xmas that will not inconvenience us much. We could not well take our friend [Matthews] out of H[ome] O[ffice] before the prorogation.' Even then, however, Matthews remained secure in his office—in fact until the end of the Government's term in 1892.

All the while Smith's health, far from improving, continued rapidly to deteriorate. Its state is reflected in the low morale shown in a letter to his wife (November 23rd): 'I am writing from the bench listening to Mr. Healy which is not at all a pleasant thing. The Irish and the Opposition are rampant, worrying us all they can, but there is an end to all trouble and all worry. It must come. . . . I have been sitting here since 3.15 and it is now 6.40—and it looks as if I should have to stay here literally all night.'

To his sister Gussie he wrote some ten days later (December 2nd): 'We have not yet settled the exact date on which we start for Monte Carlo. Business in the House drags heavily and I wish to see the end before I go. . . . I was rather done up last week, but Jenner has brought me to, and I am now feeling strong again: but all the same I shall be glad of a real rest.' Jenner in fact, was sufficiently worried to write to Lord Salisbury (December 10th): 'I have seen Mr. Smith many times (the last time this morning) and after repeated examinations I am satisfied that it is absolutely necessary for him to take rest as soon as possible. If he works on as he has done he will I feel soon break down altogether. . . .'

So Smith was finally persuaded not to wait for the Prorogation (which did not in fact take place till Christmas Eve) and to leave for Monte Carlo on December 15th, where he stayed till February 4th of the following year. Just before leaving he received the following characteristic letter from the Queen (December 13th):

The Queen has to thank Mr. Smith for all his interesting but alas! often very unsatisfactory reports of the proceedings in Parliament. She trusts Mr. Smith will insist on measures being taken to put a stop to the state of [word missing] into wh. the Home Rulers are bringing the House of Commons. It is becoming utterly impotent and contemptible.

The Queen has been so grieved to hear of Mr. Smith's health having been so tried & only wishes he had gone away sooner. She trusts he

may take a good long rest & return strong in health & resume his
arduous duties, which he performs so ably.

The Queen wd wish Mr. Goschen to report to her during Mr. Smith's
absence—daily, the proceedings in Parliament.

Where is Mr. Smith going to?

On his own side Smith's last thought before his departure was of
those loyal and devoted lieutenants whom he was leaving to carry
on the battle. Thus to Akers-Douglas, the Chief Whip, he wrote
(December 14th):

> My dear Douglas,
> I am afraid I did not today say goodbye for the present to my
> colleagues and friends on the bench to whom I owe so much. I do not
> like to go away from them while serious work remains to be done,
> but I cannot help it.
> You know well enough how much I value your help and next to
> you I value and rely on Jackson.[1]
> Pray make it clear to him that I am really very sorry I could not
> thank him today as warmly as I should have wished for all his good
> work. I could not have wished to have had a better man. He has done
> his work admirably for the Government and for the Country—and
> the whole crew are as fine a lot of fellows as any Treasury Captain
> could wish to man his Ship with.
> I hope you will pull through all right and I am sure it will not be
> the Whips' fault if you don't.[2]

Jackson's importance was indeed very real at this time, since, as
Financial Secretary of the Treasury, the main work of getting the
financial proposals of the Government through the House devolved
on him and, with Irish obstruction at its worst, he had to be almost
constantly in the House. After Akers-Douglas had shown him
Smith's letter, he wrote to the latter (December 14th) expressing
regret 'that we are not able owing to the nature of your work to
relieve you to a greater extent'. 'Anything we can do we will', he
added, '& you may rest assured we desire no more grateful leader. ...'

---

[1] M.P. (Cons.) Leeds North: Financial Secretary to the Treasury, 1886–92;
Chief Secretary for Ireland, 1891–2; created Lord Allerton.
[2] Chilston Papers.

XIII

THE UNEQUAL STRUGGLE

BEFORE Smith had started on his enforced holiday a new emergency had arisen in the Sudan, where the Red Sea port of Suakim—so miserable a place but so vital strategically—was again being besieged by the Dervishes. The necessity for a vote of supply to equip an expeditionary force for its relief brought the whole question of the British presence in that area once again under review and afforded an opportunity not only for the Opposition, but in particular for Randolph Churchill who had always held very strong views about the futility of this policy, to castigate the Government about its continuance. Smith had reported to Salisbury (December 1st):

> We have had a nasty debate about Suakim this afternoon and did not get further than rejecting Morley's motion to reduce the vote.
> Randolph Churchill put his back into making the most damaging speech he could against us, but he only carried one man with him—five others walking out. The party generally being quite sound, but it is quite clear Suakim is not popular, and I doubt very much if a proposal to withdraw the Squadron from slave trade prevention would not be carried by a large majority if men could vote by ballot. . . .[1]

Three days later, Churchill sprang a motion for the adjournment of the House when the Government were quite unprepared and was not surprisingly suspected of having tried to contrive their downfall. Smith wrote to Salisbury (December 4th) with unusual bitterness about the unscrupulous methods employed by Churchill and his military informants.

> We have had a debate tonight raised by a motion for the adjournment by Randolph based upon a statement often repeated by him that 'he knew the highest military authorities had protested against the inadequacy of the English forces about to be sent to Suakim'.

[1] Salisbury Papers.

Of course Gladstone, Harcourt and Childers supported Randolph holding that it was a most serious matter that we were acting in opposition to the views of the Military advisers to the Secretary of State.

Stanhope declined to state what had passed beyond this—that in consequence of a communication from the soldiers he had again telegraphed to Egypt.

We have therefore this new difficulty to meet—that 'the highest authorities' think it consistent with their duty to communicate with M.Ps outside the Govt. so as to enable them to question with the view of defeating the Govt. itself.

It is quite a new view of the duty of these high authorities and I regard it as incompatible with our system of Parliamentary Govt. If it is right these communications should be made to the H. of C. some new system must be devised to which I cannot be a party.[1]

However, on going away, Smith had to hand over responsibility for the handling of this affair to Goschen, who, unsupple as he usually was, managed surprisingly well. For Smith wrote from Paris to Akers-Douglas (December 16th): '. . . I did not like coming away at all but you are getting on admirably—and Goschen seems to have shown the best possible skill, tact and good feeling in dealing with Suakim and Randolph Churchill yesterday. . . .'[2] Moreover, this success on the floor of the House was capped immediately afterwards by a highly successful operation by a British force for the relief of Suakim. Nevertheless, the whole experience tempted the Government to consider whether responsibility for the defence of this outpost could not be passed to the Turks. But Smith, writing to Salisbury (December 18th), felt that 'it would not be possible to bolster up Turkish authority anywhere for any very long time, even if public opinion in England permitted us to attempt to do so.'[3]

Harcourt was leading the Opposition in the absence of Gladstone and Smith had consulted with him on the arrangements for closing the Session. Harcourt, however, had intimated that he would find it impossible to co-operate with Smith's deputy, Goschen, on account of the latter's alleged public discourtesy to him. Smith spoke to Goschen who then penned a somewhat qualified apology to Harcourt. But Harcourt returned to the charge with a length and recriminatory letter, which Goschen in turn replied to with spirit. However, the row then evaporated and explains Smith's reference to Harcourt in the following letter to Salisbury (December 24th), written from Monte Carlo:

. . . The Suakim business has gone off very well, but I doubt if you will be able to give the place up to the Turk.

[1] Salisbury Papers.   [2] Chilston Papers.   [3] Salisbury Papers.

"I DON'T CARE WHICH IT IS, YOU KNOW."

All the Moslem powers seem to be crumbling to pieces—Zanzibar & Morocco as well as Turkey.

I see that Harcourt has adhered to his arrangement with me; and the work is over for the present; but it must have been a hard week's work, and I am sorry I was out of it. Goschen seems to have managed admirably.[1]

Reviewing in his reply (December 2nd) the progress—or lack of progress—during the last Session, Salisbury once again urged a further tightening of the Procedure Rules:

We congratulated ourselves very much on having got you away when we did—for the last week of the Session was very hard work for the Front Bench in the Commons. Goschen did very well by all accounts—but he looked rather flattened out afterwards. I do hope you will make a resolute effort to secure yourself from being put into such an

[1] Salisbury Papers.

ugly fix again. There is a limit to the value even of constitutional necessities.

The few words you wrote to me about the proposed transfer of Suakim . . . entirely coincided with the direction my own thoughts were taking and I found that Goschen and Fergusson were coming to the same conclusion. Many evils both positive & negative are likely to result from Turkish occupation so long as the Turks are in their present state of weakness: and we should be held responsible for them all. Worst of all, if the Turks were kicked out by the Soudanese we should have to put them in again: & Bulgaria would be nothing to the Soudan as it would be portrayed by Gladstone's eloquence whenever we tried to do it. . . . My impression is that the lesson the Soudanese have had will last them for a year or two. . . .

Taking up his chief's point about obstruction Smith wrote back (December 31st): 'I quite agree with you that our experience of the past Session makes it absolutely imperative that we should take securities against any repetition of such evils even if we have to deal with some of our ancient constitutional forms.' Regarding Suakim he asked if the public should not be told of the actual position, as they were bewildered by press speculations and the impression grew abroad that the Government did not know their own mind. He instanced Balfour's success over Ireland: 'Balfour has gained a great deal this year by dealing with every lie and every absurdity as soon as they become current and I do not think a Govt. in these days can afford to allow distrust or erroneous impressions as to their policy to gain ground. Is there not someone in the F.O. capable of putting the case on paper and sending it to the Press. . . .'[1]

Salisbury replied (January 3rd, 1889): 'I quite agree that Balfour's contradictions & explanations did him good: but they form no precedent for F.O. Balfour was able to contradict lies effectively, because he was able to tell the facts. But I am not able to tell the facts. The situation at Suakim is only intelligible if you explain the character of the Sultan, the position & feebleness of Turkey, & the various motives & aims of Austria, France & Italy. But these are things which in public we cannot touch upon. We should therefore have to present a mutilated case, the insufficiency of which as a basis of our policy would be manifest to every eye. . . .'

With the end of January (1889) the time was at hand for Smith to go back to the grindstone. 'I am nearing the end of the longest holiday I have had for some years', he wrote to his sister Gussie (January 30th), '. . . It has done me a great deal of good—rested, refreshed and strengthened me, and I hope by care and rest in my

[1] Salisbury Papers.

work to avoid in future the sense of exhaustion which I had before I left my work in December. . . .' Nevertheless, the turning of his head towards England and the thought of the renewal of all the trials that awaited him there caused him to write to Salisbury an unusually pessimistic appraisal of the current state of British politics, ending with an offer to resign the leadership of the House and make way for another.

Private   Marseilles, Feb. 3, 1889

My dear Salisbury,

You referred a few days ago to the violence and unscrupulousness of the Opposition, and to their readiness to avail themselves of any weapon which they may find to their hands, no matter what the consequences may be.

The extension of the suffrage has brought us face to face with the most grave possibilities. It has made the extreme Radicals masters of the Liberal party, and men support a policy now from which they would have shrunk with horror ten years ago. There is also this strange peculiarity in the English mind to be taken into account. Men who are strictly honest in their transactions with their neighbours have come to regard Parliament as an instrument by which a transfer of rights and property may equitably be made from the few to the many; and there is yet another feature of the present day which is disgusting, and that is, that familiarity with crimes against property, or a class which is not their class, gradually deprives these crimes of the nature of crime in the eyes of the multitude, and even seems to create a sympathy for them.

To deal with public affairs with such an Opposition and in such a state of the public mind, the Government requires the judgment, resource and eloquence of the strongest man that can be found in the House of Commons and in the Country.

I do not think it possible to exaggerate the gravity of the struggle in which we are engaged, and I have never disguised from you my view that in such a fight, it is really the duty of the chief to put those men in the most prominent position who are best fitted to do the work. I am much stronger for my holiday, but I am not more ready of speech than I was, nor am I likely to be; and I am therefore most anxious you should thoroughly understand that, whether my health be good or bad, I am quite ready to give place to another leader, as a simple matter of duty for the good of the country, now or whenever it appears to you desirable to make a change.

I shall not refer again to the matter when we meet, unless you do so. I am with you where I am as long as you really think it best on all accounts that I should remain, and no longer.

Yours very sincerely,

W. H. Smith[1]

---

[1] Salisbury Papers.

There was no doubt about the spontaneity of the Prime Minister's reaction to this letter when he forwarded it to the Queen, adding in his own writing: 'Lord Salisbury has written to Mr. Smith to say that in his judgment it would cause the gravest prejudice to Your Majesty's service if Mr. Smith were to retire from the Leadership of the House.' To Smith himself he wrote:

Private   Feb. 5. 1889.

My dear Smith,

I am very sensible of the generous & considerate spirit in which your letter is written—& I thank for it very heartily.

But if you had heard the general impression of consternation with which the apparent failure of your health was watched by the principal men of the party, you would have had no doubt that in their judgment your retirement from the lead in the House of Commons would be one of the heaviest blows that could befall it.

I agree in all you say as to the gravity of our present condition. We are in a state of bloodless civil war. No common principles, no respect for common institutions or traditions, unite the various groups of politicians, who are struggling for power. To loot somebody or something is the common object under a thick varnish of pious phrases. So that our lines are not cast in pleasant places.

Yours very truly,
Salisbury

Smith's gloomy forebodings about England's future also found expression in a conversation at this time related by Sir Herbert Maxwell. A friend asked him if he wanted his son Frederick to go into Parliament. To which Smith is supposed to have replied 'in a tone of great gravity': '. . . England is going to be governed by three classes of men—by roughs, by men of business, and by those aristocrats who have heads on their shoulders and can use them. Freddy is not a rough, and he is not an aristocrat: if he is to go into Parliament, let him become a good man of business first.'[1] Nevertheless, owing to his father's early death, Frederick stood for his father's old constituency, the Strand, at the resulting by-election and was returned with a huge majority.

About himself, too, despite Salisbury's assurances, he continued to feel dubious and depressed, as emerges from a melancholy letter to Emily Giberne (February 24th):

. . . I am entering or have just entered in a sense on my New Year of anxious work and responsibility; and the test which is now before me is a real comfort and strength to me.

[1] Maxwell, II, 246.

I have never felt myself strong enough for the work I have to do and I should not have dreamt of putting myself forward for it. It is a burden and an anxiety, a Cross—but it is difficult sometimes to see for oneself the plain line of duty. . . .

But I can say, God help me; and 'in quietness and confidence shall be my strength'. He will take me out of my work when I am no longer required, and then will come rest. . . .

To his daughter Emily (Mrs. William Dyke Acland) he wrote also in similar vein (March 17th): 'We have trouble in politics, and I am very weary: but I must go on doing my daily work as best I can, looking for guidance and wisdom where alone it can be had, until my rest comes. I hope it is not wrong to long for it.'

Nevertheless his heart must have been warmed by the 'Memorial' presented to him shortly afterwards (March 28th) in his private room at the House of Commons by Sir John Mowbray,[1] Sir John Colomb[2] and Robert Hanbury[3] on behalf of the Conservative Party, containing about two hundred and fifty signatures and expressing 'cordial appreciation of the manner in which in the face of extraordinary difficulties' he had conducted his leadership and expressing the hope that 'this assurance of full confidence and hearty support will in some measure assist you in the continued discharge of your high but most arduous duty'.

Answering a colleague who wrote to endorse these sentiments, Smith wrote:

The whole affair came upon me as a surprise. I had no idea until a day or two before I received the memorial that my friends were signing anything of the kind and I suppose it was due to the rumours which had got abroad as to my health and my desire to retire. . . .

While they want me I am bound to stay and do the work to the best of my ability, but there are moments as you can well imagine, when one would be glad to disappear altogether from the wild turmoil of faction, and find rest in obscurity for the remainder of one's life.[4]

The 'Memorial' was followed closely by a more public tribute when he was entertained at a banquet given in the Merchant Taylors' Hall on April 10th by merchants, bankers and business men connected with the City. Here, in replying to the Chairman's speech of welcome and eulogy, Smith rose to the occasion with a speech, which, so intense was the feeling and so genuine the humility with which it

[1] M.P. Oxford University; Chairman of Committee on Standing Orders, House of Commons.
[2] M.P. Bow and Bromley.
[3] M.P. Preston; Financial Secretary of Treasury, 1895–1900; President of Board of Agriculture, 1900–3.
[4] Maxwell, II, 252–3.

was imbued, was perhaps the most eloquent and moving one he ever made and certainly far removed from the banal and complacent orations usual on these occasions.

> My friend . . . has told you that I stepped into the breach to discharge a duty which was imposed upon me. I simply responded to the call which was made upon me by my colleagues and friends, who told me that my services were required in that position. I claim no honour for doing that which was simply an Englishman's duty under the circumstances in which he found himself, and it is one of the mysteries of my life—one of those things which I have been unable to solve for myself—how it is that, having proceeded from among you, being one of you—a man of business—I have now come to be placed in a position of great responsibility, and perhaps of authority. God knows, I did not seek that position for myself. I have never sought office or honour, but I have never felt myself at liberty to decline to undertake a duty which has been imposed upon me. . . .
>
> I say most feelingly that if at times there has been weariness, if at times a sense of disgust at the difficulties with which one has to contend in the absence of that complete devotion to the country which one has a right to look for in the representatives of the people— if there has been that feeling at times, circumstances like these—the appreciation of one's fellow-citizens, the sense that they desire to do honour to one who had no expectation of receiving it, the sense that the verdict of his fellow-citizens is that he has deserved well of his country,—all this is a reward amply sufficient to cover all the sacrifices, all the sorrows, all the difficulties through which he has passed.[1]

But a few days before this, Smith had had to make a very different kind of speech in the House of Commons on the occasion of the death of the great Radical veteran statesman, John Bright. In the last three years of his life, however, Bright had come to be counted among the allies of Lord Salisbury's Government since he had broken with Gladstone over Home Rule and it was through this as much as anything, presumably, that he had earned the epitaph written by the Queen to Smith (April 2nd): '. . . The Queen truly mourns honest, good Mr. Bright.' Though Smith, on his part, had written to Salisbury (March 27th): 'Do you think it necessary or expedient to offer a funeral in Westminster Abbey to Bright? Forster was not buried there, but the funeral service was read & the body taken to Yorkshire.'

In the House, however, on the day the tribute was to be paid (March 29th), Smith's demeanour was, of course, impeccable—and, indeed, from what we know of him, it would have been entirely sincere as well. So, for one, thought the correspondent of the *New*

---

[1] Quoted from Maxwell, II, 254–5.

York Tribune, who watched the scene from the Gallery: 'The First Lord was in black; very pale; his voice uncertain; his manner that of a man on whom is laid a burden too heavy for him. He began nervously, with stumbling sentences, clearly trying not to show, but to conceal, emotion. His ten minutes' speech had almost no oratorical merit except that of sincerity, the word which during its delivery was oftenest on his lips. Mr. Bright had been almost a lifelong opponent of the party whose leader was now pronouncing a panegyric on him; but leader and party were agreed that his motives had ever been pure, his convictions firm, his loyalty absolute and complete. They lament him, and would follow reverently to his grave.'[1]

For all that, Bright's death caused the worst crisis in the always uneasy relations between the Conservatives and their Liberal Unionist allies; for his parliamentary seat was the Central Division of Birmingham, which Lord Randolph Churchill had always hankered after and about which he had had a personal understanding with Chamberlain since 1886 to the effect that in the event of a vacancy he was to be invited by Liberal Unionists as well as Conservatives to stand for it. But in the meantime Chamberlain's feelings about Churchill had altered, and, despite the continuing support for the latter of the Birmingham Tories, he decided, when Bright's son Albert came forward as a Liberal Unionist candidate for his father's seat, that he not only preferred him to Churchill but that his standing represented the only hope of saving the seat for the Unionists. 'The Gladstonians will not bring out a candidate against him although they would certainly fight anyone else', as he wrote to Akers-Douglas (March 31st).[2] In fact he begged the Tory Whip to exert utmost pressure from party headquarters upon the Birmingham Tories. But, even though Churchill himself backed out at the last moment, the latter continued to be refractory about supporting Albert Bright, until Balfour was sent down to persuade them by his famous charm. He was so successful that nearly the whole Conservative party voted for Bright on the election day (April 15th) and the Gladstonians were crushed by more than two to one.

Nevertheless, despite this and despite Churchill's barefaced desertion of them, the Birmingham Tories continued a bitter and scurrilous campaign against Chamberlain on account of his supposed 'bad faith' over his original understanding with Churchill. Chamberlain, becoming exasperated, vented his ire upon the Tory leaders at Westminster for not controlling their refractory followers and the leaders in turn showed resentment of his lack of appreciation of

[1] Geo. W. Smalley: *London Letters*, I, 161.
[2] Chilston Papers.

their tolerance of his high-handed and proprietary attitude towards all Birmingham affairs. So for months mutual recriminations continued to poison relations between the two wings of the great Unionist Alliance. Thus Akers-Douglas to Schomberg McDonnell, Salisbury's Private Secretary (April 23rd): 'There seems to be a jolly old row on at Birmingham. Joe really ought to behave well after all we have done for him—I hear from Rochester on good authority that the majority of L.Us went solid against us [at by-election], which also showed base ingratitude.'[1]

As a counter-blast to 'Joe's' laments from Birmingham the Tories decided to lodge a complaint about the apparent Liberal Unionist treachery at Rochester; for Hartington, their leader, wrote to Smith (April 29th):

> ... I spoke to Wolmer[2] about Rochester. He will make further enquiries, but as far as he knows there were a certain number of voters there who had disapproved of Mr. Gladstone's Home Rule Bills, but had never joined the Liberal Unionist Committee. These of course we have no influence with, & have never wanted as Liberal Unionists, & it was probably the support given by some of these to Knatchbull Hugessen[3] that has given rise to the idea that he was supported by the L. Unionists generally. However, as you say it is very difficult to keep the two sections together, and if anything can be suggested wh. will strengthen the alliance, I shall be very glad to co-operate. I have had a good account from Wolmer today about the Central division of Bradford which is an important constituency, and where there has been much difficulty in getting the Conservatives & L. Unionists to work together. . . .

Thus Hartington was on the whole reasonable and co-operative with his Tory allies over the extremely difficult business of trying to get the two Unionist wings to work together; but Chamberlain, though just as genuinely anxious to preserve the alliance, by his touchy and arrogant demeanour gave so much the impression of wanting to do so solely on his own terms that the common aim was always in danger of being lost amid mutual bickerings and resentments. Smith, however, always made it his business to try to see Chamberlain's point of view and, by showing candour about Conservative aims and fears, to appeal to his most co-operative instincts. Thus, when the Budget came up and Bradlaugh put down a challenging motion regarding the commutation of Perpetual Pensions, he

---

[1] Salisbury Papers.

[2] Viscount Wolmer, Chief Liberal Unionist Whip in the Commons; later, as 2nd Earl of Selborne, was First Lord of Admiralty, 1900–5, and High Commissioner for South Africa, 1905–10.

[3] Hon. Edward Knatchbull Hugessen, M.P. (Lib.) Rochester, 1889–92; succeeded father as 2nd Baron Brabourne, 1893.

made an indirect appeal to Chamberlain for support (May 15th): 'I am very anxious as to Bradlaugh's motion and the Budget, both of which stand for tomorrow. It will be a heavy blow to us if we are defeated on either; and I think to the Unionists as a whole. We have really a very good case in reply to Bradlaugh if it is listened to impartially and no Govt. can sustain a check on its Budget without being most seriously weakened.'[1]

In his private life, just after the Easter recess, Smith received another blow in the loss of his beloved sister Augusta (Gussie), who had lived on in the house his father bought at Torquay and with whom, from his earliest boyhood, he had had a much closer relationship than with any of his other sisters. In fact, owing to her considerable seniority, it had for much of his life approached a mother-and-son relationship. But he believed in their speedy reunion. 'It is very hard to part for a time in this way, but I would not have it otherwise', he wrote to his daughter Helen (April 29th).

At the same moment he received a letter of gentle warning and advice from his old friend and medical adviser, Henry Acland (April 29th):

I cannot help breaking silence now your short rest is over—to send you my expression of earnest desire, nay prayer, that you may have strength for your work, or resolution to break from it. . . .

Two things are believed by me—1st that owing to the firm, steady, quiet determination of the Government, the country is becoming more calm, and less moved by exaggeration & misconduct—and 2ndly that you might relinquish the 'Leadership' and otherwise remain the same. These are the opinions of quiet John Bull, without of course any special knowledge or opportunity. . . .

Meanwhile, all this time, the Parnell Commission had been grinding laboriously on its way. Indeed, owing to its extremely wide terms of reference, it had sat for 128 days and had examined 450 witnesses before the defence (consisting of the great Liberal lawyer Sir Charles Russell and the budding Herbert Asquith) were able to put in the witness-box the man whom they had known all along to be the forger of the 'Parnell letters' (February 20th, 1889). This turned out to be a seedy Irish journalist named Pigott, who after two days of agonizing cross-examination by Russell, fled the country, leaving a full confession behind him, and shot himself in Madrid. Parnell, meanwhile, went into the box and denied on oath the authenticity of the letters, whereupon *The Times* offered an apology, withdrew their allegations and voluntarily paid him £5,000 damages.

Needless to say this startling denouement was the cause of considerable chagrin, not only to *The Times*, but to the Government—

[1] Chamberlain Papers.

and equally of triumphant jubilation in the Irish and Liberal camps. Parnell became the hero of the hour, received a standing ovation from the Opposition in the House, was invited by Gladstone to stay at Hawarden, received the freedom of Edinburgh and a gift of £3,000, publicly subscribed towards his expenses in the affair. For the time being, therefore, the Government suffered a serious loss of face, since, although they were in no way responsible for what had occurred (except in so far as they had been dupes of *The Times*), to the man in the street the whole matter appeared to have been unequivocally settled against them. But of course, apart from the question of the authenticity of the letters, which was but one facet of the case, nothing had as yet been finally settled or decided, for the Commission sat on till nearly the end of the year and did not submit their report till February, 1890.

LORD R. CHURCHILL.

"NOT THE SHADOW OF A LEG TO STAND UPON."

Although Lord Randolph had so severely criticized the setting up of the Commission—and was to do so again when it issued its report—he was good enough at this stage to offer a suggestion for saving the Government's face over the forged letters. For he wrote to Smith (May 4th): 'Sir E[rskine] May, page 95, is worth looking at. A direction by the House to the Attorney General to prosecute *The Times* printer & publisher for libels upon certain M.Ps named would I fancy put the Parnellites between the devil and the deep sea. This course of proceeding will suggest to you many interesting eventualities. . . .' But it is difficult to see quite what these were and the Government did not adopt the suggestion.

The Government's unpleasant predicament had however made Smith think even more intently about the question of the dual status of the Attorney General or 'whether Law Officers should have private practice'. So he spoke to his colleague Lord Knutsford, who was a barrister and who in turn spoke to the Lord Chancellor. Both these men thought that the argument against changing the existing system was 'that the Law Officers by giving up private practice, lose touch with the profession, & lose, as a consequence, the high position now held by them as Heads of that profession'. Knutsford also thought that 'unless private practice is allowed the Law Officers will, on expiration of term of office, have lost their clients & their business; and that therefore the Government will not be able to secure leading men as Law Officers'. Nevertheless, a Bill *was* ultimately introduced and passed into law—though not till five years later—debarring the Law Officers from private practice.

Custom demanded that on the Queen's Birthday, May 24th, the Leader of the House should give a dinner party to his colleagues, with a member of the Royal Family as guest of honour. In this year, 1889, the occasion was slightly marred by a peculiar incident which is revealed by a small bundle of letters, marked by Smith: 'Correspondence as to Lord Randolph Churchill's non-appearance at the dinner after having accepted and having sent no subsequent intimation'. The first letter is a very natural kind of letter from Lord Randolph himself:

2, Connaught Place,
W.
May 26 1889.

My dear Smith,

I am so distressed and provoked with myself. On reading in the 'Observer' this morning the list of Ministerial banquets I was suddenly reminded that I had been engaged to dine with you last night. The engagement had completely slipped from my memory and I went and dined with my mother thinking that I was free for the evening. I pray you to forgive this apparent, but most unintentional rudeness on my part. I feel very sorry moreover to have lost what I am sure was a very pleasant party.

Believe me to be
Yours very sincerely
Randolph S.C.

From a letter from the secretary of the Duke of Clarence it appears that he, having been the guest of honour of the evening, had also received a personal apology from Churchill. Yet, in a letter to Smith, dated the next day (May 27th) Schomberg McDonnell writes: 'An invitation was sent to the Randolph Churchills last Tuesday but for some reason they did not get it till Friday night. This must have been the fault of the Post Office, and I shall make enquiries about it. . . . I missed Lord Randolph by a few minutes at the Carlton yesterday: I shall probably see him today and will explain that this unfortunate delay was in no way due to us.' This not only seems to suggest that Churchill had made an entirely different excuse to McDonnell from the one he offered to Smith, but shows that Lady Randolph was also invited—and this in turn poses the question why she did not remember the dinner even if her husband forgot.

The mystery is deepened rather than clarified by a letter from Lord Cadogan, Lord Privy Seal, commenting on the above letters

303

and remarking: 'Nothing could be more satisfactory—and I rejoice to think that in neither case was there the slightest intention on the part of anyone to exhibit any unfriendly feeling—R.C's letter is very courteous and amicable.' The strange little episode is summed up in a brief note from Lord Rowton[1] to whom Smith's secretary, Pattisson, had evidently shown the correspondence: 'How VERY odd some people are!' But probably it was but one of the several recent indications of the insidious advance of Churchill's fatal malady.

An attempt to deal with the question of 'Appanages' for the children of the Prince of Wales had, as we have seen, been made in the previous year and had had to be dropped owing to pressure of other business. Then, in the new year, Salisbury had written to Smith (January 17th): '. . . I am verging to the belief that the subject had better not be touched till the demise of the Crown. . . . Everything—except the actuarial conditions—is unfavourable now. . . . The temper of the times is bitter and unscrupulous: and those who oppose the Govt. will make a weapon against them out of anything. . . .'[2] But now a renewed request from the Queen for provision for the Prince of Wales's eldest son, the Duke of Clarence, and also for his daughter Princess Louise, who was about to marry the Duke of Fife, determined the Government to try to settle it before the end of this Session. Salisbury had written to Smith (June 6th):

> The Queen told me she was willing if we wished it to write to Gladstone herself about the Appanages—as he had 'stated to her that he thought the Royal Family were not supported on at all an excessive scale, in view of the wealth of private persons in this country'.
> I replied that I was not able to judge whether such an interposition was desirable without asking you. Of course we shall have to draft the letter.

Gladstone was indeed so favourably disposed towards the Appanages that he seconded the motion for a Select Committee (under Smith's chairmanship) to consider the Queen's requests and even suggested that a quarterly payment of £9,000 should be made to a separate account on behalf of the Prince of Wales, from which money could be assigned to the Prince's children. But then Gladstone was of course always on much friendlier and easier terms with the Prince of Wales than with the Queen. In fact he got no thanks from the latter for his loyal support—and merely succeeded in offending some of his own Radical supporters for giving it. Indeed, at one

[1] Montague Lowry Corry, private Secretary to Disraeli, 1866–81; founder of the 'Rowton Houses'; created Baron Rowton, 1881.
[2] Salisbury Papers.

point, Smith told Salisbury (July 9th) that Gladstone had been to see him and was much 'distressed and depressed', implying that he thought he ought to act with his Party over the Appanages question—whatever they decided.[1] Nevertheless, Gladstone seems quickly to have regained heart, for he sent to Smith (July 18th) a 'full statement of my views, as the best contribution I can make towards expedition in this delicate matter!' 'I think', he added, 'it has the general concurrence of my political friends on the Committee, except Mr. Labouchere & Mr. Burt[2] of whom I do not now speak as they have taken a separate line.' And again a few days later (July 21st) '. . . I should be *glad* if we can keep to ourselves all particulars of the Queen's expenditure. It is the receipt I think that the world or the House is entitled to know.' Smith, however, does not appear to have fully appreciated Gladstone's kindly intentions, for he wrote to Freddy on the same day (July 21st): '. . . I have had a rough time during this week in the Committee on Royal Grants. . . . Mr. Gladstone & John Morley are hard upon the Queen and I have been anxious not to give them an excuse for making their disagreeable speeches in the House, but I am afraid I shan't succeed.'

It was Labouchere—as Gladstone had already intimated—who was the one to be disagreeable. He had in fact submitted an independent report in which he declared that there were ample funds at the disposal of both the Queen and the Prince of Wales for the provision for the latter's children. This caused Smith to conceive the idea of enlisting the support of one whose Radical, even Republican, past might render a defence of the Royal Family peculiarly disarming: namely, Chamberlain. He therefore wrote to the latter (July 22nd): '. . . Will you follow J. Morley in the debate on Thurs. Labouchere has put down an amendment which traverses the need of my grant and Morley will endeavour to set himself right with the extreme party. I should very much like you to wait upon him.'[3] Chamberlain responded nobly to this appeal, defending the proposed grant and declaring that the Queen's income was not sufficient to provide for it. He even characterized those who opposed it as the 'Nihilists of English politics'.

However, the Government had meanwhile adopted Gladstone's proposals regarding provision for the Prince of Wales's children—abandoning their own—and had embodied them in a draft report which was laid before the Select Committee by Smith. In the debate on the report Gladstone rose magnificently to the occasion, defied his Radical dissidents and again strongly defended the case for the

[1] Salisbury Papers.

[2] M.P. (Lib.) Morpeth, 1874–1918; Secretary to Board of Trade, 1892–5.

[3] Chamberlain Papers.

Prince of Wales and his children (July 25th). Indeed, in a division he, Parnell and Sexton voted with the Conservatives against Morley, Labouchere and other Radicals.

Smith persuaded the Queen, in return for this support by Gladstone, not to press her claims for the children of her daughters and younger sons—and it was presumably on this account that he received this letter of reproof from Salisbury (July 22nd):

> My dear Smith,
> I think you bought Gladstone's vote exceedingly dear. We could have perfectly done without it. If Prince Eddy [Duke of Clarence] marries next year—which after his sister's [Princess Louise] marriage he probably will do—there will be £11,000 to divide among three princesses and one prince. . . .
> I always thought—and I told the Queen so—that she would receive more honest treatment from the House of Commons.
> But I can practically do her no good in the matter: & so I shall not mention the subject to her unless she asks me.[1]

However, the report was finally adopted, framed into a Bill and passed on August 5th. Yet, this was still not the end of the Session and Smith was showing marked signs of fatigue and ill-health. The good Dr. Acland wrote again after seeing him (July 27th): '. . . I wanted to say to you that you seemed *too* tired—and I shall have to lay or get laid some interdict on you. . . . Now you must spare yourself *all that is possible*, just as you did at Easter. . . .' And again a few days later (July 31st): 'I am concerned to hear of the disturbance you have had. It is probably due to the sudden heat coming upon your fatigue & anxiety. I hope Jenner will not be too dismal. If he is I must come up to protect you.'

Strong as was his sense of duty, such advice really coincided pretty much with Smith's inmost feelings; for he wrote to Freddy a few days later (August 2nd):

> . . . It is hot and thundery and the political atmosphere is as disagreeable as the air of London. Quarrels break out suddenly in the House as thunderstorms declare themselves in the sky and we cannot calculate on the progress which is necessary to enable us to wind up our work. I have almost made up my mind to cut and run whatever happens on this day fortnight . . . and we shall probably send the 'Pandora' somewhere so as to save time for the more pleasant part of the cruising—joining her by train. . . .

Three weeks later, however, he was still a prisoner in London and wrote despondently to Dr. Acland (August 23rd):

> . . . I hope you have not followed our parliamentary work. It has been very dreary—a very poor kind of acting or making-believe. All this week we have had Ireland to the fore—indignant patriots declaiming

[1] Salisbury Papers.

in burning language of violent indignation at one moment, and the next laughing in their cheeks [sic] at the hollowness of the whole performance. And this is the working of the British constitution in 1889, and a scientific form of Government!—but perhaps it is as good in its result as anything that could be devised—only it is impossible not to recognize an enormous waste of power and vital strength, which might conceivably be applied to better uses in the interests of the country. Forgive me: I am inclined to be despondent sometimes.[1]

The particular excitement over Ireland was connected with the debate on the Irish Constabulary Vote, when the Irish of course introduced an amendment for its reduction, and on the vote for County Court and other Irish officials, when an Irish member nearly made a physical attack on Balfour.

There was also the Tithe question—still unresolved and still sticking out like a sore thumb. Archbishop Benson had begun prodding Smith again in June by telling him that 'the position has undoubtedly become critical' and by August that 'the Agents are not prepared to encounter any longer the enormous difficulties, annoyance and injuries to which they are exposed under the present system . . .'; that 'under these circumstances it will henceforth become impossible to collect Tithe in some districts. . . . It is also clear—that the reflex effect of this on England will be most serious . . .'. Yet, although Smith wrote to Salisbury on August 6th[2] that the Tithe Bill was to be brought on after the Irish Estimates and that Akers-Douglas had a private understanding with the Irish Whip for hurrying it on, even the compromise Bill which the Government had framed failed to get through and had to be withdrawn.

Parliament was finally prorogued on August 30th and Smith was at last free to escape to the *Pandora* which awaited him off the North coast of Scotland and in which he and his family proceeded to make a leisurely tour of the Orkney and Shetland Islands. Even in this desolate region he could not altogether avoid the trammels of being a public figure, for at Kirkwall, where he and his party landed to look at the Cathedral, he was kidnapped by the Provost, carried off to the Town Hall and presented with the freedom of the burgh. The occasion elicited from him one of those felicitous and disarming speeches which were so characteristic of his more relaxed moments.

I thank you [he said, addressing the assembled worthies], because you have not made this distinction one which is attached to a particular party or creed, and because you have honoured one who has simply been the servant of the country and the servant of his Queen,

---

[1] Quoted in Maxwell, II, 256, footnote.   [2] Salisbury Papers.

in the discharge of the duty which has fallen upon him from day to day. Everyone has duties to perform: every one of you has the sense of what is right and what is wrong: and it is the sense of what, humbly speaking, I believe to be right which has carried me through so many difficulties.[1]

This perhaps too is the place to record the tribute paid to him at about this time by that shrewd and often merciless chronicler, Sir Henry Lucy. In his 'Diary' under the date-line July 8th, 1889, he writes:

It is no secret that Mr. Smith was selected for the office of Leader of the House of Commons not because he was at the time regarded as the best possible man. His character was prophetically drawn in a couple of lines written years ago.
 'Here comes a young person of excellent pith,
 Fate tried to disguise him by calling him Smith.'
. . . He has now held the post through three Sessions, and has worked upon the House of Commons the same charm which operated to advancement in the inner councils of the Conservative leaders. The House, it is true, sometimes laughs at him. But there is nothing malicious in the merriment, for it recognizes in him an honest, kindly, able man, who, free from all pretension, unaided by personal prestige or family influence, has conducted the business of the House of Commons with a success that will bear comparison with any equal period of time under more famous leaders.[2]

Balfour was at this time framing the Government's latest version of a Land Purchase Bill for Ireland (there had, as we have already seen, been the 'Ashbourne Act' of 1885), which he was to introduce in the following year and there was as much strong feeling about this among the Irish landlord section of their supporters as there was ignorance, prejudice or apathy among the ordinary English electors. Smith's close friend the Duke of Rutland had written to him before the close of the Session (July 24th):

I am very despondent about the future of Ireland, and cannot look upon the anticipated purchase of its soil by the existing race of tenants with complacency. If the process could be reversed and the landlords be enabled to buy out the tenants I should have more hope: but the bowl has been set trundling in one direction, and must, I suppose, trundle till it stops—and drops.

Another close friend, Penrose FitzGerald, the member for Cambridge, also sent him some observations on the question and in his reply (September 22nd) Smith showed that deeply rooted as was his respect for the rights of property he was ready in this case to temper

---

[1] Quoted in Maxwell, II, 257. [2] Lucy, op cit., 225.

it with that realistic commonsense which was one of his greatest assets.

> . . . I have always said that if Irish landlords as a body prefer to run the risk of a strike against rent and a refusal on the part of the Govt. of the day of the forces of the Crown to enforce payment—rather than accept a greatly diminished income, no Government would be justified in forcing through Parliament a large measure to transfer the remaining property in the land from the Proprietor to the Occupier. . . .
> I can only express my opinion, but if I was a trustee for an Irish property I should like to put my house in order and make terms with the enemy while I had the chance, but if the Government is relieved from the duty of proposing a large scheme it will escape a great danger and most serious difficulty—for any measure of the kind is certain to be most violently attacked from all sides. . . .

Nevertheless, he wrote to Akers-Douglas, the Chief Whip, who always had his finger on the pulse of the party, to find out what the latter thought about this and other current subjects of legislation (October 9th): '. . . I shall want to know what you think of Purchase, Local Government and University Education—Ireland—, before the Cabinet decide on the programme for the Session. . . .' The Whip replied: 'I will keep my ears open to be able to tell you the feeling of our men with regard to Land Purchase & University Education—my own instinct tells me they care but little about the former & dislike the latter. . . .' He also sent Smith some opinions collected by his Assistant Whip, Lord Arthur Hill, son of a great Irish landowner, the Marquess of Downshire. Lord Arthur himself wrote: 'Personally I must say that I have noticed an utter absence of desire to purchase on the part of the tenantry of this estate.' Of 'Compulsory purchase' he wrote that 'such a measure may become a necessity but at present there is no urgent demand for it and it would I think be premature'.

Another Irish landowner[1] wrote saying he thought rumours of a scheme of Compulsory Purchase were doing harm to existing arrangements under the Ashbourne Act, as tenants were holding out in hopes of getting their farms at half their real value. 'If the Unionist Party win the next General Election the crisis of the Irish Land question will have been tided over. Sale & Purchase will then proceed naturally either in the ordinary market or under the provisions of the Ashbourne Act. . . . Agitation in Ireland will be best allayed by declining to encourage the idea of fresh land departures & adhering to the gradual development of freeholders under the Ashbourne Act.' But, the writer added: 'Give the machinery of Local Govt. to Ireland, control the abuse of it by a strong central authority & by

---

[1] J. W. Ellison-Macartney, of Clogher Park, Tyrone; M.P. Tyrone, 1874–85.

altering the incidence of local taxation and the vitality of Home Rule as an election cry in England is killed.' This incidentally was exactly what Chamberlain thought too.

The person least fussed by it all was the author of the projected Bill—Balfour, who wrote to Smith from Whittinghame, his Scottish seat (October 11th):

My dear Smith,

I have been muddling away at land purchase during the holidays—and have embodied my ideas in a kind of provisional land bill which I have ordered to be sent to you.—Of course, away from books of reference and lawyers I could make no pretence to accuracy of drafting: but you will easily be able to gather my ideas. I think you will find them not out of harmony with yours: except that I have framed my bill on *voluntary* lines, in despair of being able to pass anything else. . . .

I am now in my Northern home for three days. The people (crofters) all expressing enthusiastic affection for me! I believe it to be perfectly genuine as far as it goes—but would it stand any strain? With my Irish experience behind me, I doubt it.—But to do them justice they have hitherto proved quite deaf to the voice of the Land League charmer—though naturally enough no efforts have been spared to seduce them!

Yours ever
A.J.B.

Later he wrote again (October 30th), returning a memorandum on Land Purchase by one of Smith's Irish correspondents and remarking: '. . . It does not advance the question much—but I concur (as you know) in its main contention that compulsion is impossible. I am working away hard at legislation in the intervals allowed by endless interviews with D[istrict] Commissioners, Officials of all kinds and aggrieved citizens. I am hammering away at a scheme for the congested districts: and really think I may be able to produce a presentable one, with the aid of what remains of the Church surplus!'

Ministers had returned from their summer holiday to find the 'Birmingham Row', which had sprung up in the spring over the respective candidatures of Randolph Churchill and Albert Bright for the Central Division seat, flaring up again over the East Birmingham seat, at that time held by Churchill's protégé, Henry Matthews, the Home Secretary, whom, as already shown, the Conservative leaders were anxious to get rid of. Chamberlain was not only against creating a vacancy at East Birmingham, as he considered the Unionists likely to lose the seat, but he was incensed by the smear-campaign which ever since Bright's election had been conducted against him by the 'Randolphian' section of the local Conservatives and in particular by a series of offensive articles in the *Birmingham Gazette*—of which, ironically, Richard Middleton, the Conservative Chief Party Agent, was chairman of the board of Directors.

Smith had written to Chamberlain (October 23rd) to tell him that the death of a certain Lord of Appeal 'has brought up the question of the possible elevation of Matthews to the Court of Appeal and the consequent creation of a vacancy at Birmingham' and to ask him what he thought the outcome of such a step would be, because it was 'more necessary than it has ever been to avoid any step which would weaken the Govt. in the H of C. or the country'. He then asked what would be the attitude of Chamberlain and his friends if Churchill were to stand for the vacant seat.[1] Chamberlain's reply (October 25th) was forthright—and in parts bitter. He thought it extremely risky to court defeat by creating a vacancy at East Birmingham. He did not imagine that Churchill was likely to stand, as his ambitions as well as his supporters had always been concentrated in the Central Division and 'if he were to stand for the East I would bet 2 to 1 against and I fancy many of the local Conservatives would refuse to support him'. He added, with some relish, that he had heard the Conservative organization in the Division was very bad. He then went on to complain of the articles in the *Birmingham Gazette*, which he described as 'as insulting to the Liberal Unionists and to myself personally as it is possible to conceive', and to point out the unfortunate connection with the Conservative Party Agent. 'I need not tell you', he added, 'that the effect is bad both on the Conservative party and on the Liberal Unionists, who are getting restless.'[2]

Sending this on to Salisbury (October 27th), Smith remarked: '. . . apart from his distrust of the Cons. organization there is an unpleasant tone in the concluding part of the letter. . . .'[3] And to Akers-Douglas (October 27th): '. . . He [Chamberlain] is . . . evidently very sore and if the Alliance is to last something must be done to remove the cause of complaint. . . .'[4] Middleton, too, though often inclined to impatience with Chamberlain's pretensions, fully concurred. 'Chamberlain must be squared if Birmingham is to be considered safe',[5] he wrote to Salisbury (October 28th); and on the same day to Smith: 'Unless we have Chamberlain's cordial co-operation it would be very dangerous to vacate any Birmingham seat. . . . Chamberlain's great fear is that Lord Randolph should be invited and until that is removed difficulties will always be made.' (This last observation does not agree with Chamberlain's own professed views.) Middleton disclaimed any personal responsibility

---

[1] Chamberlain Papers.　[2] Ibid.　[3] Salisbury Papers.
[4] Chilston Papers.　[5] Salisbury Papers.

for the articles and said he had 'told the editor it must be stopped', so it was eventually decided that he had better go to Birmingham to see Chamberlain and make his explanations in person. Meanwhile Smith wrote back soothingly to Chamberlain (October 30th): '. . . It is a thousand pities that the two sections of the Unionist Party cannot be brought to act cordially together in Birmingham . . .'; and again, on the same day: 'I have been talking to Middleton about the Gazette and I have told him to go down and see you and talk it out. . . . I hope you will be able to give him a few minutes, as a personal explanation is in any opinion always much more satisfactory than anything else can be.'[1]

One outcome of this meeting was the arranging of a conference between the two wings of the Unionist Party as to the future repre-

"HIS INFLUENCE ACCUMULATES THOUGH HIS PARTY DECAYS."

sentation of the city of Birmingham. But here Chamberlain brought matters to a deadlock by insisting on continued adherence to the original compact of 1886, whereby Liberal Unionists in constituencies held by them before the election of 1886 were promised the fullest Conservative support. No settlement being reached, the conference unanimously agreed to refer the question to the arbitration of Lord Salisbury and Lord Hartington. A year elapsed before the two leaders published their award, but, when they did, it fully supported Chamberlain's contention, and, although Hartington earnestly

[1] Chamberlain Papers.

advised that the Liberal Unionists in Birmingham should not insist upon the strict letter of their rights, Chamberlain remained adamant about retaining the six out of seven seats in the city which they then had. Not till eight years later—by which time Chamberlain had at last taken the plunge and joined the Government—were the Tories allowed an additional seat in Birmingham.

As Middleton sped to Birmingham to appease the Great Joe, Smith journeyed north to attend a Conservative conference in Glasgow. Here on November 5th he addressed an immense meeting in St. Andrew's Hall and, amid scenes of great enthusiasm, delivered one of those characteristic speeches which unashamedly revealed those high notions of what a politician should be, which had earned for him from his more cynical or easy-going contemporaries the sobriquet of 'Old Morality'.

> . . . Allow me to draw your attention to a peculiarity in these days which attaches to politicians. They say: 'It is not a question whether we think disestablishment is right, or nationalisation of land is right, or confiscation of houses is right; but the question is whether the majority of the people of the country wish it to be so; and if they do of course it must come to pass, and we will offer no opposition—in other words, we will facilitate the progress of measures which in our consciences we believe to be destructive and injurious, of which we personally disapprove, but which nevertheless must pass, because the people will it'. Now I am very far indeed from saying that the people through their representatives ought not to have expression given to their desires. But this is a new doctrine. A politician, a statesman, whose duty it is to lead, not to follow, whose duty is it to have a definite view on questions of the highest importance to the people at large—I say it is a new doctrine, and a very evil one, that a politician being placed in the post of leader, abdicates that position and follows where he ought to guide. . . .

Naïvely, he went on to assert that 'in old times' this kind of conduct was unheard of, which of course is palpably untrue; but, high as were his intelligence and integrity, it must be remembered that the peculiar circumstances of his boyhood had allowed him little scope for the study of history—or of anything else. Indeed, the more one reads his letters and speeches, the more one is struck by his excellent command and happy use of language—always clear, never stilted, highly individual and resourceful.

Later the same month he made a tour of the West Country, speaking at Exeter, Truro and Plymouth, finally returning to Greenlands for a few weeks' rest before facing the rigours of the next session. This was interrupted, however, by a summons to Windsor Castle, whence he wrote on December 5th to Miss Giberne:

I have been intending to write to you for a long time, but I have to confess that I have been growing idle lately, and that it has required some effort—a little mental flogging—to make my hands and my head co-operate to do anything more than the pressing necessary work of the day. We had a telegram this morning asking me to dine and sleep, and Emily also, if she was not afraid of the cold. It was very considerate of Her Majesty was it not? . . . Have you been told of our western journey? I took Emily and Helen with me for speeches I had to make at Exeter, Truro and Plymouth.

We stayed the first night at Lord Poltimore's,[1] and on our return to his house, four miles from Exeter, the Conservatives escorted us by a torchlight procession and bands of music to the confines of the city. Everybody was very kind. It was the first thing of the kind Emily had seen. I then went on to Plymouth with them and we all stayed with the Mount Edgcumbes.[2] Neither Emily nor Helen went with me to Truro; but the Cornishmen were as kind to me as the Devonians, and I wound up on my return to Mount Edgcumbe by a short speech at Plymouth, and we got home on Wednesday week after 8 days' visiting.

Since then I have been in London almost every day, 'clearing up', as on Tuesday Freddy comes down from Oxford, and we are to have people in the house and parties, to celebrate for Greenlands his coming of age last August.

It is a very great blessing to know that, although he has not the reputation of being clever or smart, he has that of being a really good fellow, and everybody, from the Head of his college down to the freshman, speaks of him with respect, and often with affection. I cannot—we cannot—be too thankful that we have been spared sorrows and troubles in our family. No one of them has yet given us a moment's anxiety, or caused a sense of shame to pass through our minds. It is a blessing to be humbly grateful for.

[1] Augustus Bampfylde, 2nd Baron; Alderman of Devon County Council; Chancellor of Primrose League, 1895.

[2] William, 4th Earl of; A.D.C. to Queen Victoria; Chairman of Cornwall County Council.

XIV

DECLINE

━━━━◆┣◆┫◆━━━━

T HE shaming exposure of the Pigott forgeries had come at a time
when the Government was approaching what is always the
critical age in any Government and the combination of these two
things had caused a continuous run of adverse by-election results
during recent months. Therefore Smith and his colleagues looked
forward to the next Session, when, amongst other things, the Report
of the Parnell Commission was to be presented, with considerable
anxiety and foreboding.

Parnell himself had made several speeches in England with full
Liberal backing and support on the platform. One such took place
at Nottingham on December 16th, when Arnold Morley, the Liberal
Chief Whip, as chairman, moved a resolution congratulating Parnell
'on the vindication of his character from the foul libels and aspersions
of *The Times*'. In acknowledging this, Parnell declared he would
rather have died under the suspicion of having written the letters
than have accepted the vindication offered him by the Government.
For, he said, under pretence of this vindication they had turned from
the personal charges to charges against his movement and his
country. In reality, he said, the Government fought from behind *The
Times* and the next Special Commission would be to try the reality
of the connection between the present First Lord of the Treasury and
'his old friend Walter'.[1]

Smith snatched another holiday on the *Pandora* at the turn of the
year and although he undoubtedly felt these imputations acutely, the
rumour that went the round of the newspapers at this time that he
intended to resign over the collapse of the forged letters case was as
devoid of foundation as its import would have been uncharacteristic.
Thus to Akers-Douglas he wrote from Messina, referring to recent
by-election defeats (January 24th, 1890): '. . . Our elections are a

[1] Annual Register, 1889 (259).

315

great bore, but they are not of our own making and if we do the best we can we must not get down-hearted because the chapter of accidents is against us. As to the New York Herald and the general election—no doubt the wish was father to the thought: but I am afraid we shall have to face trouble during the coming Session. Our programme is not a pleasant one if we wish to have smooth water. . . . I am sorry you have been seedy. Everybody has if that is any comfort, excepting the women and they don't seem to have suffered. . . .'[1]

Indeed, though Smith himself was rapidly becoming an invalid from prolonged strain and overwork, many of the other leading figures in the Unionist party appear to have been struck down by sudden illness at this juncture. Thus, Chamberlain, writing to Smith from Paris (February 6th):

> . . . I have now heard of the serious nature of the illness of both Lord Salisbury & Hartington. I am more than sorry but I hope that both patients are a long way to perfect recovery. . . .
>
> I want to have a week more leave of absence to attend to my personal affairs & hope that nothing of any serious importance will come on before then. Afterwards I will be ready to attend the House as often & as long as I can be of the slightest service. I hope you are yourself stronger after your much needed holiday, but as far as I can gather everyone has been ill except the G.O.M., who keeps on renewing his youth like the eagle & ten years hence seems likely to be a sprightly boy when we are all aged men.

In his reply Smith wrote (February 8th): 'I am very glad to hear you are returning home and I shall be still more glad to see you opposite to me in the H. of C. Hartington's absence is a misfortune . . . but he is not now seriously unwell and Salisbury is almost himself again. . . .'[2] These two letters bear witness to the great improvement in the relations between the two wings of the Unionist Party since the Conservative leaders had exerted themselves to pacify Chamberlain and to control their own recalcitrants in Birmingham.

The moment Parliament met on February 11th the Government found themselves under heavy fire and forced on to the defensive over the whole matter of the Parnell Commission and the forged letters. For, even before the debate on the Queen's Speech was begun, Sir William Harcourt raised the question of privilege, of which, he maintained a breach had been committed against the House by *The Times* in publishing and commenting on a letter allegedly written by a Member and since proved to be a forgery. Gorst moved an amendment to the effect that after so long the House declined to treat the matter as one of breach of privilege. Gladstone, however,

[1] Chilston Papers. [2] Chamberlain Papers.

declared *The Times* apology to have been inadequate and that, owing to the Government's tactics in forcing on a Commission, this was the first opportunity the House had had of dealing with the affair. Balfour strongly rebutted these accusations; but after much debate Parnell continued to insist that the Government and their supporters still wanted to pin on him the authorship of the forged letters.

To this Smith replied that Balfour's words should have made it clear 'how completely he [Balfour] joined with hon. gentlemen on the other side of the House in expressing his detestation of the forger and the forged letters and the means by which the forgery had been published'. He added: 'I wish on behalf of myself, my right hon. friends on this bench, and those who sit on this side of the House, to express our detestation of the act which has been committed and our measure of satisfaction that the hon. gentleman [Parnell] has been relieved absolutely and completely from the imputation under which for a time he laboured.' He also agreed to Parnell's demand that the word 'forged' should be inserted before 'letters' in the amendment. But even these concessions did not satisfy the Opposition and Harcourt's resolution, having been put to the vote, was negatived by 260 to 212—a majority so greatly diminished that the numbers were hailed with triumphant cheering by the Opposition.

Apart from this ominous sign of the Government's loss of prestige, it was widely felt, even on his own side, that Smith had committed a tactical blunder in not at once following Harcourt and making the reparation due to Parnell at the earliest possible moment. Moreover, into the bargain—and not very surprisingly—he had fallen foul of *The Times*. Buckle, the editor, wrote (February 14th) inviting him to meet him at the Athenaeum Club—'to avoid the notice of the Parnellite paragraphist'.

> . . . Before we meet I think it only honest to tell you that in this office we feel very sore about the language used by the Leader of the House on Tuesday night in answer to Mr. Parnell. It was neither fair nor just to speak with equal 'detestation' of the act of Pigott & the act of The Times.
>
> I will not say more. I could hardly say less, & then talk with you on friendly terms, without loss of self-respect.

Whatever may have transpired at this uncomfortable meeting, Smith evidently felt that he had allowed himself to get a little carried away on that unfortunate occasion in the House, for he now wrote (February 17th) a rather lame letter of apology to John Walter, the proprietor of *The Times*—that 'old friend' over whom he had got into such trouble earlier on in the story. The main burden of this was that he had been misreported.

. . . I fully admit that an interpretation could fairly be put upon them [his words] which would justly be offensive to you; but my colleagues who sat by me are under the impression that I did not use all the words attributed to me.

My intention was to repeat and to emphasize the observations of Arthur Balfour's in which he expressed his detestation of the forger and of his work: and if I said more and gave you pain I do not hesitate to say I am very sorry for it.

There was great excitement in the House at the time, and the Irish members sought to put words in my mouth by interruptions. I hope a fair opportunity will occur for doing justice to the motives and to the objects of the Conductors of the Times in the debate which must arise on the motion of which I have given notice this evening.

Walter thanked him rather stiffly for these assurances, concluding: '. . . I cannot complain of the adoption by the House of the term applied by the Judges to the facsimile letter; but I must be allowed nevertheless to reserve my opinion on the subject.'

Meanwhile, the long-awaited Report of the Parnell Commission was presented on February 13th, 1890. This declared, as it was obviously bound to do, that the facsimile letter was a forgery and acquitted Parnell and his colleagues of insincerity in their denunciation of the Phoenix Park murders. It found that 'the respondents collectively were not members of a conspiracy having as its object the complete independence of Ireland', but that 'some of them . . . established and joined in the Land League organization with the intent by its means, to bring about the absolute independence of Ireland as a separate nation' and that they had conspired, by means of agrarian agitation to 'impoverish and expel from the country the Irish landlords'. Also that they 'did not directly incite persons to the commission of crime, but that they did incite to intimidation, and that the consequence of that incitement was that crime and outrage were committed by the persons incited'. Further that they 'did nothing to prevent crime' and 'did defend persons charged with agrarian crime and supported their families'; though it had not been proved that they were 'intimately associated with notorious criminals' or that they 'had made payments to procure the escape of criminals from justice'.

Thus, though exonerating the Irish Members from *some* of the charges made against them in *The Times*, the Report nevertheless undoubtedly accused them of complicity and involvement, through the Land League, in agrarian crime and seditious agitation. At first, however, the Report was greeted as rapturously by the Irish press and by Gladstonian speakers in England as if it had been a complete acquittal. But this gave place to a different feeling when it was understood that the Gladstonian party in the House of Commons were disposed to object to the Report being adopted without demur. Unionists, meanwhile, naturally felt that the *raison d'être* of the Commission had been justified by the condemnation of at least a good part of the respondents' activities.

Therefore, when, on March 4th, Smith rose in the House to move the adoption of the Report, he referred to an amendment of which Gladstone had given notice in these terms:

> Sir, I think few will deny that these are grave charges and cannot permit a 'clean bill' to be given to the respondents. The amendment of the right hon. gentleman would practically be a condonation of crime. . . .

He went on to declare that it was 'no part of our intention at any time to constitute a Commission for the purpose of obtaining evidence to inflict punishment'; that 'the primary object was to obtain the truth whether the charges were true or false'. But he concluded with a weighty diatribe against the role of the Opposition in the affair.

> Are all the experiences of past generations to be set at naught? Is the mandate of an illegal association alone to determine whether legal obligations shall or shall not be discharged, which have not only been the result of contract, but have received the approval of the State itself?
>
> Sir, this prospect, afforded by the alliance of a great party with doctrines which can only be regarded as anarchical, is one which must make a man pause and hesitate. . . . If, only a few years ago, I or any of my hon. friends had ventured to prophesy that the Liberal party would be found ranging itself on the side of those whose language they denounced—whose acts they alleged to be, and believed to be, criminal—no words of condemnation would have been too strong in the mouths of our political opponents in denouncing us for such anticipation. Alas, it has come to pass. . . .

But this—unlike those impromptu addresses with their spontaneous expressions of heartfelt emotion which were so impressive—was not the sort of speech at which Smith excelled. The over-studied manner made it appear pompous and the fact that he read it from large foolscap sheets deprived it of all semblance of spontaneity. 'Nothing has been heard in recent years in the House of Commons so like a good country rector reading a prosy sermon', wrote Lucy in his 'Diary'.[1] On the other hand, Gladstone, who followed 'spoke for an hour and forty minutes at the highest level of his argumentative force and matchless eloquence',[2] ending by appealing to the Government and their supporters 'as citizens—I will not say as Christians . . .

---

[1] Lucy, op. cit., 250.   [2] Ibid.

to place yourselves in the position of the hon. member for Cork [Parnell] as the victim of this frightful outrage. . . . Is it possible . . . after all his cares, all his suffering, all that he has gone through . . . that you can fail to feel that something remains due to him.'

As it happened Gladstone's appeal was a great deal shrewder and less misdirected than might at first appear; for events were to prove that the feeling which he had referred to was by no means confined to the Opposition. The Government managed for the time being to keep their supporters in hand—though not without some pressure; but it was this uneasy atmosphere which enabled the debate on the Report to drag on for seven days and nights, to the delay of more important business and to the detriment of ministerial influence and reputation. True, Gladstone's amendment was disposed of on the fourth day; but in the division fourteen Unionists, of whom one was Churchill, abstained.

Then, on March 11th, Lord Randolph Churchill intervened in the debate with an extraordinary speech in which he bitterly inveighed against his former colleagues and reproached them with what he held to be the abortive and ominous result of the Special Commission— 'without precedent, and of evil omen to the rights of minorities and political opponents for the future'. There was of course considerable truth in much of his attack and he could at least claim to have been consistent in his attitude towards the Commission from the beginning. (He wrote to Smith just at this time and asked him to lend him the great memorandum which he had written against the Commission in 1888, so that he could have it copied and refresh his mind as to the arguments he had then used.) But, as so often before, he over-reached himself—this time by absurdly implying that Pigott had somehow been the creature of the Government and by the outrageous terms in which he expressed himself: 'What has been the result of this uprootal of constitutional practice? What has been the one result? Pigott! a man, a thing, a reptile, a monster—Pigott!—the bloody, rotten, ghastly foetus,—Pigott! Pigott! Pigott!'

This unprecedented outburst brought upon Lord Randolph the anger and disgust of his colleagues and also cost him the support of a hitherto devoted ally, Louis Jennings,[1] who had been prepared to move another critical amendment, but who now abandoned it and publicly dissociated himself from his friend. The dropped amendment was, however, moved by W. S. Caine,[2] and, though it was defeated,

[1] M.P. (Cons.) Stockport; journalist; editor of *Lord Randolph Churchill's Speeches.*
[2] M.P. (Lib.) Barrow in Furness; from 1886 represented same as L.U.; resigned 1890 as protest against Government's Irish policy; elected 1892 for Bradford as Gladstonian Liberal.

the Government's majority in the division was only 62—another sign of the loss of confidence suffered as a result of the Special Commission with all its concomitants and implications.

Meanwhile, the Queen's Speech had announced the Government's intention to return to the charge in the matter of the Tithe question and to introduce a new Bill. In the subsequent debate on the Address Gladstone had put forward the proposition that tithe was national property and that under no circumstances had either owner or occupier any right to appropriate it. Rather surprisingly, Smith immediately associated himself with this view. 'I also echo that sentiment and it will be the effort of Her Majesty's Government to present a measure to that effect', he declared.

In North Wales, where feelings about tithe ran highest, a local newspaper made this comment: 'Much of the battle of the Tithe has raged round the question which the two leaders [Gladstone and Smith] here answer emphatically. The advocates of State Churchism usually contend that tithes are the property not of the Nation but of the Church. . . . That statement [Smith's] is something like a disaster to controversialists of a certain type for Mr. Smith takes out of their mouths their most familiar weapons. "Robbery and spoilation" is a discredited cry; and how can it be "sacrilege" for the nation to use its own property as it thinks fit?' The newspaper went on to suggest that Smith's declaration of agreement with Gladstone on this point 'must have caused something like consternation among the ranks of his following. . . . His frankness will be bitterly resented. . . .'

This prediction was accurate, for Stanley Leighton, the Conservative member for Oswestry, writing to Smith on February 20th, said his words had had 'an injurious effect, especially in Wales and the borders'. Quoting Blackstone 'that the Clergy have precisely the same right to the tithes as the heir-at-law to his ancestor's estate', he added: 'It would relieve your supporters in the H. of C. and in the country from embarrassment if you were willing to give us an assurance that your opinion is in general accordance with ours, and if you would allow such a statement to be published.'

This appears to be among those misjudgments—in this, as in some other instances to be related, the term 'aberration' would hardly be too strong—which Smith's rapidly deteriorating health now tended to induce. For when shortly afterwards the Government's long-awaited Tithe Bill was introduced, it was without any explanation and there was no trace of the particular principle with which Smith had joined with Gladstone in declaring himself to be so much in sympathy. On the contrary, it was violently attacked by the Radicals and Welsh members on the ground that 'all legislation perpetuating the tithe as Church property was objectionable' and was defended on the Government's behalf by Hicks Beach declaring that 'lay tithe . . . rested upon as good a title as any other property and could no more be equitably applied to public purposes, without compensation to its owners, than could the watch in a man's pocket'. Outside, in the country, meanwhile, resolutions were adopted by angry meetings, not only of farmers and Welsh Disestablishmentarians, but even of clergy and landowners—the latter owing to the supposed concessions to Radical opinion contained in the Bill. Although, despite this, a Second Reading was agreed to by the surprising

MR. BALFOUR.

majority of 125, the Bill never got any further through being overtaken by other highly controversial measures.

A similar fate seemed likely to overtake the Government's Allotments Act (1887) Amendment Bill which was brought in in the first week of the Session (February 17th), for it was not until more than a month later that an opportunity could be found for moving the Second Reading and then the debate seemed likely to be so much prolonged that Smith had to resort to the closure to enable the Bill to be read a second time without a division. So it is not surprising to find him not over-sanguine about the introduction of the far more

322

important Irish Land Purchase Bill. Thus he wrote to Emily (March 24th):

> Arthur Balfour spoke for nearly two hours, very well and very clearly explaining his Bill and then Gladstone followed him acknowledging that the measure was a large one, comprehensive and complicated: and he asked for tables which were promised to him, and then sat down. To our immense surprise no one rose and leave was given to bring in the Bill amid cheering from our side of the House—and then we went on with other business. This is great luck and has quite raised our spirits.

But despite Balfour's brilliant presentation of it and an initially good reception all round, this Bill too became bogged down in endless debate and had to be stood over till the following Session. These frustrations, taken together with the unpleasant imputations made against the Government's motives in the Parnell Commission considerably depressed Smith, who must have allowed this to show in his reports to the Queen. For she wrote back to him from Aix-les-Bains (April 4th) thanking him for these and adding, with calculated cheerfulness: '. . . As regards *success* & majorities he must be satisfied—tho' factious opposition & bad language have certainly not been wanting. The election in Ayrshire S. was a clear gain & the one at Windsor was very satisfactory. . . .'

Shortly afterwards the Government began running into new difficulties—again largely of their own making. In his Budget of this year Goschen, as Chancellor of the Exchequer, imposed an additional tax on spirits and the proceeds of this and part of the existing tax on beer were earmarked to provide compensation (through the local authorities) for the extinction of publicans' licences. These proposals were embodied in a Bill called the Local Taxation Bill and they aroused a storm among the numerous temperance bodies throughout the country because they involved the detested principle of compensation to publicans.

Resistance to this principle was not confined to the Opposition. At the Second Reading of the Bill (May 12th) it was opposed by some of the Government's supporters, notably W. S. Caine (though admittedly he was on the point of rejoining the Gladstone Liberals), who moved an amendment refusing assent to any proposals to extinguish licences by means of public moneys. He was supported by Gladstone, who, by some subtle casuistry, escaped from pledges he had given to his Midlothian constituents in *favour* of compensation for the abolition of licences. On a division the amendment was negatived by a majority of 73; but the hornet's nest which the Government had stirred continued to buzz.

In the meantime Lord Randolph Churchill had on April 29th introduced—with what turned out to be his last great Parliamentary speech—his own 'Licensing Amendment Bill', but this, though enlightened and not unfavourably criticized by Government spokesmen, was dropped after a First Reading. He therefore then concentrated on moving amendments to the Government's Bill. Reactions to this situation are reflected in a letter from George Smith, M.P. for the Truro–Helston Division of Cornwall, to Lord Mount Edgcumbe and forwarded by the latter to W. H. Smith. He was not, declared this M.P., 'some fanatical teetotaller', but 'A loyal supporter of the Government' desperately anxious

> . . . to prevent the alienation of the large section of the Unionist Party which puts what it deems to be 'Temperance' first, & Unionism, or anything else, second.
> I can quite understand that the Government is too fully pledged to the Bill to withdraw it . . . or to alter it vitally. . . . But I shall still hope it may be possible to be conciliatory towards Lord Randolph's amendments. I wish they came from another source, but I think it will be found that his notions . . . catch the more respectable public opinion of the House which desires *substantially* to diminish the drink traffic whilst being fair to 'the trade'. . . .

But in fact a 'Memorial', drawn up by Caine, was already being circulated to all members of the Liberal-Unionist party. Addressed to Lord Hartington, it informed him of the 'strong feeling of dissatisfaction' felt in regard to the licensing clauses of the Local Taxation Bill. He was warned that if these clauses are passed, it will inevitably lead to strong dissension in our ranks' and stating that they considered the Government 'pledged not to bring forward in the present Parliament acute questions on which any large section of the Liberal Unionist party feel strongly'.

However unjustly, Smith was not escaping from a pretty large share of the blame for the ugly predicament in which the Government found themselves. The feeling on his own side is well summed up in the journal of Sir Richard Temple, the Conservative member for Evesham.

> . . . This Licensing Bill [he writes] . . . was sprung upon us without notice and without mention in the Queen's Speech. The party were justly angered at all this, which they regarded as nothing short of blundering, and which they would have stopped had they got even an inkling beforehand. Now this Licensing Bill mistake was attributed, not to W. H. Smith by his followers, but to one or more of his ambitious colleagues in the Cabinet. But our men asked each other, What is the use of him as leader if he cannot check these vagaries? The Prime Minister could hardly do so, as he sits in the Lords. The

proper—indeed the only—person to do so on this occasion was W. H. Smith, the leader in the Commons. What, then, was he about? Why did he not authoritatively interpose? These are questions which have never yet been solved. This reason and the supposed state of his health again brought up the discussion about the future leadership to the surface of men's minds. But then there would be difficulty in choosing a successor to him. His many merits and virtues remained in countless details, despite this one cardinal failure, and we rather shuddered at the thought that after all he might be forced to retire by failure of strength. . . . I should add that he is supposed to be a conciliatory moderator in all internal troubles in the Ministry, and that his forte is the judicious and often witty parrying of awkward questions.[1]

Knowing Smith, we are not surprised to find that he himself was a prey to the same sort of doubts as those expressed by Temple. Indeed, it is while he was on a cruise in his yacht along the South Coast during the Whitsuntide recess, that he seriously began to consider retiring from office. From Plymouth on May 30th he wrote to Akers-Douglas: '. . . I am afraid I shall not put in an appearance at the House on Monday. The truth is I am not much "forrader" and it may be wiser to hold on until it is really necessary that I shd. be present as is the case with the Cabinet on Tuesday.' But the next day (May 31st) he wrote to Salisbury even more unequivocally:

My dear Salisbury,
  I am afraid I may not be fit for my work when I get home. The Doctor here does not give me much hope, but I have asked Sir William Jenner to see me on my way through Southampton on Monday, if he is in those parts. If I am not fit, I should not like to stay on while another man has all the labour and the responsibility. It would not be fair to him, to you, or to my other colleagues.
  It may be only a matter of a few days, but taking one week with another, I have gone back steadily so far as the eczema is concerned, and the recent attacks have been so severe that they have deprived me of the power to do any work; but I shall see you on Tuesday at the Cabinet under any circumstances.
                                                    Yours very truly,
                                                       W. H. Smith

Jenner could not see him immediately, but wrote (June 1st):

. . . The Session has been a horrible time for you. . . . I am indeed . . . anxious about you, anxious because I am sure you will overwork

---

[1] Quoted from Maxwell, II, 277. Sir H. Maxwell says that Sir R. Temple showed him his Journal and allowed him to quote it on this point. The Journal itself does not appear to have ever been published, though Temple did later publish *The Story of My Life* (1896).

yourself & get into such health that no doctor can be clever enough to cure you.

One must speak plainly to you—Your life is a most important life to your family & also to the country. . . . There are many many men whose lives are of consequence to their families, few whose loss would be felt as yours would by the country.

Pardon me if I write strongly because I feel strongly & should never forgive myself if I did not say what I feel & in language not to be misunderstood.

Then, after seeing him, Jenner wrote again (June 3rd):

Your recent indisposition proves beyond dispute the necessity for your following the advice I have repeatedly given you, viz. that of taking more rest from your labours.

At present there is no local disease to cause grave anxiety, but your general health is such that if you had an acute attack of local disease your system would have no strength to resist it. . . .

I strongly advise you to take a holiday from work on Wednesdays and then another on Fridays, Saturdays & Sundays, going into the country on Friday afternoon & staying there Saturday & Sunday. Reflect seriously on what I have said, for there is not a word I could not prove by numberless sad, sad cases.

But, though his colleagues too joined in these entreaties, begging him to allow himself to be relieved by leaving the House early in the evening and leaving the conduct of business to a deputy, he still struggled on, scorning to remain leader in name only. Meanwhile he wrote serenely to his old confidante, Emily Giberne (June 8th):

I am not very bad, but the irritation, like some other mental irritation to which I am subjected in my work, is a little trying, but it will all come right; and when I look around me at the multitude of gifts and blessings which I enjoy, I at least have no right to complain.

My only difficulty is always to know what is best to be done. Emily would wish me to give up public work more than I feel I can do at present, and my doctors are exacting, and my difficulties in my work are great; but all these things trouble me less than they did, as I have complete trust that a higher Power will give light and guidance from day to day. . . . God bless you, my dear friend.

Returning from his brief Whitsun holiday to re-enter the fray, Smith found a letter from the Queen (June 16th) sympathizing with him in his illness: '. . . She really must urge him as strongly as she can to save himself as much as he can and not to work too much—expecially of a morng: & always to try to get some air & exercise.' Despite illness and worry, the ludicrous inappropriateness of this well-meant advice may well have caused Smith to laugh.

For, immediately, upon the House's reassembly the debate on the Local Taxation Bill was resumed and signs began to appear of the pressure which had been brought to bear on members whilst at home or in their constituencies. The majorities in favour of the controversial clauses sank to below 40 and, at length, on June 19th the Government came within an ace of defeat. It was 'Ascot Thursday' and many of the Government's supporters were away at the races. A member who was expected to hold the fort by speaking until the race-goers returned failed to rise to the occasion and the Opposition seized their opportunity by forcing a snap division. The Government's derisory majority of 4 virtually compelled the withdrawal of the licensing clauses—as was done a week later (June 26th). Such was the fate of 'a measure to which a powerful Ministry have in their fifth session pinned their fortunes', as Lucy commented.[1]

From this humiliation, it is sad to relate, the Government—and their leader in the House of Commons—moved straight on to another. In view of recent events, Smith had been consulting with experts inside and outside the House with the idea of preparing a new draft Procedure Rule under which it might be possible to suspend proceedings on any Bill under consideration in Committee and resume them at the same stage in the ensuing Session—thus obviating the appalling waste of time involved in going over the whole process again from the start, as under the existing system. He had caused considerable research to be done into the previous history of the question and earlier attempts to solve it. He had even telegraphed all British embassies to find out the practice of foreign parliaments on the point—including those of Japan, Greece, Germany, Scandinavia and the United States. But he was warned by the then Assistant Clerk to the House of Commons[2] that '... Radicals who would upset everything with a light heart ... pretend to be scared by your proposal—what they wish is to throw it over till next Session to wreck the Government Bills in this'.

However, Smith launched out in his frail barque, writing to Gladstone (June 1st):

Dear Mr. Gladstone,
   I think it right to mention to you that I shall this afternoon give notice of my intention to move a new Standing Order giving power to the House to suspend and carry over to the next Session of the same parliament Bills which have reached the Committee stage,—by motion in each case—and so that the Bills shall be taken up in the new Session for all practical purposes at the point at which they were suspended in the previous year.

Believe me,
Yours very faithfully,
W. H. Smith

[1] Lucy, op. cit., 285.
[2] Archibald Milman; later Clerk to the House of Commons.

327

When he rose in the House that afternoon to announce the proposal he said that a Standing Order to give effect to it would be placed on the table and in the event of its being adopted the House would be asked to carry over the Irish Land Purchase Bill to the next Session. Gladstone at once gave notice of an amendment, declaring that so grave a change in the practice of the House might not be made until the matter had been inquired into by a Select Committee. Labouchere followed this up by moving the adjournment of the House in order to discuss 'the serious state of public business caused by the mismanagement of the Government'. An acrimonious discussion ensued in the course of which Parnell predicted that the House would continue sitting till October and Harcourt, reading from criticisms on the mismanagement of business by the Government in a *Times* leading article, said it would be an agreeable novelty to him to adopt and speak the language of *The Times* and the House might take the comments of that 'friend of the Government' as his own speech. Eventually the motion was rejected by 233 to 181. But Gladstone's suggestion of a Select Committee to inquire into the proposed change of procedure was accepted by the Government and a motion for the appointment of such a committee agreed to by the House (June 23rd).

The Select Committee had got so far as to agree in principle that the Government's proposal would be 'a breach of the constitutional usage of Parliament', when Smith announced in the House (July 10th) that 'owing to the pressure of business' the Government did not intend to proceed with the proposed new Standing Order, although reserving to themselves absolute freedom of action in the matter. At the same time he announced the abandonment of the Land Purchase Bill and the Tithe Bill, although they would be re-introduced in the coming Session, he said.

Even *The Times*—as Harcourt had pointed out—was becoming so critical of the Government as to be inclined to believe the version of things as presented by the Opposition without question. Thus Buckle, the editor, had written to Smith (July 7th):

> I fear we must have done you—most unwittingly—an injustice in the leader of Saturday. Much assertion on the part of the enemy had led us to believe that you *did* say what, now you challenge it, I confess I cannot find anywhere reported. I am very sorry; but at the same time glad to know that the Government remain absolutely unpledged in reference to the Procedure resolution. You will see that we rectify the mistake in our leader tomorrow.

Meanwhile the Prime Minister had been writing to the Queen (June 25th):

'Lord Salisbury . . . is very anxious to induce Mr. Smith to go for three weeks abroad. In his present state of health he is incapable of a fixed resolve. . . .'[1] To which the Queen had replied (June 27th): '. . . the Queen does think that Mr. Smith's state of health and nerves renders him unfit for the position of leader, and that Mr. Goschen, or still more Mr. Balfour ought to have that place. Mr. Smith should remain, if possible, in the Government, but not in the House of Commons. . . . The Queen is most anxious to see the Government strengthened and supported and she *does* think that want of firmness in the leader of the House of Commons is most detrimental to it. . . .'

It is difficult to avoid the feeling that both the Queen and her Prime Minister were being rather hard and unfair on him in view of his repeated offers to retire—the last one only a few weeks earlier—and that if anyone was 'incapable of a fixed resolve' it was Salisbury, who on each occasion had begged him to stay on. Certainly Smith himself was still under the impression that he was wanted and needed—to the extent that his colleagues would feel badly let down by his going. At the same time he was not hell-bent on self-destruction or indulging any morbid craving for a martyr's crown, as is clear from the following letter to Dr. Acland (July 10th):

You let drop the words yesterday, 'Is the game worth the candle?' suggesting to me, as I thought at the moment, to consider whether I ought to go on with my present work in the Government; and you then went on to say that I had a very small reserve of power (or balance at my banker's, so to speak), which might be very easily overdrawn.

My position is that I am what I am in the House of Commons from no personal ambition. I fill a place in the machine of Government at the desire of my colleagues, and I am perfectly willing to drop out of it whenever in their judgment it is no longer necessary that I should remain; but a sense of loyalty to them and to the country keeps me with them so long as they want me to stay, and I am at all able to do the work.

Now it is for you to say if I am able. It would be folly and worse than folly if I cut short my life by staying on a few weeks or a few months longer as leader of the House; but if I have only to bear discomfort and wearisomeness I should not be justified in withdrawing, at the cost of serious difficulty to the Government, at the present time.

Dr. Acland replied by reiterating his warnings as to the risk of continuing at his post, but gave him hope of carrying on if timely precautions were taken. The first of these was that he should go to the French watering-place La Bourboule—which was near that other watering-place, Royat, whither Lord and Lady Salisbury

[1] *Letters of Queen Victoria*, Third Series, Vol. I, 616.

usually went. This Smith duly did, but unfortunately not till another month had elapsed, during which he was inevitably bombarded with problems and continually reminded of governmental worries. Strikes threatened—though they did not actually materialize—in both the Metropolitan Police and the Post Office and Ministers were required to answer questions on these matters in the House. Then Gladstone wrote to Smith with a pettifogging resolution 'respecting references to Peers in debate' and the tone of Smith's reply (July 15th) is indicative of the strained state of his nerves—though it is perfectly controlled and well-considered.

LORD JOHN MANNERS.

"THE NEW DUKE."

Dear Mr. Gladstone,

Is there any real necessity for raising the questions involved in the resolution you sent to me?

I am afraid it would give rise to very prolonged debate, and I do not see what possible advantage could result to the House from the discussion.

It would afford an opportunity for showing how extremely easy it is for Members to misunderstand each other, and to differ—probably with warmth—because of the misunderstanding.

Yours very truly,

W. H. Smith

He also had to receive a deputation in support of Samuel Plimsoll's[1] Merchant Shipping Amendment Act, headed by the fanatical Plimsoll himself, bearing a memorandum which began: 'If the Session ends with its present record your opponents will insist loudly and often about its alleged barrenness, and what they will call the "blundering" of the Government. If on the other hand the Government will assist me to pass the . . . Bill there will not be a single meeting of working men held in the recess that will not ring with their praises. . . .' Smith's old friend the Duke of Rutland (formerly Lord John Manners) did not much relieve his gloom by telling him (July 23rd): '. . . Lord Powis[2]

[1] M.P. (Lib.) for Derby. For years he had conducted an agitation against the sacrifice of sailors' lives through overloading and over-insuring of merchant ships and in 1876 he forced upon Disraeli's Government a Merchant Shipping Bill to prevent this.

[2] Edward James, 3rd Earl of Powis, Lord Lieutenant of Montgomeryshire.

writes in a very gloomy strain on the postponement of the Tithe Bill, and says it will drive all the small farmers into the Radical ranks and lead to an attack on Rent. . . .'

Then he blundered again, arousing a quite surprising degree of anger and irritation in his usually placid and friendly chief. 'I stated in Cabinet not once, but on two or three occasions', wrote Salisbury (July 23rd), 'that I regarded the question of having a Religious Census as an *open* question and that I intended to vote for it, if it was proposed. Cranbrook made the same statement. . . . I cannot conceive what forgetfulness induced you to speak on behalf of the whole Government in the sense you did last night. I don't see what is to be done.'[1] In his reply Smith (July 25th) mentioned in his defence the peculiar circumstances and mood prevailing in the House at the time and went on: 'I may have been wrong in my judgment but I thought it necessary to say this and a man who acts as Leader must take such a responsibility as occasions arise . . . and having said this I cannot now advise you as to what should be done [but if you think otherwise I supply you with an answer to your question by saying throw me over in the House of Lords.]'[2] These last rather desperate words were struck through on reflection, but his mortification is none the less apparent.

However, the Queen wrote him a kindly letter a few days later, which may have soothed his feelings, 'to express her deep regret at the fatigue & worry to wh. he is exposed & wh. is so bad for his health. She purposely did not ask him to come to Windsor for fear of fatiguing him . . . she hears he is to go abroad which she trusts will do him good. . . .' And indeed at last, when Parliament had been prorogued on August 12th, he obeyed Dr. Acland and went to La Bourboule, whither the Salisburys had already preceded him. 'I wish I had not got the bother of the journey before me', he wrote to Akers-Douglas (August 15th), 'I had infinitely rather go home and sleep.' But when he got there his spirits revived, he made plans for a cruise in the *Pandora* after the water-cure was finished and wrote again: 'Can I persuade you to join the yacht at Venice . . . for a three week's cruise on the Adriatic. Fitz[3] and his wife are coming and we intend to leave dull care behind and be as jolly as a whole crew of sandboys. Pray give me the great pleasure and send me a wire. . . .'[4]

A few days later (August 21st) he sent Akers-Douglas an amusing sketch of life at La Bourboule: '. . . This place is an extraordinary mixture—very few English and of the French two classes only— those who are intent on spending and those who feed on them. Prices are higher than at Monte Carlo and the Salisburys amuse me by

[1] Salisbury Papers. [2] Ibid.
[3] Penrose FitzGerald, See *ante*. [4] Chilston Papers.

grumbling at them. . . .' And to his son Freddy (August 31st) he described the curative routine: '. . . bathing once a day in a hot bath for 25 minutes and drinking Arsenic water in minute doses at the Spring three times a day . . . I have been made worse in order to be made better, and now at last I think I have turned the corner. . . .'

Thus seemingly restored he set out on the Adriatic cruise, cheered by a gay letter from Arthur Balfour—to whom he had written gloomily (September 9th): '. . . A younger man than I am and with more strength and resource is needed to deal with the crisis in Parliamentary life. We must pass our Bills in the coming Session or suffer very great discredit. . . .'[1]—and who now wrote back from Scotland (September 12th):

My dear Smith,

I rejoice to hear that your general health is much better:—I think we may confidently hope now that you will be able to throw off the eczema; and that the Autumn Session will find you strong and cheerful. I have great hopes of being able to cut down the *most essential* part of my L[and] Bill to proportions which will enable us, I will not say without difficulty, but at least without risk of failure, to force it through the House, even under our present rules. . . .

I am having a huge caucus here of Irish Officials tomorrow, to discuss potatoes & prosecutions.

With his wife and daughter Helen, Smith had joined the *Pandora* at Venice, as prearranged, and they then cruised down the Adriatic and up the west coast of Italy. 'I am really not the same man I was before I started for home and I am much better than I ever expected to be', he wrote to Miss Giberne (October 1st). They landed at Toulon on October 13th; but then he got a chill and by the time he reached Paris, on his way home, he was quite ill again. To add to the depressing circumstances of his return his sister Louisa (Lucy) died shortly after his arrival in England. 'Another Sister has gone— Louisa the widow of Rupert Sercombe', he wrote to Ford, his solicitor and friend, '. . . The doctors won't allow me to attend the funeral as the cold weather has brought out my eczema afresh and if I got a chill now and it was driven in it might be serious. . . .' Dr. Acland saw him again and was shocked. 'If you are not [better] I shall use my endeavour to get you released after this Session', he wrote (November 9th).

But within barely a month of his return Smith was plunged into a new kind of anxiety through the threatened collapse of Baring's Bank and the attendant risk of a chain reaction of disaster in the City. Goschen, as Chancellor of the Exchequer, held a conference

[1] Balfour Papers.

at the Bank of England on November 10th and declared that Government support could only be given if the Bank of England were satisfied that Baring's would prove solvent after realization of assets. Goschen thereupon left London in order to fulfil some political engagements in the North and it fell to Smith, as First Lord of the Treasury, to carry out the negotiations necessary to avert the threatened crash.

The Bank of England had reported satisfactorily on the question submitted to them and therefore Treasury support for Baring's was forthcoming. But Smith now made a most impressive personal gesture. It may be supposed that some delay in implementing the Treasury promise was anticipated—a delay which might prove dangerous to the stability of the City—and that Smith, as one of the wealthiest men in the country, felt called upon to proffer his own aid. At any rate, the circumstances are described in a letter written just after his death, by the Governor of the Bank of England, William Lidderdale, to Smith's Secretary, Pattisson (October 8th, 1891). After describing the great impression Smith had made upon him, Lidderdale continued:

. . . When I was led by some remark of his to say, 'I fear, Sir, you do not appreciate the gravity of the position', he replied, 'You are mistaken; & to prove this I will myself send you a cheque for £100,000 tomorrow morning, if you tell me to do so'.

This £100,000 was to be Mr. Smith's contribution towards averting the danger with which our finances was threatened, & it was offered some hours before the Guarantee Fund was started.

Indeed, Smith explained his motive in a letter to Lidderdale at the time (November 21st, 1890):

My motive in offering a guarantee of £100,000 was entirely a public one. I thought it would have been a national misfortune if Barings had gone down, and I was willing to incur a private risk to avert that disaster; but since I have been a member of the Government—since 1874—I have never asked for an allotment of shares in a company, or taken part in speculation, in order that as a Minister or ex-Minister it may be impossible for anyone to impute interested motives to me in any transaction I may have with people out of doors on behalf of the Government.

Following this rule, I should not ask for any share in the New Barings, but I do regard it as of great public importance that the business of the House should be kept together and carried on on the old lines (not the recent ones), and if it was necessary to that end that I should subscribe, I am prepared to do so; but for the reasons I have given, I had rather not—as a matter of course and of policy.

The date chosen for the reassembly of Parliament was November 25th and Smith had notified Gladstone that 'I propose so soon as the Address has been voted to ask the House to give the Government the whole of its time up to Christmas for the consideration of the Tithe and the Land Purchase Bills . . .'. To which Gladstone had replied: 'You will not require to be told that I view it with regret'. In fact, after the bitter experiences of the last Session the Government

CHARLES STEWART PARNELL.

looked forward to the new one with as much anxiety and foreboding as the Opposition anticipated with grim relish the opportunities it might afford for inflicting fresh damage and humiliation upon them.

But only a few days before the reassembly a bombshell had fallen which was to alter this picture beyond belief and put an entirely different complexion on affairs. Captain O'Shea, the Nationalist member for Galway, had filed a divorce petition against his wife, citing Parnell as co-respondent, as long ago as December 1889; but

334

the case had been prejudged by Gladstonians and Parnellites alike as just another vile conspiracy—similar to the forged letters—to destroy Parnell's character and wreck the cause of Home Rule. Moreover, this impression was strengthened, as it had been in the trial before the Special Commission, by the retention of the Unionist Solicitor-General, Sir Edward Clarke, as counsel for O'Shea, as well as by the latter's reputation for unscrupulousness and double-dealing. Resolutions by almost all Irish public bodies had expressed unaltered confidence in Parnell's leadership and Parnell himself, interviewed by John Morley on behalf of Gladstone, had given the impression there would be no adverse decree or even any likelihood of his temporary disappearance.

But when the case opened on November 15th, 1890, to the dismay of all his friends and allies, Parnell offered no defence and on the 17th O'Shea was granted a decree nisi, accompanied by some scathing comments upon Parnell—who made no appearance—by the judge. Nevertheless, the Irish Party and many other Irish bodies and meetings still reaffirmed their unshaken confidence in Parnell's leadership; though Gladstone hoped that he would voluntarily retire—at least temporarily—from it. But, when Parnell made it clear that he had no such intention, Gladstone, submitting to pressure from English Liberals and the 'Nonconformist Conscience', wrote a letter to Morley to be shown to Parnell—through the agency of Justin M'Carthy—asserting that his continuance as leader would render his own (Gladstone's) advocacy of Home Rule 'almost a nullity'.

But through Parnell's elusiveness M'Carthy never succeeded in communicating the contents of the letter, before Parnell was unanimously and enthusiastically re-elected leader at the Sessional meeting of the Irish Party on November 25th. Next day, however, Gladstone's letter was published and at a special meeting of the Irish Party, called at the instance of thirty-one members, Parnell was asked to reconsider his position. He refused to do so and though he managed to retain the allegiance of a portion of his party, an even larger part detached itself and set itself up under the leadership of M'Carthy. There were now therefore two distinct and mutually antagonistic wings of the old united Home Rule Party.

Immediately, as though some fearful abscess in it had at long last burst, the Parliamentary system cleared and things moved with a speed and expedition, which, after so many years of hopeless obstruction, seemed almost miraculous. The Queen wrote to Smith next day (November 26th):

... This voting of the Address in *one* night is indeed quite remarkable & certainly has not happened for many years.

The conduct of Mr. Gladstone & of Mr. Parnell & the division in
the Liberal Party are most startling facts, tho' the Queen *never* thought
Mr. Gladstone cd. continue to act with Mr. Parnell after the late
esclandre—It will greatly weaken the Radical Home Rule party.
The Queen hopes Mr. Smith is feeling strong & well?

It certainly cheered him; but he seemed as yet scarcely able to
believe in any permanent relief from the old stress and strain.
However, he was able to accept the Queen's invitation to stay at
Windsor, whence he wrote to his son Freddy (November 30th):

... Lord Hartington and the Bp. of Peterborough are here. Hartington
is in good spirits at the discomfiture of his opponents—who are equally
disagreeable to him—Parnell and Gladstone. . . . The confusion in
the Opposition ranks exceeds anything I have ever known in politics.
Probably they will recover themselves before this note reaches you,
but we are taking advantage of the absence of cohesion to press on
our work.

P.S. Dec. 5.
The confusion in the Liberal ranks continues. The Irish are going
to Gladstone today to ask him what he means by Home Rule and if
they get a plain answer out of him I shall be as much surprised as
Parnell will be. The week however has been useful to us whatever the
future may be, and on the return of the House on 22nd Jan. we shall
have already secured a good start. . . .
I have had just now to say a few words in the House expressing our
sympathy with the Speaker [on the death of his wife]. . . . The House
was most sympathetic and took what I said kindly—but there was not
a single Irishman present—so completely are they absorbed with their
own difficulties.

Smith was uncertain, however, as to the exact manner in which
this heaven-sent confusion among their opponents might best be
exploited. Thus when it came to a by-election in Ireland, he wrote
urgently to Akers-Douglas (December 9th): 'Will you get hold of
Arthur Hill[1] and consider with him and any other of our friends
what course we should take at the Election now proceeding in
Kilkenny and in any other that may occur in Ireland. Is it sound
policy to run a Unionist as against the Parnellite and his anti-
Parnellite Competitor? I rather incline to the view that we ought to
try our strength if we have any.'[2] Nevertheless, his grave and anxious
nature recoiled from anything in the nature of a Roman triumph, as
urged by some Unionists—particularly Liberal-Unionists. Thus,
when Akers-Douglas forwarded a letter from Sir Henry James
urging the adoption of a 'most enthusiastic and triumphant tone'
and speaking of 'trampling the Gladstonians under foot',[3] Smith

[1] See *ante*, p. 309.   [2] Chilston Papers.   [3] Ibid.

336

replied (December 23rd): '. . . As to Henry James . . . I think we should be more likely to do ourselves harm than good by any exhibition of over-eagerness to triumph over Gladstonians. It would possibly turn people back again. . . .'[1]

Hartington's appraisal was sober too. '. . . I congratulate you on the success of the Session', he wrote to Smith (December 13th), 'I am afraid that the Parnell split has not had any great effect on the English Constituencies, and do not hear that Bassetlaw[2] is by any means a certainty, but I hope it will be alright. . . .' However, in the event, the Conservative beat his Gladstonian opponent by 700 votes—despite the intervention of Gladstone himself with a weighty speech at Retford during his campaign. Thus Lord St. Oswald to Smith (December 19th): '. . . I think the Home Rule bubble must have really burst—but what extraordinary depths the G.O.M. has sunk to!—The result of Retford after Gladstone's visit was most satisfactory—better than I could have hoped for, tho' I always thought we should probably win. What could an Irish Parliament be like if they ever got one?'

Lord Lansdowne, the Viceroy of India—and also a great Irish landowner—was more sanguine than Hartington, but, like Smith, inclined to caution. 'The Irish Exhibition is very interesting to me', he wrote to him (December 23rd). 'It should open the eyes of the constituencies if anything will. I hope you will not be tempted into a premature dissolution—My impression is that the rift in the Irish party will widen, if they are allowed to fight their quarrels out: a general election might force a reconciliation upon them. . . .'

Meanwhile, the Tithes Bill and the Land Purchase Bill moved along with unaccustomed smoothness and celerity to their second readings—the Land Bill in particular emphasizing the change wrought by recent events, for whereas when it was first introduced in the previous summer Parnell had felt constrained to join Gladstone in opposing it, he now took great relish in accentuating his separation from him by leading his little band of personal supporters into the Government lobby. Both Bills were afterwards allowed to pass into the Committee Stage, to be resumed after the Christmas holiday, and Parliament was adjourned on December 9th till January 22nd. Thus the autumn Session which had been approached with so much trepidation by Ministers and such eager anticipation of victory by the Opposition had lasted less than a fortnight.

When he next wrote to Freddy (December 19th) Smith allowed himself to indulge in something pretty near a note of triumph: '. . . The political events of the last month are almost marvellous.

---

[1] Ibid.
[2] By-election in the Bassetlaw Division of Nottinghamshire.

The Radicals appear to be stunned and incapable of making any forecast as to the future. What will happen if Parnell beats his opponents *I* cannot tell but I should not be surprised if Gladstone threw up altogether. They say he was so angry when he was in town that no one dared come near him.'

XV

LAST DAYS

━━━━◆┣━◆━━━━

THE opening of the new year, 1891, found the question of the
Irish leadership still in the balance. William O'Brien, who had
been arrested some months earlier for sedition and had escaped to
America with the connivance of Healy, now crossed the Atlantic
again to meet Parnell in Paris with the self-appointed task of 'healing
the split' in the Irish Party. Parnell, in fact, offered him the leadership
in the event of himself resigning, but the Anti-Parnellites would not
accept this situation, suspecting that O'Brien would merely be the
tool of Parnell. While these agonizing discussions were going on
among their enemies, Balfour wrote to Smith from Dublin (January
8th, 1891) with his usual airiness:

> My dear Smith,
> I have been meaning to write to you for many days—but I spend
> my time so agreeably in the Society of Rly contractors, Poor Law
> Officials, Priests and beggars, that I have no leisure for less exciting
> pursuits!! On the whole I think things are going well: I am sorely
> hampered by the drivelling incompetence of some of the P.L.
> inspectors—and by my ignorance of the various methods in which Rly
> contracts can be drawn up! . . .
> I am very curious to see the terms of the concordat between O'Brien
> & Parnell. That they were bound to agree has long been obvious;
> because neither can at present get on without the other. But what are
> the bases of agreement? I see that Parnell means to speak at Limerick,
> Waterford, Tralee, Ennis &c—*i.e. all the places where the extremists
> are most powerful.* This does not look like abdication.

And Smith replied (January 12th) equally and, for him, unusually
lightheartedly: '. . . The Parnell row is a most delicious Comedy
for us—regarded, as I suspect, by some of the Actors, as a dreadful
tragedy. I am looking forward to the drying up of the fountain which
for so many years has quenched the thirst of some 40 or 50 Home
Rule members of Parliament. . . .' Meanwhile, just before Parliament

339

reassembled, on January 22nd, a Cabinet Meeting was held of which Smith sent (January 19th) a full account to his old friend the Duke of Rutland, who was unable to attend through illness:

My dear Duke,
. . . Although you may possibly hear from others of our colleagues, I will tell you shortly what we did—if Cabinets ever do anything. We considered somewhat alarmist telegrams from the Cape. The Boers are supposed to be about to trek into Mashonaland and set up a republic, with the connivance of the Transvaal Government. . . . We agreed a telegram should go warning the Transvaal Government that the threatened incursion would be unfriendly, hostile, and a breach of the Swazi Convention. . . .
The Budget was of course considered and your views as to the Income Tax were debated, but it was felt that having included Assisted Education in the Queen's Speech provision must be made for it and a reduction of Income Tax postponed. Both cannot be done this year. It is I think certain that if we proposed to postpone the former to the latter, we should be met by an Amendment which would unite all the men on the Liberal benches with some of our own men against us.
Every member now has his eye on the General Election and every vote is given from an opportunist point of view. The payers of school fees are more powerful from a voting point of view than the payers of Income Tax!
The Vote on Opium shows the demoralisation of the House. Men could not be induced to vote against Pease.[1] They were terrorised by the cry of immorality raised by the Sentimental and Dissenting agitators. . . .

Smith was much preoccupied with the question of 'Assisted Education'. 'I wish I could have a talk with you about assisted education', he wrote to his other oldest friend, Lord Harrowby (February 6th), 'It gives me great concern and I would be no party to it if I did not feel quite certain that if we cannot frame some scheme which will preserve Voluntary Schools, our successors will carry one which will destroy them.'[2]

Meanwhile, on February 4th, Gladstone moved the Second Reading of a Bill he had introduced to remove the disability preventing Roman Catholics from holding the offices of Lord Chancellor and Viceroy of Ireland—but removing from the Lord Chancellor the right of administering the ecclesiastical patronage of the Crown.

[1] Sir Alfred Pease (*Elections & Recollections*, 283) writes: 'On the 9th April, after years of labour and many defeats, my father [Sir Joseph Pease, Bt., M.P. Barnard Castle] at last carried his motion against the Government by 160 to 130 for the abolition of the policy of forcing Indian Opium on China and the abrogation of the Opium clauses in the Treaty with China.'
[2] Harrowby Papers.

To the more cynical among Gladstone's opponents his motive merely seemed to be to enable him, in the event of his return to power, to appoint two of his most prominent supporters, who happened to be Roman Catholics, to these two offices respectively. But apart from these considerations, Smith, in moving the rejection of the Bill, was able to point to one glaring weakness in the Bill. Declaring the Bill to be 'most unfortunate and inopportune', he said he did not know why it was proposed 'unless it be in connection with the scheme of Home Rule with which the right hon. gentlemen is connected'. But chiefly he saw it as 'the setting up of a new scheme of disability, declaring at one moment that a Roman Catholic lawyer is to be fully capable of discharging the duties of Lord Chancellor, and the next moment cutting him off from a very large proportion of the most important duties which devolve upon him'. He concluded by condemning the irresponsibility and danger of 'reviving religious controversy' by stirring questions of this kind. Whatever the merits of this argument it is at least proof of the continuing vigour and resource which the ailing Leader could still muster on occasion: though the Bill was rejected by a majority of only 47 and 27 Conservatives voted against the Government.

Furthermore, the Catholic Union of Great Britain took umbrage at the action of the Government in resisting Gladstone's measure and forwarded to Smith, through their president, the Duke of Norfolk, a copy of a motion expressing their 'deep pain' and protesting against 'the deep slur cast upon the loyalty and patriotism of the Catholics in this country'. Replying to the Duke, Smith wrote: '. . . Not only did I take pains in my speech to emphasize the fact that no one who knows English society could doubt the perfect loyalty of the Roman Catholics, but I pointed out that the constitution of Her Majesty's Government at the present time was in itself a complete answer to such a suggestion' (referring presumably to the presence of Matthews, the Catholic Home Secretary).

But a curious sidelight was thrown upon the affair by a letter which Smith received (February 23rd) from a distinguished Catholic Conservative. This person, George Lane Fox, deplored the resolution of the Catholic Union, which he said only proved that 'certain influential gentlemen have fallen into the trap cleverly laid for them by Mr. Gladstone', for 'there were only about 50 present at the meeting and most of them were liberals or liberal unionists': he himself received no invitation and did not think 'that Conservative Catholics in general knew what was in the air'.

At about this time Smith had another brush with Goschen, with whom, in common with others of their colleagues, he had never been

341

able to get on. The Government, as we have seen, was pledged by the Queen's Speech to 'alleviating the burden which compulsory education has, in recent years, imposed upon the poorer portions of my people' and intended to redeem this pledge by a Free Education Bill. Goschen, whose skill and foresight at the Treasury had been rewarded by a £2 million surplus, had referred in introducing his

THE BUDGET.

Budget, with a subacid inflection, to 'the despoiler of the public purse sitting on the Treasury Bench', meaning the Minister of Education, Sir William Hart Dyke. Smith was irritated by the tone and allowed to slip a rather tart rejoinder implying derogation of all Goschen's budgets. But immediately afterwards his usual kindness led him to express his regrets. The reply he got from Goschen must have quite chilled his feelings again:

Treasury Chambers,
Whitehall, S.W.
My dear Smith, 7/3/91.

It is like your goodness of heart to wish to remove at once any pain you may have given, and to treat your observations as a joke. I quite believe that it was 'heedlessly uttered', but it was an unintentional revelation of what was in your mind rather than a joke. If you had been satisfied, or had thought that the party had been generally satisfied, not with all, but with most of my former budgets, it would have been impossible for you to have, even heedlessly, said what you said. Of course there can be no question of an apology between you and me. What gave me pain, is not what you *said* but what I discovered you *thought*.

And pray do not think it necessary to explain away, or to disclaim. I understand your line of thought which was to my mind very clear. . . .

. . . I am absolutely sure you meant nothing unkind, nor sarcastic. But sometimes one's feelings will out & a glimpse is given of what is latent in the mind.

Don't think any more of the incident.

Yours very sincerely,
George J. Goschen

Smarting under this patronizing little homily, Smith unburdened his feelings to Salisbury who wrote back to him with jocular sympathy (March 8th):

My dear Smith,
You see the disadvantage of a good character. When I say a bitter thing, people only say its a bad habit I've got, and draw no inference from it.
But when you say a bitter thing, there is a general explosion.
Poor Goschen! He is too sensitive for this world—especially when he has got a chill on the liver. I am afraid he will insist on sweeping away our Education project for this year—as a kind of expiation for your joke.

Ever Yours truly,
Salisbury

Salisbury himself was at this time the unwitting cause of qualms and resentment on the part of Goschen. The quarrel with Portugal over the division of Central Africa which had been going on since 1886, reached such a crisis in December 1890 that war seemed imminent. Despite a very severe bout of influenza Salisbury had still insisted on conducting policy in his usual fashion—that is to say completely 'solo' from Hatfield. This had caused considerable anxiety and even a little resentment among some of his colleagues—especially Goschen, who had written an anxious note about it to Smith. Three months later Salisbury had recovered, but the crisis was still serious and Goschen was even more resentful—especially with the soreness over the Budget and Free Education still rankling. He therefore wrote irritably to Smith (March 31st):

My dear Smith,
Neither do I 'get peace during my so-called holiday', but I get some fresh air, gardening & exercise, but otherwise budgets & bothers from hour to hour.
I will not write abt budget today, except to tell you that the surplus will *not* be enough to remit 1d. in the income tax besides providing for free education. It is impossible & too risky even if it were barely possible. . . .
I am uneasy about Portugal & all the more because I know so little. It is not right that we are kept so much in the dark. . . . Do you see the despatches? I see none. . . .

343

I think Salisbury contemplated fighting there as a possibility. If the Portuguese are stubborn possibly he thinks he may leave it to the Company[1] to fight it out, but if they are beaten we may be in for something big there before we know it. When Salisbury comes back I really feel we ought to be told more. I have had some talk with him, but I don't see why we should not see Portuguese despatches to & fro as we see Egypt, South Eastern Europe & other papers. I speak only for myself: perhaps you may see more.

As you know, I am uneasy altogether as to this Chartered Warlike Company.

Yours very sincerely,
George J. Goschen

A couple of days later he wrote again (April 2nd): '. . . I sent Dawkins[2] to the F.O. to enquire about Portugal & the Chartered Coy. I enclose copy of what he writes. Most unsatisfactory. And now I read in the newspapers that the Matabele people may move. Heaven avert some great catastrophe.'

Smith must have appreciated it as a singular tribute to his unique standing among the politicians of his day when he received this invitation (March 20th) from the man who was one of his most determined opponents in the House, Sir William Harcourt: 'The Gladstones dine with us on Wednesday, April 15. . . . Is there any chance of you & Mrs. Smith being disengaged. . . . If so it would give Ldy H. & myself great pleasure if you could meet *across our table* (quite according to Parlty rules). I may mention it is not a *round table.* . . .' It is evidence of the great depth to which party differences then cut that Smith felt it necessary to consult Akers-Douglas, the Chief Whip, writing (March 28th): '. . . I am very much inclined to go. Would it frighten our friends?'[3] Evidently he went, for he observed later in a letter to Sir Henry Acland: 'Gladstone is more kindly in his personal relations than I have ever known him, but he is physically much weaker, and the least exertion knocks him over.'[4]

Goschen's nagging about the Portuguese policy was not without effect—though Salisbury affected to be surprised at any discontent about his methods. For he wrote to Smith (April 6th): 'On reading your account of Goschen's complaint that he had not seen more of the despatches to Portugal, I telegraphed Philip Currie[5] to place at

[1] Cecil Rhodes's Chartered South Africa Company.
[2] His Private Secretary. Later Sir Clinton Dawkins, K.C.B.
[3] Chilston Papers.
[4] Maxwell, II, 306.
[5] Sir Philip, later Lord Currie, Permanent Under Secretary of State for Foreign Affairs.

Goschen's disposal all the correspondence we have upon the subject. Nevertheless, I am puzzled at the complaint: for our practice with respect to Portugal has been exactly the same as that which we have always pursued, without complaint, in regard to all other parts of the world. You get the telegrams daily: & the despatches are collected & circulated from time to time, in the "confidential prints".'

Salisbury then referred to the death, which had occurred a few days earlier, of Lord Granville, the great Whig leader, who had been Lord Warden of the Cinque Ports for the past twenty-five years: 'What is Akers-Douglas worrying himself about the Cinque Ports for? It cannot be converted into a County Office for East Kent.[1] I have sent my two names in to the Queen, in order to stop certain royal suggestions that are being made, but I will not write to either of the men till I see you. . . .' Akers-Douglas had in fact already been in touch with Salisbury's Private Secretary, Schomberg McDonnell, on the subject and put forward the name of a Kentish candidate and McDonnell had replied that there would be 'a rush' for the post—especially among 'all the houseless Ministers'.[2]

But this was where he—and Salisbury—were wrong. For the Lord Wardenship was actually no office of profit for a needy minister. On the contrary, owing to the heavy expenses of running Walmer Castle, the Lord Warden's official residence, it was a considerable financial liability.[3] Salisbury suddenly discovered this when Lord George Hamilton gave his reasons for declining. He thereupon promptly bethought him of his richest, most deserving colleague and recommended Smith to the Queen. His letter to Smith (May 1st) was as blunt as it was amusing:

My dear Smith,
    On Hamilton's refusing the Cinque Ports on the ground of expense—it became evident that I had made a mistake in thinking it should be reserved as an assistance to a poor man. It is a white elephant of the whitest kind.
    I consequently asked the Queen whether she did not think you ought to be asked to take it. It is a semi-naval position—and you have been since 1876 always exceedingly popular with naval people: and I think

---

[1] Akers-Douglas was M.P. for the St. Augustine's (former 'East Kent') Division of Kent.
[2] Chilston Papers.
[3] It is true that at one time in the distant past the Lord Warden was said to derive between £3,000 and £4,000 a year from the proceeds of wreckage. But when Lord Russell had offered it to Granville in 1865 he had written: 'As you have no place on the sea perhaps you would like to be Lord Warden of the Cinque Ports. The salary is *nil* and the expense something.' (See Lord Edmond FitzMaurice: *Life of Lord Granville, I,* 488.)

the Dover people would feel complimented at the Leader of the House of Commons taking it.

I enclose the Queen's answer.

Will you take it.

Yours very truly,
Salisbury

The Queen had written that she 'highly approved' of the proposal, adding: 'No one deserves it more than he does.' Thus offered, Smith could scarcely refuse and he realized too that part of the intention was to give him a valid reason for spending some, at least, of his time in the bracing air of the South Coast, where he could literally step onto his beloved yacht at a moment's notice. The Navy was duly pleased too, as Salisbury had foretold. One of the officers who had served under him at the Admiralty wrote: 'I am sure I am not taking too much on myself when on behalf of the Navy I congratulate our old Chief. . . . It is gratifying to us to know that administering the Navy is amongst the services for which you are now Lord Warden of the Cinque Ports. . . .'

After accepting, Smith's first thought was for the feelings of his predecessor's widow, for Walmer had been the happy home of the Granvilles and their children for a quarter of a century. He therefore wrote at once (May 4th) to Lady Granville informing her of his appointment before it was made public and assuring her that 'both Mrs. Smith and I are extremely anxious you should understand that we are in no hurry to take possession of Walmer Castle and we hope therefore that you will remain there as long as it may suit your convenience to do so. . . . There is no necessity whatever for our appearance there for three or four months to come. . . .' But Lady Granville replied (May 5th): '. . . Would not you or Mrs. Smith like to see the Castle? . . . I am so fond of the dear old place that I have the vanity to wish you to see it, if possible, before we take down books & prints & make it look miserable & uninhabited. . . .'

Immediately upon the public announcement Smith was approached by the Registrar of the Cinque Ports and other officials connected with the ancient office with suggestions and proposals of various kinds. Bewildered, he turned to the man who was always at his elbow in the House, Akers-Douglas. 'If you don't object I shall constitute you my Prime Minister in regard to my new functions', he wrote to him (May 7th). 'I suppose I am not Lord Warden until a Patent has passed the Great Seal. Is that not so? Then I cannot do any act in that capacity until I produce the requisite authority. . . .'

Then, just after he had written he learned that Akers-Douglas was ill and immediately wrote a second letter giving him the same kind of advice as he himself was now continually receiving—and seldom following. 'Whatever may be the condition of other men don't attempt to leave your house until the doctor is quite satisfied you can do so without perfect safety. It would be madness for you to do so. Although I am not in the House I am keeping watch over matters and you need have no fear they will go right enough. . . .'

For, despite the alleviation of obstruction caused by the Parnell Divorce and the confusion of the Irish—or perhaps because of its very suddenness after such long-sustained effort at the highest pitch—there had now descended upon the Unionist camp a curious spell of weariness and ill-health. Probably the continual sight of the gradually failing powers of their Leader in the Commons, the illness of a number of other ministers and members, together with the knowledge that the Parliament of 1886 was running towards its term, combined to induce a certain feeling of hopelessness and fatality. Smith had written to the Duke of Rutland, with reference to the Government's defeat on the Opium Question, of the 'Demoralisation of the House', meaning that members had been swayed by the sentimental arguments of Dissenters. But on April 23rd the Duke had written back:

. . . The explanation the Whips gave you of the Opium defeat is no doubt true; but is it the whole truth? A day or two after it I heard from one of our supporters that he & others stayed away from sheer weariness of the House, and of its perpetual sittings, and this opens up to view other dangers likely to arise from attempting legislation for such a subject as Assisted Education late in the Session. Too great a strain will have been placed on private members, and the result will be that while those among them who take a lead, and really care for Parliamentary life, may remain to the end, others less ambitious, and less devoted to St. Stephens will go away and the Government will run a great risk of being left in the lurch. . . .

Meanwhile, however, Smith's appointment as Lord Warden provided the occasion for what was to be the last spontaneous demonstration from the House of the warmth of its feelings for him. For, in accordance with the rule of the day requiring members accepting 'offices of profit' under the Crown to vacate their seats and seek re-election, he had to go through the form of an appeal to the Strand electors. But he was not opposed and promptly returned to the House in triumph (May 12th). The scene was thus described by the *Pall Mall Gazette*, at that time strongly Radical in flavour and little likely to be predisposed in favour of the Tory leader of the House:

'Members desiring to take their seats will now come to the table,' shouts the Speaker in stentorian tones, and behold! there marches up to the table a member whom we seem to have seen before. He blushes, but he is not in the first bloom of his manhood: he smiles nervously in response to the ringing cheers that greet him from all parts of the House, but he goes through all the ceremonies of introduction—not with the awkwardness of a new member, but with all the grace and ease of one who has known them from his childhood up. And the curious thing is this, though he is obviously a Tory member, the whole House joins in his welcome, and grins from ear to ear with satisfaction, as at the coming of some very dear old friend. Curious? it is not at all curious; for who should this member be but the most popular man that has led the House of Commons for the last twenty years—Mr. W. H. Smith.

Two days later Smith left England to spend the short Whitsuntide recess at Cadenabbia. He returned on May 27th to receive a shower of letters from Lord Harrowby from Schwalbach in Germany (since his retirement from politics some eight years earlier Harrowby was in continual search of health at continental spas) about the Government's Free or 'Assisted' Education Bill which was about to be launched. Harrowby, it will be remembered had been closely associated with Smith in the attempt to cooperate with and influence Forster at the time of the latter's Education Act of 1870. He had also been Vice-President of the Council on Education in Disraeli's Ministry. Opposition to the present Bill came not only from the die-hard wing of the Tories, but also from the extreme individualist Liberals (such as Goschen) and from those Nonconformists who feared the 'assisted' free schools would draw pupils away from their own 'Voluntary' fee-paying schools.

'You know of course as well as I do', wrote Harrowby (June 4th), 'how very unpopular Free Education is with our Irish friends, with all the Clergy (roughly), most of the Country Gentlemen & the farmers & how most of our Educationalists believe that the Change & its consequences will be fatal to the Voluntary System. I do trust the Govt. will remember . . . that if they are to rally the Country they must at once get rid of the prevalent notion that the contest is on behalf of a doomed system & must fix in the minds of the people that the question at issue is none other than the religious & moral training of our vast population.' Smith replied (June 6th): '. . . I quite agree with you as to the line to be taken in debate. We avow, and Chamberlain is with us upon that, that we intend to preserve the Voluntary Schools and we are prepared to do battle with those who wish to destroy them. Issue will be joined upon that and if I may trust to assurances Joe Chamberlain and his friends will support us.'[1]

Indeed, when introducing the Bill on June 8th, Sir William Hart Dyke emphasized the Government's desire 'not to interfere with

[1] Harrowby Papers.

existing arrangements more than might be absolutely necessary'. For, though the majority of elementary schools would now become entirely free, the denominational school would still remain voluntary and would also benefit by a grant up to ten shillings per child.

The Government's tactics in handling the Bill were well thought out and quite subtle. Smith had been impressed by Harrowby's suggestion in one of his letters that too much pushing or commendation from their own side would be a mistake. They were opposed on this issue by so many diverse elements and complex combinations—a Conservative section headed by Howorth,[1] the advanced Radicals or 'Jacobins' under Labouchere, who in turn might influence the Irish, as well as a portion of the Liberals—that they decided to stand back and let these damage themselves by quarrelling and generally exhibiting themselves as anti-progressives, whilst bringing a few subtle pressures to bear on some of them. Thus Smith wrote to Akers-Douglas just before the Bill's introduction (June 6th):

My dear Douglas,
    Dear old Harrowby who is in a highly nervous state about the Education question, writes to me from Schwalbach that we should dissuade any of our friends who may be disposed to bless the Education scheme from doing so in too pronounced a tone on Dyke's speech—leaving the Radicals to curse as much as they like. Some support will of course be necessary but a little of Howorth's tincture will probably be more healthy than too much syrup.
    How can we get hold of the Romans? The Bill must be an enormous boon to them and they must wish to pass it at once I should think—but Sexton as Labby's tool may make it impossible. Is not Sexton to some extent under Priestly influence? Can it be brought to bear?
    Think these things over and speak to me before I go down to the House on Monday.

On the whole these calculations were pretty well justified by events, for the most sustained opposition to the Bill did indeed come from Howarth and another Conservative member named Barnet,[2] which had the effect of drawing one of the Opposition's foremost figures, Sir William Harcourt, into a warm defence of the scheme. The fact that Chamberlain, too, strongly supported it was of great influence upon the Government's Liberal allies and so—although a great many amendments were moved, some of which were adopted and some not—the Bill passed through all its stages with comparative ease and speed.

The German Emperor, William II, having, since his last visit two years earlier, rid himself of Bismarck and begun to invest himself

[1] M.P. Salford South.   [2] M.P. N. Islington.

with all those trappings of autocracy for which he had so long yearned, determined this summer to show himself to his grand-mother, the Queen, her Government and subjects in his new guise. Another object, since he had resolved to compete with British might on the seas, was to have a good look at the Royal Navy. Since his accession the Queen had become increasingly disturbed by him: she was thoroughly mistrustful of his motives and resented his brash arrogance. Now, his impending visit exasperated her in more ways than one. Salisbury wrote to Goschen, as Chancellor of the Exchequer, a letter (June 12th), which the latter passed to on Smith:

> The Queen has urged me very strongly to speak to the Cabinet with respect to her pecuniary position in regard to the Emperor of Germany's visit.
>
> He invites himself: he comes with thirty or forty attendants & he has to be entertained entirely at the Queen's cost. If it were not for State considerations of the most cogent kind, his visits would of course be discouraged. But I need not enlarge to you on the impossibility of taking that course.
>
> The Queen's position in this aspect is one of very great hardship. Up to the year 1889 she fully believed that the children of her sons would, in accordance with invariable precedent, receive a provision from Parliament. . . . But she has been roughly told she must provide for her grandsons out of her own savings. Surely it is very hard that, at this point, saving should be made impossible for her by requiring of her new & unexampled outlay, incurred purely & entirely for a political object.
>
> I think that, in justice, a vote ought to be taken to defray the cost of the Emperor's residence in London. It is as much part of the political expense of the country as the salary of the Ambassadors.

A Cabinet was held on June 20th, but Smith was only just able to get to it owing to a sudden and severe attack of gout. The faithful Miss Giberne had written to him (June 23rd) for his sixty-sixth birthday, saying: 'A friend of mine, a very valued one, though a Radical(!) to whom I mentioned your coming birthday said yesterday "Give my love to him—I believe in Mr. Smith".' He wrote back (June 24th): 'Gout has seized on my right ankle, but I am told it is good for me, which I believe, and that I shall be better in a day or two. . . . Everyone is very kind and very good to me, and I think I am as careful as I can be if I go on with my work, which I don't see my way, as a matter of conscience, yet to throw up. . . . I am 66, and have no sorrow with anyone of my children. God has been very merciful to me.'

Gladstone was not so fortunate. On July 4th his eldest son William died from cancer of the brain after two years' painful and distressing illness. At this time the Government were on the point of introducing their Clergy Discipline Bill, after a long campaign of pressure—mainly on Smith on the one side and on Gladstone on the other—from the Archbishop of Canterbury, Edward Benson. The following exchange between Smith and Gladstone offers a striking example of the strange mingling of warm, human gestures with downright, hard business which is a constant feature of our Parliamentary life. Smith wrote (July 7th):

Dear Mr. Gladstone,

Will you allow me to offer you and Mrs. Gladstone my most sincere sympathy in the heavy sorrow which has befallen you.

I have not had to part with a Son but I can well understand and enter into the feelings of those who are called upon to endure such a heavy trouble.

Mr. Arnold Morley[1] was kind enough to read me portions of a note he had from you referring to the Clergy Discipline Bill. I am grateful for the expression of your desire that your influence should be used to prevent prolonged or obstructive discussion but having regard to the intentions avowed by some Members from Wales and by others, I am afraid your Authority will be disregarded unless you are present to exercise it, and this under present circumstances seems to be hardly possible.

Believe me, my dear Mr. Gladstone,

Yours very sincerely,
W. H. Smith

Gladstone's reply on the same day, after the preliminary courtesies, was equally full of political calculation.

Dear Mr. Smith,

I thank you very much for the expression of your sympathy: and I am sure that in no case could it come more directly from the heart.

I could arrange through others for obviating the kind of opposition which has been the subject of our conferences on the Clergy Discipline Bill—and this without being myself present, to which medical objection (relating to the throat) could be taken. But I have no title to interfere with *bona fide* discussion and from what has reached me (but you are a far better judge) I had feared that the Bill could not be guaranteed against this difficulty on your own side of the House.

Believe me very faithfully yours,

W. E. Gladstone

Smith spoke what were to be his last words in the House of Commons a few days later (July 10th) in reply to a question from one of their own supporters as to whether the Government would extend an invitation to the French President to visit England—

---

[1] Liberal Chief Whip.

presumably to offset the impression created by the German Emperor's visit. Smith gave an evasive reply.

Next day, July 11th, the Prime Minister gave a great reception at Hatfield in honour of the German Emperor and Smith joined with other members of the Government in attending it—though not really fit to do so. In fact his ill and worn appearance shocked everyone so much that Balfour tried, in vain, to persuade him to send for a doctor. Lady Salisbury, however, did succeed in getting him to go to bed early in her house and to stay there over the next day. From here he wrote the following serene letter to his wife—obviously designed to allay any fears which his friends' reports might have aroused—and which has been poignantly marked by her 'His last letter to me'.

> Hatfield House,
> Herts.
> 12th July, 1891.
> 7 p.m.
>
> My dearest Wife,
>
> Everything has gone off wonderfully well today.
>
> The weather has been perfect for Hatfield, the place is looking beautiful and everybody says so, which must be very satisfactory to the Salisburys.
>
> They have been very kind to me and observing I looked tired last night Lady Salisbury urged me to go to bed early, which I did, and today I have rested a great deal in my room.
>
> The house is so crowded that many of the guests are sleeping out in the town and amongst them George Hamilton and Stanhope, but I am lodged comfortably in a quiet corner of the House.
>
> I am still uncomfortable and I am clearly not yet fit for the Iron which I shall not take again until I have seen Powell.
>
> I hope it has not been an unhappy day for you. It would have been happier for me if I had been with you, but I think it was right to come under the circumstances.
>
> Your loving husband,
> W. H. Smith

This had been indeed his last public appearance and on the following day, 13th, he returned to London exceedingly ill. After a few very critical days he rallied again and then lay for almost another six weeks at Grosvenor Place. However, he kept in touch with events. Thus his daughter wrote to Akers-Douglas: 'My Father asks me to write and ask you to be kind enough to look in and see him on your way to the Treasury this morning, if you do not mind paying him a visit in his bedroom. He is much better, and both he and we are quite in good spirits at the way he has responded to the rest and treatment, and we are grateful to you for making it easy for him to be quiet.'[1]

[1] Chilston Papers.

Goschen, too, acting again as temporary Leader of the House, took pains to keep him informed of developments. '. . . We go on slowly, but not uncomfortably', he wrote to him on July 26th. 'We hoped to have advanced beyond the present point in Supply, but it is something to have got the Irish Land Bill comfortably through. There is not much changed in the Education Bill & Dyke tells me that an hour or two will be sufficient for that. . . . We can't sit tomorrow because the Prime Minister has invited every single Conservative to Hatfield tomorrow to meet the Prince of Naples[1] & the prospect of Royalty & Hatfield will be too much for the virtue of some of the Tory democrats. . . . Whenever you wish to see me, & feel ready for a chat, you must send word to me & I shall come at once.'

One thing which Smith made sure should be unaffected by his own absence and illness was the annual fête and excursion to Greenlands, which for many years he had been accustomed to provide for the police attending at the House of Commons and for the messengers, doorkeepers and others employed there. His next thought was to write to the Queen to warn her that he might now really be compelled to give up the leadership of the House. She replied (August 6th): 'The Queen thanks Mr. Smith for his kind letter which gave her pleasure as she saw that he was better—but pain to learn that he feared he might be unable to continue ultimately in his very arduous office. He knows well how his invaluable services to herself & the Country have been appreciated by the Queen & how greatly she would grieve to lose him. Still, his health must not be sacrificed, & when the time comes he must follow the advice of his Physicians. . . .'

On August 20th he was allowed to move to Walmer Castle, his new official residence, not so much because it was this as in the hope of the sea-air restoring him. Shortly before he left he was visited by Salisbury and one or two other intimate colleagues, for whom it was to be the last glimpse of him. He went by special train, accompanied by his wife and members of his family, the engine-driver having special instructions to go slowly round curves and over points—for which consideration he was duly thanked by Smith at the other end.

Walmer, with its romantic old ramparts and gardens, its magnificent views over the Downs and Goodwin Sands and lofty tranquillity, broken only by the sound of the breakers pounding the rocks beneath and the cries of the sea-birds, would in better times have filled Smith with peace and contentment. But he could not walk or roam at will and his sense of his failing powers and imminent dissolution filled

[1] Son of King Humbert of Italy, whom he succeeded (1900) as King Victor Emmanuel III.

him with a restlessness which could only be stilled by the notion of boarding once again his yacht *Pandora*, which now lay at anchor off the Castle and which symbolized for him escape from weariness and dull care. However, the steep beach at Walmer was particularly difficult to embark from: Deal Pier was some way off and not much better and Dover Harbour was altogether too far. Nevertheless Smith was so persistent about the idea that eventually it was decided to practise embarkations from Walmer with his unfortunate doctor as stand-in for his illustrious patient. This was thus described in a letter (September 10th) from his Private Secretary, Pattisson, to Akers-Douglas.

As to the Chief himself I cannot report any real progress—on some days he seems better—then the gout reappears in another place and his temperature goes up, and the R.M. (Resident Medico) looks scared. Today he is brighter again and if the weather holds we may perhaps put him on board Pandora for a few hours steaming tomorrow. We have been rehearsing getting him on board—putting the R.M. in his chair and going through the whole performance—the first trial nearly sent the R.M. into the sea at the hoisting into the yacht—But now we can do it like clockwork. . . .[1]

Next day Smith himself was conveyed on board without mishap and spent several hours cruising in the Channel. Thereafter, whenever the weather was favourable, these excursions were repeated, himself lying or sitting on deck with his wife or daughter beside him and interestedly watching and identifying the different types and nationalities of ships which they passed. One day, to his great delight, he was accompanied on his cruise by his two faithful lieutenants, Akers-Douglas, the Chief Whip, and Jackson, the Financial Secretary to the Treasury. He still kept his eye closely on the political arena and after the Conservatives had lost a by-election at Walsall to a Radical largely through holiday-season apathy and another by-election supervened at Lewisham he had written to the Whip (August 23rd) to 'apply the Whip to the electors'. '. . . I think if you have the addresses of the absentees or any of them you might telegraph in your own name or in mine from Downing Street to any place in the three kingdoms urgently entreating them to return for the day and vote, adding that if the Conservative Electors who are absent do abstain from voting the result must be disastrous. . . .' Perhaps this desperate expedient worked, for the Unionist candidate was duly returned.

That Smith's personal predicament was but one manifestation of a more general state of physical collapse among his colleagues at this

[1] Chilston Papers.

354

time was brought home, first, by the temporary retreat of the Chief Whip to a sanatorium to 'soak in bromide', as Hart Dyke, who had preceded him there, expressed it;[1] secondly by the death at the early age of 52, of Cecil Raikes, the Postmaster General, 'from prostration and collapse due primarily to the pressure of official duties'.[2] The latter event, moreover, had other unpleasant implications to cloud Smith's last days. Raikes had been M.P. for Cambridge University, and Gorst, whose real or imaginary grievances had made him a perennial thorn in the Government's side, had hopes of succeeding him both in this seat and in his office. As Cambridge was a safe seat and Chatham, which he at present represented, a marginal one, Balfour had told him in rather uncompromising terms that he considered such a switch 'impossible' for any member or aspiring member of the Government.

Despite all his earlier troubles with Gorst it was characteristic of Smith to want now to try to be fair to him and help him. He had expressed to Salisbury the hope that something might now be done to gratify Gorst's ambitions: but he did not know that Gorst had already, again, completely alienated the Prime Minister and the Chief Whip by his embittered complaints and recriminations. Thus Salisbury wrote (September 15th) from France:

My dear Smith,
    I gather you do not like my passing over Gorst. If you feel up to it—read the enclosed.
    You told me to exhort him—you will see the result of my parental efforts.
    I think after reading the enclosed . . . you will admit that it was dangerous to 'endorse' him to the extent which such promotion would imply: & also dangerous to put him in a position where he would be able to try so many hazardous labour theories. . . .

Smith was now quite satisfied that Gorst was impossible. He wrote (September 17th) to Akers-Douglas, who had received a particularly poisonous letter from the latter:

My dear Douglas,
    Salisbury has sent me a copy of correspondence he has had with Gorst which removes all doubt in my mind that it would have been dangerous to 'endorse' him at the present moment for promotion.
    Gorst writes to Salisbury that he understands the Gov. have intervened to prevent his selection at Cambridge on the ground that he ought to hold on to the critical seat at Chatham.
    Salisbury replies that he has not had any communication with any Cambridge man as to his candidature and disdains any interference

[1] Chilston Papers.   [2] Annual Register, 1891, 177.

on the part of the Gov. and he then in a most kind way asks him to think over the effect on his own career of the independent attitude he has assumed.

Gorst's reply puts an end to the possibility of promotion.[1]

During these September days, with their frequent cruises on the *Pandora* in the Channel, there had appeared to be some improvement in Smith's condition. '. . . I am better', he had written to Balfour (August 30th), '—the doctor tells me so and I think so myself, but I cannot use my legs and I am carried about everywhere like a baby. . . .'[2] His friends, however, already feared the worst. 'Smith is not getting on at all', Akers-Douglas wrote to Schomberg McDonnell (September 13th), '—I have been to see him every week since the House rose and can see no improvement. He is quite helpless and can do no business and the doctors are still very anxious about him.'[3] And McDonnell replied (September 15th): 'The Chief refuses at present to contemplate the choice of a successor feeling no doubt that it is of no use to anticipate the inevitable day when he must do so. . . .'[4]

Nevertheless, with the aid of Pattisson he was still managing to transact a fair amount of business and on October 1st, being at sea for a few hours, he seemed so much better that members of his family who had been staying at Walmer, felt free to disperse for the time being and plans were even made for renting a house at Torquay for the winter months. Next day there was a rough sea, but he was carried down over the beach and with some difficulty placed in the gig. 'Ah! this is like life itself', he said to Blow, the *Pandora*'s captain, as he felt the motion of the boat; 'your treatment is doing me good. I feel some hopes now.'[5] But it was the last time he was on board his beloved yacht.

On Monday, October 5th, he was up and dressed and anxious to transact business, but Pattisson noticed he was in great pain and tried to dissuade him. He insisted on signing some cheques for his doctors' fees and wanted to dictate a letter to Lord George Hamilton, but felt unequal to it and gave it up saying: 'No: tell George I am not well enough to deal with it.'[6]

Next morning, Tuesday, October 6th, his condition was alarming, as his heart was failing. The absent members of his family were recalled by telegram, though they could not arrive in time to see him alive. His London doctor, Douglas Powell, arrived together with an eminent surgeon of the day, Tom Smith;[7] but he was beyond their help. He was still quite clear of mind when they withdrew and

[1] Chilston Papers.   [2] Balfour Papers.   [3] Salisbury Papers.
[4] Chilston Papers.   [5] Maxwell, II, 318.   [6] Ibid.
[7] Sir Thomas Smith, K.C.V.O. (1897); Baronet (1901).

left him with his wife, a nurse and a faithful valet and it was in their presence that he died that afternoon at ten minutes past three.

On the selfsame day, by a weird coincidence, there died—even more unexpectedly—the man whose activities might fairly be said to be in large part responsible for Smith's untimely death. In the few months since his deposition from the leadership of the Irish Party Parnell had fought unceasingly like a lion at bay. In Ireland by-elections had been fought between the conflicting factions—Parnellites and Anti-Parnellites—with a sickening ferocity; but the tide had been running too strongly of late against the man who had once been called the uncrowned king of Ireland and he was beaten again and again. The tremendous strain of these vain campaigns and the bitter emotions involved wore down his already weakened constitution. He had married Mrs. O'Shea in June, as soon as the decree nisi became absolute, and it was to her, at Brighton, that he returned to die.

The Queen had been immediately notified by telegram that, as she put in her journal, 'Good, excellent Mr. Smith had expired. Such a terrible, really irreparable loss! Such an excellent, honest, wise, reliable, conciliatory man, and so modest and simple. . . .'[1] She wired her warmest condolences to Mrs. Smith and followed this up with a personal letter (in the first person) in which she wrote: '. . . I feel most deeply for you, and fear that his unceasing devotion to his country and Sovereign has shortened his most valuable life! . . .'[2] In another letter of October 8th, which must have been addressed to Lord Salisbury, although it is among the Hambleden Papers—perhaps passed to him by Mrs. Smith—the Queen exhibits that characteristic blend of warm-hearted appreciation and brisk practicability, whilst at the same time indulging in that irresistible impulse to point a moral and trounce her especial enemies.

Balmoral Castle
Oct. 8. 1891.

The Queen deeply deplores Mr. Smith's loss wh. is a very serious one, but He cd never have continued to lead the House of Commons, that was certain; but no one expected that we shd lose him all together & his advice wd have been invaluable, even if he cd not hold active office.

He was so good, so honest, so amiable & of such a modest & unselfish character that everyone respected him & must regret him. He died from devotion to his work.

[1] *Queen Victoria's Letters*, Third Series, Vol. II, 73.
[2] Ibid.

What a startling Event is Mr. Parnell's death! But *what* a contrast! *He* was a really bad & worthless man who had to answer many lives lost in Ireland! What a monstrous speech Mr. Gladstone made! Such wicked and mischievous proposals!

But he surely has gone too far & will shock all more moderate men. He states such falsehoods.

Smith's funeral was very simple. His body was taken from Walmer Castle to Henley on the morning of Saturday, October 10th, and then to Hambleden Church. The burial took place in the new cemetery at Hambleden and, despite the heavy rain, was attended by several hundred local people, as well as his family and friends of all kinds. Meanwhile, in London, an impressive memorial service was held at Westminster Abbey, which was attended by the Queen's representative, Lord Radnor, who reported to her that there were present most of the Cabinet and Government (but not Lord Salisbury who was ill), Opposition leaders and foreign Ambassadors (but not the French) and 'great numbers of Members of Parliament, Tories and Liberals, but no Parnellites, he believes, or McCarthyites'.[1]

Next morning, Sunday, October 11th, one of his very oldest friends, Canon Ince, Regius Professor of Divinity, prefaced his sermon in Christ Church Cathedral, Oxford, with a eulogy of Smith. He told his hearers of his earliest recollection of Smith getting up at four o'clock every morning in Kilburn to go down to the family business in the Strand. 'In recalling those early days I have often thought of that verse in the Proverbs, "Seest thou a man diligent in his business? he shall stand before kings; he shall not stand before mean men".' On the same day another old friend, Dr. Warre, Headmaster of Eton, delivered a great tribute to him in College Chapel, referring, to 'the blessing, the strengthening, comforting, consoling power of such an example'.

Many other eloquent tributes were paid in letters to Mrs. Smith and her son. One which was particularly impressive owing to the sphinx-like aura surrounding its author was that received by Freddie from Joseph Chamberlain. He wrote: '. . . On many occasions I have been indebted to his kindness and generous consideration & it was impossible to know him without feeling for him a personal affection & respect which few men are privileged to win in their public capacity.' But perhaps the most impressive of all came from the man whom he had picked out, as a boy, from amongst his own employees at his Strand Offices and who through his unremitting encouragement and financial help was already on the way to becoming one of the greatest archaeologists of the day. Ernest Wallis

[1] Ibid., 75.

Budge[1]—for he was the man—wrote: 'To his example and to his help I owe nearly everything I have. . . .' Among themselves, the men who had served him and worked with him during the last few hectic years, expressed as much heartfelt grief as if they had been writing their letters of duty to his widow. 'I hardly know what to say to you', wrote Lord Dartmouth, a former Junior Whip, to Akers-Douglas (October 8th). 'This crushing blow seems to have taken all the life and heart out of me, so what must you feel, who were always with him. . . . It is a terrible calamity.' And another Junior Whip, Sidney Herbert, to the same: '. . . It is a terrible blow to us as a Party. . . . I am very, very sorry about it. He was such a kind, good man, and so thoroughly straightforward, and we shall miss him both personally and politically. . . .'

Meanwhile, the Queen had been consulting Lord Salisbury as to the appropriateness of conferring a peerage on Mrs. Smith and Salisbury had replied that it 'would be a gracious and suitable recognition of his services on the part of your Majesty, and in accordance with precedent' and that the offer would be more valued if it came from the Queen direct. The latter accordingly wrote:

Balmoral Castle.

Dear Mrs. Smith,   Oct. 12. 1891

I am most desirous as you will easily believe to give a public mark of my deep sense of the services your beloved Husband rendered to me & to his country, services which I fear shortened his valuable life.

I wish therefore to offer to you, his devoted wife, a Peerage, a Viscountcy, which I hope you will feel inclined to accept for His sake.

Truly thankful am I, to hear that you are able to bear up under your overwhelming affliction & trust that the universal mourning for your dear Husband's loss & the equally universal appreciation of his services & character will be soothing to you.

Believe me always,
Yours most sincerely,
Victoria R.I.

Emily Smith, as may be well imagined from what we know of her modest and self-effacing disposition, was not at all anxious to be dragged out of the comparative obscurity in which, despite her husband's ascent into the limelight, she had always managed to live

---

[1] In his spare time from W. H. Smith & Son he had studied and learned several ancient oriental languages. Later a subscription was raised to send him to Cambridge to which Smith, Gladstone and Sir John Stainer, the musician, were the principal subscribers. In 1887 Smith obtained Treasury Sanction for money to be provided to send Budge on an archaeological mission to Egypt and Baghdad. Budge later became Keeper of the Egyptian and Assyrian Department of the British Museum, published a number of learned books and treatises and was knighted in 1920.

and to become a viscountess, with all the implications of such a title at that time. She must have consulted her son, who was already a man of twenty-three, and who would bear the title after her and he most likely had no more desire for it than she had. She therefore confided her feelings on the subject to Lord Salisbury and asked what she should do. He replied as follows (October 14th):

Dear Mrs. Smith,
I was very glad when I heard from the Queen that she intended making the proposal which you mention, and I warmly advocated it. I think you ought to accept it. In so doing I am convinced you will be doing what *he* would have wished & what he would have thought to be your duty. It is good for his country and for the world that such a career as his should be held up to general admiration and respect by the Sovereign of the Country, in the most conspicuous manner: and that it should receive her emphatic and solemn commendation in the manner in which that tribute is usually paid in the cases of the highest merit. I know that if God had willed that he should live beyond the period of his active political career, it was his intention to have accepted a peerage: for I had spoken to him about it. This was not to be: but it would not be well that his merit should, on that account, not receive public and formal recognition.
There are more precedents than one for the course proposed to you. If I remember rightly a similar step was taken in the case of Mr. Canning, who died also unexpectedly while still filling the office of Leader of the House of Commons. It was a matter of great regret to me that I was not able to be present at the ceremony on Saturday. On the day he died I was taken with a very violent, though transient malady—& was for the time very ill: & on Thursday, when it would have been necessary to start in order to be present in London on Saturday, I was too ill to move with safety. I therefore had no choice. So sudden & terrible a shock made it hard to throw off the illness.
Believe me,
Yours very truly,
Salisbury

So next day (October 15th) Mrs. Smith wrote to the Queen that '. . . In obedience to Your Majesty's most gracious wish that I should accept a Peerage at your hands I beg most respectfully and gratefully to do so "for his sake". For myself my wish would have been to bear his honoured name as now, till I might join him again, but I cannot only think of myself. . . .' Lady Hambleden, as she now became, taking her title from the village adjoining their country home, 'Greenlands', lived on quietly for another twenty-two years, comforted in her bereavement by the great consolation of seeing their son Freddie, who succeeded her as second Viscount Hambleden in 1913, following exactly in his father's footsteps—carrying on as

M.P. for the Strand, directing and expanding the family business and devoting his spare time with great zeal to philanthropic interests— especially the voluntary hospitals. Moreover, of their four daughters, two were especially distinguished and honoured for their good works.

When depressed and disgusted by public affairs, Smith as we have seen, would frequently recall and give thanks for the happiness of his family life and the excellence of his children. These blessings and his faith in a merciful, all-wise, all-seeing God bore him up till the very end of his life. He stands out in an age noted for stern and remote fathers, to whom their children often became virtual strangers or even enemies, for he quite clearly inspired as much affection and friendship in his own children, as he did in the men with whom he had to do in his public life. The secret was, of course, that he was a good husband and father first and always—and a businessman and politician afterwards. His great virtues in the first capacity spread into and influenced the other. But he was no mean businessman or politician for all that—as this book has tried to show.

BIBLIOGRAPHY

BIOGRAPHICAL WORKS (Arranged in Order of Subjects)

AKERS-DOUGLAS, ARETAS: See CHILSTON, VISCOUNT.
ASQUITH, 1st Earl of Oxford and Asquith:
  Life of Lord Oxford and Asquith, by J. A. Spender and Cyril Asquith,
  Vol. I (Hutchinson, 1932).
  Fifty Years of Parliament, by the Earl of Oxford and Asquith, Vol. I
  (Cassell, 1926).
  Memories and Reflections, by the Earl of Oxford and Asquith, Vol. I
  (Cassell, 1928).
BALFOUR, 1st Earl of:
  Arthur James Balfour, 1st Earl of Balfour, by Blanche E. C. Dugdale,
  Vol. I (Hutchinson, 1936).
  Chapters of Autobiography, by Arthur James, First Earl of Balfour
  (Cassell, 1930).
BEACH, SIR MICHAEL HICKS: See ST. ALDWYN, EARL.
BEACONSFIELD, Earl of:
  Life of Benjamin Disraeli, Earl of Beaconsfield, by W. F. Monypenny
  and G. E. Buckle, Vols. V and VI (Murray, 1910–24).
  The Earl of Beaconsfield, His Life and Times, by A. C. Ewald, Vol. II
  (Mackenzie, 1881).
  Letters of Disraeli to Lady Bradford and Lady Chesterfield, ed. Marquess
  of Zetland, Vol. I (Murray, 1929).
CAINE, WILLIAM SPROSTON:
  W. S. Caine, M.P., A Biography, by John Newton (1907).
CAMBRIDGE, H.R.H., GEORGE, 2nd Duke of:
  *The Royal George: The Life of H.R.H. Prince George, Duke of
  Cambridge*, 1819–1904, by Giles St. Aubyn (Constable, 1963).
CARNARVON, 4th Earl of:
  Life of Fourth Earl of Carnarvon, 1831–1890, by Sir Arthur Hardinge,
  Vol. III (Humphrey Milford, Oxford, 1925).
CHAMBERLAIN, JOSEPH:
  Life of Joseph Chamberlain, by J. L. Garvin, Vols. I and II (Macmillan,
  1932–3).
  A Political Memoir, by Joseph Chamberlain, ed. C. H. D. Howard
  (Batchworth, 1953).

BIOGRAPHICAL WORKS

CHILSTON, VISCOUNT:
Chief Whip: The Political Life and Times of Aretas Akers-Douglas, First Viscount Chilston, by Eric Alexander, 3rd Viscount Chilston (Routledge and Kegan Paul, 1961).

CHURCHILL, LORD RANDOLPH:
Lord Randolph Churchill, by Winston S. Churchill (new edn., Odhams, 1951).
Lord Randolph Churchill, by Robert Rhodes James (Weidenfeld and Nicolson, 1959).
Lord Randolph Churchill, by Lord Rosebery (Humphreys, 1906).
Speeches of Lord Randolph Churchill, 1880–1888, ed. Louis J. Jennings, 2 vols. (Longmans, 1889).

CHURCHILL, LADY RANDOLPH:
The Reminiscences of Lady Randolph Churchill, by Mrs. Cornwallis West (Edward Arnold, 1908).

CRANBROOK, 1st Earl of:
Gathorne Hardy, First Earl of Cranbrook: A Memoir, by A. E. Gathorne Hardy, 2 vols. (Longmans, 1910).

DEVONSHIRE, 8th Duke of:
Life of Spencer Compton, Eighth Duke of Devonshire, by Bernard Holland, 2 vols. (Longmans, 1910).

DILKE, SIR CHARLES WENTWORTH, BT.:
Life of the Rt. Hon. Sir Charles W. Dilke, Bart., M.P., by Stephen Gwynne and G. M. Tuckwell, 2 vols. (Murray, 1917).
Sir Charles Dilke: A Victorian Tragedy, by Roy Jenkins (Collins, 1958).

DISRAELI, BENJAMIN: See BEACONSFIELD, EARL OF.

ELPHINSTONE, SIR HOWARD:
The Queen thanks Sir Howard: The Life of Major-General Sir Howard Elphinstone, V.C., K.C.B., C.M.G., by his daughter, Mary Howard McClintock (Murray, 1945).

GLADSTONE, MARY:
Mary Gladstone (Mrs. Drew): Her Diaries and Letters, ed. Lucy Masterman (Methuen, 1930).

GLADSTONE, VISCOUNT:
After Thirty Years, by Viscount Gladstone (Macmillan, 1928).

GLADSTONE, WILLIAM EWART:
Life of William Ewart Gladstone, by John Morley, Vols. II and III (Macmillan, 1903).

GOSCHEN, 1st Viscount:
Life of George Joachim Goschen, First Viscount Goschen, 1831–1907, by A. R. D. Elliot, 2 vols. (Longmans, 1911).

GRANVILLE, 2nd Earl:
Life of Granville George Leveson-Gower, Second Earl Granville, K.G., by Lord Edmond Fitzmaurice, 2 vols. (Longmans, 1905).

GRIMSTON, ROBERT:
Life of the Hon. Robert Grimston, by F. Gale (Longmans, 1885).

HAMILTON, LORD GEORGE:
Parliamentary Reminiscences and Reflections, by Lord George Hamilton 2 vols. (Murray, 1916–22).

HARCOURT, SIR WILLIAM GEORGE VENABLES VERNON:
Life of Sir William Harcourt, by A. G. Gardiner, 2 vols. (Constable, 1929).

HARDY, GATHORNE: See CRANBROOK, EARL OF.

HARTINGTON, MARQUESS OF: See DEVONSHIRE, DUKE OF.

HEALY, TIMOTHY MICHAEL:
Letters and Leaders of My Day, by T. M. Healy, 2 vols. (Thornton Butterworth, 1928).

IDDESLEIGH, 1st Earl of:
Life, Letters and Diaries of Sir Stafford Northcote, First Earl of Iddesleigh, by Andrew Lang, 2 vols. (Blackwood, 1890).

JAMES OF HEREFORD, LORD:
Lord James of Hereford, by Lord Askwith (Benn, 1930).

JEUNE, MRS.: See ST. HELIER, LADY.

LABOUCHERE, HENRY DU PRE:
Life of Henry Labouchere, by A. L. Thorold (Constable, 1913).
Labby: The Life and Character of Henry Labouchere, by Hesketh Pearson (Hamish Hamilton, 1936).

LONG, 1st Viscount:
Walter Long and his Times, by Sir Charles Petrie (Cassell, 1936).

MAXWELL, SIR HERBERT:
Evening Memories, by the Right Hon. Sir Herbert Maxwell of Monreith, Bt. (Maclehose, 1932).

MIDLETON, 1st Earl of:
Records and Reactions 1856–1939, by the Earl of Midleton (Murray, 1939).

MORLEY, 1st Viscount:
Recollections, by John, Viscount Morley, 2 vols. (Macmillan, 1917).

NEVILL, LADY DOROTHY:
The Reminiscences of Lady Dorothy Nevill, ed. Ralph Nevill (Edward Arnold, 1906).

NEWTON, LORD:
Retrospection, by Lord Newton (Murray, 1941).

NORTHCOTE, SIR STAFFORD: See IDDESLEIGH, EARL OF.

O'CONNOR, THOMAS POWER:
Memoirs of an Old Parliamentarian, by T. P. O'Connor, 2 vols. (Benn, 1929).

PALMERSTON, 3rd Viscount:
Life of Henry John Temple, Viscount Palmerston: 1846–1865, by E. Ashley, 2 vols., 1876.

PARNELL, CHARLES STEWART:
Charles Stewart Parnell: His Love Story and Political Life, by Katherine O'Shea (Mrs. Parnell), 2 vols. (Cassell, 1914).
Life of Charles Stewart Parnell 1846–1891, by R. Barry O'Brien, 2 vols. (Smith, Elder, 1898).
Parnell and his Party, 1880–90, by C. Cruise O'Brien (Oxford University Press, 1957).

BIOGRAPHICAL WORKS

PEASE, SIR ALFRED EDWARD, BT.:
Elections and Recollections, by Sir A. E. Pease (Murray, 1932).

PONSONBY, SIR HENRY FREDERICK:
Henry Ponsonby: Queen Victoria's Private Secretary, by Arthur Ponsonby (Macmillan, 1942).

REDESDALE, 1st Lord:
Memories, by Lord Redesdale, G.C.K.O., K.C.B., 2 vols. (Hutchinson, 1915).

ST. ALDWYN, 1st Earl:
Sir Michael Hicks Beach, Earl St. Aldwyn, by Lady Victoria Hicks Beach, 2 vols. (Macmillan, 1932).

ST. HELIER, LADY:
Memories of Fifty Years, by Lady St. Helier (Edward Arnold, 1909).

SALISBURY, 3rd Marquess of:
Life of Robert, Marquis of Salisbury, by Lady Gwendolen Cecil, Vols. II, III and IV (Hodder and Stoughton, 1931–2).
Salisbury, 1830–1903: Portrait of a Statesman, by A. L. Kennedy (Murray, 1953).

SMITH, WILLIAM HENRY:
Life and Times of the Rt. Hon. William Henry Smith, M.P., by Sir Herbert Maxwell, Bart., M.P., 2 vols. (Blackwood, 1893).

VICTORIA, QUEEN:
Letters of Queen Victoria. Second Series, Vols. II and III; Third Series, Vols. I and II.
Concerning Queen Victoria and Her Son, by Sir George Arthur (Robert Hale, 1943).

WEST, SIR ALGERNON:
Recollections, 1832 to 1886, by Sir Algernon West, 2 vols. (Smith, Elder, 1899).

WOLFF, SIR HENRY DRUMMOND:
Rambling Recollections, by Sir H. D. Wolff, 2 vols. (Macmillan, 1908).

WYNDHAM, GEORGE:
Life and Letters of George Wyndham, by J. W. Mackail and Guy Wyndham, 2 vols. (Hutchinson, 1925).

OTHER WORKS

BARNES, J. T.: *Free Trade in Books: A Study in the London Book Trade since 1800* (Oxford University Press, 1957).

BAUMANN, ARTHUR A.: *The Last Victorians* (Benn, 1927).

ENSOR, (SIR) R. C. K.: *England, 1870–1914* (Oxford University Press, 1936).

GOOCH, G. P.: *History of Modern Europe, 1878–1919* (Cassell, 1928).

GORST, HAROLD E.: *The Fourth Party* (Smith, Elder, 1906).

HANHAM, H. J.: *Elections and Party Management: Politics in the Time of Disraeli and Gladstone* (Longmans, 1959).

HEARNSHAW, F. J. C.: *Conservatism in England* (Macmillan, 1933).

LUCY, (SIR) HENRY W.: *A Diary of the Salisbury Parliament, 1886–1892* (Cassell, 1892).

MARRIOTT, SIR J. A. R.: *Modern England, 1885–1945*: *A History of My Own Times* (4th edn., Methuen, 1948).

MUIR, J. RAMSAY: *A Brief History of Our Own Times* (George Philip & Son, 1935).

PHILLIPS, W. ALISON: *Modern Europe, 1815–1899* (5th edn., Rivingtons, 1921).

POCKLINGTON, G. R.: *The Story of W. H. Smith & Son* (London, printed for private circulation, 1937).

SANDARS, J. S.: *Studies of Yesterday, by a Privy Councillor* (Philip Allan, 1928).

SMALLEY, GEORGE W.: *London Letters, and some others*, 2 vols. (Macmillan, 1890).

SPEARMAN, DIANA: *Democracy in England* (Rockliff, 1957).

TREVELYAN, G. M.: *British History in the Nineteenth Century and After* (new edn., Longmans, 1944).

YOUNG, G. M.: *Victorian England: Portrait of an Age* (Oxford University Press, 1936).

INDEX